KU-143-905

Macrodynamics:
Fluctuations and growth

Macrodynamics: Fluctuations and growth

A study of the economy in equilibrium and disequilibrium

Pierre-Yves Hénin

Routledge & Kegan Paul

London and New York

First published in Great Britain in 1986
by Routledge & Kegan Paul plc
11 New Fetter Lane, London EC4P 4EE
Published in the USA by
Routledge & Kegan Paul Inc.
in association with Methuen Inc.
29 West 35th Street, New York, NY 10001
Set in Times Roman 10 on 12 point by
Hope Services, Abingdon
and printed in Great Britain
by TJ Press (Padstow) Ltd
Padstow, Cornwall

First published as Macrodynamique: fluctuations et croissance
© Ed. Economica, 1981
This translation © Routledge & Kegan Paul 1986
No part of this book may be reproduced in
any form without permission from the publisher,
except for the quotation of brief passages
in criticism

Library of Congress Cataloging in Publication Data

Hénin, Pierre Yves.
Macrodynamics, fluctuations and growth.
Translation of: Macrodynamique, fluctuations et
croissance.
Bibliography: p.
Includes index.
1. Equilibrium (Economics)   2. Economic development.
3. Macroeconomics.   I. Title.
HB145.H4613 1986   339.5   85-11865

British CIP data also available

ISBN 0-7102-0663-1
ISBN 0-7102-0664-X (pbk.)

Contents

Part Two

BEHAVIOURAL DYNAMICS

Part Three

GROWTH

Preface

This work is the outcome of several years' teaching as a professor of Economics at the University of Paris. It results from the conviction that it is neither possible nor honest to teach macroeconomic dynamics without first introducing students to contemporary studies and approaches. Already, these works form the basis for debate on the regulation of industrialised economies and are invoked to justify political decisions.

Rightly or wrongly? How can one say, without once having followed the line of reasoning and without having made the effort to understand the principles, if not the details, of the analytical method?

In order to provide the student with this 'door' to contemporary macroeconomics, it was necessary to present as comprehensive a work as possible. Because of this, it will sometimes go beyond the syllabus of a Bachelor's or Master's degree in Economics, and may constitute a useful reference work for more advanced students, young post-graduates undertaking research and economists wanting to broaden their knowledge of a technical field, so relevant to current affairs.

The second edition includes some very sensible modifications. There is a more integrated treatment of macroeconomic equilibrium models, both classical and Keynesian, and a fuller development of their dynamic analysis. The study of inflation is more far-reaching and so too is the presentation of 'new classical' theories, based on rational expectations. Some account is taken of developments in 'crisis analysis', and of the character of contemporary disequilibria. Lastly, a more systematic presentation of modern disequilibrium theory is given.

The author would like to thank all those, and in particular Professor R. Bodkin of the University of Ottawa, who have facilitated his task by passing on their comments on the first edition. Naturally, we add the usual disclaimer absolving them from any responsibility for the errors and deficiencies which remain.

Foreword

by F. II. Hahn

Economics, like, one suspects, many other disciplines, is subject to waves of fashion. Not long ago it was the theory of growth and optimum growth which attracted most of the young and aspiring. Now it is Rational Expectation, Asymmetric Information and Incentive Compatibility. There is really nothing very wrong with this process. Indeed, an economist could easily justify it by an appeal to increasing returns to intellectual endeavours. But as theories and knowledge accumulate there is some danger that past achievements are forgotten or only dimly recalled. There *is* a great deal wrong with that!

This danger is particularly acute in macroeconomics. A good example here is the fact that Robertson's contributions keep getting 're-discovered'. But more serious is the fact that very few of those contributing to the 'new' macroeconomics now fashionable seem to know what Keynes and the economists working in the Keynesian tradition had to say and why. Consider the currently held theory that there is no trade-off between unemployment and inflation. In examining this proposition one finds that it says that inflation cannot increase employment beyond the level which Keynes and Beveridge called 'Full Employment'. But it was never proposed by them or anyone else that there was a trade-off at this level. Indeed, Keynes in *How To Pay For The War* went out of his way to make this clear. But this is just one example, and there are very many others. The consequence is that the 'new' macroeconomists no longer know the arguments which were deployed against those who proposed similar theories in the 1930s.

This book could be a remedy, because it sets out these arguments clearly and gives an account of the theoretical work which preceded that of the new macroeconomists and of some recent efforts in that tradition. It will make a very good text in those University departments of Economics which want their students to learn Economics and not just the latest theory from the latest pre-print.

Introduction

The aim of this book is to undertake a macrodynamic analysis, that is to say a study of the determinants of general economic movements: fluctuations and growth. This theme encompasses one of the most active fields in contemporary economic thought and has given rise to a considerable volume of work. The controversies which it excites, albeit technical, scientific or ideological, frequently find an echo in political thought or debate, although this necessarily entails some occasionally excessive simplification of the theories in question.

Before discussing the content and the plan of this work, we will delimit its scope through a discussion of the elements of dynamic and macroeconomic analysis, on the one hand, and fluctuations and growth, on the other.

1 DYNAMIC ANALYSIS

The static-dynamic divide relates to methods of analysis, denoting a property of the theories or models utilised. Static analysis considers a given state of an economic system as the result of the interaction of a certain number of determining factors at a given moment. In doing this, it relies on models in which time does not figure among the variables considered. It is applicable to states considered to be in equilibrium, that is states in which there is an exact balance of the various forces acting upon the system, and thus no resultant net tendency towards change.

Comparative statics proceeds by comparison of virtual equilibrium states, introducing no temporal references whatsoever. In its strictest form, this type of analysis would never elicit a statement such as, 'If taxes fall, consumption will rise' but rather one of the following form: 'If taxes were lower, consumption would be higher.'

Dynamic analysis aims to take account of the reality of a moving economy, which adjusts from period to period. It, therefore, involves theories or models in which time intervenes as an essential variable.

The history and thought of dynamic analysis suggest that the static-dynamic divide may in fact hide two distinct, basic views:

(a) Either we may consider, along with Harrod, that dynamics is the study of an economy in evolution, in the process of long-term growth. This idea does not exclude the possibility of a regular evolution, along an equilibrium growth path. So, in this field, we therefore tend to encounter theories or models which lie very close to statics, in which the levels of variables have been replaced simply by their rates of growth, without the intervention of leads and lags.

(b) Or, alternatively, we may consider, along with Hicks and Samuelson, that dynamics is the study of movements and adjustments born out of disequilibrium situations. Hence, leads and lags should be incorporated into models, although the concept of long-term evolution need not necessarily appear.

These two conceptions of dynamics clearly meet when it comes to discussing growth disequilibria.

2 MACROECONOMIC ANALYSIS

A second dichotomy separates microeconomic from macroeconomic analysis. This division is sometimes represented in terms of opposing aims: the former accounting for the individual behaviour of agents, while the latter concerns itself with the economy as a whole, taken in its entirety. However, Walrasian general equilibrium theory, which is without question a product of microeconomics, clearly constitutes a representation of the economy in its entirety.

It is their methodologies which permit us to specify more closely the distinction. Schematically, microeconomics proceeds by describing modes of behaviour and then aggregating the observed relationships, whereas macroeconomics would first aggregate and then construct its explanatory relationships. Nevertheless, many relationships thus posited by macroeconomics are in fact based upon the logic of rational individual behaviour.

It is quite evident that macroeconomics amounts to more than an aggregation of individual behaviour and actions, as is shown by the 'savings paradox' called to mind by Keynesian theory. By definition, an individual enriches himself by saving but society as a whole may become poorer if all consumers simultaneously raise their rates of saving: the fact is that a general rise in savings has consequent effects upon income, which do not occur, or rather are negligibly small, in the case of a rise in savings on the part of a single consumer.

On the other hand, it was considered, sometimes too easily, that macroeconomics could directly postulate behavioural relationships of an immediate significance at the aggregated level. Aggregate modes of behaviour were said to be of a social nature, reducible to individual actions.

The disadvantage of this 'globalist' conception of macroeconomics, frequently found in the works of so-called Keynesians, is that it depicts the economy as a machine made up of aggregate variables rather than as a network of manifold components acting upon partly co-ordinated and partly contradictory plans.

Within this 'globalist' perspective, one would consider the basic problem of macroeconomics to be the co-ordination of aggregate quantities such as savings or investment. Would it not be better to take as the basic problem the co-ordination of individual behaviour, of which the adjustment of aggregate quantities is only a symptom? This distinction we will meet again on several occasions.

Macroeconomics has nothing to gain from cutting itself off from the foundation laid for it by the analysis of individual behaviour, as long as this behaviour is not taken as a pure, unconditioned expression of individual objectives but as broadly determined by a set of constraints arising from the nature of the operation of the economy as a whole: for there would be resource constraints, of course, and others too in a disequilibrium context, in which an idealised model of market forces would no longer be applicable.

One contemporary macroeconomic approach is searching for non-naïve microfoundations, but the difficulties involved are serious and require complex solutions. As a result many developments rely on aggregate relationships which are not sufficiently well-founded, or alternatively on arbitrary transposition of relationships established at the microeconomic level.

In any case, the split between microeconomics and macroeconomics has been exaggerated and it is no longer possible to teach them as distinct subjects. We will see, for example, how modern disequilibrium theory leads to the integration of the multiplier, a typical macro-economic tool, and the theory of consumer choice – the cornerstone of the microeconomics paradigm. To be more precise, over and above any question of their aims or methodologies, the true distinction between microeconomics and macroeconomics lies in the problems they address and the practical application that is made of them. Microeconomics is concerned with the problem of the allocation of resources, whereas it is the problem of regulating economic activity which explains the specific characteristics of macroeconomics. Actual macroeconomic forecasting work and the debate over the 'fine tuning' of stabilisation policy provide a more certain definition of the field of macroeconomics than the unending debate on aims and methodologies.

3 ECONOMIC MOVEMENTS: FLUCTUATIONS AND GROWTH

Those economic movements which are observable present a complex profile and a rather dubious regularity. One of the aims of our analysis will be to represent them as the outcome of a combination of multiple components with different amplitudes and periodicities. Again we will take as our reference point a mathematical result, often applied in physics.

A temporal process is described as 'stationary' (in physics the term is a 'standing wave' pattern) when the characteristics of its cycle are unaffected by time: a time series may be made 'stationary' through the elimination of a trend term. Now, any stationary temporal process, observed over T periods can be expressed as a sum of strictly 'periodic' components, with different amplitudes and periodicities, at their maximum equal in number to T; this is what is called a Fourier series. In general, a good approximation will be obtained if only a limited number of periodic components is adopted: this is the principle of the statistical technique known as spectral analysis of time series.

Without explicitly employing a mathematical method, the analysis of economic movements follows a similar path by distinguishing between cyclical components and a trend component.

The trend component, which since modern times has been positive in the West, is analysed in terms of growth. Its study forms the subject of Part Three of this book. In addition to the concept of growth, defined as the trend increase in indicators of the level of production, there has also been advanced the notion of 'development', whose aim is to take account of the structural modifications and qualitative change required and implied by such a movement in the long term.

For about a century (1850–1950), economic theory endeavoured to analyse recurrent movements in activity in terms of fluctuations of a cyclical character, similar to the 'periodic' components found in mathematical reasoning. As a result, movements are classified in terms of three principal types of cycle:[1] a medium-term or Juglar cycle, a short-term or Kitchin cycle and a long-term or so-called Kondratieff cycle. To these we may add an annual cycle formed by the ensemble of seasonal factors, and a hypothetical building cycle with a periodicity of some twenty years.

The main type of fluctuation in capitalist economies (the Juglar cycle) can be seen to occur quite regularly from 1815 to 1937, with a periodicity of some 8 years. Similarly, the Kondratieff cycle, whose length would be of the order of 50 years, corresponds quite well to observable data for the period 1790 to 1940, and some people discern in the present crisis a trend shift back to this cycle, after the expansion of the post-war years up to 1973. The Kitchin cycle is the name given to a more frequent cycle, with a periodicity of about 40 months.

The cycle approach has led to some very full morphological studies, in particular on the part of the researchers of the NBER. J. Shiskin (1967)[2] and G. H. Moore (1980) give an exposition of some post-war developments of this approach, extended to the case of growth cycles by Ilse Mintz. The cycle approach received less interest between World War II and recent years, being challenged by Keynesian theories aiming more at causal explanation and at structural prediction than at the description of temporal regularities. So we will only occasionally address ourselves to the problem of the cycle in this sense.

4 THE PLAN OF THE BOOK

This book will involve four parts. In the first, devoted to the development of macroeconomics, we will study in turn the 'grand dynamics' of Marx and the Classics, and pre-Keynesian theories of the business cycle before discussing the Keynesian revolution and its implications. The second part will deal with behavioural dynamics and will consider the reformulation of three important aggregative functions for consumption, investment and the demand for monetary assets. In the third part, we will tackle the concept of growth: its representation and its sources, the problem of its stability and regulation, and lastly various questions connected with the optimal pattern of growth and its limits, in particular those arising from the scarcity of non-renewable resources. The last part of the work is tied up with the analysis of short-term instabilities, of a more temporary character. Having shown the contribution of models to business cycle dynamics, we will deal with the analysis of inflation and unemployment with references to the modern 'new classical' paradigm, to neo-Marxian analysis of the 'crisis', and to neo-Keynesian disequilibrium theory.

Part One
The Development of Macrodynamics

The advisability of beginning the study of any field of economic analysis along historical lines is debatable. Certainly such a circuitous course is not justified if past studies are considered only as error-ridden accounts, which merely anticipate contemporary analysis. Yet, to see in the evolution of economic thought only a perpetual recommencement of the same debates and a perpetual reproduction of the same divisions suggests an excessively pessimistic view of the scientific status of economic analysis. Like any other discipline, economic science has progressed through alternating constructive development with discontinuous reorganisation of its visions of reality around new paradigms. Thus, current models may be studied as much from the contemporary (synchronistic) point of view of their structures as from the historical (diachronistic) perspective of their origins.

We will study the development of macrodynamics up to the so-called Keynesian Revolution. Three stages in this development can be distinguished. With the 'great dynamics' (W. J. Baumol, *Economic Dynamics*, Macmillan, 1959), there appeared the aggregative systems of interpretation of economic movement of Ricardo and Marx. The pre-Keynesian period witnessed a burgeoning cluster of works devoted to the study of growth and business cycles from a disequilibrium perspective. And lastly, it was through the Keynesian Revolution and the dual process of neoclassical synthesis and counter-revolution which followed it, that macrodynamic analysis reached what appeared, ten years ago, to be its definitive form.

1 Great Dynamic Theories of the Past

The earliest representations of the complete network of economic activity were constructed by Boisguilbert and later by the physiocrats, in terms of the circulation of wealth. Without ignoring the genuine dynamic aspects of their work, relating in the former case to the nature of crises, in the latter to the accumulation of capital, we will instead restrict ourselves to a presentation of the grand systems of interpretation of economic movement advanced by the English Classical economists, in particular Ricardo, and by Marx. Clearly, this account does not aim to give a complete historical picture of the work of these authors, such as might be found in a more specialised work.[1]

1 THE RICARDIAN DYNAMIC MECHANISM

David Ricardo, who wrote at the end of the Napoleonic Wars, was the principal representative of the English Classical school founded forty years previously with the publication of Adam Smith's *Wealth of Nations*. This book laid down quite clearly the two components which, these writers believed, constituted economic movement: growth, led by capital accumulation and culminating in a steady state, and short-term fluctuations which market mechanisms themselves would resolve, to the extent that they were allowed into play.

A The growth process and the constraints on growth

The English Classical economists witnessed the 'take-off' of the British economy in the first industrial revolution. They identified the accumulation of capital as the engine of growth, a process which seemed to them to have a limited life-time and to be destined to culminate in a stationary state.

In Smith's view it was the division of labour[2] which permitted the accumulation of wealth, but the division of labour also implied that in contrast to the traditional artisan, the industrial labourer could no longer live from the sale of his own produce. His wage had to be advanced to him from a subsistence fund, which along with the instruments and materials he required, constituted the capital stock.

Profit was at once both the source and the objective of the accumulation of capital – hence the emphasis placed on the distribution of income in Ricardo's analysis. 'It is as impossible for the farmer or manufacturer to live without profits, as it is for the worker to exist without a wage. The motivation to accumulate will diminish with every reduction in profits.'[3]

It is not possible to introduce Ricardian dynamic theory without first briefly outlining Ricardo's position on the question of value. Beginning from an initial reaffirmation of the labour theory of value, in its strict form, he first assumes that the exchange value or natural price of reproducible goods is determined by the quantity of direct and indirect labour required for their production. But he then points out that a significant role is also played by the distribution of costs between wages and profits, which is linked to the mean gestation period of capital in the production process under consideration. Therefore, Ricardo only adopts labour-value as an approximation.

But, conscious of the unsatisfactory nature of this solution, Ricardo searched all his life for an invariant standard of value, which would not itself be affected by changes in the distribution of income, and so could provide an absolute reference point from which to measure the value of other goods.[4]

For want of a solution to this problem, Ricardo assumed in the first presentation of his analysis that there was only one basic commodity (that is to say, only one commodity used in the production of all others) which was at the same time the product of the agricultural sector and the sole means of subsistence of labour: corn. This good was thus employed as the unit of measurement for every variable. Income was distributed between landowners who received rent, wage workers and capitalists – that is, farmers and manufacturers who collected profits. The latter were considered a surplus, rents and wages being determined 'up-stream'. Ricardo believed that the 'natural wage' which prevailed in the medium to long term, would stabilise at the subsistence level, determined by custom as well as by physiological considerations. The strategic component was the movement of property rent.

Property rent was said to result from the difference in fertility of different types of soil, and thus had a differential character. Like all classical writers, Ricardo accepted that decreasing returns prevailed in agriculture and constant returns prevailed in industry. So, strictly speaking the labour theory of value could not be applied to corn, because it implied constant returns. Ricardo applied it at the margin, assuming that the natural price of corn was the labour cost of the most costly output, obtained on the least fertile land. Thus, on all other lands, there was a divergence between the price of corn and its cost in terms of wages and profits, and this was rent.

Now, in this model when output rises, less fertile lands are brought into cultivation and the labour-cost of corn rises. Hence, total output in terms of corn increases less than employment. Furthermore, an increasing proportion of total output is seized by rent. Kaldor's classic diagram[5] illustrates the dynamics of the determination of rent and distribution.

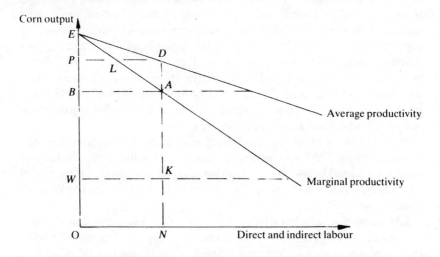

Figure 1.1

The respective axes represent direct and indirect labour (labour and capital in modern terminology), which are assumed to vary together (in fixed proportions), and output in the agricultural sector, assumed to be made up solely of corn. As a result of diminishing returns, the average productivity of labour (direct and indirect) decreases, so marginal productivity must be less than the average. The total level of output from a level of employment N is found either by multiplying ON by average productivity (giving the area of $ONDP$) or by integrating the marginal productivity function between O and N (giving the area of $OEAN$), which implies that the triangles EPL and LDA are congruent (given that the average marginal productivity schedules are assumed to be linear).

The remuneration, in wages and profits, for one unit of direct or indirect 'labour' in standard terms is just equal to its marginal productivity at N, that is the distance *NA*. If it were not, marginal land would not be exploited or it would not be truly marginal. The total cost of corn production in wages and profits measured in corn is thus determined by the area of the rectangle *OBAN*. So, by subtraction property rent is found to be equal to the area EBA. It is well worth noting that rent is here determined by the difference between the productivity of marginal land and that of the most fertile land, or in other words, by the slope of the marginal productivity function – that is, by purely technical factors.

How the cost of production *OBAN* is divided between wages and profits is quite simply determined. The fact that the real wage rate, in terms of corn, is predetermined implies a total value of wages equal to the area *OWKN*. Profits are simply a residual over and above this – *WBAK*. As wages are advanced over an average period assumed to be one year, the annual wage flow is also equal to the society's wage fund. In the absence of fixed capital, the rate of profit is thus equal to the ratio of the areas *WBAK/OWKN*.

We may complete the dynamics of the model by noting the dual causality of the wage fund equation $W = wN$.

In the short term this equation determines the wage rate. Capital accumulation entails an increase in the market wage rate, which, on account of the Malthusian population principle, will lead to a population expansion which will bring the wage back to its natural, subsistence level. In the long term, the wage fund equation operates as a demand function for productive labour $N = W/w$. Accumulation of capital will then result in increased employment of direct and indirect labour. The margin between the average and marginal productivity of labour will grow, so rent will signify a proportionately increasing levy. With a constant real wage rate and falling marginal labour productivity, it is clear that the share of profits can only contract.

Another standard diagram, presented by Baumol,[6] illustrates this evolutionary process. Total output is now measured on the y-axis. This output grows at a decreasing rate but consistently faster than the total cost of production (output minus rent or alternatively wages plus profits). Wages, expressed in corn, are proportional to employment and equal to wN. Hence, we obtain the graph in Figure 1.2.

If *F(N)* is the total output of corn, $N \, dF/dN$ is the total cost of production $((ON \times NA)$ on Kaldor's graph), so rent comes to $N(F/N - dF/dN)$ and profit to $(dF/dN - w) N$. We assume that profit is entirely reinvested in the form of the wage fund.

$$\Delta K = [(dF/dN) - w]N \quad \text{therefore} \quad \Delta N = \tfrac{1}{w} \, [dF/dN) - w)N$$

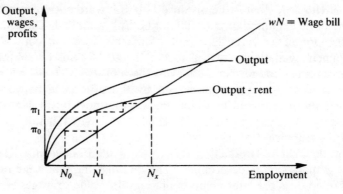

Figure 1.2

and the rate of growth of capital and employment is equal to:

$$\frac{\Delta K}{K} = \frac{\Delta N}{N} = \frac{1}{w} \frac{dF}{dN} - 1 = \frac{dF}{dK} - 1$$

The expression DF/dK represents the 'apparent' productivity of capital, as labour is the only factor of production. The rate of growth is nil at the level of employment where marginal labour productivity is equal to the subsistence wage.

At the initial level N_0, the profit π_0 is produced; so in the following period a level of employment $N_1 = N_0 + \pi_0/w$ is registered, yielding a profit of π_1.

The process continues until the maximum employment level N_x is reached, where there is no profit and thus no accumulation. In fact, it might be seen as desirable to show the fact that growth actually stops before the profit rate reaches zero. Thus the most correct formula is to incorporate a minimum rate of profit ρ, required to maintain capitalist consumption. This would be applied to the wage function as follows: $w(1 + \pi)N$, yielding a level of capital accumulation:

$$[(dF/dN) - w (1 + \rho)] N.$$

This line of argument was considerably significant in strengthening classical economists in their belief that the growth induced by the industrial revolution was only a transitory phenomenon.

Ricardo tried to give it a more general significance at the technical level by considering a multi-good economy with values denoted in money terms. Some interesting implications arose from this but also some confusion. Because profit varied inversely with wage costs and the volume of the latter was exogenous, only the production costs of goods required for workers' consumption influenced the determination of the rate of profit, which was not affected by the conditions of production of other goods (luxury goods). However, for the Ricardian scheme to work wage goods had to be subject to decreasing returns, otherwise the wage rate, with its volume in goods remaining constant, could not increase regularly in value as the proof required.

At the social and political level, this analysis clearly pointed to rent and its beneficiaries as the potential enemies of industrial growth. It was in the interests of manufacturers to lower the cost of consumer wage goods through massive imports of agricultural commodities from countries endowed with an abundance of fertile land. So, Ricardo's analysis came at an opportune moment to strengthen the case of those who called for the abolition of the 'Corn laws' (preventing the importation of wheat), whose claims were not in fact satisfied until 1846.

Free trade was thus seen as a way of delaying the prospect of a stationary state. It is worth recalling that it was the defence of free trade which inspired another famous Ricardian theory – the theory of comparative costs, which showed that, contrary to the view of the Mercantilist school, trade brought mutual gains.

One might ask if technical progress was not similarly of a type which would raise marginal labour productivity and permit permanent growth: Ricardo himself did not think so. In agriculture, technical progress, which in the short term effectively reduces rent, would be halted by landowners; while in industry, it would take the form of mechanisation, that is to say the substitution of capital for labour, generating technological unemployment.

To understand the Ricardian line of thought, one must remember that, in Ricardo's view, wages were part of the gross product but not the net product of society. Mechanisation enabled the net product of society and hence profits to increase, but also entailed a reduction in the wage fund and the gross product with which it was replenished each year. 'As the ability to employ labour and maintain a population depends always on the gross product of a nation and not on its net product, the demand for work-hands will necessarily diminish, the level of population will become excessive, and the working classes will enter a period of anguished impoverishment.'[7]

In fact, the examples quoted by Ricardo seem weak and, in order to draw any firm conclusions from this reasoning, it would be necessary to specify its assumptions more clearly.[8] Nevertheless, Ricardian thinking on the effects of mechanisation did exert a strong influence, in particular on Marx.

B Self-regulation of the system

The Ricardian analysis of growth led its author to defend liberal ideas which were favourable to manufacturers – the engineers of the industrial revolution. Similarly, Ricardo lent his authoritative support to liberal theories relating to the automatic short-term regulation of the economy. Essentially, these simply demonstrated that market mechanisms could efficiently resolve any possible disequilibria, so that there was no need for State intervention. Ricardo's role in the defence of this theory consisted in supporting the 'law of markets' and the quantity theory of money.

Although the law of markets had been expounded by preclassical writers, it was through J. B. Say and J. S. Mill that it received its definitive formulation. In its earlier exposition, the assertion that products served as mutual outlets for demands merely expressed an understanding of the links between the different participants in the economic cycle; for the latter writers, however, the idea that supply created its own demand made it possible to declare that in the aggregate there could be no excess supply – only disequilibria due to imbalances, for which the best remedy to apply was to allow prices of goods to fall when there was excess production, and to rise when there was excess demand.

Ricardo's position was very clear.[9] Under no circumstances could insufficient demand be a hindrance to production or the accumulation of capital, which could only be restricted by the increased production cost of wage goods.

At the time, Malthus was opposed to Say's law and emphasised the persistent risk of over-production. Unlike Ricardo, he rejected the explanation of value in terms of labour[10] and conducted his analysis in terms of supply and demand, which led him to adopt a less one-sided view of the determinants of prices and output. He laid stress on the two dimensions of so-called 'effective' demand: willingness to buy and the availability of buying power; he was also afflicted by an illusion common to many under-consumption theorists.

In Malthus's view, saving was a generator of over-production, not in the modern sense, in which savings would tend to exceed investment, but, on the contrary, because savings were entirely invested. In fact, one should point out that he shared Adam Smith's belief, 'that that which is saved is as surely consumed as that which is expended'. Savings were entirely invested, that is to say included in the wage fund and, as such, spent on consumer wage goods. So effectively, saving replaced unproductive consumption with consumption by productive workers. Disequilibrium did not arise from a reduction in demand – which did not occur – but from an increase in supply due to the activity of the productive workers additionally employed.[11]

The logic of Malthus is interesting in that it dictates a standpoint on rent completely at odds with Ricardo's. The landed gentry played a socially useful role in so far as they used the macroeconomic surplus in an unproductive manner, thus avoiding a supply glut, given the unchanged demand situation. In this view, the abolition of the Corn Laws would have led the English economy to generalised crises of over-production.

In any open economy following liberal policies, there is an additional means of regulation, operating at a more global level. It is based on the influence of the quantity theory of money. This old concept, first expounded by J. Bodin in the sixteenth century and later by D. Hume in the eighteenth century, was given its traditional format by Ricardo. J. S. Mill expressed this form as follows:

$$MV = PT.$$

This formula shows that the product of the stock of money in circulation times its velocity of circulation is equal to the product of the general price level times the volume of transactions. As both the volume of activity and the velocity of circulation are exogenously given, the general price level will be proportional to the money supply.

But under a gold-standard regime – a liberal policy prescription *par excellence* – the money supply will itself vary with the balance of trade as denoted in gold. So, if English prices in terms of gold were to rise excessively, there would be an ensuing trade deficit, an exodus of gold and hence a reduction in M and a fall in prices. If, on the other hand, English prices were too low, a trade surplus would prevail, accompanied by an influx of gold, an expansion of the domestic money supply and a compensating rise in prices.

There had probably never been presented such an idyllic and apparently simple image of the self-regulating properties of the liberal capitalist system. Ricardo's influence was to hold sway for a consider-able time and the Peel Acts succeeded in strictly limiting to a modest sum the amount of money which the Bank of England could bring into circulation over and above the sum corresponding to the stock of gold.

The Ricardian system only achieved its apparent rigorousness at the expense of some analytical simplifications, which rather weakened it theoretically. Nevertheless, it held a curious fascination for economists who repeatedly stated their verbal allegiance to it while at the same time developing analytical critiques of it.

2 THE DYNAMIC TREND IN MARX

Marx's 'grand dynamic system' surpassed that of Ricardo in its scale and in its impact on the present day. As it is written from a methodological perspective totally different from that of other schools of economic thought, to present and, above all, assess it on the same basis presents a rather intricate problem. However, behind the different conceptualisations, it is often the same determinants which are being analysed and which we find again and again.

Marxian dynamic theory relates specifically to the capitalist mode of production, that is to say a form of social organisation in which the wage relation is the dominant relation of production. The driving-force of the system is the extraction of surplus-value, in the form of profit, and its accumulation. The process of capital accumulation will be studied first; and we will then linger a while on the question of the fundamental laws, underlying the development of the system.

A The accumulation of capital

Just as with classical writers, it is the accumulation of capital which is the essence of capitalist economic growth in Marx. But 'capital' does not simply denote a stock of the means of production and the means of workers' subsistence, because it also represents the other party to the wage relation. Furthermore, the accumulation of capital is bound up with the notion of 'reproduction' – a notion whose scope is extended from the purely physical meaning given to it in the writing of the Physiocrats to encompass the reproduction of the actual relations of production. Before starting on this point, it might be useful to briefly recall the underlying concepts of the theory.

1 Underlying concepts

The capitalist economy is a market economy and in it goods become 'commodities' – mere supports of exchange value abstracting from their use value. The value of commodities corresponds to the quantity of abstract (homogeneous) labour socially necessary for their production. But here, Marx ran up against the same problem which had confronted Ricardo: the problem of the influence of the structure of those costs tied to the structure of capital. He resolved the problem by introducing a distinction between value and the normal exchange ratio, which he called the price of production. He admitted that the price of production would exceed value in manufacturing processes which embodied a lesser proportion of direct labour, and vice versa.

The structure of capital is not studied so much in terms of its technical composition – the combination of labour and the material means of production – as its value-composition or organic composition, which is the ratio of capital devoted to the material means of production (constant capital) to capital devoted to wages (variable capital). It is the organic composition of capital which governs the ratio of values to prices of production. In fact, value may be broken down into paid labour (wages, including those with which indirect labour is remunerated) and unpaid labour (or surplus-value), which is proportional only to the variable capital employed, while the price of production may be broken down into wages (the price of production of the means of subsistence) and profits, which are proportional to the whole of employed capital.

Thus a dual level of analysis is developed. The purpose of value, which no longer coincides with exchange ratios, is to identify surplus-value as the difference between the amount of labour supplied and the amount of labour paid for, which is the value of labour power, and as such is equal to the labour time necessary for its reproduction.[12] This is considered the fundamental level, essential for the analysis of the mode of production. In contrast, the concepts of profit and the price of production are met only at the level of circulation, as the forms in which value and surplus-value are realised, that is to say transformed into money. To the capitalist and the non-Marxist analyst only this level is apparent. There thus arises a new problem because, while for Marxists the objectivity of these concepts is quite illusory, one cannot deny their relevance for the analysis of the operation of the system, as it is precisely with respect to these categories that agents' decisions are made.

2 Reproduction

The basic analysis of the operation of the system relies on the distinction between two forms of 'circuit'. In the simple circuit, of monetary exchange, a commodity is transformed into money through sale ($C - M$), then the money into a commodity through purchase ($M - C$). As the items exchanged are equivalent to one another, this process entails no change in value. On the other hand, when money circulates as capital, it is initially employed in the form of *labour power* and the means of production ($M - C$) but when the value of output is realised through sale, it is the value of *labour* and the means of production which is relevant, thus surplus value is included. So we have $C' - M'$ with $M' > M$.

Combining these two cycles permits reproduction to occur with the means of production and workers' means of subsistence being replaced, and a profit also being attained. Simple reproduction occurs when the capital mobilised in each period is identical, all of surplus-value being consumed. The following diagram[13] illustrates the four phases of this process.

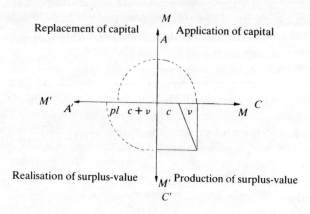

Figure 1.3

Initially, money capital is transformed into the capital commodities c and v, constant and variable capital. The process of production is analysed as a process of extraction of surplus value at the rate $T = \frac{s}{v}$ hence the line in the second quadrant has a slope of $1 + T$. The sale of the commodities produced permits their value to be realised (3) and this is then allocated (4) partly to capital replacement and partly to capitalist consumption.

The accumulation of a proportion of surplus-values permits capital accumulation and enables reproduction of the system on a larger scale. The same diagram may be used to represent this case, if we suppose that a fraction of α of surplus-value is accumulated and assume, for simplicity of presentation, that this is solely in the form of variable capital.

Reproduction, which is a condition of survival of the capitalist mode of production, is not certain to occur, as it presupposes the satisfaction of certain conditions which are continually called into question by the contradictory nature of the system.

B The laws of motion

The general development of the system is governed by the materialist conception of history, according to which man 'produces' society and its mode of organisation by producing the material conditions for his existence. Thus, it is the development of the material forces of

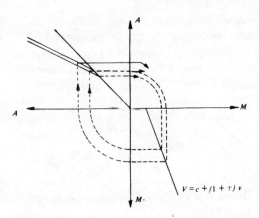

$$V = c + (1 + T) \, v$$

Figure 1.4

production – labour power and the techniques of production – which plays the driving role and which, at a certain stage, comes into conflict with the social relations of production and with the legal and ideological superstructures of society. The capitalist mode of production is subject to certain deep-seated tendencies which exemplify the inevitability of this contradictory mode of development and which are themselves expressed in the 'laws of motion' of the capitalist system.

The concept of a 'law of motion' shows quite clearly the originality of the Marxist methodology as compared with the conventional scientific method. In the words of Karl Popper[14] the philosopher, the influence, explanatory value and theoretical and empirical content of a scientific law are the greater, the more possible outcomes it excludes and the broader the class of feasible observations capable of refuting it. The 'laws of motion', on the other hand, are not intended to be empirically refutable but merely to establish the primary of certain basic tendencies over secondary counter-tendencies, even if the influence of the latter might locally or temporarily dominate the historical development of the system.

The basic trends of the system are expressed in three fundamental laws: the tendency of the rate of profit to fall, the tendency towards growing impoverishment and the tendency towards increased concentration of capital.

1 The tendency of the rate of profit to fall

This classical belief, justified in Smith by the limited opportunity for investment and in Ricardo by the rising cost of wage goods, is found again in Marx, based on the nature of technical progress itself.

Marx believed that technical progress, in the form of mechanisation, would necessarily entail some change in the organic composition of capital $\frac{c}{v}$. In fact, technological development would effectively combine labour with ever-increasing quantities of the material means of production, a process which would be reflected in the organic composition of capital,[15] though possibly in a rather roundabout way.

If we adopt an expression for the rate of profit ρ in terms of the rate of extraction of surplus-value τ and the organic composition of capital,

$$\rho = \frac{pl}{c+v} = \frac{\tau v}{c+v} = \frac{\tau}{(c/v + 1)},$$

it is apparent that a rise in c/v with surplus-value constant implies a fall in the rate of profit.

There are certain forces which tend to counteract this trend: first, an increase in the rate of surplus-value extraction, in particular through the relative growth of surplus-value (through a reduction in the labour time necessary for the reproduction of the labour force, hence in remunerated labour time) and the faster circulation of capital, second, a relative fall in relation to wage consumption in the value of the elements making up constant capital. But these counteracting forces are themselves limited in the long term.

One point remains to be cleared: if technical progress lowers the rate of profit, why do capitalists undertake it? Because the competition to which they are subjected obliges them to innovate, says Marx. The first to put a new technique into operation will derive an increased profit from it, but as the value of profit falls, others will have to follow at the risk of being eliminated. Then nobody will realise any more than the reduced rate of profit corresponding to this new organic composition. In fact, the argument neglects the effect of technological progress occurring simultaneously in producer goods industries. This will permit those who are slow in innovating to buy their machines more cheaply.

The most controversial point of the law is the inevitability of the rise in the organic composition, and more particularly the inevitability of the relative movement of the values of producer and consumer goods. To discuss this matter more deeply would require some specification of the assumptions relating to technical progress and its relative rate in the producer and consumer good sectors. In this respect, one might quote J. Robinson's contribution,[16] though C. Bettelheim's essay presents the advantage of lying close to Marxist theory. Introducing an exogenous productivity growth trend, he establishes that the rate of profit will tend to conform to a limit equal to the quotient of the rate of growth – given by the growth of employment plus the growth of productivity – divided by the rate of investment of surplus-value.

Certain Marxists[17] have criticised results of this kind on the grounds that they hide the contradictions between capitalists as well as the fundamental contradiction between capital and labour.

As regards the current implications of this controversy, it is worth emphasising that Marxist writers believe that the principal factors counteracting the falling tendency of the rate of profit may be found by studying the circumstances under which depreciation of the value of constant capital occurs. Thus, the concept of depreciation occupies a central place in contemporary Marxist work and will be examined more closely later.[18]

2 The tendency towards increasing impoverishment

This Marxist law may also be said to have Classical roots. The Malthusian population principle prevented wages from remaining consistently above a 'subsistence level', which, although defined in terms of custom rather than purely in terms of physiological needs, had a basic demographic significance. The German Lasalle interpreted this as the iron law of wages being imposed upon labour.

Marx, however, could not attribute a purely demographic significance to the concept of impoverishment as if it were a natural and unavoidable law: it had to appear as a law specific to the capitalist system. Thus, in his eyes the principal driving force in the process was not absolute overpopulation (in relation to resources) but relative overpopulation (in relation to variable capital).[19] So his argument is an extension of Ricardo's analysis of mechanisation. Intercapitalist competition in the development of techniques entails the substitution of constant for variable capital – machines for men – without any apparent compensation. Hence, there arises a group of technologically unemployed people, an industrial reserve army which permits capitalists to determine the wage rate.

We will not examine whether the character of this impoverishment would be relative or absolute, the former involving a reduction in the value of workers' consumption, and the latter a reduction in the goods available for workers' subsistence. Marx's writings seem to admit of both possibilities.[20] In any case, increasing impoverishment is always backed by increasing proletarianisation – that is to say, the concentration of the means of production in an increasingly limited number of hands.

3 The tendency towards increasing concentration

The third fundamental tendency of the capitalist mode of production is for capital to become increasingly concentrated in a limited number of decision-making centres. There are two elements at work here. Strictly speaking, concentration denotes increase in the size of individual capital units, that is to say, the development of larger and larger units of production. It is the requirements of technical development which produce this process. In addition, there is the centralisation of capital, resulting from the merging of individual capital units. The development of the joint-stock company has given quite a fillip to this process, as has the development of the large corporation in more recent years. More generally, one might see the centralisation of capital as one of the essential functions of the financial intermediary.

Centralisation dispossesses the small owners of the means of production, uniting them with the mass of the proletariat. It also reduces the social base of capitalism and anticipates the socialisation of the means of production. As Marx put it, 'the expropriators shall be expropriated'.

Concentration and centralisation of capital are incorporated into the Marxist analysis as a way of characterising the stage of development with which specific modes of growth or regulation of the system are associated. Thus, Lenin[21] saw imperialism as the method of expansion of a capitalist system at a stage of development dominated by financial capital as described in Hilferding's analysis,[22] while the phrase 'state monopoly capitalism' has been coined as a way of describing the contemporary stage of development, characterised by systematic state intervention and a high degree of monopoly.[23]

3 CAPITALIST CRISES

In England, Marx witnessed the first of a new type of economic crisis, resulting not from the chance failure of agricultural production but from disequilibria in economic activity. In his view, such crises were a manifestation of the contradictory nature of capitalist development. It has often been said that Marx had no integrated theory of crises, and that is true. However, there is in Marx some examination of the nature of equilibrium conditions and of the possibility of crises, and this is as important as the analysis of the actual form of these crises.

A The formal conditions for reproduction

The process of reproduction, both simple and expanded, was illustrated above in a format which made clear the different phases of the process, by placing emphasis on the organic composition of capital. In order for reproduction to occur, certain ratios must be established between the capital devoted to the manufacture of the means of production (sector I) and the means of consumption (sector II) respectively. In fact, the value produced in each case may be broken down into constant capital consumed, variable capital and surplus-value[24]

$$V_1 = c_1 + v_1 + pl_1$$
$$V_2 = c_2 + v_2 + pl_2$$

In simple reproduction, the value assigned to consumer goods is $v_1 + v_2 + s_1 + s_2$, while $c_1 + c_2$ represents the value of producer goods used. In order that the value of production should coincide with the value of each good used, it is therefore necessary that:

$$V_2 = c_1 + c_2 \quad \text{and} \quad V_2 = v_1 + v_2 + pl_1 + pl_2,$$

or, that the equilibrium condition

$$c_2 = v_1 + pl_1.$$

should hold.

This determines the ratio which must be established between sectors in order to make simple reproduction possible. In expanded reproduction, the pattern is modified in so far as a fraction α_1, of total surplus value is accumulated in the form of constant capital, while the fraction α_2, accumulated in the form of variable capital,[25] represents an additional expenditure on consumer goods, just like the fraction directly consumed $(1 - \alpha_1 - \alpha_2)$. Hence, the equilibrium condition becomes:

$$c_2 + \alpha_1 pl_2 = v_1 + (1 - \alpha_1) pl_1$$

There are two interpretations suggested by these models. In the first place, it is the scheme of expanded reproduction which presents the basis for R. Luxemburg's theory that capitalist development requires external markets. According to her, unless there is a credit-backed demand for an equivalent sum outside the system, there is no way of financing the investment demand corresponding to accumulated surplus-value, as this surplus cannot be used to finance any purchases before being realised.[26] The error in her reasoning consists of imposing a notion of time sequence on an equilibrium condition which relates to simultaneous flows. This becomes apparent when it is observed that an equivalent external demand would introduce an error in the other direction, accumulated surplus-value being realised twice over.

In other respects, certain writers, H. Denis[27] in particular, believe that these conditions can be likened to the savings-investment identity in Keynes. But one might note that non-realisation of these conditions is not incompatible with the law of markets, which is not the case with the Keynesian proposition. In fact, the equilibrium condition for reproduction might be better likened to another Keynesian condition laid down in the *Treatise on Money*,[28] which says that expenditure on investment should be equal to the cost of investment $(I = I')$.

Without directly constituting a theory of crises, these reproduction models lay down conditions for the proportional development of the system, which if violated would threaten the process of capitalist reproduction. Each proportion to be respected presents a further opportunity for crisis.

B The possibility of crises

It would seem unusual to assert the possibility of crises, if we were only attempting to assess the empirical existence of this possibility. In fact, the problem is to judge whether a crisis may occur for reasons exogenous to the operation of the system or if, on the contrary, it is inherent in the very rules of the system's operation. Marx confirmed the possibility of crises by rejecting Say's law, and by pinpointing certain properties of the capitalist system, which, in his view, demonstrated its fundamentally contradictory nature.

His rejection of Say's law is fierce, which is understandable, given the vindicatory image of the operation of capitalism which this law presented in opposition to 'market-saturation'[29] theorists, but it is also analytically sound. The law of markets relies on each individual assuming a dual role as both a producer, selling products or at least services, and a consumer, operating as a purchaser. It was quite easy for Marx to point out the illusory nature of this apparent symmetry: though consumption is undertaken by both capitalists and the mass of productive workers, production, or at least the decisions concerning it are undertaken only by a minority of agents.

Moreover, monetary exchange in the *CMC* circuit takes place through the medium of currency. This implies the separation of the exchange cycle into two distinct acts – a sale and a purchase. The problem of co-ordinating these different acts then arises. For a liberal economist, the problem is doubly resolved. In the first place, since the purpose of any sale is exchange, that is to say the acquisition of another good, every sale will inevitably be followed by a purchase of the same sum. Secondly, according to Adam Smith, individual decisions will be spontaneously co-ordinated by the market 'as if by an invisible hand'. On the first point, Marx retorted that the reason for a sale might lie more in the desire to realise value by transforming it into money, than in the desire to buy. There would then be no synchronisation between sales and intended purchases. On the second point, his conflicting view of the operation of the system stands diametrically opposed to the liberal notion of harmony.

> Nothing could be more foolish than the dogma that because every sale is a purchase, and every purchase a sale, the circulation of commodities necessarily implies an equilibrium between sales and purchases. If this means that the number of actual sales accomplished is equal to the number of purchases, it is a flat tautology. But its real intention is to show that every seller brings his own buyer to market with him. . . . No one can sell unless someone else purchases. But no one directly needs to purchase because he has just sold. . . . These two processes lack internal independence because they complement each other. Hence, if the assertion of their external independence proceeds to a certain critical point, their unity violently makes itself felt by producing – a crisis.[30]

Once the *CMC* circuit is broken, its effect will be magnified in two ways, developing into a crisis. Firstly, the breakdown of the purchase–sale link will jeopardise the whole chain of the circuit. Secondly, the crisis of circulation will affect the actual *MCM'* circuit, that is to say the process of the engagement and reconstitution of money capital. Thus, a crisis of circulation becomes a crisis of reproduction.

C The determination of crises

The prior lack of co-ordination between the different agents in a capitalist economy, each guided by contradictory plans, creates a permanent possibility of crisis, but it is not sufficient to provoke one, that is to turn this possibility into a reality. There are various more direct causal factors which must come into play, which determine more immediately the incidence, the form and the role of crises. The relevant arguments may here be grouped under three headings: 'overproduction and underconsumption', 'overcapitalisation', and 'the technical peculiarities of capital'.

1 Overproduction and underconsumption
The tendency of the system towards overproduction illustrates the contradiction between its capacity, recognised by Marx, for developing

productive forces and its inability to increase consumption to the same extent. Thus, overproduction and underconsumption are closely linked.

Underconsumption is a factor permanently constricting the possibilities for the realisation of surplus-value in sector II. It is a corollary of pauperisation, of the downward pressure on wages under the weight of the 'industrial reserve army'. Hence, there is a growing disparity between society's absolute capacity to consume and the actual capacity to consume of the masses.[31] Thus, overproduction is never absolute, overproduction with respect to needs – but essentially relative – overproduction with respect to the possibilities for the realisation of profit in the capitalist economy.

Overproduction is manifested by a fall in the rate of profit, but in no way will this induce any compensating variation in output. On the contrary, capitalists might react by increasing production still more in order to maintain profit levels despite reduced unit margins. This, necessarily temporary, development helps to transform what is initially a trend towards permanent depression into a cyclical movement.

2 Overcapitalisation
We have seen in the context of reproduction models that the maintenance of equilibrium presupposes the achievement of certain ratios between the output of the means of production and the output of the means of consumption. Now, in a time of capitalist expansion, everything conspires to ensure an unequal development of the two sectors. The growth of sector I tends to accelerate as the result of a rapid accumulation of capital, which largely takes the form of a rise in the organic composition. On the other hand, sector II will find its development constrained by the less-than-proportional growth of variable capital. In other words, it suffers directly from the tendency towards underconsumption.

Once again, the resulting overcapitalisation expresses not an absolute surplus of accumulated means of production, but a surplus of capital with respect to the possibilities for valorisation.

This disproportionate development cannot continue indefinitely. Indeed, it is the resulting crisis which, by restraining accumulation of the means of production, restores the required balance in the rates of development of the two sectors.

3 Capital rigidity
The ability to correct disproportionalities is restricted by the rigidity of capital – 'the prisoner of its fixed element'. A certain part of the means of production, the fixed capital, is not renewed in each cycle but periodically as depreciation occurs. In fact, in addition to normal,

purely technical, depreciation there is economic depreciation – obsolescence – which implies for the means of production 'the need for constant replacement, although it may not have undergone its material lifetime'.

The replacement of fixed capital reveals a cyclical pattern,[32] which Marx thought might be represented by a period of ten years. However, it is not this length of time which is important but the fact that 'this rotational cycle provides a sound basis for periodic crises'.

4 Common characteristics

The various determinant factors described above do not constitute alternative causes as such, but combine to make up cumulative processes. Thus, a crisis affecting sector I as a result of the breakdown of accumulation generates a fall in the variable capital engaged in this sector, and hence induces a contraction of activity in sector II.

Another factor common to these various determinants is that they constitute complementary manifestations of the law of the tendency of the rate of profit to fall. It is in this respect that we can understand from the Marxist analysis the functional role of crises in the operation of the capitalist system.

A crisis is not only a costly illustration of capitalist contradictions; in Marx's view, it also provides a temporary solution to them, it 're-establishes the disturbed balance for the time being'. In contemporary terminology, it is a constituent element of the means of regulation of the system.

The functional character of crises is connected with the explanation of the recovery. This relies essentially on the recovery of the rate of profit under the influence, certainly, of an increase in the rate of extraction of surplus-value, which unemployment would permit, but, above all, under the influence of the reduction in the organic composition of capital, through the writing off of a proportion of constant capital and, more significantly, through its devaluation. Undoubtedly, it is on these conflicting tendencies affecting the rate of profit which we must focus in order to develop some understanding of the Marxist concept of a crisis.

> The barrier to the capitalist mode of production is manifested in the way that the development of labour productivity involves a law, in the form of the falling rate of profit, that at a certain point confronts this development itself in a most hostile way and has constantly to be overcome by way of crises.[33]

Out of the whole Marxist analysis, it is the theory of crises which has most impressed writers not sharing his general approach. At the turn of the century, it was, in particular, the theme of overcapitalisation and disproportionate development which was taken up again. Then, Marxist influence on the analysis of fluctuations went through a long period of eclipse, before reaffirming itself again in recent times. In the revival of Marxist analysis, the emphasis is on the concept of capital devaluation and the role of crises in the 'regulation' of the system.[34]

2 Pre-Keynesian Theories of Growth and Fluctuations

From the end of the eighteenth century up to the present time, it is possible to discern recurrent patterns of economic activity. These cyclical movements seem to have been particularly regular between 1815 and 1929, and were felt in turn in all the countries affected by the industrial revolutions. In fact, from the end of the eighteenth century up to 1848, depressions remained agricultural in origin, though their main effects were seen in the industrial sector. Only after 1860 do they appear as basically industrial depressions.

The slumps of 1787, 1816, 1826 and 1847 were all the results of falling agricultural output. Through various transmission mechanisms, most importantly declining spending power in the country and shortages of capital, industrial output was affected, leading to bankruptcies and unemployment. Even so, most of the unemployed were still country dwellers who had never worked in industry. These phases saw the distinction between artisans and workmen harden in the wake of mechanisation.

Between 1857 and 1940, no fewer than eleven worldwide depressions can be counted: 1857, 1864–6, 1873–7, 1882–4, 1890–93, 1900, 1907, 1913, 1920–2, 1929–34 and 1937. The first two of these mainly affected Britain, France and the United States. Germany and Austria came into the picture about 1873. Up to 1890, waves of railway construction seem to have been the determining factor, while after that date financial instability becomes dominant. Thus in 1893, a wave of bankruptcies led to the closure of 600 banks, stimulating the organisation of the American banking system. The depression of 1900 missed out the USA, but for the first time spread to Russia. That of 1913 was interrupted by the First World War, whilst that of 1920 belonged to the phase of post-war readjustment. In October 1929, the Wall Street Crash heralded the deepest and lengthiest depression yet known, while the 1937 slump was mainly felt in the United States, as Europe prepared for war.

It is hardly surprising that economists, confronted by this regular occurrence, should have attempted to formulate a theory of the trade cycle. However, at a time when neoclassical analysis was being developed around the concept of equilibrium, theories of fluctuations were not easily to be assimilated. Some attempts at integrating such theories do exist, to an extent underestimated by some recent writers, but the law of markets was deeply rooted in thinking at this time, and systematically thwarted such attempts.

We shall first study the main alternative theories of fluctuations, moving on to examine the position reached when the Great Depression broke. Finally, a section will be devoted to growth theory, then dominated by Joseph Schumpeter.

1 THE MAIN ALTERNATIVE THEORIES OF FLUCTUATIONS

In the absence of consensus, various theories invoking different mechanisms were proposed. A brief survey of the main contributions might distinguish three approaches, respectively viewing crisis as a monetary phenomenon, as a symptom of overcapitalisation or as a consequence of underconsumption.

A Economic crisis as a monetary phenomenon

Speculation and slump in financial markets were features of successive stages in the cycle, so it is no surprise that depression was first ascribed to monetary causes. Such was the view of the first writer to concentrate on fluctuations, the French doctor, Clément Juglar (1862).

Variations in the money stock depend on the demand for credit, which expanded rapidly during the nineteenth century. The expansion of credit follows a cyclical pattern because during the upturn credit increases faster than does economic activity. In particular, money supplied to the system by discounting bills of exchange, themselves rediscounted at the central bank, causes the latter's portfolio of bills to grow faster than its gold reserves, and so to restrain further expansion. This causes problems for agents needing credit for transaction purposes, leading to bankruptcies which in turn hit the banks, so that the pyramid of credit collapses as quickly as it rose up. In this way a financial balancing mechanism operates, and is a precondition for further expansion.

We shall proceed by describing the transmission mechanism which translates credit fluctuations into real effects. In Hawtrey's analysis,[1] this transmission occurs principally through inventories. The analysis presumes that the quantity equation, with constant velocity of circulation, holds. Fluctuations in the money supply M govern the cycle of boom and slump. By lowering interest rates, banks can stimulate recovery; the direct effect on industry is probably quite small, but that on wholesalers and middle-men is likely to be substantial. They react by increasing stocks and in so doing place orders which will stimulate production. Expansion could continue indefinitely if credit were not eventually squeezed again; this, however, is inevitable under a gold standard. As the financing needs of firms continue to increase, particularly because of *lagged* wage increases, the slowdown becomes recession. With prices falling, the contraction is self-perpetuating. When stocks and labour recruitment have fallen back, a fall in interest rates can once again stimulate recovery.

Other analyses, such as that of Hayek to which we will return later on, allow for an interest rate effect on fixed capital investment. Of studies of the financial determinants of instability, paradoxically, that of Irving Fisher should be mentioned. Paradoxically, because Fisher is remembered most for his reformulation of the quantity theory; he considered, however, that this theory dealt only with '*normal and definitive*' effects. But 'just as periods of transition are the rule and those of equilibrium the exception' (Fisher, 1911, p. 71), the mechanism of exchange is nearly always dynamic rather than static. Money then affects the volume of output and speculation, financed largely by borrowing, ensues.

The cumulative increase of borrowing during expansion makes its indefinite continuance inconceivable. Moreover, overindebtedness aggravates deflation, since it affects people's expenditure and the price of assets during recession, while repayments to the banking system lead to an automatic reduction in the amount of money in circulation. The course of the 1929 crisis, as of the more recent one, illustrates the relevance of this analysis and the need to preserve a place for money at the heart of the financial structure of the economy.

B Overcapitalisation

The notion of overcapitalisation derives directly from Marx, at least from a set of early writings in which he described overcapitalisation relative to available savings. A second set of writings distinguishes overcapitalisation relative to demand.

1 Overcapitalisation relative to savings

The first person to suggest a theory of fluctuations in terms of overcapitalisation was the Russian Marxist, M. Tugan-Baranovsky (1913). His theme was the inability of the capitalist system to regulate the flow of savings, so as to meet the requirements of accumulation. He compared the action of a piston in a steam-engine:

The accumulation of liquid capital has an effect which may be likened to the role of steam in a cylinder. When the pressure exerted on the steam by the piston reaches a level sufficient to overcome its own inertia, the piston is set in motion, rises to the end of the cylinder simultaneously uncovering a passage which allows the steam to escape, and returns to its initial position. Similarly, liquid capital will accumulate until a certain level of pressure is reached where links are built with industry and it is thus mobilised, but once the capital is spent industrial activity returns to its former level.

A. Spiethoff and G. Cassell developed this theory. In their view, expansion is not only stimulated by growth in the output of producers' goods; it may even determine that output. However, the process cannot continue indefinitely, not because of insufficient demand to require the use of new equipment but, on the contrary, the problem arises in the availability of certain means of production. Spiethoff sees insufficient output of intermediate products confronting overproduction of durable goods. Cassell sees the pool of savings becoming inadequate to sustain accumulation.

The typical modern boom signifies neither over-production nor under-estimation of consumer demand or fixed capital requirements, but over-estimation of the supply of capital or volume of savings available for the long-term management of the fixed capital produced. (reprinted in *Readings in Business Cycle Theory*)

Let us keep in mind the main features of this line of thought: firstly, the idea of an imbalance between output and demand, while explicitly rejecting a global maladjustment; secondly, the notion that expansion could be prolonged by increasing savings. It is apparent that Keynesian theory would be considered revolutionary.

2 Overcapitalisation relative to demand
Because of market rigidities and lags in capital formation, capital formation and hence the creation of productive capacity does not behave as a simple proportion of needs as they arise. This is the theory which was argued by A. Aftalion and J. M. Clark and which was the precursor of the accelerator, itself the forerunner of today's investment functions.

The Frenchman believed that the increasing length of the period of production under capitalism generated a lag between the investment decision and its consequences. Investment, decided according to current needs, visible in high prices and profits, would in fact be brought into effect under different economic circumstances. During a phase of expansion,

> the scarcity of consumer goods along with the persistence of high prices and profits leads the entrepreneur to suppose that there is a continuing scarcity of capital goods. He cannot but bear witness to the non-satisfaction of current needs, and yet is unaware that in terms of production potential they are already oversatisfied. Why not order still more capital goods if there are not enough items for consumption? Overcapitalisation thus occurs simultaneously with and indeed is incited by underproduction of consumer goods. This is the direct cause of misallocations arising from capitalist protraction of the production process. (Aftalion, 1909)

He illustrates his argument with the well-known example of the stove loaded with too much fuel when it was cold, but not replenished thereafter on the grounds that the room was already warm.

To this lag, however, must be added the fact that the annual flow of investment is a function not of the level of output, but of its variations. Changes in the rhythm of accumulation therefore represent changes in demand, as J. M. Clark (1917) pointed out. This principle is essential to the understanding of market cycles. If demand for consumption goods increases at a decreasing rate, demand for capital goods will fall. Similarly, provided that no spare capacity exists, a slowing of the fall in output will lead the output of capital goods to increase once again. The accelerator effect proper is joined by an amplification effect which is more pronounced the more capital-intensive the consumption goods sector is.

This principle is one of the few emerging from the economic literature of that time to have become established among the tools of present-day analysis.

C Underconsumption

Here too Marx is relevant, but far from exclusively so. The theory of underconsumption can be traced back to Sismondi, Malthus and Lauderdale. Neither is it without enemies: G. Haberler, in his 1936 compilation 'Prosperity and Depression', spoke for all the orthodox economists when he concluded that 'these arguments put forward under the name of "underconsumption" are partly irrelevant for the explanation of the short cycle and partly covered by other theories.'

The modern commentator, on the other hand, at least if he is a Keynesian, notes the criticisms of Say's law and the notion of excessive savings at the moment of crisis. Moreover, these writers brought into focus the problems of identifying the relationships among savings, investment and the level of activity. Several technical contributions stand out, notably those of the English economist Hobson and of the Americans Johansen, Foster and Catchings. Hobson's contribution (especially 1895) is of interest in explaining a cyclical, rather than evenly and consistently depressive, impact of excess savings. Inequality of incomes generates high rates of savings, this inequality increasing over the expansionary phase in favour of profits. In that case, even if an equilibrium is possible with any given constant savings rate, it cannot be maintained with an increasing rate of savings.

In discussing excess savings, it is important to define our terms carefully. Do we mean excess savings actually invested or a tendency for savings to exceed investment? Hobson appears to be a prisoner of the former conception. Excess savings are manifest (in this view) in large amounts of idle capital during the slump. Excess savings relative to employable capital cumulate in an economy in which increasing inequality of incomes depresses demand.

The analysis of Foster and Catchings, who were original thinkers, proceeds in terms of monetary flows and seeks to identify the factors jeopardising realisation of the 'consumption-production equality'. This equality is not directly endangered by savings, since these go into investment or stockbuilding and lead eventually to wage payments. However, a disequilibrium arises when surplus production finds its way to the market. The value of this output is not currently available in the form of consumers' spending power, as it was distributed and spent in the previous period. Thus, the difference between money allocated for immediate or current consumption and that which is invested is that instead of being initially used to buy consumer goods, investment funds are set aside for the production of additional consumer goods (Foster and Catchings, 1900, p. 284). Here we can recognise Malthusian reasoning, and the objections levelled against Malthus may be re-used. Nonetheless, Foster and Catchings did bring out the idea that regular growth is needed for equilibrium in a capitalist economy,[2] which was forcefully to reemerge in the discussions surrounding the early post-Keynesian growth models of Domar and, above all, Fellner.

Only the third of the writers mentioned, Johansen, managed to escape from the orthodoxy of semi-automatic investment of savings and so allow excess savings to increase relative to investment (Johansen, 1908). Savings create a deficit in demand which needs to be filled by investment. However, of the three possible uses of savings (hoarding, purchase of existing assets and purchase of new assets) only the third creates demand. The argument is fallible, because it neglects the indirect implications of the first two uses, but has the virtue of overcoming a central obstacle to the genesis of modern macroeconomic theory.

2 THE 'STATE OF THE ART' AT THE TIME OF THE DEPRESSION

The main types of explanation outlined above had their defenders even as, after 1929, the deepest depression since the industrial revolution was in full swing. However, it seems most useful to describe a contribution illustrating the most advanced synthesis attained at that point by the traditional theory of fluctuations. Friedrich von Hayek's work may be viewed as a culmination of pre-Keynesian 'normal science'. In contrast, Keynes's *Treatise on Money* is representative of the first tentative steps along alternative routes, of that 'extraordinary research' of which a scientific revolution is born.[3]

A Hayek: a synthesis

The analysis of crisis proposed by Hayek[4] incorporates the elements of disproportionality, overcapitalisation and monetary disequilibrium. It begins from an anti-globalist premiss, holding it futile to look for causal relationships between aggregates. Thus a variable such as the general price level is of no significance: an explanation of economic movements can only be found in the structure of prices and of output.

The structure of output is characterised according to the 'Austrian' theory of capital, while the specification of monetary relationships owes its elements to Wicksell. The analysis of the cycle which follows from these assumptions confirms and reinforces the orthodox pre-Keynesian conclusions.

1 The structure of output
In the Austrian School's theory of capital, capitalist production depends on the intermediate use of non-produced means of production. When we speak of a 'more capitalistic' process, we imply a lengthening of the process. Thus capital, which by its origin is the total of purchases of original factors (a generalisation of the classical 'wage-fund'), takes the form at any given moment of intermediate products 'in the process of maturation', before the cycle ends in an output of consumption goods.

Hayek used a diagram suggested by Jevons to illustrate the stages of the process (Figure 2.1). Progressive investment of non-produced means of production leads to a steady accumulation, from one period to the next, in the value of capital invested, until the consumption goods stage (represented by the base of the triangle) is reached.

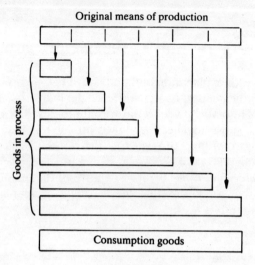

Figure 2.1

The most 'roundabout', most capitalistic, methods of production are more efficient physically, thereby enabling increased, though delayed, output of consumption goods. The productivity of intermediate processes allows a positive rate of return, but one which decreases as the duration of the process increases. A more capital-intensive technique will therefore only be profitable so long as the rate of interest is below the rate of return. A fall in the rate of interest will, as a result, normally lead to the adoption of new techniques. This will lead, reasoned Hayek, to a temporary fall in the output of consumption goods, with fewer processes arriving at maturity, to be followed by an increase in such output due to the greater efficiency of the new processes. If this temporary substitution of producer goods for consumer goods is validated 'ex ante' by agents' decisions, if it results from voluntary savings, expansion can proceed without any problem. If, on the other hand, this substitution is imposed by entrepreneurs borrowing, leading to forced savings, an unbalanced process is set in motion. When the increased purchasing power reaches consumers, they are in a position to express an increased demand for consumption goods inconsistent with the capital intensification now underway.

This conflict leads to the premature abandonment of the longest processes, the capital being liquidated: this is the essence of the crisis. It is interesting to note that this analysis conforms with the theory of insufficiency of savings, since the abandonment of the most roundabout processes is compelled by the shortage of intermediate goods to maintain them, at least at a price preserving profitability.

2 Monetary equilibrium

Fluctuations in the accumulation of capital stem, according to a theory borrowed from Wicksell (1898, 1935), from a disturbance of monetary equilibrium. Indeed, in monetary equilibrium, all savings are voluntary, so that there is no constraint on the movement of resources into more roundabout processes.

Wicksell's theory of monetary equilibrium, whose influence was to be crucial, was built on the foundations of his critique of the Quantity Theory. He effectively believed that the velocity of circulation of money proper[5] was unstable since, under certain institutional conditions, it is possible to reduce the use of money through control of credit and thus to affect its velocity of circulation. The demand for credit of the banking system is governed by the difference between two rates: the supply price of bank credit, or money rate of interest, and a rate which Wicksell defined first as a 'natural rate', which would equalise savings and investment in an economy without money, and then as a 'normal' rate: the equilibrium interest rate on loanable funds in a monetary economy. In a simple credit economy, the supply of credit would equal savings and so interest would be inelastic: a disparity between the 'monetary' and 'normal' rates of interest would quickly be resolved by an adjustment of the monetary rate. With an administered credit system, an exogenous money stock is added to savings to form the supply of credit, whose elasticity is thereby considerably increased; equalisation of rates is then accompanied by important changes in the means of payment available to firms, and hence in their demand for investment goods. In the end, if the banks are not constrained by their reserves of inside money (a 'pure credit economy' in Wicksell's terms) the supply of credit is perfectly interest-elastic. The money rate no longer plays a regulatory role, and a cumulative increase or decrease may develop.

Hayek retained the idea of a disparity between these rates as a driving force behind the processes of expansion and contraction, as well as the role of credit in allowing a demand for produced and non-produced investment goods in excess of voluntary savings. Demand is then pushed above the value of goods supplied, leading to increased prices and a rationing of consumers – a forced saving. Equality of these interest rates represents monetary equilibrium.

3 A representative synthesis

Hayek's analysis is a good example of a strand in pre-Keynesian thinking, including the conceptual blocks overcome by the General Theory but also keenly aware of the problems of the structure of prices and of output, which Keynes's work was to obscure, at least when taken at too aggregative a level, and which recent work has sought to rediscover.

It seemed clear to Hayek that the main determinant of variations in output was in changes to the nature of factor employment – to the structure of output – rather than their level of employment. In his view, when the banks' rate of interest fell below its equilibrium level, factors would be diverted towards the production goods sector, reducing output of consumption goods rather than increasing employment of factors. It is of importance to note, incidentally, that this view does not at all conflict with the law of markets.

The inculpation of excess savings as the root of the crisis obviously leads to economic policy prescriptions diametrically opposed to the Keynesian principles which had until recently prevailed since the war. A policy of public works in a situation of underemployment was therefore viewed as a false remedy.The public borrowing needed to finance such a policy would, in Hayek's view, merely draw upon a given well of savings in the economy, starving private investment. The only result would be to replace a productive use of these savings with an 'unproductive' one.

An anecdote related by Joan Robinson exemplifies this view and the debate which ensued. Seeking to counter Keynes's increasing influence, Robbins had invited Hayek to present his theory in England. After the lecture Richard Kahn, a colleague of Keynes, asked him: 'Do you mean that if I get up now and go out and buy, say, a raincoat, that will worsen the depression?' 'Yes,' replied Hayek, 'it would require a long mathematical development to prove it, but that is exactly what I mean.'

B A new direction: Keynes's *Treatise on Money*

Written in 1930, the *Treatise on Money* marked a turning-point in Keynes's thought. In it, alongside a more advanced monetary analysis illuminating the elements of the *General Theory*, may be found an important treatment of income determination and of the relationship between savings and investment.

To help him dispute the automatic equality of investment and savings, Keynes proposed a particular definition of these concepts. Income, E, is equal to factor costs: wages and entrepreneurs' normal profits. C and I being effective expenditure on consumption and investment respectively, and hence also the corresponding income of entrepreneurs, 'profit' clenches the difference between this income and the costs of production, say $Q_1 = C - C'$ for consumption goods and $Q_2 = I - I'$ for investment goods.

Savings, S, are defined as income not spent on consumption ($S = E - C$), so that investment I automatically equals the sum of savings and profits, $S + Q$. Thus equality of savings and investment is no longer an accounting identity, but a condition of macroeconomic or, in Keynes's term, monetary equilibrium.

The explicit aim of the tract was to explain price movements: Keynes accordingly proposed fundamental equations which he hoped would replace the Quantity Theory.

Let π be the general price level and $O = \dfrac{I + C}{\pi}$ the total volume of output. Since $I + C = E + Q$, the cost of factors plus profits, we obtain an expression for π.

$$\pi = \frac{E}{O} + \frac{Q}{O} = \frac{E}{O} + \frac{I - S}{O}$$

Similarly, denoting the price of consumption goods by P and their volume by R, we have by definition $C = PR = C' + Q_1$. By means of a simplification (illegitimate in fact), Keynes chose his units so as to equate the monetary cost of consumer goods C'/R with that of total output, E/O, giving the price equation:

$$P = \frac{E}{O} + \frac{Q_1}{R} = \frac{E}{O} + \frac{I' - S}{R}$$

Thus we can see that prices are determined by costs ('income inflation') and by profits ('profits inflation'), the latter being measured by the gap between investment and savings for the general price level, and by the gap counting instead the production cost of investment for the prices of consumption goods only.

Changes in incomes are however considered when Keynes develops the paradoxical consequences of his analysis which cast doubt on the orthodox means of returning to equilibrium. Thus, if producers reduce investment to avoid making a loss, they reduce total expenditure by the same amount, so that their revenue falls and their loss correspondingly increases. This is the end result of the parable of the banana plantation. Symmetrically, if entrepreneurs increase their investment spending, they will increase revenue and profits without needing to reduce consumption: Keynes compared the biblical story of the 'widow's cruse' while Kalecki expressed it by the famous axiom 'The workers spend what they get, the capitalists get what they spend.'

There is no need to point out the extent to which these examples oversimplify, particularly in their treatment of production costs. The important point is that price adjustments are no longer alone, with the level of output itself appearing as a variable. This occurred only gradually to Keynes; witness Joan Robinson's (1932) appositely titled commentary *Theory of Money as Analysis of Output*. Seeking to construct a theory of money, Keynes had opened the way to a theory of the level of national output.

3 GROWTH: SCHUMPETER

The frequency and scale of recessions may have disguised the long-term trend towards increasing output. This is doubtless one reason for the relative scarcity at this time of work on growth. In fact, it is quite noticeable that growth was not so much absent from the thoughts of the main economists in the period 1870 to 1930 as scattered through their theory: it was not systematically integrated. Joseph Schumpeter (1912) proposed a theoretical system which paved the way for a theory of growth which, while undoubtedly straying beyond the bounds of neo classical theory, still retained it as a foundation. Indeed, Schumpeter managed to combine his marginalist theory with a profound understanding of the historical approach, and of Marxism.

His analysis begins from the image of a 'circuit', by which he denotes an economy operating under unchanged conditions from one period to the next and from which profits are excluded. 'Evolution' is distinct from the circuit in that it involves not only quantitative growth but also qualitative change in goods and in techniques. The engine of evolution is innovation which, with the aid of credit, provides a role for the entrepreneur.

A Innovation and enterprise

In the static neoclassical world described, for example, by Walras, the entrepreneur is the agent who organises production by bringing together the various productive services needed in order to output a finished product. For Schumpeter, however, the entrepreneur's task was not the repetitive organisation of productive combinations but essentially the introduction of new combinations, which he called innovation.

Innovation here is not simply the increase of knowledge of feasible techniques, but is defined at once more narrowly and more widely. More narrowly, in the sense that it relates only to the technology actually used, but more widely in that it is not confined to changes in manufacturing techniques. Five categories of innovation are in fact distinguished:

1 Manufacture of a new product
2 Introduction of a new method of production
3 Opening up a new market
4 Exploitation of a new source of raw materials
5 Introduction of a new method of organising production

What these five mechanisms have in common is that they represent qualitative change, justifying for Schumpeter the essentially discontinuous nature of innovation. 'You can add as many post-chaises as you like – you'll never end up with a railway.'

Without discarding the traditional functions of the entrepreneur in co-ordinating factors of production or matching supply with demand, Schumpeter saw practical innovation as his essential function. The essential discontinuity of the process requires a decision-maker, someone endowed with power, as represented by the four historical types listed by Schumpeter: the modern manufacturer-trader, the captain of industry in the industrial revolution, the manager and the founder in the limited companies of the late nineteenth century.

Unlike the Walrasian entrepreneur, 'who makes neither profit nor loss', Schumpeter's entrepreneur does make a profit, a reward for the innovatory function allowed by the temporary monopoly which the new combination confers on him. Profit is not, however, his sole motivation: he also desires power and possesses an instinct for creation. Concentration of capital tends, on the other hand, to bureaucratise innovation and to deprive the decentralised firm of its most basic justification. Pursuing the logic of his argument, Schumpeter was to identify here a factor casting doubt on the very survival of capitalism (Schumpeter, 1944).

B The evolution mechanism

The innovator does not, any more than does the Walrasian entrepreneur, own the resources he needs from the word 'go'. He needs to obtain them; by means of borrowing, he needs to get hold of factors of production previously used in traditional combinations to redirect them to new ones. Through the exercise of his power, he will with the help of credit 'remove them from the circuit'. If evolution is in progress, credit might correspond to the use of earlier savings. Alternatively, in the transition from the circular flow to evolution, credit corresponds to creation of new means of payment by the banks. The banker is the intermediary between the entrepreneur and the owners of means of production. Inflation will arise from the process of redirecting resources from traditional activities both as a consequence of excess demand for factors of production and wage goods, and as a means of financing innovation through credit derived from forced savings.

This evolution mechanism is of interest purely as a concept, as well as for its implications regarding the problems of demand creation and of fluctuations.

An image of capitalist growth as a continuing process of restructuring is presented, with old combinations disappearing to be replaced by new. This image is certainly enlightening. However, Schumpeter was also seeking a logical solution to questions of the day relating to the problem of finding markets, and to imperialism. While he did not exclude the opening up of a new market from his list of possible innovations, neither did he make it a precondition for evolution. In fact his analysis shows that credit can provide sufficient purchasing power to accommodate innovation within the economy and to allow the innovator his profit. Thus, Schumpeter thought that imperialism stemmed from the historical constant of power relationships rather than from a need for new markets specific to capitalism.

Moreover, the essential discontinuity of innovation provides a key to unlock analysis of growth and fluctuations. Each cycle could correspond to a 'wave' of innovations, expansion occurring when new borrowing was financing innovation. During the boom, inflation presents the transient illusion of possible coexistence of old and new techniques, but crisis reveals the need to eliminate old combinations, which happens during the depression phase. Conditions then again become favourable for a new series of innovations. (Schumpeter also thought that innovations could explain long (40–50 year) cycles – so-called Kondratieff waves.)

Schumpeter's contribution to growth theory was to stand out on its own for some time. Apart from a few contributions which laid the foundations for modern theories of optimal growth (e.g. Ramsey, von Neumann), growth only re-entered the mainstream of economic analysis with Harrod's work in the aftermath of the Keynesian revolution.

3   The Keynesian Revolution

The publication in 1936 of the *General Theory of Employment, Interest and Money* represented a fundamental break with the past and led over the space of a few years to the birth of modern macroeconomics. Keynes's ideas, however, have been simplified and occasionally distorted, leading to a distinction between 'Keynesianism' and 'Keynes's economics' (cf. Leijonhufvud, 1968), each in turn having many different interpretations. Without wishing to play down the simplifying nature of 'Keynesianism', it is difficult to share the view of purists for whom all the weaknesses of modern macroeconomics derive from its infidelities to the teachings of the Master. Keynes himself was at times ambiguous or obscure – a side effect of his powerful intuition. He probably pursued purely aggregative reasoning too far in the *General Theory*, in response to criticisms of his *Treatise on Money*.

We shall look first at the main ideas of the *General Theory* and of the so-called 'Keynesian' expositions of national income determination. Keynes's theories will then be compared with neoclassical analysis, and we shall see how Keynesianism led to the use of true macroeconomic policy instruments.

1 THE *GENERAL THEORY* AND KEYNESIANISM

The main aim of the *General Theory* was to provide a theory of the level of national output and employment, a problem which was largely passed over by the Marshallians such as Pigou, for whom it reduced to an analysis of partial equilibrium on the labour market. While Keynes's analysis, based on the principle of effective demand, remained faithful to Marshall's methodology, incorporating a sequential system of markets, Hicks's presentation (to be further developed by other Keynesians) reintroduced a simultaneous interdependence of markets.

A The general theory of employment

Keynes believed that employment was not determined by the confrontation between supply and demand in the labour market, since wages are not equal to the 'supply price' of labour – its marginal disutility. Instead, employment is determined by equilibrium in the aggregate markets for goods and services, to which the Marshallian tools of partial equilibrium analysis are applied. The principle of effective demand determines the level at which equilibrium is reached, with markets operating iteratively.

1   The principle of effective demand

It is worth briefly recalling the analytical method of Alfred Marshall in which Keynes was steeped. Marshall did not study markets in terms of demand and supply curves for quantities but in terms of demand and supply prices. 'The price required to call forth the exertion necessary for producing any given amount of a commodity, may be called the supply price for that amount during the same time.' (Marshall, 1890) Notice that 'price' here denotes a total value of a quantity rather than a price per unit. Symmetrically, the demand price for a quantity is the maximum sum for which buyers are willing to acquire this quantity. Equilibrium is reached when the two values are equal.

At a quantity for which the demand price does not reach the supply price, 'sellers receive less than is sufficient to make it worth their while to bring goods to market on that scale' (ibid., p. 34). With the inequality reversed, sellers have an incentive to increase the quantity offered for sale on the market. When the supply and demand prices are equal, the quantity sold tends neither to increase nor decrease, it is in a state of equilibrium.

Keynes applied this analysis to the whole goods market. However, rather than introducing a volume index defined for all goods and services, he used employment as a direct indicator of the level of activity – without important consequences for the logic of his argument. Additionally, he measured macroeconomic flows of receipts and expenditure in terms of wage-units.

The global supply price for a given level of employment, $Z(N)$, is the minimum amount of expected receipts required for employers to employ at that level.[1] The global demand price for a given level of employment $D(N)$, is the total of receipts expected by entrepreneurs at this level of employment. It differs from the Marshallian idea of a demand price only in that it does not require the expenditure actually made by consumers, but only the expectations of entrepreneurs.

From here, there is a striking parallel with Marshall's own reasoning:

> Now if for a given value of N the expected proceeds are greater than the aggregate supply price, i.e. if D is greater than Z, there will be an

incentive to entrepreneurs to increase employment . . . up to the value of *N* for which *Z* has become equal to *D*. Thus the value of employment is given by the point of intersection between the aggregate demand function and the aggregate supply function; for it is at this point that the entrepreneurs' expectation of profits will he maximised. The value of *D* at the point of the aggregate demand function where it is intersected by the aggregate supply function, will be called *the effective demand* . . . This is the substance of the General Theory of Employment, which it will be our object to expand . . . (Keynes, 1936, p. 25).

Figure 3.1 (cf. Davidson and Smolensky, 1964, p. 145) is a suggested illustration:

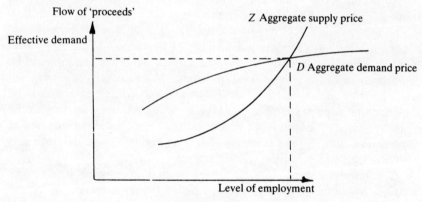

Figure 3.1

While for a devotee of the 'law of markets', supply price and demand price will coincide for any level of employment, in Keynes' theory there is only one equilibrium level. Notice that equilibrium output equals demand so long as entrepreneurs correctly forecast the amount of revenue which a given level of employment will provide. The two may diverge if there are forecasting errors, but the latter do not play an important role in the *General Theory*.

One special feature of Keynes's reasoning should be noted. 'Entre- preneurs' are invoked as a unique information and decision centre in the economy. The underlying image is the fiction of a collective entrepreneur vested with the sole power to determine output and employment.[2]

Application of the principle of effective demand leads to description of an equilibrium in which unemployment can persist – an equilibrium in the sense that there is no incentive for entrepreneurs to alter their decisions. Such an equilibrium also depends on the state of short-term expectations: that is, on a combination of information, intuition and psychological factors which lead entrepreneurs to expect a greater or lesser revenue from a given level of employment.

To survey the determinants of the value of aggregate demand, we move on to an overview of the main themes of the *General Theory*.

2 Determination of output and employment

The determinants of the volume of output and employment are found in the value of aggregate demand and its relationship with the aggregate supply price. Consumption and investment are the main components of aggregate demand, to which government expenditure and export demand can be added in a more general framework.

Consumption is a function of current income, in particular wages paid out by firms, justifying the increased revenue expected to accompany any increase in employment. Keynes believed this increase would remain less than proportional to increases in distributed income (see below, chapter 4, section 1). Investment, on the other hand, would be independent of the current level of income, being exclusively determined by the state of long-term expectations and the interest rate. It will be higher the more favourable are long-term expectations relative to the current price of investment goods, and the lower is the current rate of interest on longer-term borrowing such as bonds (whose determinants will be studied in chapter 5).

The current rate of interest is determined as a function of expectations over long-term rates and of existing money balances, which can be used to buy bonds and securities. Liquidity preference can in effect lead people to hold balances in monetary form, thus depriving themselves of interest but hoping for speculative gains when the rate of interest rises and the price of securities falls. The more important the money stock, the more liquidity preference is satisfied and the more people demanding securities, the higher will be their price and so the lower the rate of interest.

When these factors are taken each in turn, the various markets are seen to be interconnected. First, an exogenous supply of money, determined by the central bank, meets a largely speculative and interest-elastic demand for money. A stock equilibrium is then reached in the money market, and determines the rate of interest.

Given the state of long-run expectations and the supply price of capital goods, this rate then determines the level of private firms' investment which, along with government expenditure and possibly exports, constitutes the autonomous element of aggregate demand and stimulates primary employment. Expenditure, mainly by consumers, is induced by the first round of employment and income creation and leads via the multiplier process to an additional income. Total income or output is then derived from this process. Employment eventually reaches the level which entrepreneurs consider necessary to produce this output, in the light of the techniques and equipment available.

Figure 3.2 summarises the process

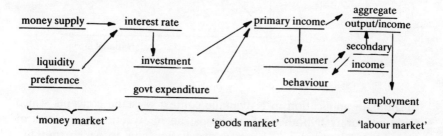

Figure 3.2

The dissemination and interpretation of Keynes's ideas owed much to popularising and expository writings such as those of Alvin Hansen, Lawrence Klein and Paul Samuelson, themselves influenced by the work of John Hicks, Oskar Lange and Franco Modigliani, who sought a theoretical reconciliation between Keynesian and neoclassical doctrines. The word 'Keynesianism' has come to be used to designate vulgarising works which spawned the exposition of Keynes generally to be found in English and American textbooks. Two types of presentation are associated with this school: the 45° diagram, and the *IS-LM* model.

3 The 45° diagram

Used notably by Samuelson (1976), this method centres on a graphical representation of the static multiplier. It incorporates two relationships:

(a) equality of output E (identical to national expenditure) with national income Y at all points along the 45° line;
(b) an expression for national expenditure (or output) as the sum of investment I, given exogenously, and consumption, which is a function of income: $C = C_0 + cY$.

Figure 3.3, while in itself unimpeachable, illustrates the dangers of proceeding from simplified illustrations. Some writers, seeing an excess of aggregate expenditure over income at the level of income R_o, deduced the existence of an 'inflationary gap' which could be corrected by an increase in national income. Similarly, to the right of the intersection there would be a deflationary gap. This represents an

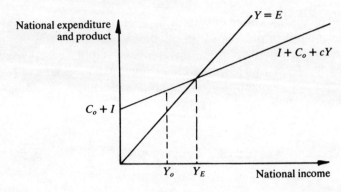

Figure 3.3

illegitimate application in a dynamic context of static concepts which describe purely hypothetical situations; an interpretation in terms of global supply and demand curves of relationships to which they are unsuited. In fact, the diagram serves only to indicate that Y_E is the national income associated in equilibrium with the autonomous expenditures C_0 and I, assuming the consumption function given.

In other words, the 45° diagram merely gives an illustration of the static multiplier, taken from the reduced form of the model:

$$Y = R$$
$$Y = I + C = I + C_0 + cR$$

whence the well-known expression

$$Y = (I + C_0) / (1 - c)$$

The multiplier appeared in Keynesian literature in 1932, first as a relationship between an increase in primary employment produced by a programme of public works, and the secondary employment induced by it (Kahn, 1932) then in its familiar form. As a static formulation, the multiplier only serves to determine the unique level of national income compatible with autonomous expenditure, given the propensity to consume. A dynamic interpretation, and a widening of the scope of the analysis to take in monetary and budgetary factors, would increase its usefulness.

4 The dynamic multiplier

Static analysis seeks to find the level of income compatible with autonomous expenditure. Dynamic analysis is concerned with the path of income resulting from a given pattern of autonomous expenditure. The lags in the process of inducing additional demand are therefore of fundamental importance.

One simple assumption is to introduce a one-period lag between a flow of income and the consequent flow of consumption, according to the relationship:

$$C_t = cY_{t-1} + C_o$$

An increase in investment at time t then leads to waves of additional consumption:

$$\Delta C_{t+1} = c\Delta I_t$$
$$\Delta C_{t+2} = c\Delta I_{t+1} = c^2 \Delta I_t$$
$$\cdots\cdots\cdots\cdots\cdots\cdots\cdots\cdots\cdots$$
$$\Delta C_{t+n} = c\Delta C_{t+n-1} = c^n \Delta I_t.$$

The cumulative effect is, asymptotically,

$$\sum_{\theta=0}^{\infty} \Delta C_{t+\theta} = \Delta I_t \sum_{\theta=0}^{\infty} c^{\theta} = \frac{1}{1-c} \Delta I_t \quad \text{pour} \quad c < 1$$

The cumulative effect of the dynamic multiplier is equal to that of the static multiplier. It can be shown that the same relationship shows the movement of equilibrium income if the increase in investment at t were maintained in all succeeding periods.

At this point, the reader might spot a paradox. On the one hand, the multiplier re-establishes the equality of savings and investment, which only, therefore, *tends* to occur in the above example. On the other hand, that equality is necessary *ex post* in each period. The solution lies in the distinction between effective savings – income not consumed, and so including the automatic adjustment of money balances – and desired or planned savings, a given proportion $1 - c$ of any increase in income. Thus at the end of period $t + 1$ the increase in investment ΔI_t is balanced by planned savings $(1 - c)\Delta I_t$ plus an increase in balances $c\Delta I_t$, which forms an automatic, unplanned saving. As the process converges, the whole of investment comes to be balanced by 'normal', or planned, savings.

B Keynesianism and the *IS-LM* model

We have seen in the 45° diagram an early 'didactic' formulation of Keynesian theory, whose apparent simplicity turned out to be misleading. The illustration suggested by Hicks with the *IS-LM* model is of markedly greater interest and importance, though it too is open to criticism. The *IS-LM* model is an algebraic and graphical representation of relationships set out more or less explicitly by Keynes in the General Theory, incorporating an interaction between the money market and the market for goods and services to determine simultaneously national income and the rate of interest. The model was later extended to take account of the labour market, the price level and financial assets other than money or real capital.

1 The IS-LM *model*
The *IS-LM* model depicts the simultaneous attainment of equilibrium in the markets for money and for goods and services. It starts with a closed, single-good economy with a single asset, claims on which are a perfect substitute for real capital. Stocks, wealth and productive capital are taken as given as, to begin with, is the general price level.

(a) The market for goods and services – In a closed economy, the whole value of output is equal in value to income and thus also consumption and savings, whilst the value of demand is split between consumption and investment. It follows that equality of savings and investment coincides with equilibrium in the goods market. The relationships which hold in equilibrium may be specified as follows, variables being expressed in real terms, given the assumption of constant prices.

$I = I(i)$ Investment is a decreasing function of the rate of interest.
$S = S(Y)$ Savings are an increasing function of income.
$I = S$ In equilibrium, the two are equal.

Solving this model in three equations and four unknowns produces a relationship $Y(i)$, the *IS* curve in Figure 3.4.

The *IS* curve represents the pairs of values of national income Y and the rate of interest i compatible with the attainment of equilibrium in the goods market.

(b) The money market – The exogenous money supply M_o has to satisfy a dual demand: a transactions and precautionary demand $M_1(Y)$ and a speculative demand $M_2(i)$, a function of the rate of interest. The total demand for money is thus:

$$M = M_1(Y) + M_2(i)$$

while the equilibrium condition may be written $M = M_o$.

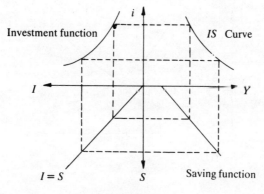

Figure 3.4

Since the value of M_o is given, the system has three unknowns M, i and Y, and two equations. Again there is one degree of freedom in the solution and the set of solutions is defined by a function $Y(i)$ called the *LM* curve and drawn as in Figure 3.5.

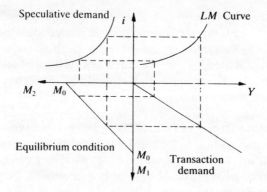

Figure 3.5

Global equilibrium is determined by the intersection of the *IS* and *LM* curves, which gives a pair of values of i and Y compatible with a simultaneous equilibrium in the goods and money markets.

In comparison with the exposition of the *General Theory* given earlier, it is notable that the *IS-LM* system incorporates an interaction between markets, whereas the original Keynesian concept was of sequential effects. The relationship behind this 'loop' is the demand for transaction balances, which leads to a feedback from the goods market to monetary equilibrium. It seems unfair to criticise Hicks for introducing this relationship, which was explicitly set out by Joan

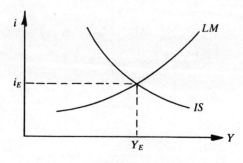

Figure 3.6

Robinson herself in the Introduction to the *Theory of Employment* in 1937:

> A rise in prices and incomes leads to an increase in requirements for money balances in the active circulation. This tends to reduce the amount available for inactive balances and so causes the rate of interest to rise. (Robinson, 1937, p. 17)

It is true that the rejection of this interaction by 'purist' disciples of Keynes was based on the primacy of effective demand based on expectations, in determining income. But if these expectations are systematically fulfilled, if indeed they are self-fulfilling, then it is logically correct to introduce the equality of expected and actual income, which once again introduces interdependence between the markets.

To the extent that Keynes himself believed errors of foresight, while certainly not impossible, to be inessential and thought that his theory would stand up to the assumption of perfect expectations,[3] the interdependence of the *IS-LM* system is appropriate, but it must, at least in its static form, prove inadequate to analyse the consequences of errors of foresight.

Before returning to consider further objections to *IS-LM*, we must look at its extension to a 'full Keynesian model' through the addition of a supply side.

2 The full 'Keynesian model'
The *IS-LM* model is completed by adding in a short-run production function $Y = F(N)$ or, logically equivalent and more in the Keynesian spirit, an employment function $N = F^{-1}(Y)$; for example, using functions for supply and demand of labour.

Demand for labour must satisfy the 'first postulate of the classical economists', the equality of the real wage and the marginal product of labour:

$$W_d = dY/dN$$

However, Keynes believed that wage-earners could only measure their reservation wages, corresponding to the marginal disutility of work, in nominal terms,* hence the supply price of labour

$$w_O = w(N)$$

With a given level of output and price, this specification leads to overdetermination of the system, and is usually incompatible with equality of the supply and demand wage. Leaving until later an examination of possible ways out of this indeterminacy, consider now the case in which the labour market determines the general price level, for an exogenously given real output. Figure 3.7 explains the story.

The falling demand price of labour mirrors diminishing returns to the scale of production. The supply price of labour has an ambiguous interpretation. Keynes inherited the tradition of English economists in laying emphasis on the individualistic notion of disutility of labour; as a concession to reality, however, he preferred to interpret the disutility curve as representing the sensitivity of union wage demands to the level of employment. Since the supply price is specified in nominal terms and the demand price in real terms, their equality would implicitly determine the general price level p as cotangent of the angle α, in Figure 3.7.

Thus, for any level of employment, a pseudo-equilibrium of the labour market, equalising the supply and demand prices of labour and thus 'satisfying' both unions and firms, is possible and would determine the general level of prices.[4]

It does, however, appear difficult to produce out of this process the general explanation of the price level in Keynesian theory; firstly because it relies on an equality of supply and demand wages inconsistent with the existence of involuntary unemployment unless the labour supply is perfectly inelastic, and secondly because it assumes that real income is determined independently of the price level, which requires the peculiar assumption of a money supply constant in real value.

We must now consider this feedback of the labour market onto the goods and money markets – a feedback which occurs through the price mechanism and introduces a more general interdependence, suggesting conformability with the structure of neoclassical models.

---

* Variables defined in money (nominal values) will be noted by lower case letters.

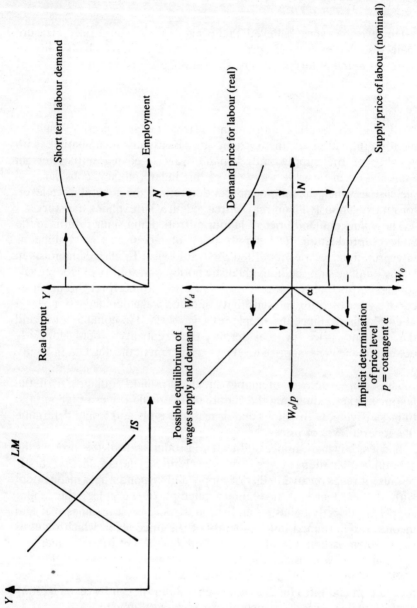

Figure 3.7

2 KEYNESIAN THEORY AND NEOCLASSICAL ANALYSIS

The *General Theory* was consciously polemical towards the work of what Keynes called the 'classical' economists, who accepted Say's law and whose exemplar was Pigou. Commentators have, rather carelessly, identified those theories rightly criticised by Keynes with neoclassical theory as a whole. A more detailed study suggests a more qualified conclusion.

A systematic comparison of neoclassical and Keynesian worlds begins with a discussion of Say's law and a simple neoclassical model, and will focus on the possibility of mechanisms automatically restoring equilibrium.

A Say's law and Walras's law

Say's law of markets is definitely not just a logical necessity of the neoclassical system of analysis. Walras's law, however, a different proposition, plays an important part in general equilibrium analysis.

Walras's law proceeds from the aggregation of the budget constraints faced by all agents in the economy. In a general equilibrium framework, all possible resources arise from the supply of goods, services, money or securities, while all jobs correspond to demand for goods, services, money and securities. The equality of endowments and the ways to which they are put under the individual's budget constraint implies equality of his supplies and demands, an equality which must be conserved after aggregation.

The required equation, taking n goods of price p_j; a single service (labour); securities and money, is:

$$\sum_{j=1}^{n} p_j(D_j - S_j) + w(D_l - S_l) + p_s(D_s - S_s) + D_m - S_m$$
$$\equiv 0$$

Walras's law does not imply perpetual equilibrium. It may continue to be satisfied even in the absence of equilibrium in certain markets. It means only that if one market is in disequilibrium then:

(1) at least one other market must also be in disequilibrium, and
(2) the sum of the values of excess demands in other markets is numerically equal and of opposite sign to the value of excess demand observed in the market being considered.

Since the importance of this law is at issue, we must be very clear about the conditions required for it to hold. Walras's law is satisfied so long as only demands and supplies satisfying agents' budget constraints are allowed. Hence a demand to buy on credit does not violate the law since the demander is implicitly supplying a security representing his total debt. It is indeed possible to construct models which do not include this assumption, but their interpretation may turn out somewhat tricky. We shall return to Walras's law when dealing with the modern theory of disequilibrium in chapter 12.

For the next part of our discussion, we shall provisionally abstract from securities. In their absence, Walras's law implies Say's law if and only if the excess demand for money is identically equal to zero $(D_m \equiv S_m)$.[5] Therefore,

$$\sum_{j=1}^{n} p_j (D_j - S_j) + w(D_l - S_l) \equiv 0$$

a relationship which could be called 'Say's law in a production economy'. In a pure exchange economy, the term for labour disappears and we are left with the equality of aggregate supply and demand of all goods.

This case corresponds to two distinct assumptions made by most of the 'Classical' economists. They either considered a barter economy with money assumed away; or else money was allowed to exist, but was never demanded for its own sake, only for exchange and so by definition matched by an equivalent supply.

Unemployment being defined as an excess supply of labour, Say's law asserts not its impossibility but its temporariness provided market mechanisms function normally. To cancel out the value of excess demand for goods, an equal excess supply of labour is needed. There is consequently a tendency for output and employment to rise, and for the real wage and the supply of labour to fall. Thus market mechanisms must spontaneously re-establish full employment.

Walras's law leads to a different conclusion. An excess supply of labour may find its counterpart, not in excess demand for goods, but in an excess demand for money, an unsaturated desire to hold money balances:

$$\sum_{j=1}^{n} p_j (D_j - O_j) + w(D_l - S_l) + (D_m - S_m) \equiv 0$$
$$= 0 \qquad\qquad < 0 \qquad\qquad > 0$$

Thus a global equilibrium, or rather a partial equilibrium in the market for all goods, may exist persistently with unemployment. Keynesian theory is compatible with Walras's law, though with the proviso that unemployment could only persist in a horizontal region of the *LM* curve corresponding to Keynes's 'liquidity trap'.

Introducing the market for securities extends the range of possible disequilibria.

B The Keynesian and neoclassical models

Hicks's 1938 article was among the first to parallel the Keynesian and neoclassical models of static macroeconomic equilibrium. Since then, expositions of this sort have multiplied, and the most convenient way to make sense of them is to start from a general formulation, showing the restrictions which give rise to each individual model.

1 A general macroeconomic model

Whilst the particular relationships we specify do not affect the main argument, later developments will be facilitated by the use of linear or log-linear formulations, combining simplicity of exposition with a sufficient degree of generality. The symbols used all denote variables measured in real terms unless otherwise indicated, with all parameters being positive.

In the market for goods and services we have the following equations:

$$C = cY - bi + C_O$$

$$I = I_0 - ai$$

$$Y = C + I = F(N)$$

$$\Rightarrow I = S = (1 - c)Y + bi - C_O$$

In the money market, we have

$$M_d = mY + L_O - li$$

$M_d = m_o/P_d$, where m_o is the nominal money supply; while the labour market is described by

$$N_d = N_d(W, P) \text{ where } W \text{ is a nominal wage}$$
$$N_s = N_s(W, P)$$
$$N_d = N_s$$

For a given price level P and money supply m_o, we can, by looking at equilibrium in the goods and money markets, construct an *IS-LM* model.

The relationship obtained expressing equilibrium income Y as a function of P can clearly be interpreted as a decreasing function of aggregate demand, $Y_d(P)$, if a, l and m are all non-zero.

Similarly, employment, wages and aggregate supply $Y_s(P)$ are determined by solving $Y = F(N)$ and the labour market equations for different values of P. Under our assumptions about the signs of the parameters, $Y_s(P)$ is an increasing function.

Macroeconomic equilibrium of the general model can therefore be examined in terms of aggregate supply and demand and as a function of the general price level, as in Figure 3.8.

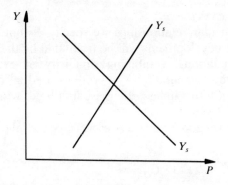

Figure 3.8

The introduction of special restrictions into this general model on the one hand introduces possibilities of separation of equations so that several variables can be determined autonomously rather than simultaneously; but on the other hand causes some sets of equations to be overdetermined, jeopardising the realisation of full employment equilibrium.

2 'Classical' and 'Keynesian' variants
The general model set out above might be labelled 'neoclassical' in the sense that it relies on rational behaviour of agents and involves regulation through the price mechanism. The 'classical' model, to use Keynes's term in the *General Theory*, is taken to mean a particular case corresponding to a set of restrictions as follows:

(a) There is no money illusion in the labour market, so that $N_s = N_s(W/P)$ and $N_d = N_d(W/P)$.

(b) The demand to hold money is not appreciably affected by the rate of interest, so that l is zero.

(c) Savings depend only on the interest rate.

These assumptions lead to the model becoming redundant. The labour market alone determines the real wage, employment and therefore equilibrium output. The equalisation of savings and investment represents arbitrage in the intertemporal allocation of resources without affecting the level of current output. Meanwhile the money market determines the general price level according to the traditional quantity theory.

The 'classical' model thus defined may be represented by Figure 3.9.

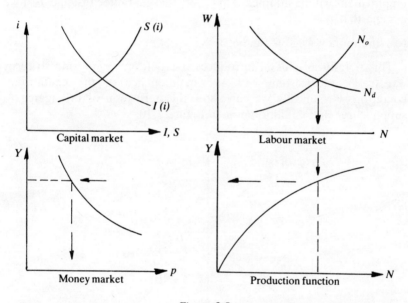

Figure 3.9

The three restrictions (a), (b) and (c) suffice to produce all the pre-Keynesian liberal conclusions. In particular, it is only possible to raise employment by reducing the wages demanded by workers – by, in effect, lowering the labour supply curve.

It is also quite straightforward to specify the restrictions needed to derive the so-called Keynesian model from the general model:

(a') Workers have a – possibly total – money illusion $\left(\dfrac{\partial N_s}{\partial(1/P)} < \dfrac{\partial N_s}{\partial w}\right)$

(b') Current savings are not significantly influenced by the level of the interest rate $(b = 0)$.

Under these assumptions, a full Keynesian model with endogenous prices is obtained. Moreover, if

(c') the demand for transactions balances is negligible *(m = 0)*, and
(d') the money supply is fixed in real terms $(m_o/P_o = \text{constant})$,

a sequential determination of the macroeconomic variables is obtained, the order being $i, I, S, Y, N, w/P, P$. If, on the other hand, restriction (d') is not assumed, the determination of the general price level introduces a 'loop', so that equilibrium can be thought of in terms of the equalisation of global demand and supply expressed as functions of price.

The endogeneity of prices and wages in general guarantees that full employment will be attained. However, this guarantee disappears if we assume that

(e') the money wage is rigid at w_o.

This rigidity in general introduces overdetermination, and so turns out to be inconsistent with the maintenance of the equilibrium condition. Graphically we can show the derivation of the aggregate supply curve and equilibrium as in Figure 3.10.

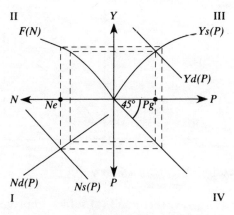

Figure 3.10

In quadrant I, demand for labour is shown as a function of prices, for given W_o. An aggregate supply function $Y_s(P)$ in quadrant III is derived via the production function in II, and this intersects the demand curve $Y_d(P)$ derived as before from the *IS-LM* system. There is no endogenous mechanism to ensure that the price level P_g given by equilibrium of the good market would be consistent with the equilibrium level of employment N_e. If in addition assumption (d') is introduced, aggregate demand $Y_d(P)$ is horizontal and the supply curve determines only the general price level, as discussed earlier.

The formal analysis of the model thus underlines the crucial role of wage rigidity in allowing unemployment to arise. Is flexibility of all prices then a sufficient condition for full employment?

C Can unemployment persist indefinitely?

Keynesian theory asserts that a state of unemployment may persist in a capitalist economy because there is not always a market mechanism to absorb it. This is the idea of an underemployment equilibrium, which we saw corresponded to equilibrium in the market for goods and services – a global equilibrium in the sense that it holds on aggregate but only partial in the sense that it neither includes nor implies equilibrium in the money and labour markets. By definition, an equilibrium is a state in which there is no net tendency towards change and therefore it tends to persist. While it is easy to associate Keynes's theory with the crisis of 1929, and this connection has often been made, it is worth remembering that Britain's historical experience since 1920 had been one of prolonged depression rather than sudden crisis. This may help to explain the secondary status accorded discussion of the cycle in the *General Theory*.

A relevant framework for discussion is provided by the introduction of price and wage flexibility.

1 Wage and price flexibility
We begin from an initial position of underemployment in a Keynesian model, for price level P_1 and wage w_1.

Real sector equilibrium is determined in the first quadrant and implies a level of employment N_1. If firms are on their demand-for-labour function N_d, this level of employment is consistent with a real wage w_1/P_1. Unemployment or excess supply of labour is equal at this wage rate to:

$$N_s(w_1/P_1) \mid P_1 - N_1$$

In line with Keynesian assumptions, the level of the labour supply curve depends on the price level (since it is a function only of the nominal wage): for a price level P_2 below P_1, the supply curve $N_s(w/P)|P_2$ would be below the curve $N_s(w/P)|P_1$.

However, with price P_2 lower than P_1, the real value of money balances is higher, equivalent to a higher money supply. The corre-

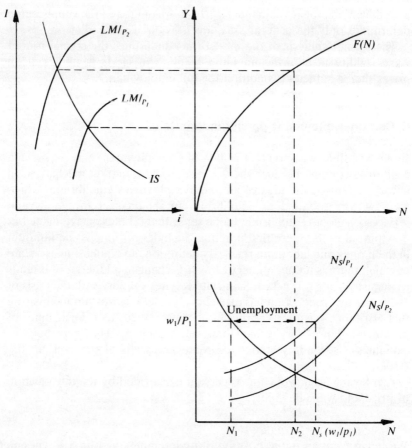

Figure 3.11

sponding *LM* curve will therefore be higher, allowing a lower interest rate and a higher level of output.

Consider the case of total flexibility of wages and prices. Excess supply of labour tends to bring down wages and therefore to increase employment and firms' output.[6] The fall in wage costs and increase in supply allow prices to fall and thus increase the value of money holdings, shifting the *LM* curve upwards. More real balances are available for speculative purposes, causing the interest rate to fall and permitting investment – and hence effective demand – to increase. Since there is simultaneously an increase in the output which can be produced at a profit, and in that which is demanded, a higher macroeconomic equilibrium position will be reached. Let us now provisionally alter the assumption made earlier regarding the supply of labour.

If wage-earners have no money illusion (or very little), the labour supply curve is unchanged, or changed only slightly. If, then, prices and wages vary independently, full employment equilibrium will be restored. Since there are degrees of freedom in the adjustment, the real wage will adapt to ensure full employment and the general price level is established at the level where effective demand suffices for full employment.

We can therefore see the assumptions under which automatic return to equilibrium can be justified in a Keynesian model. These include the absence or weakness of money illusion among wage-earners; and at this point diverge from the *General Theory*.

If the flexibility of prices and wages is incomplete, and only has a single degree of freedom, the above result is no longer guaranteed. Flexibility of a single price or price-ratio will not in general be enough to bring two markets into equilibrium. Suppose, for example, that the money wage alone fell: effective demand would not increase to balance the increase in aggregate supply.

Similarly, if money illusion is reintroduced into the labour supply, the same process, while increasing actual employment, increases the supply of labour by lowering the supply curve N_s. The realisation of full employment is thereby delayed and possibly even forestalled. Indeed, though of largely academic interest, if the impact of the fall in N_s exceeds that of the increase in the level of *LM*, taking into account the elasticity of these curves as of *IS* and N_d, then the fall in prices and wages may increase unemployment even though it raises employment.

Wage and price flexibility in the absence of money illusion, as well as allowing a spontaneous return to full employment, brings back some important properties of the neoclassical model.

The level of employment and of output is then determined on the labour market alone, by the intersection of stable (i.e. independent of the price level) supply and demand curves. To the level of output thus determined there corresponds a unique value of investment, and so a unique interest rate. The money market then determines only the general price level. Thus we are back to the quantity theory and the neutrality of money which is its corollary: employment, output and the rate of interest are independent of the quantity of money, which determines the general price level. Figure 3.12 illustrates this process.

The equilibrium level of employment N^* determined in the labour market generates equilibrium real output Y^* which in turn determines the rate of interest i^* via the *IS* curve, which represents effective demand. The price level is then established at p^* giving existing money balances the real value required for monetary equilibrium, corresponding to the point $[Y^*, i^*]$ at which the *LM* curve is brought to intersect the *IS* curve.

2 Criticisms and justifications of the stability results

Confronted by this liberal argument for a spontaneous return to equilibrium through the mechanism of wages and prices, the Keynesians raised five objections to it while the liberals constructed an argument justifying their view. The first Keynesian objection – that wage-earners are subject to money illusion – has been discussed. The second concerns distributional effects; the third expectations, the fourth, interest-rate rigidity and the fifth, the consequences of debt revaluation. The neoclassical argument called up to the liberal cause was the converse of the last-mentioned effect: called the 'Pigou effect', it appeals to the favourable effect of a revaluation of credit.

If wages fell, as Keynes believed they would, faster than prices, there would be distributional consequences. Reducing the share of wages in total income tends to lower the propensity to consume of the population as a whole and so also lowers effective demand for a given total investment. It tends to reduce equilibrium output and so increase unemployment (Keynes, 1936, p. 261).

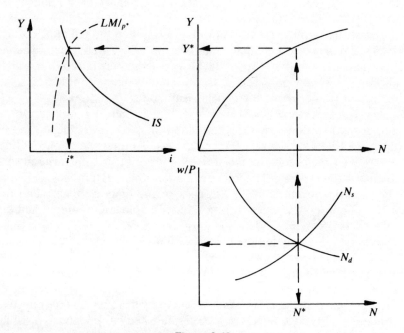

Figure 3.12

The third objection relates to expectations. A fall in the present level of prices and wages must be considered in the context of their future prospects. If the fall in current wage levels leaves expectations of future prices and wages unchanged, it is highly favourable to effective demand since it increases current profits and expected profits from investment. If, on the other hand, it is expected to have a strong effect on prices, it downgrades expected profits in the short term and, if it is expected to persist in the future, reduces the marginal efficiency of capital (ibid., especially pp. 263–5).

The fourth objection is linked to the existence of the 'liquidity trap'; that is, a minimum interest rate, i_o, at which the speculative demand for money becomes infinite: at this rate, no one holding money wishes to exchange it for securities. The rate of interest then becomes inelastic with respect to increases in the real value of balances and a fall in the price level no longer stimulates an increase in investment and effective demand. Graphically, the *LM* curve has a vertical section, whose shifts have no effect on equilibrium output.[7]

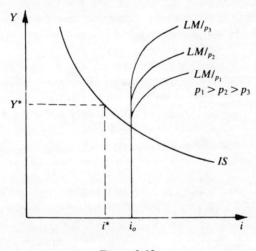

Figure 3.13

When full employment income Y^* requires an interest rate i^* below i_o in Figure 3.13, price flexibility does not suffice to guarantee that it will be attained. Figure 3.13 suggests that an upward shift of *IS* then becomes necessary.

While the 'liquidity trap' has attracted an amount of attention somewhat out of proportion with its empirical importance, the fifth Keynesian objection has been generally neglected in the literature. It relates to the consequences, adverse for effective demand, of re-valuation of debts. Let us go back to Keynes himself:

> On the other hand, the depressing influence on intrepreneurs of their greater burden of debt may partly offset any cheerful reactions from the reduction of wages. Indeed if the fall of wages and prices goes far, the embarrassment of those entrepreneurs who are heavily indebted may soon reach the point of insolvency – with severely adverse effects on investment. Moreover the effect of the lower price-level on the real burden of the national debt and hence on taxation is likely to prove very adverse to business confidence (ibid., p. 264)

From this discussion it emerges that, for Keynes, the downward rigidity of prices and, above all, of wages was not so much the outcome of a social or institutional constraint, as it was for Pigou, as a normative economic policy prescription.

Oddly enough, the main argument advanced by the neoclassics in defence of the liberal theory was the counterpart of the last Keynesian objection against it. Pigou (1943) and Haberler, in particular, stressed that a fall in the price level would raise the real value of government and external credit held by agents, in particular that of money. This increase in wealth would induce an additional demand as required for the restoration of full employment.

Once again in the *IS-LM* framework, the Pigou effect leads to an upward shift of the *IS* curve due to a fall in prices. There thus exists a price level allowing full employment to be reached even in the presence of a liquidity trap and a rate of interest inelastic at i_o. Liberal writers attached great importance to the Pigou effect, since it served to reinforce the stabilising effects of price flexibility. In their view, persistent unemployment could only be a result of institutional wage and price rigidities which were to be condemned and removed.

It should first be pointed out that, while Keynes never accepted the Pigou effect, he in fact deduced a very similar relationship since known as the 'Keynes effect'. This denotes the following sequence of events: first, a fall in prices raises the value of money holdings, and liberates idle balances which held up the interest rate. Investment is thus stimulated, and then we are just left with a shift in the *LM* curve and its consequences. But the Keynes effect goes further. The fall in the interest rate increases the price of bonds, so increases wealth. This windfall gain increases consumption. Like the Pigou effect, then, the Keynes effect taken as a whole implies an upward shift of the *IS* curve.

Let us stop to consider the respective impact of the Pigou effect and of the Keynesian objection concerning revaluation of debts. Reasoning at the aggregate level and considering only monetary assets, there will be an exact balance between the two and hence zero net effect if all money is paid out in settlement of private debts (internal money); some writers have suggested this as a justification for Keynes's negligence of the Pigou effect (e.g. Johnson, 1962, p. 343).

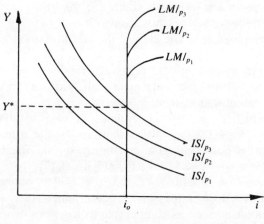

Figure 3.14

If we look at wealth effects, the problem is to find out whether the total of revaluable debt held by private agents exceeds their total credit – in other words, whether they are net debtors towards the government and external sectors. The question can, however, only be confined to an examination of wealth stocks if agents are perfectly free to rearrange their planned receipts and expenditure. However, there are important expenditure flows which are fixed in nominal terms in advance – such as interest and principal repayments and rents. Revaluation of these would have a strongly deflationary effect: if the recent recession had led to a fall in prices of about 20 per cent – half that experienced in the US in the 1930s – the position of many debtor firms and households would have become critical – as happened to American farmers in 1933–5. It is clear that in practice this depressive effect by far exceeds the stimulative effect of revaluation of credits. While capital gains have a gradual effect, spread out over time, bankruptcies represent a sharp constraint, a discontinuity in the spending opportunities of agents and a downward pressure on the price of real assets.

3 Keynesian unemployment and 'equilibrium'

The set of Keynesian arguments convincingly refutes the liberal belief in an automatic return to equilibrium. Could we nevertheless use the word equilibrium to describe situations of lasting unemployment? The point has been much disputed. Thus, for the neoclassics, according to Mark Blaug (1981), 'it is simply a contradiction in terms to speak of an under-employment equilibrium.'

We saw earlier that there is a global equilibrium in the sense of a partial equilibrium in the goods market, but not a general equilibrium. So there are tendencies towards change in the other markets and we need to explain why they are not strong enough to bring the economy back to full employment. The case of the labour market is particularly unsettling.

If there were no institutional real-wage rigidities, we would expect unemployment to cause the real wage to fall. Various stories have been devised to forestall that change.

An early effort (Klein, 1947) postulates an inelastic labour supply at given nominal wage W_o (see also Allen, 1967). For a fixed price P_o, unemployment is perceived as a shortfall below the maximum labour supply for that wage rate, N_s (W_o/P_o) (Figure 3.15).

The problem with this theory is that it considers only a fixed price level. Taking as it does employment as determined solely in the labour market, it cannot be seen as comparable to Keynes's own ideas.[8]

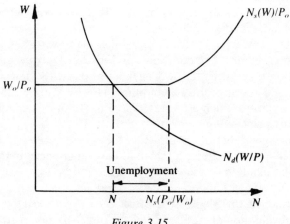

Figure 3.15

A similar interpretation, but one potentially much more fertile, was suggested by Patinkin (1965). He takes the labour demand curve, rather than its supply curve, as being kinked, and possessing a zone of inelasticity.

While the 'normal' demand curve, drawn as a dotted line, would correspond to equalisation of marginal productivity with the real wage, the kinked demand curve is derived under the additional constraint of

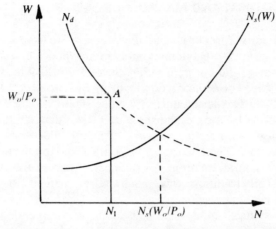

Figure 3.16

effective demand; firms take account of the fact that they cannot sell all the output which appears to be profitable under present conditions of wages and prices (ibid., pp. 322–3).

Suppose that the labour market is currently at A, with real wage W_o/P_o. Could a fall in wages reduce unemployment? Certainly not by increasing employment beyond N_1, but possibly so by reducing the supply of labour. This, however, still requires that the reduction in the real wage does not lower effective demand through distributional effects, which would tend to move the kink in the demand function to the left and to reduce the level of employment (see also Hansen, 1970, pp. 141–7).

Patinkin's analysis is set squarely in a disequilibrium context and therefore seems to turn its back on Keynes. But at the same time, it shows that disequilibria generate further constraints on behaviour and so opens the way to the renewal of Keynesian theory achieved by the modern theory of equilibria with rationing (as we shall see in chapter 12).

To the question of whether a situation of persistent Keynesian unemployment is an equilibrium our preferred reply will be that it has been historically and logically productive to view it as such, so as to argue against the neoclassicists the non-automatic regulation of the system; but that technically speaking this is a narrow-minded view since it rests on an application of Marshallian partial equilibrium to all goods. Compared with general equilibrium, Keynesian situations are disequilibria, representing a particular case of weaker co-ordination, of restricted equilibrium in which agents are subject to extra constraints.

3 KEYNESIANISM AND MACROECONOMIC POLICY

Keynesian theory, formalised and interpreted as we have seen, provided a rationalisation for economic intervention policies whose earliest examples, before the outbreak of the Second World War, were largely empirically based. Becoming dominant in Britain after 1945 with the Beveridge Plan, Keynesian influence made steady progress in the USA in the 1950s, to become established after 1961 under the Democratic administration. In French post-war economic doctrines, Keynesian influence was mixed with a distinctive political and intellectual tradition, one noticeably different from the dominant ideas in the Anglo-Saxon countries. This tradition was much more inclined towards direct planning of economic activity.

In the technical field, rationalisation of interventionist policies stimulated the development of structural models seeking to measure the expected effects of monetary and fiscal policy. This required elaboration of the Keynesian model towards a fuller integration of financial variables and endowments. Apart from these technical developments, Keynesianism was always clearly linked to an appreciation of the macro-economic obligations of the state.

A Multipliers in the full Keynesian system

The static multiplier corresponds to the 45° diagram exposition. The dynamic multiplier operates in the process of equilibrating macro-economic flows. Using a full Keynesian model and its *IS-LM* representation enables us to analyse these multipliers better by integrating monetary aspects. It is also a convenient framework for discussing the action of the fiscal instruments, public expenditure and taxation, favoured in Keynesian-inspired economic policies.

We consider a linear model, without loss of generality insofar as it can be considered as an approximation in the neighbourhood of an initial equilibrium of some given model. The model of sections I and II is therefore rewritten, and completed by adding in government expenditure G and T proportional to income in the ratio t. The model is thus:

$$\left. \begin{aligned} C &= c(Y - T) + C_o \\ I &= I_o - ai \\ Y &= C + I + G \\ T &= tY + T_o \end{aligned} \right\} \quad \textit{IS} \text{ block}$$

and

$$M_1 = mY$$
$$M_2 = L_o - l_i$$
$$M_o = M_1 + M_2$$

$\left.\right\}$ *LM* block

Since the whole analysis is carried out in terms of fixed prices, all magnitudes may equally be taken as real without further restriction.

Both blocks being under-determined, we get a set of solution pairs *(Y, i)* defined by:

$$Y = \frac{C_o + G + I_o - cT_o}{1 - c + ct} - \frac{a}{1 - c + ct}i$$

for the *IS* curve whose (negative) slope is given by the coefficient $-a$, measuring the impact of the interest rate on investment via the multiplier; and

$$Y = \frac{M_o - L_o}{m} + \frac{l}{m}i$$

for the *LM* curve whose (positive) slope is equal to the quotient of the coefficient on speculative demand and that on transactions demand, *m* (Bowers and Baird, 1971, ch. VII).

The general solution of the model is obtained by solving the system formed by the *IS* and *LM* equations for *Y* and *i*. We find, for the value of income:

$$Y = \frac{l(C_o + G + I_o - cT_o) + a(M_o - L_o)}{l(1 - c + ct) + am}$$

and for the rate of interest:

$$i = \frac{m(C_o + G + I_o - cT_o) - (1 - c + ct)(M_o - L_o)}{l(1 - c + ct) + am}$$

The multipliers for the elements of autonomous demand, investment, government sector and autonomous private consumption may then be derived:

$$\frac{\partial Y}{\partial G} = \frac{\partial Y}{\partial I_o} = \frac{\partial Y}{\partial C_o} = \frac{l}{l(1 - c + ct) + am}$$

$$= \frac{1}{1 - c + ct + a\ \dfrac{m}{l}}$$

This multiplier is lower than the simple multiplier because the denominator is increased by two positive expressions. The first of these results from the tax at rate t on distributed income, playing a role equivalent to an increase in the rate of savings. The second term represents monetary restraint.

The multiplier is calculated here for a given money stock. The increase in income induced by autonomous spending requires an increase in active balance M_1, and thus a reduction in speculative balances, leading to an increased interest rate and a fall in investment.

This effect is known as 'crowding-out' of private by public expenditure, in the sense that part of the additional public expenditure simply replaces private investment. The crowding-out effect was already the kernel of the British 'Treasury View' before the war, which held that public works would replace private investment rather than constituting a net increase in capital formation. Paradoxically, if, as in the 'Classical' model, savings move positively with the rate of interest, the crowding-out effect is reduced.

It therefore seems that the simple Keynesian multiplier overestimates the increase in income which would result from an increase in autonomous expenditure, in the absence of an accommodatory monetary policy.

If, on the other hand, monetary policy is applied on its own, and consists of an increase in the money stock with a constant level of autonomous expenditure, its impact on income is given by the multiplier:

$$\frac{\partial Y}{\partial M_o} = \frac{a}{l\,(1 - c + ct) + am} = \frac{1}{m + \dfrac{l}{a}\,(1 - c + ct)}$$

This multiplier has a value lower than that implied by the quantity theory viewed as a theory of nominal income. The main effect is felt indirectly, via the interest rate and investment. We can see that, in fact, the importance of the money and expenditure multipliers respectively hinges on the absolute value of the term a/l. If this is small, the fiscal multiplier approaches its maximum value and the money multiplier is small. Conversely, a high level of a/l gives a higher money multiplier, close to the predictions of the quantity theory, and a lower value of the multiplier on autonomous expenditure.

a/l is in effect the coefficient which measures the sensitivity of investment to the money supply:

$$\frac{\partial I}{\partial M} = \frac{\partial I}{\partial i} \Big/ \frac{\partial M_2}{\partial i} = \frac{-a}{-l}$$

It varies directly with the interest elasticity of investment and with the flexibility of the interest rate relative to the money supply. If investment is elastic and the interest rate flexible, *a/l* is large and monetary policy will be relatively more effective than direct action on autonomous demand, for example through budgetary policy. If, however, the interest elasticity of investment is low, as many Keynesians believe it is, and a liquidity trap operates, even approximately, monetary policy will have little effect compared with fiscal policy. This 'elasticity pessimism' is the conjuncture which has led 'Keynesians' to emphasise fiscal policy while neglecting monetary policy. This choice of assumptions was to expose Keynesians to the critique of Friedman who could easily attack a theory according to which money 'doesn't matter'.

Whilst monetary and fiscal intervention can be proposed as alternatives, they can equally be viewed as complements. If the money supply is unchanged, a monetary constraint will reduce the multiplier and the effectiveness of a purely fiscal policy. An accommodating monetary policy aimed at maintaining a constant rate of interest through the expansion of the money stock, *dM*, in proportion to the increase in public expenditure *dG*, could be set as a target. Such a policy would seek to make the total differential of the interest-rate equation equal to zero:

$$di = \frac{m}{l(1 - c + ct) + am} dG - \frac{(1 - c + ct)}{l(1 - c + ct) + am} dM = 0$$

from which we obtain the formula for the monetary expansion needed:

$$\frac{dM}{dG} = \frac{m}{1 - c + ct}$$

The change in output resulting from such a policy is then:

$$dY = \frac{l}{l(1 - c + ct) + am} dG + \frac{a}{l(1 - c + ct) + am} \frac{dM}{dG} dG,$$

or, using the money expansion ratio derived from above:

$$dY = \frac{1}{1 - c - ct} \, dG,$$

which is just the usual value of the multiplier in the presence of an income tax. The value of the full *IS-LM* Keynesian model is to show that the multiplier can only take its traditional value in the case where accommodating monetary policy is used in conjunction with fiscal policy.

Regarding fiscal policy, it is important to explore the consequences of financing extra expenditure through taxation. To keep the exposition simple, we shall consider a once-for-all lump sum tax dT_o, with the marginal tax rate t being assumed to be zero. We will further assume, without going into the details, that an accommodatory monetary policy, stabilising the rate of interest, is operated. The change in output is then

$$dY = \frac{1}{1 - c} \, dG - \frac{c}{1 - c} \, d \, T_o.$$

In the case of a balanced budget $dT_o = dG$, we have:

$$dY = \frac{1 - c}{1 - c} \, dG = dG.$$

This result is called 'Haavelmo's theorem of the balanced budget': the multiplier on public expenditure financed by an extra tax is equal to one.

B Developments of the Keynesian model

The analysis set out above rested on a set of assumptions which limit its generality. In particular, prices and wealth were assumed constant. Developments of the Keynesian model allow us to widen the analysis to include changes in these variables.

1 Multipliers with flexible prices
We shall deal here only with a model with flexible prices but given money wages, which *a priori* will generate involuntary unemployment. Derivation of the multipliers with flexible prices is more complicated (see Burrows and Hitiris, 1974, pp. 91–119), but it is easy to show that price flexibility will in general tend to reduce the real effects of fiscal or

monetary policy. To do this, we will consider Figure 3.17 in terms of aggregate supply and demand. An increase in public expenditure G, in the nominal money supply M_o, or a reduction in taxes will each increase aggregate demand for any price level.

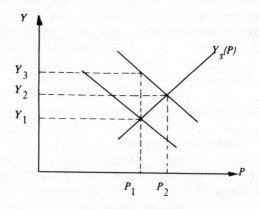

Figure 3.17

Equilibrium income increases from Y_1 to Y_2 but with a price increase from P_1 to P_2. The final impact on income $(Y_2 - Y_1)$ is therefore lower than would be the case $(Y_3 - Y_1)$ with fixed prices, the split between real and price effect of the shift in demand being commanded by the price elasticity of supply.

2 Wealth effects and public expenditure
By assuming the various stock variables constant, the traditional discussion of the *IS-LM* model obscured several aspects of monetary and fiscal policy. Even if we only consider the short term and ignore increases in wealth resulting from private investment (cf. Turnovsky, 1977), it would be difficult to ignore the consequences of government actions for the financial wealth of private individuals. In particular, Christ (1968) and Blinder and Solow (1973) stressed the need to take account of the state's budget constraint, which requires any deficit $G - T$ to be financed either by money creation, dM or bond issues, dB.

$$G - T = dM + dB$$

To follow the implications of this point, it is necessary to think of an economy with three assets; with money M, real capital with a required rate of return r and bonds with a yield rate i. Fiscal or monetary policy measures then produce, besides the effects already described, wealth and substitution effects relating to the value and composition of asset holdings.

For example, a supply of money through open-market operations is usually associated with an unchanged fiscal stance; that is, a constant deficit with $dM + dB = 0$. In that case, there is no private wealth created (neglecting the variation in the value of bonds caused by the change in interest rates) by changes in the state's liabilities, only a reorganisation of portfolios through substitution of money for bonds (in the case of expansionary monetary policy). The effect of such a policy is to shift the *LM* curve to the right.

A policy of public expenditure financed by monetary expansion $dG = dM > 0$, leads to a rightward shift of both *IS* and *LM*, as in the case of accommodating monetary policy outlined earlier.

The case of additional expenditure financed by public borrowing, $dG = dB > 0$, is the one in which crowding-out effects are most pronounced. Even in this case, though, more detailed analysis leads one to qualify that conclusion.

Two effects are well known to begin with: the expansionary effect of dG shifting the *IS* curve to the right, and the crowding-out effect in the usual sense due to the extra demand for money for transactions leading to an increase in interest rates.[9] Shifting the *LM* curve to the left, the latter effect tends to mitigate the former.

Consideration of portfolio effects includes wealth and substitution effects. Households find their wealth holdings increased by increased claims on the state dB, which may lead them to increase consumption (shifting *IS* to the right), and also their demand for money, bonds and capital (shifting *LM* to the left).

Thus, as opposed to the transactions effect which always tends to crowd out private expenditure, the portfolio composition effect may imply a reinforcement of the expansionary effect of public expenditure (B. M. Friedman, op. cit.; Cohen and McMenamin, 1970, pp. 322–36). The mechanism may be described as follows.

An increase in transactions demand for a given money supply requires an increase in the rate of return on real assets, r, in order to restore equilibrium. An increase in the supply of bonds requires a corresponding increase in demand not entirely justified by the wealth effect: households, for a given set of interest rates, would not hold the whole of their increase in wealth dB in the form of bonds. i therefore has to increase and the rate of a return on the competing asset, r, has to fall. If bonds are a close substitute for capital, the demand for bonds is highly elastic with respect to r and the tendency for r to fall due to the excess supply of bonds is very weak. The need for money market equilibrium is paramount, so the required rate of return on capital increases and the net portfolio effect is a crowding-out effect. However, if bonds are wider substitutes, the sensitivity of r to excess demand for money is weaker than it is to excess supply of bonds. The second effect is dominant and r falls, stimulating investment. In this case reallocation of wealth strengthens the effect of fiscal policy, and works against the crowding-out phenomenon.

Figure 3.18 deals with each of these cases with the reallocation of wealth opposing or reinforcing the crowding-out effect (of transactions demand).

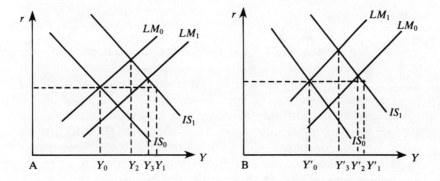

Figure 3.18   A If bonds are close substitutes for money
B If bonds are close substitutes for capital

Increases in government expenditure, dG, and induced increases in wealth $dB = dG$, shift IS to the right to IS_1. In the absence of a monetary restraint, the increase in income would be $(Y_1 - Y_0)$. The crowding-out effect of transactions demand increases the required rate of return, reducing equilibrium income by $(Y_2 - Y_1)$. The wealth effect is favourable in case A, where bonds are a close substitute for money $(Y_3 - Y_2 > 0)$, but unfavourable in case B, where bonds are more substitutable for fixed capital $(Y_3' - Y_2' < 0)$.

C Some notes on Keynesian intervention policies

The Keynesian argument starts from an empirical proposition: that market forces are incapable of ensuring the spontaneous self-regulation of the capitalist system so as to maintain full employment of resources. From this is deduced the need for a deliberate policy of intervention to provide the necessary adjustment. This intervention, however, is strictly limited.

Indeed, in Keynes's own view, the failure of the system was not in efficiently allocating resources, but in guaranteeing their full employment.

> To put the point concretely, I see no reason to suppose that the existing system seriously misemploys the factors of production which are in use. . . . It is in determining the volume, not the direction, of actual employment that the existing system has broken down. Thus I agree with Gesell that the result of filling in the gaps in the classical theory is not to dispose of the 'Manchester System', but to indicate the nature of the environment which the free play of economic forces requires if it is to realise the full potentialities of production. (Keynes, 1936, p. 379; see also Minsky, 1975, ch. VIII)

So we can see that the Keynesian theory is very different from the ideas which underlay, for example, French planning in its early stages. It is in fact neo-liberal by nature, in that it describes the political and economic framework for a practical liberalism.

We can thus begin to understand the extremely aggregative structure used in the *General Theory*: it was appropriate for the points to be made. It is fully in accord with Keynes's thinking to emphasise global intervention rather than selective measures, because the desired results deal only with aggregates and interfere as little as possible with resource allocation through the market mechanism.

It remains true that Keynes's theory and Keynesianism thereafter themselves set up obstacles into which they would eventually collide. Their approach in terms of aggregate supply and demand, for example, leads logically to a symmetrical view of inflation and unemployment. The current problems encountered by policies which they inspired illustrates the need for an advance beyond the Keynesian system.

Part Two
Behavioural Dynamics

In a decentralised economy, macroeconomic developments follow largely from the behaviour of different categories of agents. The construction and measurement of relationships capable of taking account of these behaviours is an integral part of the macroeconomic analysis. More particularly, it is undertaken with the aim of introducing these relationships into a model, after due econometric estimation. The relationships which we are going to study were established principally between 1950 and 1970. They are characteristic of this period of 'neo-classical resurgence' in the face of triumphant Keynesianism and present an undoubted unity. In the first place, they typically keep implicit the problems of passing from microeconomic to macroeconomic analysis and the functions proposed at the aggregate level follow all too frequently from simple transpositions of relationships established at the microeconomic level. Secondly, the development of these relationships allows for the progressive emergence of a series of dynamic factors related to the temporal structure of behaviour, formally expressed in lag structures.

In these studies, the concept of disequilibrium was first presented in the form of prolonged adjustment towards a norm. In more recent times, the disequilibrium perspective has led to the consideration of the additional constraints limiting the range of decisions open to agents by comparison with that offered within a general equilibrium framework.

Here we will first study the behaviour of consumption good purchases, then of factor demands, in particular the demand for investment goods and finally behaviour with regard to financial assets, notably money.

4 The Consumption Function

The consumption function first appeared in Keynes's *General Theory* as an element in the determination of aggregate demand. While, clearly, such a function would have served no purpose in an approach which had retained Say's law, in which there is no place for an autonomous determination of aggregate demand, it is, nevertheless, only recently that the conceptual relationship between this function and the neo-classical demand functions has been made explicit. This reconciliation is forced upon us, once we abandon a strictly aggregative perspective by undertaking even a minimal breakdown of household consumption, albeit simply into durable and non-durable goods.

In our presentation, we shall first deal with the aggregate Keynesian function, then present models based on the theory of inter-temporal consumer choice, before later incorporating into the analysis the influence of liquidity variables and transaction constraints.

1 THE DEVELOPMENT OF THE AGGREGATE KEYNESIAN FUNCTION

In the *General Theory* an aggregate relationship is postulated between consumption expenditure and income, both terms being measured in wage units. This relationship, still called the propensity to consume, is regulated by a series of objective and subjective factors.[1]

Its form is specified in a famous passage, in which Keynes declares:

> The fundamental psychological law, upon which we are entitled to depend with great confidence both *a priori* from our knowledge of human nature and from the detailed facts of experience, is that men are disposed, as a rule and on the average, to increase their consumption as their income increases, but not by as much as the increase in their income. That is to say, if C_w is the amount of consumption and Y_w is income (both measured in wage units) ΔC_w has the same sign as ΔY_w but is smaller in amount,
>
> i.e. $\dfrac{dC_w}{dY_w}$ is positive and less than unity.[2]

Further on, it is true, the conditions relevant to this latter relationship, called the marginal propensity to consume, are presented as an approximation, able to replace the fundamental psychological law, 'not indeed with absolute accuracy but subject to qualifications, which are obvious and can easily be stated in a formally complete fashion'.[3] Although certain passages suggest a decrease in the marginal propensity itself, other developments relevant in particular to the multiplier, treat this relation more as a constant, which would justify the linear form generally given to the Keynesian function in subsequent works:

$$C = cR + C_o$$

with $0 < c < 1$ and $C_0 > 0$, which implies an income elasticity of consumption of less than one,[4] and so a decrease in the average propensity.

Such is the relationship which post-Keynesian works, both theoretical and applied, have put into practice and which M. Friedman contests in favour of the permanent income hypothesis.

A Post-Keynesian functions

The Keynesian consumption function came at an opportune moment to be written onto the research programme of econometricians, whose first macroeconomic studies, with research led by Tinbergen on behalf of the League of Nations, are practically contemporary with the *General Theory*. The estimates undertaken yield ambivalent results with regard to the Keynesian hypothesis. More precisely, there appears a conflict between two categories of results. When the data are collected through household surveys, a positive intercept on the vertical axis is indeed obtained – that is an estimate for C_o, which implies an elasticity less than unity. On the other hand, studies based on aggregate time series data[5] yield a regression line passing through the origin, implying a C_o term not significantly different from zero and a constant average propensity given by the regression line.

The doubt thrown upon the hypothesis by this result was deepened by the failure of the Keynesian function when applied in a predictive manner. Its use, notably by Smithies,[6] led in fact to a substantial underestimation both of the propensity to consume and of the multiplier. Since then, several explanations have been proposed in an attempt to reconcile the hypothesis with the many aspects of the 'empirical evidence'. Leaving aside the proposal of Smithies himself to introduce a trend factor, three approaches stand out in restoring a

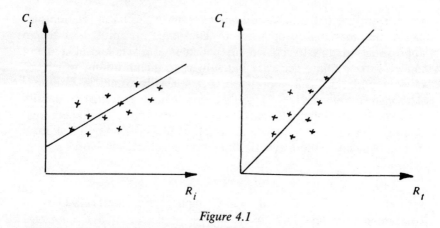

Figure 4.1

clearer theoretical insight into the issue – the relative income approach and the ratchet effect and habit formation approaches.

1 Relative income

The concept of relative income has been developed by J. Duesenberry and its practical application pursued by D. Brady and R. Friedman. The theory of relative income postulates that a houschold's propensity to consume is dependent on its position in the income ladder; Duesenberry established that such a relationship is compatible with the theory of consumer choice as long as there is an interdependence of individual preferences, that is to say as long as the consumption of other households (alternatively the mean consumption of the group) figures as a variable in the utility function of the consumer. Functionally we may write:

$$C_i = aR_i + b(\bar{R} - R_i) + c \qquad \text{with } 1 > a > b > 0$$

where R_i denotes the consumer's own income and $\bar{R}$ the mean income of the group to which he is conscious of belonging.[7] The propensity to consume personal income is $a - b$, which is the figure measured in studies of any single-period cross-section of the population. On the other hand, in an aggregated time series, the term disappears through aggregation and the estimated propensity is a, which is higher than that obtained in cross-section.

2 The ratchet effect

Duesenberry advanced the hypothesis of an irreversibility of consumption decisions over time. 'It is more difficult for a family to reduce its consumption from an initially elevated level than it is to refrain from executing significant purchases for the first time.'[8] So there is included within the consumption function a 'bench-mark' level of income R_o, which might be for example the maximum income level attained in the past. Thus, we may obtain the following expression, which underlines the formal kinship with the relative income theory.[9]

$$C_t = aR_t + b(R_o - R_t) + c \qquad \text{with } 1 > a > b > 0$$

In a depression situation $(R_t < R_o)$, the propensity to consume from current income is $a - b$; in the long term, bench-mark income does not differ from actual income and the marginal propensity to consume is equal to a.

Once again the discrepancy in the statistical results is explained. The bench-mark income level R_o here represents a temporal reference, while a social reference $\bar{R}$ is kept in the relative income theory.[9]

3 The theory of habit formation

It has been proposed to substitute in place of R_0 in the previous formula, a past level of consumption as the point of reference. Taking the actual consumption of the previous period as this reference value, we have the function proposed by T. M. Brown in 1952.[10]

$$C_t = aR_t + bC_{t-1} + c \qquad 0 < a < 1 \; ; \; 0 \leqslant b \leqslant 1$$

A non-zero value of the coefficient b expresses a behavioural inertia, resulting from the formation of consumption habits. Habits evolve at a speed inversely proportional to the value of the coefficient b. An increase in Y from an initial stationary state $(R_{t-1} = R_{t-2} = R_{t-T}...)$ is translated in the first period into an increase in consumption of $a(dR_t)$.

(The relationship dC_t/dR_t one would call the short-term marginal propensity to consume and it is equal to a.) But the adjustment of consumption will continue over subsequent periods:

$$\Delta C_{t+1} = ab \; R_t$$
$$\Delta C_{t+2} = ab^2 \; R_t.$$

Or in total:

$$\Delta C = \sum_{\theta=1}^{\infty} \Delta C_{t+\theta} = a(1 + b + b^2 + ... + b^\theta + ...) \Delta R_t$$
$$= \frac{a}{1-b} \Delta R_t.$$

The relation $a/(1 - b)$, called the long-term propensity to consume, is greater than the short-term propensity to consume a, for $0 < b < 1$, that is if behavioural inertia is neither zero nor infinity. This result can equally be obtained assuming stationary conditions where:

$$C_t = C_{t-1} = C_{t-\theta}, \quad \text{for any value of } t.$$

Therefore:

$$C_t = aR_t + bC_{t-1} + c = \frac{a}{1-b}R_t + \frac{c}{1-b}$$

The short-term propensity to consume is thus the product of two distinct factors – the long-term propensity to consume multiplied by the coefficient of adjustment $(1 - b)$.

Brown's model is formally very significant. It presents, for the first time, a type of 'auto-regressive' or distributed lag model, which illustrates a so-called geometrical lag structure, with the coefficients of the lagged values of the explanatory variable following a geometrical progression of common ratio b. Developing the expression for C_{t-1}, then that for C_{t-2}, we obtain in fact the following relation:

$$C_t = a \sum_{\theta=0}^{\infty} b^\theta R_{t-\theta} + c/(1-b)$$

This lag distribution has been named the Koyck distribution, after the Dutch economist who applied it in 1956 to the investment process.

The relative income, ratchet and habit formation effects have in common the fact that they do not so much contradict Keynesian theory as seek to perfect it, in particular by providing a more profound treatment of psychological and sociological factors.[11] Milton Friedman with his permanent income theory advocated a diametrically opposed course.

B Permanent income and the critique of the Keynesian function

The permanent income theory, propounded by M. Friedman in 1957, has eclipsed the preceding interpretations and now constitutes the principal reference point for the analysis of the macroeconomic consumption function. In fact this theory combines different elements of analysis: a statistical model, a reference to the theory of consumer choice and a derived staggered-lag structure. In this section, we shall consider only the first of these; the other two will be discussed in the following section. In many respects, the permanent income theory, in putting into question the multiplier, represents a definite stage in the programme of work undertaken by Friedman since 1947.

1 The statistical model of consumption

Friedman's hypothesis is that consumer rationality implies a determinate[12] and proportional relationship between the permanent components of income and consumption:

$$C^p = kR^p$$

k being equivalent to the marginal propensity to consume, given that the elasticity $e^{C_p}_{R_p}$ is equal to one. To the permanent components are added the transitory components C^t and R^t, though there is no correlation either between them or with the permanent components. The transitory elements correspond to receipts or expenditures, which are out of the ordinary, unpredictable and non-recurrent (that is, without autocorrelation).

With these assumptions, it is easy for Friedman to demonstrate that use of the Keynesian function yields a biased estimator of the true propensity k. In fact the method of least squares leads to an estimated value of:

$$\hat{a} = \frac{COV(C, Y)}{VAR(Y)}$$

when the theoretical value of k is:

$$k = \frac{COV(C^p, Y^p)}{VAR(Y^p)}$$

We may show that:

$$\hat{a} = k \frac{VAR(Y^p)}{VAR(Y)}$$

or as Y_p and Y_t are uncorrelated:

$$\hat{a} = k \frac{VAR(Y^p)}{VAR(Y^t) + VAR(Y^p)} < k.$$

Least squares regression, when applied to the Keynesian function, underestimates the propensity to consume, and the greater the variance of transitory income in relation to the variance of permanent income, the greater is the underestimation. As transitory elements carry a greater weight in cross-sectional data, it is natural that these data should yield a greater bias (a lower estimated value) than that obtained in time series data. In this way, Friedman brings his contribution to the debate surrounding the explanation of divergent estimates, demonstrating once more that a ratification of the Keynesian function based on cross-sectional data would be illusory. On this point one must beware of an error sometimes committed. Contrary to what has been written at times, it is not the 'dynamic' character of time series data as opposed to the 'static' character of single-period cross-sections, which is at the root of this result. On the contrary, observations in cross-section (with the same degree of aggregation) capture more of the variance in permanent elements because differences between individuals are more fundamental and more long-lasting than are variations in data relating to one individual. But, in addition, time series data are aggregated and aggregation provides some compensation for individual disturbances, which also reduces the degree of transitory variance.

2 The multiplier called into question
The Keynesian consumption function has as a direct purpose the aim of providing a foundation for the mechanism of the multiplier. The doubt thrown on the former could not be without consequence for this essential instrument of the Keynesian analysis. We shall show that Brown's reformist thesis implies a wakening of the short-term multiplier, while Friedman's more critical approach leads to an affirmation of the multiplier's overall instability.

C The time structure of the multiplier effects

Let R_t, national income, be the sum of investment and consumption, which is assumed to follow Brown's function:

$$R_t = aR_t + bC_{t-1} + I_t$$

An expansion of investment dI_t creates an additional income in the period of:

$$dR_t = adR_t + dI_t = \frac{1}{1-a} dI_t$$

The measure of this immediate effect is called the short-term or impact multiplier. But the process persists even if the stimulus dI_t is not maintained.[13]

$$dR_{t+1} = \frac{b}{1-a} \quad \frac{a}{1-a} dI_t$$

The sequence of these effects is traced out by 'dynamic multipliers'.[14] As regards the ultimate effect, the sùm of the dynamic multipliers, we have:

$$dR = [1 + \frac{a}{1-a}(1 + \frac{b}{1-a} + \frac{b^2}{(1-u)^2} + ... + \frac{b^\theta}{(1-a)^\theta} + ..)]dI$$

whence:

$$M = \frac{dR}{dI} = 1 + \frac{a}{1-u} \sum_{\theta=0}^{\infty} (\frac{b}{1-a})^\theta = \frac{1-b}{1-a-b}$$

M is the cumulated or long-term multiplier. It holds equally as an equilibrium multiplier in considering a stationary situation in terms of income and consumption. When b belongs to the interval $(0, 1)$ (exclusive of limits) the long-term multiplier is always greater than the short-term multiplier.

Thus the introduction of lags in consumer behaviour leads us to a revision of the multiplier mechanism. Empirically, we note that, through the interplay of dynamic multipliers, delays interrupt the reaction of income to variations in autonomous demand. Without fundamentally undermining Keynesian mechanisms, this analysis casts doubt on the efficacy of the economic policy measures which they inspire. We shall see that Friedman extends the critical scope of this analysis.

D The instability of the multiplier

While showing that the delays necessary for variations in autonomous expenditure to exert their influence constitute, in his eyes, an insurmountable handicap to the exercise of discretionary economic policy, Friedman, through the theory of permanent income, also questions the actual mechanism of the multiplier by asserting the instability of the relationship upon which it is based.

In his view, the only determinate relationship (if rate of interest changes are small, it is also stable) is between permanent consumption and permanent income. Given this fact, the relationship observed between actual income and actual consumption, and therefore the multiplier itself, must be unstable. Their values change over the course of the cycle, so to use them to calculate the magnitude of required interventions would be particularly inappropriate.

Let us consider, for example, government expenditure undertaken within the context of a counter-cyclical programme. For the agents who will receive corresponding sums in the form of income, these sums amount to transitory resources, destined by their nature not to be maintained. The propensity to consume this income is theoretically zero and in practice quite low. Thus a new criticism is added to the obstacle of a delayed reaction of autonomous demand to discretionary policy.

These arguments will be discussed more deeply below in connection with the explicit formulation of an expectations formation process. However, underlying the development of a statistical critique, there appears to be a reference to the neoclassical theory of inter-temporal consumer choice.

2 INTER-TEMPORAL CHOICE AND THE CONSUMPTION FUNCTION

In Keynes, saving appears as the residual element in the allocation of income. Nevertheless, there is a neoclassical tradition going back at least as far as Walras, in which saving is considered as the allocation of a part of income in response to a demand for future goods: hence the theory of choice is applicable to consumption-savings arbitrage in the allocation of current income.

The permanent income theory is constructed with reference to this approach, which has also provided an inspiration for other hypotheses such as that of the life cycle. More generally, it leads us to the introduction of wealth as a determinant of current consumption. A brief recollection of the theory of inter-temporal choice will precede our exposition of its implications for the macroeconomic consumption function.

A The reference model: inter-temporal consumer choice

We will suppose, at the cost of great simplification, that consumer behaviour may be reduced to a choice between present consumption C_0 and future consumption C_1. The consumer has preferences over the whole range of pairs (C_0, C_1) and these preferences are assumed to be regular and therefore representable by a utility function $U(C_0, C_1)$, giving rise to a set of indifference curves in the space (C_0, C_1), which satisfy the usual conditions of the theory of consumer choice.[15]

The resources of the consumer consist of a present income R_0 and a future income R_1. If no transfer of purchasing power is possible, the consumer's budgetary constraints amount to the inequalities:

$$C_0 \leqslant R_0 , \qquad C_1 \leqslant R_1 .$$

If it is possible to transfer purchasing power from the present to the future, in the form of deposits, these constraints become:

$$C_0 \leqslant R_0 \qquad C_1 \leqslant R_0 + R_1 - C_0$$

A transfer of purchasing power from the future to the present requires the possibility of borrowing. The pure theory of inter-temporal choice, following I. Fisher,[16] assumes the existence of a perfect financial market, in which it is possible to borrow and lend without limit, at a constant single rate of interest i. Under these conditions, the consumer is now only confronted by one budgetary constraint, which indicates that his discounted expenditure should not exceed his discounted income, that is to say his wealth.

$$C_0 + \frac{C_1}{1 + i} \leqslant R_0 + \frac{R_1}{1 + i} = W_0$$

This equation defines a 'wealth line', which is at the frontier of the pairs of values (C_0, C_1) attainable by the consumer. The latter in choosing his preferred combination of present and future consumption, given his wealth constraint, reaches the following solution:

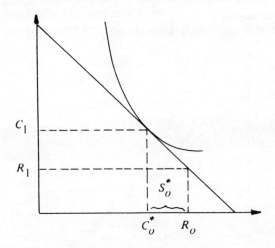

Figure 4.2

The optimal consumption pair (C_0^*, C_1) leaves savings of $S_0^* = R_0 - C_0^*$ which maximises utility subject to the condition of equalising the marginal rate of substitution between present and future consumption with the interest factor $(1 + i)$ – the absolute value of the slope of the wealth line.[17] In this solution, with preferences given, it is clear that consumption and savings depend only on the absolute level and the slope of the budget constraint, that is to say on the wealth of the consumer and the rate of interest:

$$C_0 = C_0(W_0, i) \quad ; \quad S_0 = R_0 - C_0(W_0, i)$$

We may accept that neither present not future consumption are inferior goods, so that consumption is an increasing function of wealth.[18] The effect of the interest rate is more ambiguous.

A variation in i will be reflected in the diagram by a rotation of the wealth line around the point (R_0, R_1). It leads to both an income effect and a substitution effect. Let us remember that the substitution effect is always negative, entailing a reduction in demand for the good whose price has risen. An increase in the rate of interest will lead to a steeper slope (in absolute value) of the wealth line: so, for a given level of utility and therefore an unchanged indifference curve, we get a point of tangency further to the left, representing a reduction in current consumption and an increase in savings. It is only in terms of this partial effect, that one can consistently affirm that consumption is a decreasing function and savings an increasing function of the rate of interest.

In fact, for every consumer who is initially either a borrower or a lender, the variation in the rate of interest will also have an income effect, which will be positive for a creditor and negative for a debtor.[19]

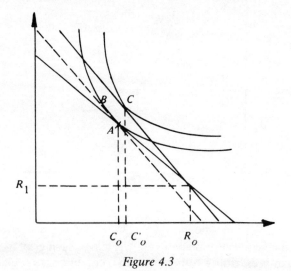

Figure 4.3

This effect may act counter to the substitution effect and possibly dominate it. The example in the graph illustrates the case of a rise in the rate of interest modifying the decisions of a lender. The substitution effect reduces consumption and increases savings and therefore future consumption (the shift AB), while the income effect (the shift BC) increases present and future consumption but reduces saving.

We see, then, that the usual hypothesis which depicts saving as an increasing function of the rate of interest, may be invalid if household consumers, as a whole, are net creditors. It is, nevertheless, traditionally accepted.

B Permanent income: theoretical content

While he does refer to the theory of inter-temporal consumer choice, M. Friedman does not express consumption as a function of wealth. In its place, he puts an indicator of the level of the wealth constraint which should be homogeneous with income. The solution may be easily found in the two-period case.

The income Y_p which, when earned in each period, has the same discounted value as the effective revenue is called permanent income. The data Y_p and i are sufficient to define the wealth constraint in its entirety. We note that for a vector (R_0, R_1) of given effective incomes, permanent income is a function of the rate of interest. More generally, permanent income is that intensity of the constant flow of income, which has the same discounted value as the record of effective incomes over a given economic time horizon T. Friedman's definition is as follows:[20]

$$\sum_{t=1}^{T} \frac{R_t}{(1+i)^t} = \sum_{t=1}^{T} \frac{R^p}{(1+i)^t} = R^p \sum_{t=1}^{T} \frac{1}{(1+i)^t} = R^p \frac{(1-i)^{-T}}{i}$$

With an infinite time horizon, the following relation is established between wealth and permanent income:[21]

$$W_0 = \frac{R_p}{i} \rightarrow R_p = iW_0$$

Thus, Friedman will retain as his consumption function the expression $C_0(R_p, i)$. In addition, he assumes that the utility function is homogeneous, which ensures that indifference curves are homothetic, that expansion paths are straight lines and therefore that the trade-off between present and future consumption is independent of the level of wealth.[22] So we may write:

$$C_0 = k(i) R_p$$

We may complete this definition with regard to the determinants of the propensity to consume k, by the addition of, on the one hand, the portmanteau variable u – an indicator of tastes, age and family situation – and, on the other hand, the expression w denoting the relation between non-human wealth (other than discounted wages and salaries) and permanent income. This part of wealth, which provides a better insurance against uncertainty, has a positive influence on consumption. Whence, we have the final expression:

$$C_0 = k(i, w, u) R_p,$$

which as a final hypothesis, relating to the independence of the distributions of w and u with respect to R_p, permits us to transpose to the macroeconomic level.

The life-cycle hypothesis, developed in particular by F. Modigliani in collaboration with Ando and Brumberg, provides another expression derived from the neoclassical theory of consumer choice. In the microeconomic sphere, it illustrates an apparent evolution of the propensity to consume, determined by the age of the consumer. In the aggregate sphere, it explicitly retains wealth as a variable in the consumption function.

After aggregation, the following function is obtained:[23]

$$C_t = aR_t^L + bR_t^E + cA_{t-1}$$

where R_t^L denotes current wage and salary income, R_t^E average expected income from wages and salaries, and A_{t-1} present net assets. For practical application, it is often assumed that expected income R_t^E is proportional to current income R_t^L. This variable thus disappears from the equation.

The following estimate has been obtained by the aforementioned authors in the American case:

$$C_t = 0.7 R_t^L + 0.06 A_{t-1}$$

As R_t^L represents about 75% of total income, we may establish the short-term marginal propensity to consume to be $0.7 \times 0.75 = 0.525$. In contrast, assets and income grow in unison in the long term, which, if the average ratio A_t/R_t is of the order of five, implies a marginal propensity to consume of $0.525 + 0.06 \times 5 = 0.825$. These values tally with empirical observations. So, the life-cycle theory may also be considered to provide a satisfactory explanation of the paradoxes which have been met since the first studies on the Keynesian function. Furthermore, while yielding at least equivalent results at the empirical level, the life-cycle hypothesis provides a richer theoretical framework than the theory of permanent income, particularly for the analysis of the development of consumption in the growth process[24] or of the role of financial constraints.[25] 'For these reasons,' we may conclude along with Ott, Ott and Yoo, 'the hypothesis of Ando and Modigliani can be considered a step forward both in relation to the absolute income hypothesis and the permanent income hypothesis.'[26]

Under these circumstances, the success of Friedman, to whom a majority of authors continue to refer, seems above all due to the powerful empiricist connotations of his theory.

C Permanent income and expectations

The theoretical determination of permanent income does not lead directly to a method of statistical evaluation. So it is not surprising that Friedman slips quickly towards a more empirical definition, taking permanent income as the normal income expected within a given economic time horizon. He thus accepts that his evaluation results from an adaptive expectations process of the form:

$$R^p_t - R^p_{t-1} = \alpha(R_t - R^p_{t-1}) \qquad 0 < \alpha < 1$$

The consumer corrects his evaluation of permanent income from one period to another by a fraction α of the divergence observed between his current and permanent incomes. This divergence may, in fact, correspond to a transitory income receipt or to an error in the evaluation of permanent income. The adaptive expectations process amounts to taking the proportion α as corresponding to transitory income and the proportion $(1 - \alpha)$ as corresponding to the change in permanent income.[27]

It is therefore possible to provide an auto-regressive expression for permanent income, that is an expression which takes the form of a distributed lag distribution:

$$R^p_t = \alpha R_t + (1 - \alpha) R^p_{t-1} \qquad \text{(auto-regressive form)}$$

$$R^p_t = \alpha R_t + (1 - \alpha) \alpha R_{t-1} + (1 - \alpha)^2 \alpha R_{t-2}$$
$$+ (1 - \alpha)^3 R^p_{t-3},$$

or, developing the function up to infinity:

$$R_t^p = \alpha \sum_{\theta = 0}^{\infty} (1 - \alpha)^{\theta} R_{t - \theta}.$$

Note that coefficients with lagged values are weighted to an extent, which decreases in accordance with a geometric progression of common ratio $(1 - \alpha)$. Substituting this auto-regressive expression for permanent income into the consumption function, we obtain:

$$C_t = k(\alpha R_t + (1 - \alpha)R_{t-1}^p)$$

or:

$$C_t = k\alpha R_t + (1 - \alpha) C_{t - 1}$$

This expression is practically identical to Brown's function, which we have previously encountered. Clearly, Friedman's equation does not contain any constant term, but this is not a feature derived from the concept of permanent income itself nor from the adaptive process on which he relies to calculate it. The absence of a constant and the value of the elasticity of consumption consequently adopted are directly implied by the specific hypothesis of a homogeneous utility function.[28] However, it is the difference in interpretation, rather than the difference in form, which seems more significant. In Brown's view, a normal level of consumption C_t^* is associated with a given income, but as a result of consumption habits and behavioural inertia, this level of consumption will not be reached, until a slow adjustment process has been completed. In Friedman's view, consumer rationality implies that an optimal spending programme will immediately be put into action. There is no 'adjustment' other than in the process of assimilating the new information conveyed by variations in current income.

To conclude, the theory of permanent income results in fact from the partial combination of three models: econometric models with errors in variables which interpret transitory income as an observational error in the true explicative variable; permanent income; auto-regressive models derived from adaptive expectations and the neoclassical theory of inter-temporal choice. Its success is largely the result of this synthesis of theoretical and econometric contributions.

3 CONSUMPTION, WEALTH AND LIQUIDITY

After a Keynesian period in which emphasis had been placed on the influence of income, a series of empirical studies, related to the theories of permanent income or the life cycle, have affirmed the primacy of wealth as a determinant of consumption. Remembering that these theories question the value and stability of the marginal propensity to consume, it appears that it is the actual validity of the multiplier which is being challenged. It is, therefore, interesting to ask to what extent this neoclassical approach is comparable with Keynesian theory, and what relationships link the multiplier and the theory of consumer choice.

Empirically, it is useful to note that the volume of liquid assets held by households has been mentioned as one of the possible causes of the increased level of consumption in the United States in the post-war period – a level unforeseen by the Keynesian function. In fact, during the war American households had accumulated liquid assets (principally Treasury bonds), whose positive influence on aggregate consumption has been established by certain econometric studies.[29]

Nevertheless, the positive influence on consumption of monetary or other liquid balances can be interpreted in several ways. The first, long predominant in standard works, attributes this influence to a wealth effect. The analysis in terms of real balances is a good example. A second interpretation, bringing to the fore the notion of liquidity, is proving fertile ground for a realignment of Keynesian theory in relation to neoclassical theory.

These two interpretations will be studied in turn.

A The real balance effect

In its macroeconomic impact, the real balance effect lies at the heart of the debate on the stability of full employment equilibrium. In terms of analysis, it implies that the real value of money balances held at the beginning of a period, let us say M_0/P_0, should be introduced as a variable in the consumption function.

For advocates of the real balance effect, such as Patinkin, its justification is clear. Money is both one of the components of the 'initial endowment' – the wealth – of agents and at the same time a good furnished with a utility – an indirect utility, to be sure, but one which provides the basis for a demand, which acts in competition with the demand for goods and bonds. By virtue of this, a fall in prices leads to an increased evaluation of balances, which is translated into a rise in consumption. Any other expansion of wealth might generate a similar effect. Patinkin distinguishes clearly between his writings and those which 'give the impression that it is real balances in themselves which influence consumption rather than real balances as a component of total wealth. As we have consistently underlined, it is this latter meaning which is implied by our analysis.'[30]

According to this point of view, the real balance effect and the wealth effect of a proportional variation in all prices are synonymous.[31] The two notions differ in the case of non-proportional variations in prices because the real balance effect then encompasses, in addition to the wealth effect, the influence of a possible substitution effect.[32]

Why place real balances in this privileged position among the elements of wealth? Because the real value of this component is a function of the general level of prices, which is not the case for real assets and only partially so for financial assets.

Patinkin's analysis does not see the real balance effect as the consequence of a portfolio reshuffle. Let us consider an example to clarify this point.

Take a consumer with initial deposits of £1,000 at his disposal, corresponding to his desired balance. From other resources, he consumes £3,000 each year, a sum equivalent to 6% of a £50,000 wealth holding. There occurs a 10% fall in the general level of prices, thus the real value of the cash balance settles at £1,111. The wealth effect suggests a forecasted increase in consumption of 6% of £111, let us say £6.66. The impact of a reshuffle would be quite different. If the demand for money is a given fraction of wealth – here 2% – the surplus balance of £1,111 − (0.002 × 50,111) = £109 will be spent on the purchase of assets and so to some extent on durable consumption goods.

The problem, more generally, is knowing whether the real balance effect is permanent or transitional. Certain authors have pointed out, in opposition to Patinkin, that the cash balance retained should no longer figure in long-term demand functions, that is to say should no longer be considered an influence on equilibrium consumption. Therefore, in the short term it would be better to make consumption depend on the margin between effective and desired real cash balances:

$$\frac{C}{P} = f\left(\frac{M_0}{P} - \frac{M^*}{P}\right).$$

In this instance, opposition to the classical approach is not fundamental but perhaps essentially semantic. Patinkin would refuse to grant the above equation the status of a demand function in the neoclassical sense but would accept equivalent formulae under the title of adjustment conditions.[33] The role of the real balance effect in disequilibrium remains far from being bereft of ambiguity.

The difficulties stem from the fact that in this analysis money – or liquid assets – are characterised solely by their nominal fixed values –

hence the sensitivity of their real values to the general price level. The property of liquidity, characteristic of these assets plays no role either in the genesis or the aftermath of the real balance effect.

B The impact of inflation

The debate over real balance effect remains linked with its historical background of the Great Depression with price falling to some extent. The concern now has shifted towards the impact of inflation, with high rates being experienced even in business depression. The theoretical answer is that, if inflation is perfectly anticipated, its impact has still to be analysed in terms of wealth effects, but further effects arise from unanticipated inflation.

As shown by Angus Deaton (1977), unanticipated inflation results from the impossibility for the consumer to distinguish between relative and absolute price changes. It introduces a disequilibrium in the wealth-consumption allocation. Actual saving ratio depends upon the desired saving ratio, and the ratio of actual to planned value for both real income and prices (in logarithm). Simplifying Deaton's model, we may write

$$\frac{s}{y} = \left(\frac{s}{y}\right)^* - \beta \log \frac{y/p}{(y/p)^*} - \gamma \log \left(\frac{p}{p^*}\right)$$

The β coefficient is one if there is no revision in consumption plan due to the departure of the actual income to its reported level, which corresponds to Robertson's 'automatic lacking' if income regulations are stationary. The γ coefficient measures the degree of money illusion. Introducing a partial adjustment assumption for econometric estimation on US and British quarterly data, for a period from the 1950s to the mid-1970s give substantially (op. cit., p. 905).
For the US

$$\Delta\left(\frac{s}{y}\right) = 0.0083 + 0.453 \, g_{y,t} + 0.553 g_{p,y} - 0.240 \left(\frac{s}{y}\right)_{t1/4}$$

and for the UK

$$\Delta\left(\frac{s}{y}\right) = 0.0062 + 0.732 \, g_{y,t} + 0.594 \, g_{p,t} - 0.219 \left(\frac{s}{y}\right)_{t1/4}$$

where $g_{y,t}$ and $g_{p,t}$ denote respectively the rate of growth of real income and price. The use of data on actual inflation did not allow Deaton really to test the effect of unanticipated inflation, while he provides convincing empirical evidence for an effect of actual inflation and good theoretical support for a negative effect of unanticipated inflation on consumption.[34]

C The liquidity effect

In order to appraise the validity of neoclassical theory, in terms of permanent income or the life cycle, it is necessary to measure carefully the full significance of these hypotheses. Assume there exist 'perfect' markets for all assets, including financial and 'human' assets. By 'perfect', one usually understands a situation in which an agent can buy or sell without limit at a constant price. Under this one condition, total wealth indeed becomes the only constraint on the consumer's expenditure horizon. It is equivalent to saying that all the elements of his portfolio are perfectly liquid.

Liquidity denotes the threefold property of an asset of being marketable at a fixed price without delay and without cost. Moreover, the liquidity of the portfolio is strengthened if the agent has at his disposal the means by which to run into debt, thus avoiding the sale of tangible assets or permitting total expenditure to exceed total receipts at certain phases of the life cycle. In particular, human assets not being transferable but only their services, only indebtedness permits the anticipation in consumption of future wage income.

It is sufficient to consider the case of imperfect financial markets,[35] for example a limit on household borrowing or on rapidly increasing amounts borrowed, in order for a liquidity constraint to intervene in the process of inter-temporal utility maximisation, alongside the wealth constraint.

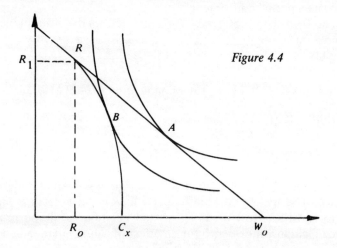

Figure 4.4

In the above diagram, two distinct hypotheses are presented regarding the borrowing possibilities confronting the consumer. If he is considered solvent and the market is therefore perfect, he may through borrowing attain any point within the segment RW_0 and so is only confronted by the single constraint of wealth. Thus, consumption is given by the point of tangency A. If he is considered barely solvent and runs up against rapidly increasing rates of interest, his possibilities for current consumption are limited by the curve RC_x. His decisions must satisfy a liquidity constraint over and above the wealth constraint, so he can only reach point B, with lower levels of consumption and utility than in the preceding situation.[36]

When the liquidity constraint is satisfied, actual consumption becomes a function of the level of this constraint and no longer only (if at all) a function of wealth. There are three factors determining the level of the liquidity constraint: the value of the flow of current receipts, that is to say current income, the significance of the liquid assets held at the beginning of the period and lastly, the capacity to run into debt. Each of these elements plays a role in the liquidity constraint and so should figure in the consumption functions of the agents who have satisfied this constraint.

However, it is clear that the endowment of liquid assets can only have a once and for all effect, whereas income is constantly replenished. The capacity for indebtedness will itself be most often formulated in terms of stocks but may equally well be determined in terms of flows. If the constraint remains satisfied for a long time, then clearly current income will be the principal source of liquidity. Thus Tobin remarks:

> For a liquidity-constrained household, income is a source of cash, and changes in income will be almost completely reflected in changes in consumption spending in a short time. For a wealth-constrained household, one year's income is by itself a small part of total wealth; like other variations in wealth, changes in current income will be shared among this year's consumption and all future years. Only if changes in current income inspire significant changes in estimates of future income and thus in total wealth will there be a large response in current consumption.[37]

There is a clear definition of the scope of Keynesian and neoclassical theories!

D Consumption in a disequilibrium situation

Liquidity is not an intrinsic characteristic of assets. It is as much the result of the organisation and operation of markets. Thus in a general equilibrium framework, arising from a Walrasian 'tâtonnement' process or from a process of recontracting in the style of Edgeworth, all assets enjoy maximum liquidity.

In fact, in a model of this kind nobody can be prevented from undertaking a transaction through not being able to realise the full value of personal assets. By definition, all exchange propositions may be revised if they do not achieve an equilibrium and, when exchange is undertaken, every offer finds its counterpart. So only the value of resources – of wealth in a multi-period context – can limit consumption possibilities. In particular, every worker is assured of finding employment of the desired duration at the current wage rate. Therefore, only the value of present and future labour-time figures in the worker's demand functions.

Everything is changed when, in the absence of a 'tâtonnement' process, exchange occurs outside of equilibrium. A consumer could see his expenditure plans realised and yet be unable to pay, finding himself unemployed when the offer of his labour could not be accepted.[38] In this case, actual receipts in the period are less than the desired receipts which correspond to the optimal consumption programme. R. W. Clower first drew attention to this point:

> If realized current receipts are considered to impose any kind of constraint on current consumption plans, planned consumption as expressed in effective market offers to buy will necessarily be less than desired consumption as given by the demand functions of orthodox analysis.[39]

The theory of consumer choice implicitly assumes a 'tâtonnement' process in considering that the full value of agents' endowments may be realised and transformed into current consumption. Therefore, the theory keeps only prices and the initial level of endowments as the variables in its demand functions. Modern disequilibrium theory, on the other hand, considers that the absence of a 'tâtonnement' process will force agents to undertake non-equilibrium exchanges. Certain agents will then be rationed and so will not be able to realise their plans and exert their 'notional' demand. Their actual receipts are governed by the transactions constraints, which they meet, and, in turn determine the 'effective' demand, which results from utility maximisation under the double constraint of wealth and transactions (or liquidity) limitations. In such a situation, the level of actual receipts, and in particular of current income, must enter as variables in the consumption function.

Thus, the concept of a transactions constraint in a disequilibrium situation permits us to justify the Keynesian consumption function on the same basis as the theory of consumer choice, once the scope of the theory has been broadened by consideration of this additional constraint.

It is no doubt interesting to focus on the transactions constraints which the involuntarily unemployed must face in the labour market, as the parallels with Keynesian analysis are particularly evocative. But one should not isolate this factor too much.

The unemployed can in fact consider their situation as transitory, in which case neither their permanent income nor their consumption would be appreciably affected. That remains true so long as there is a possibility of financing current consumption through the sale of non-human assets or through borrowing. Should these non-human assets be equally illiquid, then the transactions constraint will be strictly binding and effective demand will have to be geared to effective receipts.

In order for consumption to be a function of actual receipts, so that the multiplier will operate, it is not sufficient that there should be unemployment – illiquid labour – it is necessary that a general illiquidity of portfolios should be prevalent. 'The multiplier emerges from this analysis as an illiquidity phenomenon,' says Leijonhufvud,[40] who deduces from this that the multiplier cannot operate in time of recession as long as agents have reserves of liquid balances, such as savings deposits, at their disposal.

In this way, Leijonhufvud, and J. Tobin, alike illustrate how modern analysis has harnessed the contributions of Keynesian and neoclassical theory within the disequilibrium perspective.

5 Investment and Factor Demand

Although the consumption function governs the value of the multiplier, it is the investment function which determines an essential component of the multiplicand. As, in addition, capital formation is subject to large random fluctuations, it is not surprising that a significant volume of work should have been devoted to it.

We will here deal principally with productive investment, which is a particular case of factor demand by firms. Thus, developments relevant to the demand for labour will also be included in this chapter.

While the investment function can initially be studied as a demand function for capital goods, we may alternatively interpret it as an expression of the equilibrium positions of the capital goods market. Contemporary approaches consider investment as resulting from a disequilibrium adjustment process. We will recall in turn these three aspects of investment.

1 INVESTMENT AS THE DEMAND FOR PRODUCTIVE CAPITAL

Our first level of analysis of investment is based directly on the concept of producer's factor demand in microeconomic theory. Reference to this theory is useful in that it provides a framework, which permits us to describe clearly the different constraints, in particular on techniques of production. A brief recollection of the notion of the production function and its properties will permit us to deduce some simple forms of the investment function and, moreover, to illustrate the particular conditions underlying the accelerator mechanism.

A The production function as an expression of technological constraints

The concept of the production function may be initially defined in terms of a single unit of production, whose activity can be described as the transformation of inputs[1] into products or outputs. From the point of view of economic analysis, a technique is characterised entirely by the given quantity of inputs and outputs with which it is associated. A technique lying within the bounds of the technological knowledge of the time is said to be 'possible'. A possible technique is 'feasible' if the quantity of inputs it requires does not exceed their availability. It is 'efficient' if, out of all the techniques using no more than a fixed amount of input, it produces the maximum output, and if, out of all the techniques able to produce at least this same volume of output, it requires the least inputs.

The production set is made up of the range of possible techniques. The efficient techniques form its frontier. Taking the case of a product y with n inputs, numbered x_1 to x_n, the phrase 'production function' would describe a function f, which satisfied the following conditions:

$$y \leqslant f(x_1 \dots x_n) \quad \text{if} \quad (y, x_1 \dots x_n) \text{ is a possible technique,}$$
$$y = f(x_1 \dots x_n) \quad \text{si} \quad (y, x_1 \dots x_n) \text{ is an efficient technique.}$$

Thus the production function is the equation of the production possibility frontier; its projection on the input plane[2] is the isoquant. This function is characterised by certain properties regarding returns and substitution possibilities.

B Properties of production functions

In the multi-input case, returns are defined by considering a proportional variation in all inputs. They may then be qualified as 'returns to scale'. These returns are increasing (constant or decreasing) when the variation in output is more than (equal to or less than, respectively) proportional to the variation in inputs. A homogeneous function is unique in that returns to scale are identical at every point,[3] that is for every input mix and every level of output. Returns are increasing, constant or decreasing according to whether the degree of homogeneity is greater than, equal to or less than one.

A non-proportional variation in inputs may be broken down into a proportional variation plus a change in proportions – an input substitution – occurring at a constant level of output. The marginal rate of substitution measures the ratio of the required variations in inputs. Its algebraic form is easily derived from the following equation for an isoquant, x and z denoting two inputs:

$$dy = \frac{\partial f}{\partial x} \, dx + \frac{\partial f}{\partial z} \, dz = 0$$

whence, we have:

$$\frac{dx}{dz} = -\frac{\partial f}{\partial z} \Big/ \frac{\partial f}{\partial x}$$

A necessary condition for the minimisation of production costs is that an input mix should be maintained such that the marginal rate of substitution is equal to the ratio of input costs. Consequently, when producers follow this rule, the relative proportions of inputs (the input mix) will be modified in response to a variation in factor costs, to an extent determined by the relative substitutability of inputs. The elasticity of the input mix with respect to the marginal rate of substitution, that is to say with respect to the factor cost ratio, when costs are minimised, is called the elasticity of substitution, denoted by σ:

$$\sigma = \frac{d(x/z)}{x/z} \Big/ \frac{d.MRS}{MRS}$$

The uniform constancy of this relationship, that is to say for every level of production and every input mix, is a characteristic of the so-called CES[4] a family of production functions, which have the formula:

$$y = a[\delta x^{\frac{\sigma-1}{\sigma}} + (1 - \delta)z^{\frac{\sigma-1}{\sigma}}]^{\frac{v\sigma}{\sigma-1}}$$

Simplified expressions are obtained for particular values of the elasticity of substitution σ. Thus, we may represent perfect substitutability ($\sigma = \infty$) by a linear function, for $v = 1$:

$$y = ax + bz,$$

where marginal productivities are constant. An intermediate case very frequently met is where $\sigma = 1$. This represents the famous Cobb-Douglas function, in fact first proposed by Wicksell:[5]

$$y = a c x^a z^b,$$

where the ratio of average to marginal productivity is constant (that is to say the elasticity of output with respect to the inputs). These different relationships have remained almost unchanged in macroeconomic applications.

It is worth noting the strict nature of the definition of a production function, which theoretically is only an expression of technological information. In fact, macroeconomic applications assume preliminary aggregation, which raises delicate problems of such great importance that certain writers completely deny the validity of the production function at the macroeconomic level. We will tackle these problems in chapter 7.

C Factor demand

It is usual to assume that producers maximise profits through production cost minimisation, particularly when they are operating in competitive markets where they can influence neither the price of their output nor the price of their inputs.

Formally, the problem of minimising the cost of producing a given output y involves $n + 1$ unknowns − the n quantities of inputs and the marginal cost of production as measured by the Lagrange multiplier associated with the constrained production function. Its resolution permits us to disentangle $n + 1$ conditions, the first n indicating the required ratios of marginal productivities and factor costs and the final one constituting the production function. Factor demand functions are generated mathematically by this system of $n + 1$ equations. They relate the optimal quantity of factors to be employed to the n costs of these factors and to the level of output to be secured thereby. Let us consider the example of a Cobb-Douglas function, combining an employed labour force N with the productive capital K, respective costs being w, the wage rate, and u, the cost of capital usage.[6]

Minimisation of production costs yields the following conditions, where λ denotes the marginal cost of production.

$$u = \lambda \frac{\partial y}{\partial K} = \lambda a \frac{y}{K}$$

$$w = \lambda \frac{\partial y}{\partial N} = \lambda b \frac{y}{N}.$$

Resolution of this system leads to the following values for the desired levels of employment of labour and capital:

$$K^* = a \frac{\lambda y}{u} \quad ; \quad N^* = b \frac{\lambda y}{w}.$$

The problem with these formulae lies in the fact that the marginal cost λ is not observable. However, profit maximisation under competitive conditions requires a level of production, at which marginal cost is equal to market price p, which can then be substituted for it in factor demand functions.

$$K^* = a\frac{py}{u} \quad ; \quad N^* = b\frac{py}{w} .$$

These expressions demonstrate clearly that factor demand results from two separate variables: firstly, the level of output to be secured, which is the source of factor demand for the purpose of extending production, and secondly, the relative cost of the factor, which is the source of factor demand for the purpose of input substitution. Under constant returns, these two elements can be separated.[7] It may be noticed that, as a consequence of constant returns to scale, the Cobb-Douglas function implies an elasticity of factor demand with respect to output equal to one, and an elasticity with respect to factor cost equal to minus one. In the case of labour, for example:

$$E^{N^*}_{y} = \frac{\partial N^*}{\partial y} / \frac{N^*}{y} = 1 \quad ; \quad E^{N^*}_{w} = \frac{\partial N^*}{\partial w} / \frac{N^*}{w} = -1$$

It is important to note that this formula for factor demand raises a problem of interpretation. If there is in fact profit maximisation, the volume of output y is itself endogenous. It cannot be taken as given but merely expressed as a function of prices and factor costs. A factor demand function rigorously defined should be expressed uniquely in terms of price and cost variables but obviously such a formula, while justified at the microeconomic level, would not be immediately operational at the macroeconomic level. To be sure, numerous authors retain the level of output as an explanatory variable in factor demand but, without additional hypotheses, this variable cannot be accepted as exogenous in the statistical sense of the word.

D The accelerator and the development of the desired capital stock

In the static framework considered above we were examining what optimal levels of factor use should correspond to given values of output, prices and costs. In a dynamic framework, it is necessary to investigate the optimal path of evolution of these input quantities as a function of the time profile of output and prices. The criterion used would be the minimisation of discounted cost, or the maximisation of the present value of a flow of net, distributable profits.

The latter criterion is used in D. Jorgenson's classic model.[8] Net capitalised wealth is defined as follows:

$$W = \int_{t=0}^{\infty} (p_t Y_t - w_t N_t - p_{kt} I_t) e^{-it} dt.$$

i is a given, constant rate of interest, I_t is gross investment in volume and p_{kt} the price of capital goods. Maximisation is subject to two constraints: on the one hand the production function, of the Cobb-Douglas form, for example, and on the other hand the equation for the change in capital stock. This expresses capital accumulation as the difference between gross investment and depreciation, occurring at the rate δ:

$$\frac{dK}{dt} = I_t - \delta K_t$$

Maximisation of W under these two constraints yields the target path for desired capital and optimal employment. As the capital stock figures both in the initial level K_t and in the increase dK/dt, we are confronted with a dynamic optimisation problem compelling a trade-off between present distributable income and an increase in capital, and thus future output and incomes. Resolution of the model, through calculus of variations, leads to results very similar to those of the static model. The only difference lies in the value adopted by the user cost of capital, which becomes:

$$u_t = (i + \delta)p_{Kt} - \frac{dp_k}{dt} = (i + \delta - \pi_t)\, p_{Kt},$$

where π_t is the current rate of increase in capital good prices. This result indicates that, in order to arrive at an optimal target path for the stock of capital, it is sufficient at each moment to apply static decision-making rules, integrating variations in the prices of capital goods into the calculation of the user cost of capital.

Up to now, we have merely considered the optimal level of productive capital, that is to say the demand for accumulated capital. As Haavelmo[9] has forcefully pointed out, that is not sufficient to determine the total investment flow in each period.

The simplest solution is to assume that producers will exert an investment demand, which permits them at each moment to maintain the stock of capital at the desired level. Thus, ignoring replacement investment,

$$I_t = dK_t{}^*$$

which, with a Cobb-Douglas function, gives:

$$I_t = d(a\frac{p_t y_t}{u_t}) = a\frac{p_t}{u_t} \cdot dy_t + ay_t\, d(\frac{p_t}{u_t})$$

In particular, with p_t/u_t unchanged, constant returns to scale and w_t/u_t unchanged, we have:

$$I_t = kdy_t, \text{ or in alternative notation, } I_t = k(y_t - y_{t-1})$$

This investment function is well known, under the name of the accelerator.

The accelerator considers net investment to be proportional to variations in output, which, under the assumptions of the model, is itself always equal to demand. Its development, by J. M. Clark, dates back to the beginning of the century.[10]

There are six conditions for the validity of the accelerator:

1 Output adjusts immediately to demand.
2 There is no idle capacity in production.
3 The supply of capital goods is perfectly elastic. (It may be limitlessly extended without delay and at a constant price.)
4 The supply of the means of finance is perfectly elastic at a given cost, which is less than the return on investment.
5 The production function is homogeneous of degree one, and so exhibits constant returns to scale.
6 Either: the production function has fixed coefficients with a zero elasticity of substitution.
   Or: the factor cost ratio is constant.

The various conditions laid out seem especially severe, because they exclude the possibility of idle capacity and the phenomena of disequilibrium adjustment and capital-labour substitution. Equally, let us note that in postulating a perfect elasticity of supply for both capital goods and finance, these conditions place all the determinants of variations in investment on the demand side. It is this point of view that we are now going to put to the test.

2 THE INVESTMENT FUNCTION AND THE CAPITAL GOODS MARKET

Having studied the investment function as a derivative of the demand function for productive capital, we must now take a less one-sided look at the determinants of capital formation.[11] Aggregate investment stabilises at the level at which the capital goods market settles, albeit in equilibrium or disequilibrium. In addition, it seems to be strictly related to the market for loanable funds. We will thus pursue our analysis of investment by considering these two markets.

A The capital goods market

We will present a partial equilibrium model of the capital goods market, keeping the Marshallian terminology of supply prices and demand prices.

The demand price of a given volume of equipment is the price at which producers would be prepared to acquire that quantity. So for a consumption good, determination of the demand price relies on an evaluation in terms of marginal utility; the demand price for capital goods depends on the possibilities for profit opened up by their acquisition. Let R_t be the quasi-rents from exploitation expected over a horizon of T periods of use, and let i be the rate of interest. The discounted value of the quasi-rents is therefore:

$$V = \sum_{t=1}^{T} \frac{R_t}{(1 + i)^t} = P_K = p_K K$$

Clearly, V is the maximum a producer would consent to spend in order to acquire the corresponding stock of equipment, that is to say it is the 'demand price' P_k (in the Marshallian sense) of this capital.[12] Hence, we obtain the expression for the unit demand price of a stock of capital K:

$$p_K = \frac{1}{K} \sum \frac{R_t}{(1 + i)^t}$$

As the opportunities for profitable investment are limited, quasi-rents rise at a decreasing rate as K increases. So the unit demand price p_K decreases for every increment in K. Furthermore, with K and therefore R given, p_K is a decreasing function of the rate of interest. This relationship may be represented by a set of demand price curves, each associated with a different level of the rate of interest.

The demand for investment goods at the price p_K will be equal to the difference between K and K_h, the capital inherited from previous periods, after accounting for depreciation. So the above demand price curve will be valid for investment, after proper translation. Introducing the producers' supply price curve for capital goods, we obtain the market equilibrium diagram.

The market equilibrium positions as a function of the rate of interest generate a curve $I(i)$ known as the Keynesian investment function.

In fact, the above diagrams do not appear in Keynes's *General Theory* undoubtedly because, in order to provide a simpler exposition than in his *Treatise on Money*, he did not want to give an explicitly two-sector

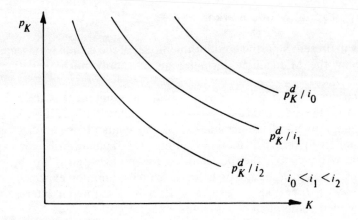

Figure 5.1

structure to his theory.[13] Consequently, he resorts to a formula which is strictly speaking a 'reduced form' of the preceding model. The concept of the marginal efficiency of capital expresses equilibrium of the capital goods market and serves to clear this market. The concept can no longer be defined, if the market settles in a disequilibrium position.

Let the following be the expression for the demand price in the Marshallian sense, at a discount rate r:

$$P_K^d = \sum_{t=0}^{T} \frac{R_t}{(1+r)^t}$$

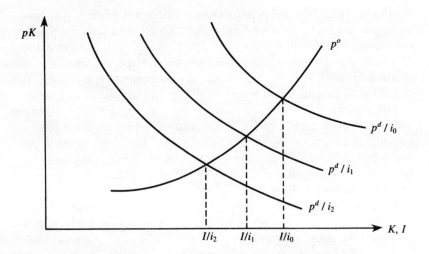

Figure 5.2

and let P^0 be the 'supply price', that is the money value p_0I at which this volume of equipment would be supplied. The solution of the system formed by the above equation and the equilibrium condition $p^0 = p_k^0$ determines a particular value of r known as the marginal efficiency of capital, defined by Keynes as 'that rate of discount which would make the present value of the series of annuities given by the returns expected from the capital-asset during its life just equal to its supply price'.[14]

The reduced equation for the above model is thus $r = r(I)$. Marginal efficiency decreases with the level of investment as a result of diminishing returns and an increasing supply price. Keynes here seems confused on two points. Firstly, he uses the expression for the demand for capital as synonymous with marginal efficiency, whereas he has just shown that a rise in the supply price leads to a decrease in marginal efficiency, which confirms, as has been indicated above, that he is dealing with a locus of equilibrium points.[15] Secondly, the marginal efficiency of capital is defined as an internal rate of return, whereas Keynes uses it as a marginal rate of return. This is obviously apparent in the following quotation:[16]

> Thus Professor Fisher uses his 'rate of return over cost' (in fact the marginal rate of return) in the same sense and for precisely the same purpose as I employ the 'marginal efficiency of capital'.

At this stage, it may be interesting to bring together the two types of investment function we have encountered – the Keynesian function and the accelerator:

$$I_t = I(i_t)$$

and

$$I_t = k \Delta Y_t$$

Are these formulae contradictory or complementary? As we have shown, the validity conditions of the accelerator rule out any possible role for the rate of interest, while at the same time they assume a total absence of factor substitution and an unlimited supply of funds at constant cost. It is still more paradoxical that demand should be ignored in the Keynesian function. In fact, in Keynes's theory the marginal efficiency of capital is conditioned by demand considerations, but this conditioning relies upon expectations rather than on any magnitude observable within the period. Furthermore, Keynes considered 'the state of long-term expectations' as inelastic with respect to current variables. There exists a marginal efficiency curve and therefore an investment function for each state of long-term expectations. Let $\bar{Y}_t$ be expected future demand. Then, the Keynesian hypothesis may be formalised as follows:

$$r_t = r(I_t)|\tilde{Y}_t \quad \text{whence} \quad I_t = I(i_t)|\tilde{Y}_t$$

$$\text{with} \quad \frac{d\tilde{Y}}{dY_t} \approx 0 \quad \text{therefore} \quad \frac{dI_t}{dY_t} \approx 0$$

So it is the hypothesis of the inelasticity of expectations with respect to current variables, which makes investment independent of variations in demand in Keynes's theory. On the other hand, long-term expectations and the marginal efficiency schedule are very sensitive to the 'state of confidence',[17] which can fluctuate strongly and is the principal cause of the random variability of investment. 'I suggest that a more typical, and often the predominant, explanation of the crisis is, not primarily a rise in the rate of interest, but a sudden collapse in the marginal efficiency of capital.'[18]

B The financial constraints on investment

The Keynesian function and the accelerator have in common the fact that they neglect the role of financial factors in the determination of investment. In order to analyse these factors, it is useful to recall the basis of the monetary theory in Fisher's model.

The model of Fisher and Hirschleifer[19] incorporates investment decisions into a general framework of inter-temporal consumer choices. It considers that each agent has at his disposal initial resources S_0 and a set of investment opportunities at decreasing rates of return, expressed by the function $R(I)$.

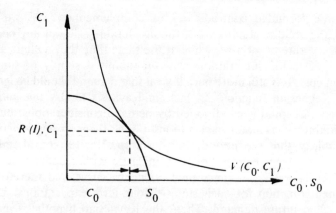

Figure 5.3

When each agent is taken in isolation, current endowments will be shared between current consumption and investment, future consumption being equal to the gross return on investment. The introduction of a perfect financial market permits the separation of savings and investment decisions, and the latter become independent of the time preferences of the consumer. It is clear from the diagram further on that, in order to maximise utility by attaining the highest possible indifference curve, one must first position oneself on the highest possible wealth line; that is to say one must take the investment decisions, which will maximise the discounted value of quasi-rents and thus the wealth of the consumer:

$$W_0 = \frac{R(I)}{1+i} - I + S_0$$

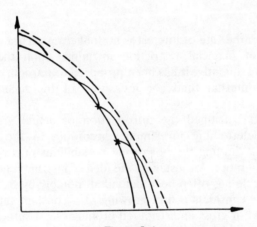

Figure 5.4

The maximum is attained where $dR/dI = 1 + i$, with a rate of return ($dR - dI/dI$) taken to be equal to the rate of interest. Our diagram establishes both the rationality of our investment criterion (the maximisation of present discounted value) and the concomitance of this criterion with the equalisation of the marginal rate of return and the market rate of interest.

But these results depend crucially on the existence of a perfect financial market, where one may borrow and lend without limit at the same, constant rate. In an imperfect financial market, with credit rationing and increasing rates of interest, the wealth constraint is no longer a straight line but an envelope of curves, each one corresponding to a different level of investment.

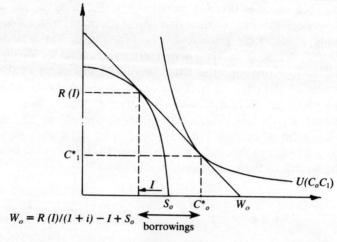

Figure 5.5

In this case, the rate of interest is no longer an accurate indicator of the degree of financial restriction intruding upon the investment function. Consequently, it has been proposed to introduce measures of the flow of internal funds or indicators of the financial state of companies.

M. Kalecki[20] justified the introduction of actual gross profit as a variable determining investment, according to the principle of increasing risk limiting the borrowing possibilities of a company of a given size. In France, for instance, the idea of internal funding having a determining role has often been defended, notably by R. Courbis.[21]

This author considers a firm growing at a constant rate g. It must achieve a level of gross undistributed profits at least sufficient to repay its borrowings, which implies a minimum rate of self-financing α_m.

Let $I_t = D_t$, thus investment is totally financed by the loan, and $A_t \geqslant R_t$, thus repayments are covered by self-financing. Each year, the proportion of $1/T$ of debts not outstanding is repaid.

$$R_t = \sum_{\theta=1}^{T} \frac{D_{t-\theta}}{T}$$

Now:

$$D_{t-\theta} = I_{t-\theta} = I_t (1+g)^{-\theta} \text{ , as } I_t \text{ grows at the rate } g.$$

Therefore:

$$R_t = \frac{I_t}{T} \sum_{\theta=1}^{T} (1+g)^{-\theta} = I_t \frac{1-(1+g)^{-T}}{g}$$

and the value of the minimum rate of self-financing A_t/I_t is:

$$\alpha_m = \frac{1 - (1 + g)^{-T}}{g}$$

$I_t^F = 1/\alpha_m A_t$ is the level of investment financially achievable given the self-generated finance A_t.

Given these assumptions, it is not surprising that there is some uncertainty over the explanatory value of profits or liquidity variables in the investment formula. R. Courbis reasons *a priori* that they would be a determining influence in sectors subject to external competition, where sale price could not be controlled.[22] An old but important study by J. Meyer and E. Kuh had concluded that investment constituted one use of the funds remaining after distribution of dividends. An extension of their work by J. Meyer and Glauber resulted in the idea of investment being determined by demand, in periods of good fortune, and by the availability of funds in periods of recession.[23] The most complete comparisons of the role of demand and the role of profits have been conducted by R. Eisner, who shows that demand is the principal determinant in the long run, although profits may appreciably alter the pattern of incidence of investments.

Eisner's results are in the main confirmed by the French studies of P. A. Muet and G. Oudiz. The former, in a simulation of investment over the period 1954–76, found the accelerator effect was always dominant as an explanatory factor.[24] The estimates of the latter 'demonstrate that transitory variations in profits have a more significant effect, which corroborates Eisner's hypothesis according to which profits have a substantial influence on the date at which investments are undertaken, without affecting their mean level in the long term'.[25]

However, the notion of profits as the principal determinant continues to be defended by authors taking their reference from Kalecki, J. Robinson or the Marxist approach. Thus J. Mazier,[26] using a network of models estimated from time series of between fifteen and twenty years, explains the rate of accumulation by reference to the relationship between self-financing from capital or capital growth, and the rate of borrowing. The quality of the statistical results is poor for the type of data and one may question the explanatory or causal value of the positive borrowing coefficient, which is difficult in this case to conceive of as an exogenous variable.

Moreover, there are two serious ambiguities which affect the explanatory importance of profit variables in an equation for investment. Firstly, their significance: do they measure the profitability of investments, as was earlier thought? One would be seriously mistaken to see any link between the hypothesis of profit maximisation and the declared influence of realised profits upon investment. Expected demand or stock market valuations would be better indicators of the potential profitability of investment. Should we alternatively consider profits solely as a means of finance? In that case, one would have to be assured that they are definitely exogenous with respect to investment, whereas there are a number of reasons for believing that investment and profits are jointly determined at the aggregate level.

The rationale for indicators of financial solvency is different. Traditional financial theory[27] considers the cost of finance capital as an initially decreasing and later increasing function of the amount of borrowing. For those firms interested in working within the area of increasing marginal cost of funds, an indebtedness indicator with a negative sign must be introduced into the investment equation. A variable of this kind has been developed by Duesenberry and later applied by Lintner and Locke-Anderson.[28]

It is to be noted that the traditional theory of finance, on which this hypothesis is based, has been undermined by the renowned discovery, by F. Modigliani and Miller, of a case in which financial structures are 'neutral', that is to say without any effect on the cost of capital or on real decisions. Justification for their result lies in the perfect substitutability, which would exist in a perfect financial market, between the incurrence of debt on the part of firms and on the part of their shareholders. This result will only hold in the absence of a risk of bankruptcy. The discussion surrounding the theories of Modigliani and Miller has made apparent the importance of fiscal policy as a determinant of the cost of capital and the overall structure of finance. The level of corporation tax on profits and the rate of redemption of public debt have been incorporated into numerous studies as components in the user cost of productive capital.[29]

Thus, at present there does not seem to exist a sufficiently general and coherent study of investment within an imperfect financial environment. Satisfactory theoretical foundations for such an approach have, however, been laid down by P. Zagamé,[30] in the context of a microeconomic model of optimal accumulation under different forms of financial markets.

3 INVESTMENT AS AN ADJUSTMENT PROCESS

Contemporary investment functions neither omit supply factors, as in the first approach we presented, nor explicitly introduce them, as in the preceding section, but rather classify them among the conditions tending to modulate capital stock adjustment. In this view, emphasis is put on the time profile of the adjustment process and the lag distributions which describe it. Characteristically, contemporary studies combine these lag structures with the equation forms previously discussed. But they themselves call for renewed justification of these equations, in particular in terms of adjustment costs. In fact, the notion of adjustment has been successfully applied to the demand for labour, which had been considered a quasi-fixed factor.

These points will be developed in turn.

A The flexible accelerator and capital stock adjustment

The assumptions of the accelerator ensured that at any moment the effective capital stock K_t coincided exactly with the capital stock required for the current level of production $K_t^* = k\ Y_t$, or for net investment:

$$I_t = K_t^* - K_{t-1} = k(Y_t - Y_{t-1})$$

In 1951, Goodwin[31] introduced the hypothesis of a partial adjustment of effective to desired capital:

$$I_t = b(K_t^* - K_{t-1}) = bk\ Y_t - b\ K_{t-1} \qquad 0 \leqslant b \leqslant 1.$$

Or, taking $I_{t-1} = K_{t-1} - K_{t-2}$ from both sides of this equation, we have:

$$I_t = bk(Y_t - Y_{t-1}) + (1-b)I_{t-1}$$

The first of these expressions we will call the capital stock adjustment equation, and the second, which is auto-regressive in I_t and due to Koyck,[32] the non-linear accelerator. It is worth noting its formal analogy with expressions deduced from an adaptive expectations hypothesis: net effective investment is obtained by the interaction of a coefficient b applied to required investment, given by the simple or 'naive' accelerator, and a coefficient $(b-1)$, which is applied to the investment figure from the preceding period. Adjustment is immediate and complete where $b = 1$, nil where $b = 0$.

By way of analogy with the consumption function, we could qualify the coefficient bk as a short-term accelerator, verifying that the long-term accelerator is equal to k.

In order to do that, let us develop the auto-regressive form into a distributed lag formula:

$$I_t = bk \, \Delta Y_t + (1 - b) \, bk \, \Delta Y_{t-1} + (1 - b)^2 \, bk \Delta Y_{t-2}$$
$$+ (1 - b)^3 \, I_{t-3}$$

$$I_t = bk \sum_{\theta = 0}^{T} (1 - b)^\theta \, \Delta Y_{t-\theta} + (1 - b)^{T+1} \, I_{t-T-1}$$

The long-term accelerator will indicate the sum of investments I_t, I_{t-1} ... induced by a given variation in output ΔY_t, that is for an infinite time horizon and for ΔY_t constant at a level $\Delta \overline{Y}$:

$$\sum_{\theta = 0}^{\infty} I_{t+\theta} = \Delta \overline{Y} \, bk \sum_{\theta = 0}^{\infty} (1 - b)^\theta$$

It is easy to return from the distributed lag form to the auto-regressive form, as the reader will verify by taking from the expression for I_c the distributed lag expression for I_{t-1}, multiplied by $(1 - b)$:

$$I_t - (1 - b) I_{t-1} = bk \left[\sum_{\theta = 0}^{\infty} (1 - b)^\theta \, \Delta Y_{t-\theta} - \sum_{\theta = 1}^{\infty} (1-b)^\theta \, \Delta Y_{t-\ell} \right.$$

A manipulation of this kind is known as a Koyck transformation.

An interesting variable associated with the Koyck lag distribution is the notion of the mean lag for the realisation of investment. In fact a fraction b of investment is realised without delay ($\theta = 0$), a fraction $b(1 - b)$ with a delay of one period, and the remaining fractions $b(1 - b)^\theta$ with a delay of θ periods. The mean lag θ is the weighted sum of these delays:

$$\bar{\theta} = \sum_{\theta = 0}^{\infty} \theta \, b(1 - b)^\theta = \frac{1 - b}{b}$$

an expression which tends towards 0 as b tends towards 1 (immediate adjustment) and towards infinity as b tends towards 0 (no adjustment).

We have already met the geometrically weighted or Koyck lag distribution while on the subject of the consumption function. It is widely used because of its great simplicity, but, for all that, it is not completely satisfactory. In effect, it assumes that over an infinite time period a variable will exert an influence, which decreases in a regular fashion according to the pattern in Figure 5.6.

This is a very rigid structure and it may not fit empirically. It has been shown in numerous applications that it tends to underestimate the coefficient of inertia $(1 - b)$ and thus the mean adjustment delay. In fact, it is too much to assume an influence stretching over an unlimited time period and decreasing regularly. Intuition suggests that in certain

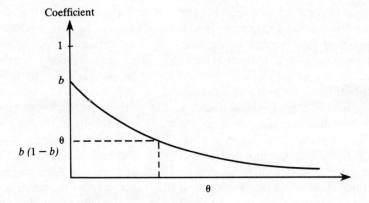

Figure 5.6

Figure 5.7

cases a distribution of the form shown in Figure 5.7 may be more pertinent.

In this case, we can see that superimposing a Koyck structure would result in systematic errors, overestimation (of *b*) in the near and distant periods and thus underestimation of mean lag.

We might envisage adopting a very general format:

$$I_t = \sum_{\theta = 0}^{T} a_\theta \ \Delta Y_{t-\theta}$$

where the $T + 1$ coefficients (denoted by a_θ) would not be constrained to follow any distribution pattern. By refusing to constrain *a priori* the shape of the distributed lag, one would avoid biasing the results of empirical study. But we must realise the illusory nature of this solution. Estimates of the a_θ would be very inaccurate at the econometric level, as there would be a strong correlation between the different lagged values. This simply illustrates that, in general, a sample does not carry enough information[33] to permit the determination of a high number of

parameters of a lag distribution, and *a priori* specification of the shape
of the distribution aims precisely to make up for that lack of information
by limiting the number of parameters to be estimated. So *a priori*
information (either theoretical or drawn from other studies) is substituted for the empirical information carried by the sample. The Koyck
distribution is very useful in this respect, because it is entirely defined by
estimation of the single parameter b. Given these properties, it is not
surprising that it cannot fit every form of lag distribution.

The solution consists in introducing *a priori* restrictions, which
constrain the lag distribution less strictly. To this end, two methods have
been proposed, that of Jorgenson and especially that of Almon. These
methods have a common basis in that they both consider the coefficients
of a distributed lag of length T to be like the coefficients of a polynomial
of degree $r \leqslant T$. They use the following symbolic notation:

$$L\, x_t = x_{T-1} \quad , \quad L^2\, x_t = x_{t-2}$$

$$\Sigma\, a(\theta)\, x_{t-\theta} = A(L)\, x_t$$

where $A(L)$ designates a polynomial in L, of the form:[34]

$$A(L) = \alpha_0 + \alpha_1\, L + \alpha_2\, L^2 + \dots + \alpha_r L^t$$

Jorgenson reasons that we may approximate any infinite lag distribution
$A(L)$ by the ratio of two finite polynomials.

$$A(L) = \frac{B(L)}{C(L)} = \frac{\beta_0 + \beta_1 L + \beta_1 L^2 + \dots + \beta L^k}{\gamma_0 + \gamma_1 L + \gamma_2 L^2 + \dots + \beta L^k}$$

This function produces a 'rational' lag distribution. With the above
notation, the investment model becomes:

$$I_t = A(L)\, \Delta Y_t \quad \text{or} \quad C(L)I_t = \Delta Y_t.$$

The first relationship may be said to be the final form of the model
formed by the second expression, which can be developed as follows:

$$I_t = \sum_{\theta=0}^{k} b(\theta)\, \Delta Y_{t-\theta} - \sum_{\theta=1}^{l} c(\theta)\, I_{t-\theta}\,.$$

The model, therefore, has auto-regressivity of order l and a freedom of
movement with respect to the exogenous variable Y_r, on average of the

order $k + 1$. Its application presupposes the estimation of $k + 1 + l$ coefficients. Approximation of the unconstrained general polynomial $A(L)$ may be made as close as one desires: for this purpose, it is sufficient to increase the values k and l. But it is clear that one would again come up against problems of collinearity among the predetermined variables (that is both the exogenous and endogenous lagged variables). In practice, it is difficult to retain more than two lagged variables ($l = 2$), but k may be increased (up to six).[35]

The second current method of characterisation of distributed lags is due to Shirley Almon.[36] Starting from the premise that it is, in general, possible to represent a distribution of length T by a polynomial of degree r – significantly less than T – the method consists of putting in place of the estimates for the T inertia coefficients, the estimates for the $r + 1$ coefficients of the polynomial of degree r. It is thus possible, using polynomials of different degrees, to obtain numerous profiles of distributed lags.

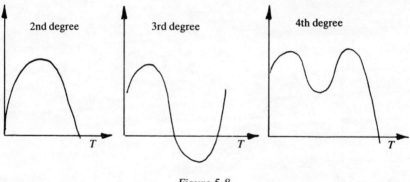

Figure 5.8

When the Almon method is employed, the maximum lag T, the degree of the polynomial r and any possible constraints at outlying values of the distribution are specified *a priori*, in such a way as to compel the curve to pass through zero at $\theta = 0$ and/or $\theta = T$, in other words nullifying the influence of the explanatory variable in the initial period and after T periods.

An interesting hypothesis to consider is the case where the lag distribution is not rigid but modulated by a single economic variable. Coefficients can then be expressed as follows:

$$a(\theta) = a^0(\theta) + a^1(\theta) . x_{t-\theta}$$

P. A. Muet and P. Zagamé[37] have estimated a model in which delays in delivery of capital equipment, with respect to orders for capital goods z_t are themselves a function of the level x_t of spare capacity in production:

$$I_t = \sum_{\theta = 0}^{T} [(a^0(\theta) + a^1(\theta) x_{t-\theta}] z_{t-\theta}$$

$$= \sum_{\theta = 0}^{T} a^0 z_{t-\theta} + \sum_{\theta = 0}^{T} a^1(\theta) x_{t-\theta} z_{t-\theta}$$

$$I = A^0(L) Z + A^1(L) X . Z$$

Thus, the variable lag structure leads to the adoption of two distributions, one bearing upon the explanatory variable z_t, the other upon the product of this variable and the factor x_t, which regulates adjustment. The authors obtain significant results, illustrated in Figure 5.9.

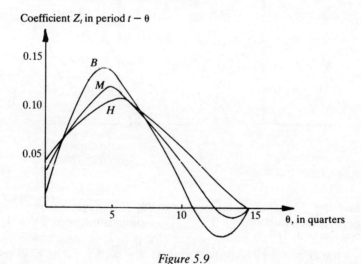

Figure 5.9

The three curves represent the profiles of investment realisation (delivery of ordered goods) in depressed circumstances (curve B, with spare capacity X_t of 25%); moderate circumstances (curve M, spare capacity of 20%) and prosperous circumstances respectively (curve H, spare capacity of 15%).[38] The average delivery delay is therefore 3.4 quarters in depressed circumstances, and 4.6 quarters in moderate circumstances, increasing to 5.4 quarters in prosperous circumstances.[39]

B Contemporary investment functions and some associated problems

We have discussed lag distributions as possible extensions to the flexible accelerator. Clearly, they may be married with other hypotheses, relevant in particular to the definition of desired capital. In this respect, Jorgenson's model is representative of modern work on the investment function.

Combining Jorgenson's rational lag distribution with the expression for desired capital obtained by dynamic optimisation using a Cobb-Douglas function (see above), the following expression is obtained, where fK_{t-1} represents replacement investment:

$$I_t = \sum_{\theta=0}^{k} b(\theta)\, \alpha\, \frac{P_{t-\theta}}{u_{t-\theta}}\, \Delta Y_{t-\theta} - \sum_{\theta=0}^{l} c(\theta) I_{t-\theta} + fK_{t-1}$$

This formula has been highly influential. However, some objections to it have been established, typical of contemporary debates over the investment function. We will recall three of these, which relate to the choice of production function, the exogeneity of production in the equation, and justification of the adjustment process.

1 The choice of production function

To retain a Cobb-Douglas function with constant returns to scale implies, on the one hand, a long-term elasticity of capital with respect to output of one and, on the other hand, a long-term elasticity with respect to its user cost of minus one. Thus, should some fiscal policy measure lower the cost of capital use by 5%, this would tend to exaggerate substitution effects, while preventing consideration of any possible economies of scale. R. Eisner and I. Nadiri[40] therefore employ in preference a CES function, without constraining *a priori* the value of the elasticity of substitution σ. The level value of desired capital is then:

$$K_t^* = k_0 \left(\frac{u_t}{p_t}\right)^{-\sigma} Q_t^{1/h}$$

where h is the degree of homogeneity of the production function.

The findings of the authors reveal that the elasticity of capital with respect to its user cost is rather small (in absolute value) and that adjustments in response to variations in relative costs are slower than adjustments in response to variations in output.

The substitutability assumption may be weakened by utilising the 'putty-clay' hypothesis, in which substitution is limited to the installation phase of equipment. This has three consequences for the derivation of the investment function.

(a) It becomes necessary to distinguish between lag distributions applied to demand variables and those applied to relative prices.
(b) User cost may be redefined as a function of the anticipated lifetime of equipment, which depends mainly on the rate of interest and the expected rate of wage increase.
(c) The lifetime of capital equipment being endogenous, the assumption of a constant rate of replacement cannot be maintained.

While the first point has been observed since Eisner and Nadiri, the second has been studied theoretically[41] but not fully applied with econometric specifications.[42] As regards the latter point, endogenisation of replacement needs within an empirical model seems necessarily to present a problem of formidable complexity.[43]

A more precise specification of the putty-clay hypothesis may be obtained in terms of net investment function of the form

$$I_t = \sum_{\theta = 0}^{m} b(\theta) \, \Delta K_{t - \theta}^*$$

which by developing $\Delta K_{t - \theta}$ for a CES production function give for the putty-putty case

$$I_t = k_0 \sum_{\theta = 0}^{m} b(\theta) \, [(\frac{u_t}{p_p})^{-\sigma} \Delta Y_{t - \theta} - \theta Y_{t - \theta} (\frac{u_{t - \theta}}{p_{t - \theta}})^{- (\sigma + 1)} \Delta (\frac{u_{t - \theta}}{p_{t - \theta}})]$$

On the other hand, the 'putty-clay' hypothesis excludes any direct influence of the *changes* in real user cost

$$I_t = k_0 \sum_{\theta = 0}^{m} b(\theta) \, (\frac{u_t}{r_t})^{-\sigma} \Delta \, Y_{t - \theta}$$

Finally, let us recall the limiting case of a 'clay-clay' technology, i.e. the flexible accelerator

$$I_t = k_0 \sum_{\theta = 0}^{m} b(\theta) \, \Delta \, Y_{t - 0}$$

Here factor costs do not appear either in level, or in terms of changes. It is worth noting that a full consideration of the putty-clay hypothesis would involve the following feature: the 'user cost' of capital, meaning the required marginal productivity of capital in a new plant, has to be redefined as [Ando, Modigliani, Rasche, Turnovsky (1974)]

$$\mu_t = q_t(r - w_t)/[1 - e^{(w_t - 2)}T_k]$$

The expected rate of increase in wage w_t is substituted to $q_{(t)}$ in the expression of real discount rate and the usual constant depreciation rate σ is replaced by an 'annuity factor', a function of the expected life time of plant, a variable endogenous in the optimal division of finance. However, econometric studies of investment retaining the putty-clay hypothesis do not make use of all implications deduced above, particularly of the endogenous determination of the life time of capital stock.

2 The exogeneity of output variations

Jorgenson's model is often presented as a neoclassical model *par excellence*. Now, in the neoclassical problem of profit maximisation, output is an endogenous variable in the same way as factor demand. Therefore, the inter-temporal optimisation model employed by Jorgenson[44] is inconsistent with this theory in considering the time-path of demand evolution as given. It would be more accurate to adopt an indicator of the position of the demand curve and possibly also of the elasticity of demand, if there is not perfect competition.

It is unquestionably more practical in applied economics to consider output as exogenous. Thus, two arguments – one empirical, the other theoretical – have been advanced to support this practice.

At the purely statistical level, there are tests, which permit assessment of the existence of a causal dependency between two variables.[45] By applying these tests to monthly data, C. Sims demonstrated that the exogeneity hypothesis had not been invalidated empirically.[46]

An idea more interesting in its implications is H. Grossman's belief that disequilibria in the goods market would result in the exogeneity of output.[47] Where in fact, the market served by an enterprise settles with an excess supply remaining, the rule of voluntary exchange implies that the level of transactions is determined by demand.

In this case producers are restricted in the quantity they can supply. It is possible to show that their investment behaviour will consist of progressive adjustment within the bounds of this constraint, according to a mechanism which follows the pattern of the flexible accelerator.[48]

Grossman's method of dynamic optimisation in the presence of quantity constraints has been extended by P. Zagamé. Relying on the mathematical technique of optimal control, he spells out the different forms of investment behaviour associated with various environmental specifications, relating to the degree of imperfection in the markets for goods, factors and means of finance.[49] In this way it is possible to distinguish between notional and effective (constrained) demand,

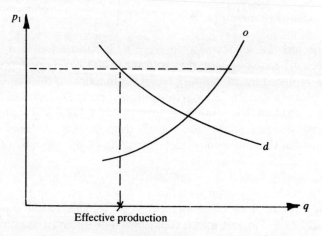

Figure 5.10

according to the terminology of modern disequilibrium theory. This approach lays fertile ground for empirical studies, as the various studies of P. A. Muet[50] illustrate.

3 Justification of the adjustment process

In Jorgenson's view, the growth path of desired capital K^*_t is determined by a process of dynamic optimisation. The path of effective capital is derived from this by the introduction of a lag structure representing an adjustment process, whose existence is proven in particular by the presence of delays in the supply of capital goods.

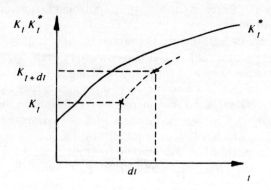

Figure 5.11

At each moment, the firm will be adjusting towards the target $K^*_{t + dt}$, which is considered the optimum level of capital to attain. But

K^*_{t+dt} is optimal in period $t + dt$, if and only if one is actually at the level K^*_t in period t. It is inconsistent to take as a target in a process of incomplete adjustment a growth path which is optimal only in the absence of constraints.

The solution is straightforward. If there are constraints and costs which justify gradual adjustment, these should be introduced into the dynamic optimisation model and not superimposed upon its results. This step is taken in the theory of adjustment costs.

For any firm to adjust its capital stock more rapidly entails costs, known as adjustment costs. Firstly there are external costs, which take the form of expenses arising mainly from the fact that, as the firm will be confronted with an imperfectly competitive market, it will pay more dearly for investment goods. But similarly there are internal costs, due to the fall in productivity which will be experienced during the period of reorganisation and training of labour. In the presence of internal costs, the production function becomes $F(K, N, I)$ with $\delta F/\delta I < 0$, while the assumption of external costs leads to the following expression for investment expenditure:

$$C(I) = p(I)I \text{ with } p(I) = p_0 + cI$$

which implies

$$C(I) = p_0 I + cI^2.$$

Introducing this quadratic cost function into Jorgenson's optimisation problem, the discounted profit to be maximised becomes:

$$W = \int_{t=0}^{\infty} (p_t\, Y_t - W_t\, N_t - p_0\, I_t - C I_t^2)\, e^{-it}\, dt,$$

whose resolution by calculus of variation leads to the condition:

$$p_t\, \frac{\partial Y}{\partial K} = (i + d)(p_0 + 2 . cI).$$

If the production function has constant returns to scale, $\delta Y/\delta K$ is a function of the ratio W/P, which in this simple model[51] is assumed constant. Substituting in this expression and simplifying, we obtain the following expression for optimal investment, which is under these assumptions independent of time:

$$I^* = \frac{Pf(W/P) - p_0\,(i + d)}{2\,c\,(i + d)}.$$

This constant level of investment implies a limiting stationary value for the stock of capital of $K^* = I^*/d$, d being the rate of depreciation. The resultant value of net investment I_t is:

$$I_t = d(K^* - K_t),$$

the difference between gross investment and replacement capital dK_t. At this stage it is satisfactory to have obtained a formula similar to the flexible accelerator: similar but not identical since we are here dealing with adjustment towards a fixed target – a stationary capital stock K^*. It has been shown[52] that, with a flexible target K_t, all future values of exogenous variables, prices and demand constraints must be incorporated in the investment function. In fact these future values being unknown, forecasts must be attached to them. A feasible specification, one might say, could take the form:

$$K_t^* = f(\tilde{Y}_t, (\frac{\tilde{u}}{P})_t, \tilde{g}_Y, \tilde{g}_u),$$

where $\tilde{Y}_t$ and $(\tilde{u}/P)_t$ are forecasts of the level of the demand constraint and the real cost of capital usage, $\tilde{g}_Y$ and $\tilde{g}_u$ forecasts of their weighted mean rates of growth. When these forecasts depend little on current values but rather on the 'state of confidence', we are once again confronted with the Keynesian hypothesis.

As a reconciliation of the modern investment function with Keynesian theory, one must note the recent contribution of J. Tobin,[53] who takes the credit for explicitly reintroducing the role of asset prices. In the *General Theory*, equilibrium investment is determined in such a way as to ensure that, at each moment, the demand price of every asset is in line with the current rate of interest, and so equal to its theoretical market value and its supply price, that is to say its replacement cost. If one shifts from this equilibrium as a result of unforeseen changes and incomplete adjustments due to supply delays and adjustment costs, then the two prices will differ. The ratio q_t of the market value of existing assets to their replacement cost thus determines the incentive to invest, measured by the difference $q_t - 1$.

The factor $q_t - 1$ is a simple function of the margin between K^*_t and K_t and of the investment projects already adopted and in the course of realisation. Supposing $\bar{K}^*_t$ is the desired level of capital as a function of expectations of long-term demand, then the effective stock of capital may be expressed thus:

$$K_t = \frac{B(L)}{C(L)} (q_t - 1) + \bar{K}_t^*,$$

where $B(L)$ is the distributed lag arising from delays in delivery of equipment, and $C(L)$ the distributed lag between $(q_t - 1)$ and the resultant divergences from the level of capital desired in the long term. If the structure of supply lags $B(L)$ is geometric (a Koyck distribution), net investment is explained by the following simple, contemporary relationship:

$$K_t = \gamma(q_t - 1) + \Delta \bar{K}_t^* ,$$

where γ is a function of the parameters of $B(L)$ and $C(L)$. In fact, the following equation was used in the econometric study by A. Ciccolo:

$$\frac{I_t}{K_t} = \gamma(L)(q_t - 1) + \frac{\Delta \bar{K}_t^*}{K_t} .$$

The distribution of the q_t variables proves very significant,[54] but the estimated lags are important, which confirms the notion of a weak investment response in the short term to economic policy measures.

C Labour as a quasi-fixed factor

Labour has long been considered a variable factor, *par excellence*, the firm being assumed to be able at each moment to adjust the volume of manpower which it employs to the optimal level. This hypothesis would correspond more to the case of a producer, who relied solely on temporary work agencies and had no employees of his own. In fact, labour is a quasi-fixed factor, 'that is to say a factor whose total cost is partly variable and partly fixed'.[55]

The fixed costs are the costs of recruitment, hiring and training. The marginal productivity of labour should cover not only variable (wage) costs, but also recuperation of these fixed costs. Thus, even from the point of view of their economic advantage firms are not justified in taking on or laying off workers in proportion to variations in their output. Employment regulations and trade union pressure tend to intensify these costs and further limit adjustment possibilities.

Denoting the flows of manpower entering and leaving employment by $\overset{\circ}{N}{}^+$ and $\overset{\circ}{N}{}^-$ respectively, the function for total wage costs takes the form:

$$C_t(N, \overset{\circ}{N}{}^+, \overset{\circ}{N}{}^-) = wN_t + v\overset{\circ}{N}{}_t^+ + u\overset{\circ}{N}{}_t^- ,$$

which would justify an asymmetrical adjustment of manpower, according to whether the required variation were positive or negative:

$$N_t = b^+ (N_t^* - N_{t-1})^+ + b^- (N_t^* - N_{t-1})^-.$$

As N^*_t cannot be observed, the majority of empirical studies retain a classical format with partial adjustment, the coefficient b being unchanged both for a rise and a fall.[56]

The formula for desired employment N^*_t can be derived from a production function embodying some substitutability, with the wage rate introduced as an additional variable. In certain studies, it is preferred to take account of capital-labour substitution simply through the introduction of a trend factor T. We then have:

$$N_t^* = aY_t + bT + c$$

The speed of employment adjustment differs significantly over different countries and periods (slow in France and the UK, fast in West Germany and the USA). Moreover, it appears to be a determinant factor in the cyclical evolutions.[57]

Incomplete adjustment introduces a 'phase displacement' between output and employment. Employment picks up late in periods of expansion but suffers contractions in activity to a lesser extent and at a later stage. As a result, the average productivity of labour N_t/Y_t follows a cyclical pattern, which affects the movement of company profitability. For a number of years, the 'employment cycle' has been particularly studied by French economists.

To illustrate this cycle, it is convenient to consider not the actual partial adjustment equation but rather the following relationship adopted by the authors of the STAR model. We will round off its coefficients:

$$\overset{\circ}{N}_t \approx 0,6\,\overset{\circ}{Y}_t - 0,2\,\overset{\circ\circ}{Y}_t$$

where $\overset{\circ\circ}{Y}_t$ is the rate of acceleration of production – the change in the rate of growth. Under this formula, the more stable the pattern of growth, the greater will be the proportionate change in employment.

For the same value of Y_t, 5% for example, there would be a slower rate of employment growth, if production was accelerating by 2% than if it was decelerating by 2% (2.6% as opposed to 3.4%). Following this calculation through systematically, the employment cycle is created. Four phases in this cycle may be distinguished.

1 The expansion phase, characterised by a substantial increase in

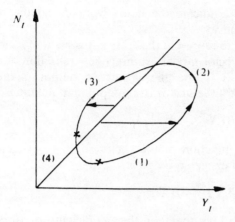

Figure 5.12

productivity growth because expansion of output precedes employment growth.

2 The end of expansion and deceleration, which are accompanied by a deterioration of production conditions due to the slowdown of productivity growth and the utilisation of less productive equipment.

3 The phase of falling output growth, accompanied by decreasing labour productivity.

4 The rationalisation period during depression, in which reduction in manpower and elimination of the least efficient production units permits a recovery in productivity, which precedes the real recovery.

Although not very stable in any definitive sense, this cycle illustrates how partial adjustment processes generate cyclical phenomena.

D Cross-adjustment of factors

The pattern of employment adjustment, like the speed of capital stock adjustment, is but one of a number of factors determining random evolutions. For a long time, macroeconomic analysis has proceeded as if these adjustment processes could be considered independently. Clearly, we cannot maintain this hypothesis. A lag in capital adjustment could be reflected in a slower speed of adjustment of production to demand. In fact, a constraint on the production function of the following type must at all times be satisfied:

$$Y_t = f(N_t, H_t, K_t, V_t)$$

where H_t and V_t indicate the hours worked and the rate of capital utilisation respectively.

We undertake to represent the cross-adjustment of factors through an auto-regressive vector model – a direct generalisation of the non-linear accelerator.[58] Let X_t be the vector of output quantities actually demanded and X^*_t the vector of the optimum quantities. Then:

$$\Delta X_t = B(X^*_t - X_{t-1})$$

or, X^*_t being a function of the vector Y_t of m exogenous variables (factor costs and expected output):

$$\Delta X_t = BAY_t - BX_{t-1}$$

The matrix B brings together the coefficients of direct and cross-adjustment. If it is diagonal, we will again be dealing with a flexible accelerator and a partial adjustment of employment as studied above.

An interesting property of this model is that it provides the theoretical foundation for a rational lag structure of the type which Jorgenson employs, whereas previously only the Koyck distribution had received theoretical justification. In the symbolic notation used above, the level of factor demands becomes:

$$Y = BAY - (I - B)LX,$$

where I denotes the unit matrix. In its final form, that is as a function only of the exogenous variables Y, the expression is a distributed lag equation:[59]

$$X = [I - (I - B)L]^{-1} - BAY.$$

Following Cramer's rule, the terms of the inverse matrix can be expressed as a ratio of two determinants, hence two polynomials in L of maximum degree $n - 1$ for the numerator and n for the denominator, which is precisely the general expression for a rational lag structure.

The applied studies conducted on the basis of this formula by Nadiri and Rosen in the United States and M. Pouchain in France,[60] confirm the existence of such a process of dynamic co-determination of factor demands.

6 Financial Behaviour and the Demand for Money

Money is the only financial asset which appears explicitly in the Keynesian model and, although contemporary macroeconomic models generally offer a more detailed representation of the financial sector, characterisation of the behavioural relationships of agents with regard to money remains the principal subject of controversy in this field.

The classical school proposed a functional analysis of money. A monetary asset was said to be characterised by three functions: that of a standard of value or unit of account – money is the good in which prices are quoted; that of a means of payment or mode of currency – it is the means of 'passing on' riches (Boisguilbert); and lastly the function of a store of value – the means of postponing the exercise of purchasing power. The notion of money demand appeared in Walras under the name of the 'desired balance'. It was presented as analogous to a demand for stocks of goods and likewise was based on the provision of 'inventory services'. The development of this approach takes us past the Cambridge formulation of the Quantity Theory and through the Keynesian analysis of the motives for money demand.

At the beginning of the twentieth century, there were two opposing currents among defenders of the Quantity Theory: on the one hand, writers like I. Fisher, who maintained an approach in terms of transactions in which the holding of money resulted more from the technology of exchange than from any specific behaviour of demand, and on the other hand, A. Marshall and his disciples Pigou and Keynes,[1] in whose opinion the velocity of circulation was not a technical or institutional constant but rather a behavioural parameter related to a demand for money, which was a function of income, wealth and prices. While keeping the notion of a demand for money in the *General Theory*, Keynes by introducing the speculative motive brought an element of instability to the concept, which prevented its integration with the Quantity Theory in the way the more traditional Cambridge view had permitted. The Keynesian reformulation of the theory placed emphasis on the multiplicity of motives for the demand for money: transactions, precaution and speculation. At the same time, it toned down the functional approach, whilst reinstating the 'store of value' function, whose opposition to Say's law Classical economists had not seen. All modern analysis since Keynes is characterised by this orientation.

We will initially study the demand for money as a component in a portfolio of risky assets. Then we will return to the specific view of the Keynesian function as a way of behaving under uncertainty, before dealing with the Monetarist viewpoint – the outcome of a conception of money as an asset – and the critique of this viewpoint, which has been strengthened by the recent revival of the functional approach.

1 THE ROLE OF MONEY IN A PORTFOLIO OF RISKY ASSETS

When emphasis is placed on the store of value function, the demand for money balances becomes treated like the demand for a financial asset, distinguished by its degree of liquidity. Seen from this perspective, the demand for money is the outcome of a set of rules regarding the optimal composition of a portfolio just as the demand for a good is the outcome of a set of rules regarding the optimal allocation of income. The latter are laid down in the theory of consumer choice.

The law of equalisation of marginal utilities subject to the relative prices of goods is replaced by the principle of equalisation of the marginal rates of return on assets. This effectively maximises the total return on a portfolio of a given value. In adopting this approach, we must initially make clear the components of the return on money and compare this return to that on other assets. We will then elaborate the treatment of risk suggested by portfolio theory before contemplating the general formula for the demand functions of financial assets.

A Liquidity and the return on money

Application of the law of equalisation of marginal returns presupposes an analysis of the components of these returns sufficiently complete to permit comparison of the advantages derived from the retention of different assets, which are highly heterogeneous by nature. There are six components, which may be positive or negative:

1 A flow of final services, from which the consumer derives some utility and which may be evaluated by means of an imputed rent. It is specifically durable consumer goods which earn this type of return.

2 A flow of productive services, coming from a contribution to a technical process of production: this type of return is specific to investment goods.

3 A flow of monetary receipts, which may be constant or variable, certain or risky, finite or infinite. More specifically, this is usually a matter of interest on loans or dividends on shares.

4 A relative appreciation (or depreciation) of the asset, its transfer price rising with respect to some numéraire, which may be money or the goods. Such capital gains form an essential part of the return on shares, but also affect physical assets (real estate, works of art, etc.) and in a negative sense, money.

5 A risk premium, tied to the level of inconvenience which the hazards involved in an asset's return entail for the holder. This premium enables a comparison of the returns on assets embodying risks of different natures and magnitudes. Its study is more sophisticated in the context of portfolio theory.

6 A liquidity premium, corresponding to the evaluation of the liquidity differential between assets. The notion of liquidity is bound up with the conditions under which an asset can be transformed into money, and its definition comprises the following three dimensions:
  - the transfer value of the asset must be certain;
  - it must be possible to exercise the monetary purchasing power of the asset without delay;
  - realisation of the asset's value must be costless.

By applying these criteria, the reader will be able to verify the 'liquidity hierarchy' of the following assets: physical assets (plant and equipment), shares, bonds, deposit accounts, current accounts.

Having described these six components, it is possible to place money within the spectrum of assets held. At first sight even the phrase 'the return on money' may seem contradictory, as it is a traditional rule of financial systems that monetary assets bear no interest at all, while, on the other hand, the holding of money entails a significant capital loss in a period of persistent inflation. Certain writers[2] maintain that money yields productive or final services and thus resembles a producer or consumer good. Another school of thought includes all the services rendered by money within the notion of liquidity, as a way of highlighting their uniqueness. In both cases, it is impossible to undertake a direct evaluation of the imputed worth of these services. It is only possible to deduce this indirectly from the opportunity cost of holding money. When a portfolio is in equilibrium, the imputed marginal rate of return of money is equal to that of every other asset, bonds for example, and equal to the real opportunity cost of holding money. It could thus be estimated from the nominal rate of interest on government securities, at least in a situation where stability of interest rates was anticipated and the capital value of these bonds could be considered as certain.

All these concepts require closer examination. We must first clarify the treatment of risk, then that of uncertainty (in section 2) and lastly (in section 3) come to the contemporary elaboration of the 'circulatory' role of money.

B The contribution of portfolio theory

Portfolio theory in the technical sense of the term was born in 1952 out of the works of Markowitz and was applied to monetary analysis by J. Tobin in 1958. It is based on an unusual but relatively manageable formalisation of risk.

In the course of their work on the theory of games,[3] von Neumann and Morgenstern proposed a very general criterion for decision-making by agents who were formulating subjective probabilities in a situation of uncertainty. They demonstrated that agents whose behaviour is assumed to satisfy certain axioms of coherence and continuity of choices do maximise mathematical expectations of utility.

Portfolio theory considers utility as a function of the mathematical expectation and the variance of returns from wealth. This hypothesis may be justified either if the distribution of risky returns follows a normal pattern, or if the von Neumann-Morgenstern utility function is quadratic, of the form:

$$U(R) = aR^2 + bR.$$

The mathematical expectation of this function $E(U(R))$ is expressed as a function of the expected return $E(R)$ and the standard deviation σ_R, in the following way:

$$E[U(R)] = b E(R) + a[\sigma_R^2 - E(R)^2].$$

Concavity of the utility function $(a < 0)$ corresponds to 'prudent' behaviour, illustrating an aversion to risk. It may be represented by a set of indifference curves of the following form (Fig. 6.1).

In making decisions over the allocation of wealth, each agent considers a certain number of risky assets, each bearing a co-ordinate $[E(R), \sigma_R]$ relating to the expected return and the standard deviation of this return, which is taken as a measure of the risk on the asset. Money may be considered as an asset with no return and no risk,[4] thus it is represented in the diagram by the origin. Combining money and a risky asset within a portfolio, in the proportions α and $(1 - \alpha)$ respectively, produces an asset with a return of $(1 - \alpha) E(R)$ and a risk $(1 - \alpha) \sigma_R$. In

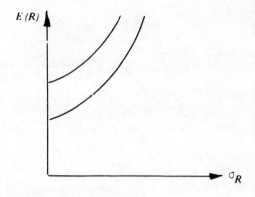

Figure 6.1

general there is a variety of risky assets and combining them produces a spreading of risk.

Consider two risky assets with expected returns of $\bar{R}_A$ and $\bar{R}_B$, and risk factors σ_A and σ_B. Let σ_{AB} be the covariance of their returns. A portfolio P combining them in the proportions α and $(1 - \alpha)$ offers an expected return of:

$$\bar{R}_P = \alpha \bar{R}_A + (1 - \alpha) \bar{R}_B,$$

which has a variance of:

$$\sigma_P^2 = \alpha^2 \sigma_A^2 + (1 - \alpha)^2 \sigma_B^2 + 2\alpha (1 - \alpha) \sigma_{AB},$$

or, denoting by r_{AB} the correlation coefficient between the returns of the two assets,

$$\sigma_P^2 = \alpha^2 \sigma_A^2 + (1 - \alpha)^2 \sigma_B^2 + 2\alpha (1 - \alpha) \sigma_A \sigma_B r_{AB}.$$

The properties of the portfolio will depend on the degree of correlation between the returns of the assets. In the case of perfect correlation $(r_{AB} = 1)$, the risk on the portfolio is given by linear combination of the assets' risk factors.

$$\sigma_P = \alpha \sigma_A + (1 - \alpha) \sigma_B.$$

But if the degree of correlation falls short of this maximum, the risk on the portfolio is less than the combined risk of the assets. There is a gain which justifies diversifying portfolios with risky assets. In an extreme case where there is perfect negative correlation between the returns of the two assets, it is possible by combining them to obtain a portfolio with a certain yield.

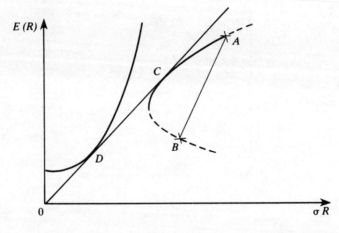

Figure 6.2

Figure 6.2 represents the optimal portfolio of risky assets in the case where money is the only asset with no risk. The segment AB shows the combinations of risk and return possible when the assets A and B are perfectly correlated. The curve ACB represents the locus of combinations in the more general case (where $-1 < r_{AB} < 1$). The continuous part of this curve describes the set of efficient portfolios of risky assets, that is to say the portfolios involving the minimum risk for a given expected return or, equivalently, the portfolios embodying the maximum return for a given level of risk.[5]

Any assimilation of money into an efficient portfolio will be represented by a point on the segment leading from the origin to the point on the curve AB corresponding to this portfolio. It is quite obviously apparent that there is only one risky portfolio which can be combined with money in an efficient manner: that corresponding to the point C, the only point at which a ray from the origin is tangent to the curve ACB. This result implies that the optimal combination of risky assets is independent of the preferences of the investor, who will only adjust his portfolio in response to his risk aversion by choosing to keep a more or less significant part of his wealth in the form of a risk-less asset. It was Tobin, in particular, who set forth this 'separation theorem' of portfolio theory.

The optimal mixed portfolio of shares and money is ultimately determined by the point which maximises the investor's utility, while taking account of his investment possibilities: that is to say, the point situated on the highest indifference curve which has a point in common with the segment OC. If D is the point of tangency which fulfils this condition, then the ratio *CD/CO* measures the proportion of wealth held in the form of money.

In this way portfolio theory justifies the retention of money, where it is the only certain asset, as a way of spreading the risk of holding wealth, but the contribution of this theory is not limited to that. Following the work of Sharpe and Lintner, the analysis of individual portfolios has been broadened into a theory of financial markets, which has permitted specification of the structure of rates of return required of different assets as a function of their riskiness.

C The demand for different assets

The analogy drawn above between the demand for assets in the context of the allocation of wealth and the demand for goods in the context of the apportionment of income suggests the nature of the variables to be introduced for the construction of the demand functions of financial assets: to wit, the rate of return of the asset under consideration, the total value of the wealth to be allocated and the rates of return on complementary and alternative assets.

The structure of rates of return can be as easily analysed from the point of view of the riskiness of assets as from their term structure. Demand functions have in general been constructed according to the principle of partial adjustment towards a desired level.

1 The rate of return on risky assets
The theory of financial markets, deduced from portfolio theory, has permitted specification of the equilibrium rates of return required of assets, bearing different risks. The expected return $\bar{r}_A$ required of the asset A, in order that it should figure in the market portfolio F, is a function of the rate of return i on the risk-less asset (zero, if we are dealing with money), of the market cost of risk (the slope of the line OC in Figure 6.2) – let us say $(\bar{r}_M - 1)/\sigma_M$, and of the covariance σ_{AM} between the return on the asset A and the return on the market portfolio. This might be expressed as follows:

$$\bar{r}_A = i + \frac{\bar{r}_M - i}{\sigma_M} \times \frac{\sigma_{AM}}{\sigma_M}.$$

In other words, for a given level of risk as measured by the dispersion of returns, the return required of an asset is lower the less its returns are correlated with those of the rest of the assets.

2 The term structure of rates of return[6]

The question of term structures – the structuring of assets' rates of return according to their dates of maturity – has been the subject of a considerable volume of literature. It is not our purpose to summarise it here but merely to recall the principal arguments.

The fundamental approach, or anticipation thesis, considers a long-term rate as the result of the combination of all the anticipated short-term rates. The underlying idea is that the return expected of a long-term investment as measured by the interest factor $(1 + R)^T$ must be the same as the anticipated return from a short-term investment renewed successively over the same period. Thus, denoting by $\tilde{r}_t$ the rate of return anticipated in period t and compounding this from the present period to period T, the long-term return must be equal to the product:

$$(1 + \tilde{r}_1)(1 + \tilde{r}_2) \dots (1 + \tilde{r}_t) \dots (1 + r_T) = (1 + R)^T = \prod_{t=\pi}^{T}(1 + \tilde{r}_t),$$

where Π is the product operator. A formalisation of this kind may be applied to the problem of formulating hypotheses regarding the process of formation of expectations over future values of the short-term rate: the assumption of a gradual revision of expectations according to an adaptive process is often adopted.

The 'anticipation theory' approach would be fully warranted under an assumption of a certain future, or in a case where investors were indifferent to risk. To avoid this assumption, Hicks introduced the notion of a term structure of interest rates incorporating a risk premium, which increased regularly with the duration of a claim. The risk premium introduces an asymmetry between immediately observable long-term rates and expected future short-term rates.

Although the risk premium hypothesis seems realistic *a priori*, it has not received any solid backing from the econometric studies conducted on the subject. Furthermore, there are logical difficulties involved in justifying a regular increase in the risk premium in terms of aversion to risk.

Other works have introduced supplementary elements into the explanation, in particular the consideration that there is not perfect substitution between bonds with different maturity dates, but merely a limited substitutability. Following this lead, Culbertson introduced the idea of a segmentation of the market for financial assets, while Modigliani and Sutch incorporated the notion of the 'preferred habits' of various categories of investors.

The literature on the term structure of interest rates relates mainly to the formulation of nominal rates. The Fisher equation is the name given to the relationship which expresses the nominal long-term rate as the sum of a real rate and the anticipated rate of inflation.[7]

Having specified the structure of assets' rates of return in terms of risk and maturity, we may return to the formulation of their demand functions.

3 *Financial asset demand as a dynamic process*

Static analysis leads to the construction of demand functions, which indicate the amount of each asset to be held in equilibrium – an amount by definition equal to that which investors would wish to hold, given the current values of rates of return and of their wealth. For any asset A, such a demand function[8] would have the following form:

$$D_A^* = f(r_A, r_B, ..., W)$$

where r_B ... denotes the return on alternative or complementary assets and W the value of investors' wealth.

In fact, every reallocation of wealth by an economic agent involves transaction and information costs. These may be studied as adjustment costs, in the same sense of the term as we employed in the context of the theory of investment. As a result of these costs, a divergence of the actual structure from the desired structure of wealth is translated not into a full and immediate adjustment but only into a partial adjustment in the period under consideration. Thus, dynamic or short-term asset demand functions have the following form:

$$D_{A,t} = b(D_{A,t}^* - D_{A,t-1}),$$

where b is an adjustment coefficient lying between zero and one inclusive. While this adjustment process implies a Koyck lag distribution, it is possible to assume a more flexible structure allowing for a more general lag distribution.

Though more satisfactory than the static formula, this expression has a shortcoming in that it assumes short-term adjustments of assets to be independent of each other, while at the same time recognising their long-term substitutability. Now, the budget constraint alone introduces a manifest interdependence of the various asset demands: every acquisition must be financed by reduced holdings of some other asset (very possibly money) and the proceeds of any surrender of assets must again be put to use. Thus we may be led directly to consider demands for financial assets as the result of a process of cross-adjustment, representable by a vector auto-regressive model, each equation of which has the form:

$$D_{A,t} = f(r_A, r_B, ..., W, D_{A,t-1}, D_{B,t-1}, ...).$$

The pioneering work of Brainard and Tobin[9] on models of this kind preceded, in historical terms, the development of cross-adjustment models for factor demand[10] and paved the way for contemporary studies on the demand for financial assets.

2 THE DEMAND FOR MONEY IN THE FACE OF UNCERTAINTY

By integrating the demand for money within the framework of the problem of optimal diversification of a portfolio, modern theory has fostered an analysis in terms of the risk of variability in returns, as measured by the variance of expected returns from the portfolio. Despite its advantages at the technical level, this cannot be considered an exhaustive approach: in particular, it certainly does not take full account of the role of speculation, which in Keynes's view is the basis for liquidity preference.

At the heart of the debate lies the old distinction, attributed to Knight, between risk and uncertainty. Whereas risk distinguishes a situation, in which a set of probabilities can be attached to a number of eventualities, uncertainty refers to a state where the information available is insufficient to identify the range of possible outcomes or in any case to ascribe a probability to them. Modern writings on decision-making under uncertainty, by relying on an extensive use of the notion of subjective probability, have blurred the significance of this distinction, to which Keynes accorded great importance. In fact, in his *Treatise on Probability*, he depicts uncertainty as a multi-dimensional phenomenon, of which subjective probabilities are only one facet. In addition, each agent confers varying degrees of belief in these probabilities, which express the trust accorded to assessments of a speculative nature. G. L. S. Shackle tried to develop a conception of uncertainty from the Keynesian viewpoint. As we have seen with respect to investment, as a first approximation this conception of uncertainty is expressed in a weak elasticity of long-term expectations to variations in the current values of variables to be predicted. This idea is central to the analysis of the speculative demand for money, which we will be studying with regard to its microeconomic foundations and its macroeconomic implications. Lastly we shall look at the criticisms of Tobin's attempt to reinterpret it in the light of portfolio theory.

A The speculation motive in Keynes

In contrast to the role of diversification, which serves as a cover against the risk of variability in returns, the behaviour of the Keynesian speculator is aimed at undertaking inter-temporal arbitrage with a view to extracting capital gains. Speculation does not lead to maximisation of current returns, but to a gamble over asset prices, which implies betting on their future movement. By virtue of this, there is no sense in it, unless there is some diversity in expectations due to the agents active in the market having different conceptions of the future. Speculating, said Keynes, is taking advantage of the fact that one knows better than the market what the future has in store.

In Keynes, speculation pits the demand for liquid assets in the broad sense[11] against the retention of durable assets. For the purposes of our argument, we will consider money and irredeemable government bonds.

The nominal annuity R_o from the government bond is constant and equal both to the product of its nominal value V_o and its nominal yield r_o, and to the product of its current value V and current yield r:

$$R_o = r_o V_o = rV.$$

Thus, the current value of bonds is adjusted in each period as a function of the current yield in such a way as to ensure the same rate of return for all bond-holders:

$$V = \frac{R_o}{r} = V_o \frac{r_o}{r} .$$

The anticipated value of bonds is then a function of the rate of interest forecast for the following period – $\tilde{r}$. We denote the relative capital gain by g:

$$g = \frac{Vr/\tilde{r} - V}{V} = \frac{r - \tilde{r}}{\tilde{r}} ,$$

which has a positive value if a fall in the rate of interest is expected $(r > \tilde{r})$ and a negative value if an interest rise is anticipated $(r < \tilde{r})$. In these conditions, the total anticipated return on a bond-holding is the sum of the interest received and the prospects of capital gain $r + g$, whereas the return on money balances is nil. It is therefore in the investor's interest to hold bonds as long as $r + g$ is positive:

$$r + g = r + \frac{r - \tilde{r}}{\tilde{r}} > 0,$$

that is to say as long as the current rate of interest is greater or only slightly less than the anticipated rate:

$$r > \frac{\tilde{r}}{1 + \tilde{r}}.$$

Application of this rule leads to retention of the whole of one's wealth either in the form of money or in the form of bonds, according to the respective values of the current and anticipated rates of interest. The microeconomic function for the demand for money implied by this analysis is thus as follows, with W_i denoting the amount of wealth to be allocated.

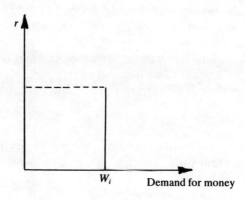

Figure 6.3

This result depends crucially on the inelasticity of the anticipated rate $\tilde{r}$ to the current rate r. Nevertheless, J. Tobin has shown[12] that the principle of an 'all or nothing' allocation is not affected by the assumption of 'viscosity' in the relationship between the current and anticipated rates, provided that the derivative $d\tilde{r}/dr$ remains less than unity.

It remains to be seen how the Keynesian demand for money function is derived from this decision-making rule.

B Derivation of the macroeconomic demand for money function

Let us first imagine a situation in which all economic agents shared the same opinion about the future level of yields. The aggregate demand curve would then have the same shape as the microeconomic demand curve above, and there would be no simultaneous holding of money and bonds, except in the case where the current yield was equal to

$\tilde{r}/(1 + \tilde{r})$. In such a case, the supply of money would not be able to influence the rate of interest in any way whatsoever.

On the other hand, a regular demand curve would appear, on introducing some disparity between the rates expected by different agents. Let us assume a regular distribution of expectations according to the following function:

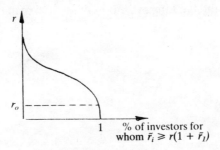

Figure 6.4

To pass from this function for the distribution of opinions to the demand for money function, one must superimpose the associated pattern of wealth distribution W_i. If the richest people are the most optimistic with regard to the growth of future yields, the function will display a levelling off at each end; if wealth and expectations are independent, the demand for money function will have exactly the same shape as the distribution of opinions above.

This result presents a striking example of a methodological principle which is often ignored: the shape and properties of an aggregate relationship are just as much the result of the distribution of particular characteristics across the population as of the pattern of microeconomic relationships, over which aggregation is undertaken. There are numerous applications of this principle but they are in general less clear-cut. In a similar way, it has been shown that the aggregate production function reflects the mode of distribution of capital between firms (Houthakker), and the consumption function the distribution of income between consumers (Borch).

Up to now, we have assumed that a constant value of wealth was being submitted for reallocation. In fact this value is a decreasing function of the rate of interest. So the slope of the demand curve for money is thus less steep than in Figure 6.4 and its point of intersection with the x-axis is further to the right.

In this case, let us examine the consequences of the existence of a critical rate of interest r_o, sufficiently low to ensure that nobody expects either a fall or even continued stability. At a current rate equal to or lower than r_o, no more people will hold bonds, as their return will not compensate for the prospect of capital losses. So the demand for money becomes highly interest-elastic.

To pass from here to a strict conceptualisation of the liquidity trap, one must assume that agents' demand for money is no longer constrained by their wealth – that they are able, for example, to borrow money through the banking system in order to expand their speculative balances.

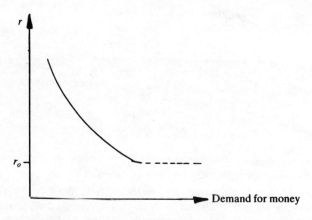

Figure 6.5

The Keynesian notion of an absolute preference for liquidity is thus formally dependent on an assumption which is rather unrealistic at the institutional level. However, this does not seriously affect the principle, as the significant point for actual analysis is not the existence of an infinite demand for money – possibly a multiple of total wealth – but the tendency to withhold an increased proportion of wealth in monetary form, for the purpose of speculation, when the rate of interest seems low in comparison with expected rates, which may be a frequent occurrence in a depression situation. A mode of behaviour, aimed at developing a high degree of liquidity in wealth under these circumstances, is compatible with observations over recent periods, in which households have expanded their holdings of liquid assets despite the stagnation of their incomes.

It remains true that, in so far as it implies a behaviour of the individual involving the exclusive holding of money or bonds, the Keynesian theory of liquidity preference seems hardly satisfactory. Furthermore, this theory relies on a disparity between the current and normal long-term rates of interest. Leontief, in particular, has objected that such a disparity should normally resolve itself, so that in equilibrium liquidity preference would be nil. J. Tobin has consequently sought to reformulate the theory of liquidity preference within the framework of portfolio theory.[13]

C Liquidity preference reinterpreted

Tobin's approach consists of transcribing in terms of portfolio theory, the elements of the choice between the holding of money or bonds, as a function of the current level of the rate of interest.

The return r_f on the portfolio is a random variable, a function of the fraction, α, of the portfolio held as money and of the total return on bonds in interest (r, given) and capital gains, g, itself a function of the future rate of interest and thus also random:

$$r_f = (1 - \alpha)(r + g).$$

The risk on the portfolio is deduced simply from the standard deviation of capital gains:

$$\sigma_f = (1 - \alpha)\,\sigma_g.$$

The set of feasible risk-return co-ordinates as a function of α is represented by a straight line passing through the origin with a slope of $(r + g)/\sigma_g$. A rise in the current rate of interest r increases this slope, thus shifting to the left the equilibrium position determined by the point of tangency of the locus of possible risk-return co-ordinates with an indifference curve.

In Figure 6.6, the left-hand quadrant illustrates the different equilibrium positions of the portfolio, when the rate of interest is rising. The right-hand quadrant permits us to derive the implications for the demand for money. With the rate of interest at the level r_1, the locus of possible risk-return co-ordinates is shown by OC_1, which is tangent at T_1 to an indifference curve, thus determining the optimal balance α_1. A higher level of the rate of interest, r_2, leads to an equilibrium position T_2, which implies a reduced holding of money (α_2). The sequence of equilibrium positions as a function of r produces a liquidity preference curve, which is, in conformity with Keynesian analysis, a decreasing function of the rate of interest.

Tobin's reinterpretation offers the manifest advantage of not implying an unrealistic 'all or nothing' rule of wealth allocation by economic agents. On the other hand, it presents the disadvantage of not capturing precisely the fullness of the Keynesian concept of uncertainty, which

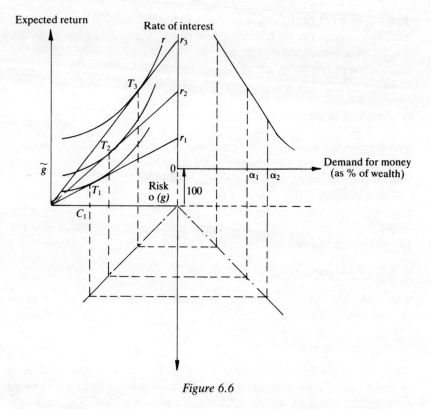

Figure 6.6

cannot be reduced to a probabilistic 'risk of variability'. As a result, a satisfactory theory for Keynesian speculative demand, incorporating a richer concept of uncertainty, still remains to be developed.

3 THE MONETARY ECONOMY AND THE MONETARIST VIEWPOINT

An essential place in the post-Keynesian development of works relating to the demand for money is occupied by the monetarist formula of Milton Friedman. Faithful to Alfred Marshall, he considers the demand for money function as the basis of the quantity theory of money, and thus, indirectly, of his interpretive framework for macroeconomics. But, because he stretches to the extreme the concept of money as an asset, Friedman clearly meets the limits of this approach. So one might consider that any fundamental criticism of the monetarist approach should incorporate, in addition to disequilibrium phenomena and the notion of the monetary economy, contemporary thinking on the revival of the functional approach.

A The demand for money in Friedman

In the eyes of the father of the Chicago school, the demand for money arises from the optimisation problem of wealth allocation.

> To the ultimate wealth-holding units in the economy, money is the one kind of asset, one way of holding wealth. To the productive enterprise, money is a capital good, a source of productive services that is combined with other productive services to yield the products that the enterprise sells. Thus the theory of the demand for money is a special topic in the theory of capital . . .[14]

As a demand for a source of producer and consumer services, the demand for money is derived from the maximisation of a constrained utility function, in the context of the theory of consumer choice. However, the maximisation model does not appear in Friedman. He is content to deduce from the analogy with the demand for goods the list of variables to be introduced, to wit the total wealth, the prices or returns of other assets, and the tastes and preferences of consumers.

Total wealth, W, corresponds to the discounted value of all the sources of revenue or services held by the agent. This wealth is related in a simple way to permanent income Y_p, a concept which is in one sense broader than current income, as it encompasses non-monetary elements, and in any other sense narrower, as it excludes transitory elements.

$$Y_p = W.r.$$

The rate of interest, r, is the ratio of income to wealth, or, at least, approximately as the identity is exact only where wealth represents the capitalised value of income over an infinite time horizon.

There are four alternative (or complementary) assets considered by Friedman: bonds, equity shares, capital goods and human capital.

Let r_b be the yield of bonds. Their capital value is inversely proportional to this rate of interest, so their return in terms of capital appreciation is a function of the rate of growth of r_b. Hence the total return of a bond is:

$$r_b - \frac{1}{r_b} \frac{dr_b}{d_t}$$

The return on an equity includes, in addition to the dividend yield r_c and the capital gain $\dfrac{1}{r_c}\dfrac{dr_c}{dt}$, the rate of increase in prices $\dfrac{1}{P}\dfrac{dP}{dt}$, whence we obtain the complete expression:

$$r_c + \frac{1}{P}\frac{dP}{dt} - \frac{1}{r_c}\frac{dr_c}{d_t}.$$

For physical assets, Friedman keeps only their nominal rate of appreciation $\dfrac{1}{P}\dfrac{dP}{dt}$. With regard to human capital, for which there is no directly observable price or return, the ratio w of 'non-human' wealth (physical and financial assets) to human endowment is directly introduced.[15].

Lastly, a variable u covers a set of implicit factors, which may be treated as random, such as tastes and personal characteristics.

The following expression for the demand for money results from this analysis:

$$M = f(P, r_b - \frac{1}{r_b}\frac{dr_b}{dt}, r_c + \frac{1}{P}\frac{dP}{dt} - \frac{1}{r_c}\frac{dr_c}{dt}, \frac{1}{P}\frac{dP}{dt}; w, \frac{Yp}{r}; u)$$

Like all demand functions derived from the theory of consumer choice, this relationship is homogeneous of degree zero with respect to prices and nominal income[16] (or wealth). It can thus be expressed as a function of demand for real balances, in terms of real income or otherwise as a function of the velocity of circulation of the following type:

$$\frac{Y}{M} = v(r_b, r_c, \frac{1}{P}\frac{dP}{dt}, w, \frac{Y}{P}, u).$$

One should not be deceived by this rather heavy functional expression: it simply corresponds to a certain stage of reasoning by a writer, who has always preferred simplified formulae to excessively complex mathematical expressions. In fact, the structure of interest rates is never incorporated in econometric studies; indeed it is rare that even a single rate should be. Efforts at estimation are focused on the properties of the relationship between money and permanent income and, secondly, on the influence of inflationary expectations.

Permanent income is the explanatory variable favoured in Friedman's work, in which he establishes two essential properties for monetarist theory.

1 The demand for money function is stable, cyclical variations in the income velocity of circulation being explained by the relationship between current and permanent income. Furthermore, although both the consumption function and the demand for money function may be affected by the same source of random instability in the relationship between current and permanent income, the relationship between money and current income is empirically more stable than the relationship between consumption and current income. This result is the foundation for the monetarist proposal to replace the Keynesian multiplier with the quantity theory.

2 In Friedman's view, the demand for money is highly elastic with respect to permanent income – of the order of 1.8.[17]

The author interprets this result as revealing that money is indeed a luxury, which some might consider a tautological and above all superficial response to the problem of the increasing monetarisation of developed economies.

Certain studies have sought to estimate the significance of the current level of prices. However, it is essentially through the medium of inflationary expectations that inflation affects the demand for money. Cagan, who carried through pioneering work in this field, is intellectually close to Friedman. He retained the assumption that expectations are revised periodically according to an adaptive process, thus, if $\tilde{\pi}_t$ is the anticipated rate of inflation:

$$(\tilde{\pi}_{t+1} - \tilde{\pi}_t) = b(\pi_t - \tilde{\pi}_t) \qquad 0 < b < 1.$$

When introduced into the demand for money function, this assumption leads to an auto-regressive or distributed lag formula.

As has been seen with regard to investment, the treatment of expectations as an adaptive process is not the only hypothesis leading to the formulation of dynamic models. The same structure may arise from a partial adjustment model. In the present case, we are thus led, in the same way as G. C. Chow[18], to distinguish between a long-term demand for money function, following the logic of statics in maintaining balances at their optimal level, and a short-term demand for money, resulting from a process of gradual adjustment of effective balances according to the following relationship:

$$M_t = bM_t^* + (1-b)M_{t-1}.$$

In this case, the margin between effective and desired balances subsists in part from period to period, which will in effect slow down the transmission through the economy of an initial impulse of a monetary character.

It is worth noting that the adaptive expectations hypothesis of Friedman (with regard to income) and Cagan (with regard to prices) is not incompatible with a partial adjustment process such as Chow's. We may show that the combination of these two hypotheses leads to a model of the following type, which is auto-regressive of order two:

$$M_t = b\beta k Y_t + [(1 - b) + (1 - \beta)]M_{t-1} + (1 - b)(1 - \beta)M_{t-2}$$

where k denotes the coefficient of the desired balance, b the coefficient of partial adjustment and β the coefficient of revision of expectations. Such a model has been successfully utilised by E. L. Feige[19] in the United States.

The analogies with the investment function should not be surprising in so far as money is here considered solely as an asset. But, nowadays, this conception of money is itself contested.

If one intends to impose the restriction of a long-term unitary elasticity of money demand for M_1 with respect to nominal income, it is relevant to consider an 'Error Correction Mechanism' as the following 'preferred' equation estimated by D. Hendry (1979, p. 239) on British quarterly data 1963–1977.

$$DL\ (M_t/P_{r-2}) = 0.86\ DL\ (\overline{y/p}) - 0.119\ DL\ (\bar{r}) - 0.90\ DL\ (P_{t-2})$$
$$+ 0.54DL(P_{t-3})$$
$$- 0.096 \log\ (M_{t-2}/Y_{t-1}) - 0.035 \log\ (r_{t-2})$$

where DL denotes the proportional rate of change (time derivatives of the logarithm) and $(\overline{y/p})$ or $(\bar{r})$ are three quarters moving averages of y/p and r. The results imply the following elasticities of the demand for real balances.

Table 6.1

E. with respect to	Real income	Interest rate	Inflation rate
short run (1 quarter)	0.28	− 0.04	0
long run	1	− 0.35	− 5

B The revival of functional analysis

In Friedman's monetarism, the reduction of the role of money to that of an asset, a commonplace component of a portfolio, is taken to its extreme. To a lesser degree, however, this conception is widely shared in post-Keynesian writings and it is worth recognising the fruitfulness of this affirmation of the store of value function as a criticism both of the concept of the money veil and its corollary, Say's law, and of the mechanistic transactions approach. Nevertheless, it seems that to define money *a priori* as an asset renders appreciation of its unique characteristics rather difficult, which explains the contemporary revival of analyses of the transactionary role of money.

1 The demand for transactions balances as an inventory requirement
The first works in this field, attributed to Baumol, lie within the tradition of the Keynesian transactions motive and reunite household transaction demand – the income motive – with firms' demand – the business motive.[20] Baumol's argument derives from the theory of inventory control.[21] The purpose of a transactions balance is to meet the problem of the lack of co-ordination between flows of receipts and expenditures. The optimal sum of this holding is determined in such a way as to balance its opportunity cost (in terms of the interest-yielding investment foregone) with the fixed cost, b, of the loans or asset transfers which must be engineered, when withdrawals exceed deposits. Let the magnitude of each encashment made at the cost b be $2M$. If expenditures follow a regular pattern, the mean balance will be M. If the sum of expenditures over the period is T, the total cost of holding balances and undertaking financial operations is:

$$c = \frac{bT}{2M} + iM,$$

which is minimised with the optimal balance

$$M = \sqrt{\frac{bT}{2i}}.$$

Baumol's analysis suggests the existence of economies of scale in transactions balances, which empirical studies do not clearly confirm.

This type of analysis, relating to the optimal management of funds, has witnessed some considerable development, of which the work of Orr and Miller[22] is typical; but it is a digression from the problems of macroeconomic conceptualisation of the demand for money.

2 The reduction of transaction and information costs
Another approach looks for a deeper understanding of the role of money in *exchange*. Initially, this approach seeks to evaluate the cost reductions which money facilitates. Taking as a reference point the

model of a barter economy, these analyses bring out the concepts of transaction and information costs and introduce uncertainty.

In a situation of perfect information, the transfer of a claim over future goods would be adequate for the settlement of any transaction. In a context of uncertainty, this claim must be made concrete and become subject to certain conventions, which guarantee it a definite value. In these conditions, transactions involve costs, which economic agents seek to reduce. There are two ways open to them to do this: on the one hand, they may reduce the cost of each transaction, and on the other hand they may limit the maximum number of transactions necessary for a certain reallocation of goods.

The cost of a transaction is linked to the guarantees which must accompany its settlement. For a long time, this guarantee was ensured by the intrinsic value of the means of settlement employed – metallic money. Demonetisation reduces transaction costs if it is accompanied by a social guarantee, which may be substituted for the intrinsic value of the means of payment itself.

Limitation of the number of transactions supposes that it is always possible to achieve a direct exchange between the initial holder of a good and its ultimate holder. Now, the barter economy assumes that a set of indirect exchanges is undertaken, in which a seller accepts in payment a good which he does not wish to keep, but proposes to re-exchange; monetary exchange permits a society to do away with the need for indirect exchange, and thus facilitates a considerable reduction in costs.

Uncertainty means a situation in which information is costly. Money may be seen as permitting a reduction in the information costs borne by agents. The economisation on information costs made possible by monetary exchange derives firstly from standardisation of the means of payment and secondly from the considerable simplification of the search for co-contractors, which direct exchange enables. Whereas in a barter economy with n goods, each seller must visit $n - 1$ markets to become acquainted with the conditions of exchange open to him, in a monetary economy it suffices to visit the market in which the good under consideration may be exchanged for money.

It has been pointed out, with reason, that the Walrasian paradigm assumes the image of a clearing-house, in which all settlements take place between agents through the general clearance of debits and credits. This device gives rise to a centralised, simultaneous process of exchange. In the absence of such a centralised process, it is money which ensures the centralisation of information on the other party in a transaction, as its value is independent of the character of the co-contractant. Similarly it permits realisation of a series of exchanges, in so far as the level of cash, which clearly reflects the exchanges undertaken, ensures respect of the budgetary constraint.[23] Thus, the role of money is essential for the functioning of a decentralised economy.

These general principles may be treated in different ways at the technical level.[24] They may, for example, lead to the reintroduction of an analysis of money from the point of view of its 'circulatory' role.

3 The demand for money within the circulation process

In a context of wealth allocation between assets, the transaction function of money designates a source of services which comes to be included in a comparison of rates of return. On the other hand, in the context of circulation, integration of the transaction function is immediate; indeed, traditional analysis frequently employs the term 'circulation function'. Before we may derive the consequences of this outlook, which in fact suggest a redefinition of the notion of the demand for money, there is a distinction to be made between the means of exchange (or circulation) and the means of settlement.

A means of exchange is a good or a claim generally acceptable against the transfer of a good or a bond, thus rendering transaction possible. A means of settlement[25] effectively clears a debt or liability. In this sense, credit is a means of exchange – it permits the realisation of a transaction – but only settlement in money eventually ensures payment. Without doubt, the concept of the means of settlement permits the most precise characterisation possible of the specific features of money as an asset.

The emphasis placed on money as an asset illustrates the predominance of an allocative approach. When the economic process is visualised as a circuit, monetary variables are considered more as flows rather than stocks, held at any given moment. The distinction is often masked through an arbitrary hypothesis in which the velocity of circulation is assumed to be equal to one.[26] If money circulates once in each period, its value as a transaction flow is exactly equal to the sum of cash held. Arbitrary conventions of this kind have most certainly harmed the explanatory value of circulation models.

Two examples will serve to illustrate the redefinition of the demand for money inspired by a circular flow approach: the notion of the 'finance' motive in Keynes and Tsiang's conception of the demand for money.

The 'finance' motive appeared in Keynes's work as a complement to the well-known motives of transaction, precaution and speculation. It indicates a demand for money for the purpose of financing subsequent investment: 'If one decides to increase investment, the complementary finance will constitute an additional demand for money,' wrote Keynes in 1937.[27] In fact, commentators have often likened the 'finance' motive to the transactions motive. However, two differences remain. Firstly, the 'finance' motive is defined essentially as a flow and the cash stock, to which it gives rise, is of its nature extremely unstable; and secondly, the 'finance' motive is linked to planned operations, whereas the transactions motive depends on the transactions currently being effected, as the following passage from Keynes makes clear: (in the *General Theory*) 'it is true, I admitted of the effect of an expansion of actual activity on the demand for money, but I did not admit of the effect of an expansion in planned activity, which in fact is superimposed on the latter.'[28] There, there is certainly the idea of two distinct motives, 'superimposed' on one another to yield the total demand for money.

Tsiang clearly interprets the 'finance' motive as opposed to the traditional conception of the demand for money.[29]

> For money, unlike other goods, is not merely wanted for its services or utilities as an asset to hold *after* all the transactions in the current period are settled, though this would be the case with the asset demand for money for which the function of money as a liquid store of value is the primary consideration. Money, however, is not merely a store of value, but also a necessary medium of exchange; money is demanded to finance the planned transactions yet to be carried out. This is what Keynes called the demand for 'finance', which he regarded as some peculiar kind of demand for money, but which is really nothing but the transactions demand for money proper.

In this author's view, the demand for money is not the final cash balance, the net sum of all transactions in the period, which he proposes to call instead 'the net acquisition of money through exchange', but the cash each person must acquire at the beginning of a period in order to cover planned expenditure. Yet here Tsiang adopts Robertson's hypothesis of a period of observation the same length as the circulation period. For him, then, the initial demand for money and the circulation flow in the period are identical. In general, this type of analysis depends crucially on hypotheses which are largely arbitrary, as the essential feature of monetary operations is their continuity. It serves to illustrate both the benefits and the problems of the circulation flow approach.

C Disequilibrium and the monetary economy

The reinterpretation of money in the context of the analysis of exchange processes has drawn attention to the relationships which might be established between money and disequilibrium. Certain writers maintain that reliance on monetary exchange might be a permissive cause of disequilibria, or at least would make their occurrence more likely. It seems to us that both the monetary economy and disequilibria have a common origin: the absence of a centralised method of co-ordinating activities and organising exchange.

R. W. Clower[30] developed a theory, according to which the monetary economy appears essentially as a restricted form of the barter economy. Employing a format of binary relationships, he defines a non-empty, reflexive exchange relationship for a set of goods. A money-good is such that it can be exchanged against any other good. Thus, a barter economy is one in which every good is money and where the exchange relationship is transitive. 'We now define a monetary economy as a system embodying at least one money-good, but a non-transitive exchange relationship.'[31] In fact, Clower essentially preserves the concept of a pure monetary economy, characterised by the existence of a single money-good.

In a conceptualisation of this kind, the monetary economy appears to impose a considerable restriction on the exchanges practicable by comparison with the barter economy – a restriction which generates disequilibrium possibilities. The unemployed cannot find firms to employ them for a money wage, while producers cannot find clients capable of paying in money for their consumer goods. In a barter economy, disequilibria of this type could be resolved by paying the wage in kind.[32] In passing, we may note that the problem is twofold: in the example cited, there is a deficiency of the means of payment and a non-transmission of information on agents' respective wants. We will return to this question in the context of disequilibrium theory.

G. L. Shackle himself defends the notion of the causal role of money in disequilibria:

> It is only when we introduce an autonomous means of payment, which is not restricted to a representation of current output, but exists or intervenes in and of itself, outside of the list of products, that total demand and total supply can be unequal. It is money which destroys the necessary equality between these two magnitudes, which is inevitable in a system of barter or virtual barter.[33]

In this writer's view, disequilibria arise more precisely from the concurrence of uncertainty and money – uncertainty encourages deferment of purchases, money provides the means of doing so through its function as a store of value.

Nevertheless, it would be paradoxical to believe that money increases the probability of disequilibrium by comparison with a hypothetical barter economy. In fact, both the existence of disequilibria and the need for money arise from the absence of a centralised mechanism for the co-ordination of agents and the organisation of exchange. The form such a mechanism should adopt is well known: what is required is the combination of a Walrasian 'tâtonnement' process and a general clearing-house for the claims and liabilities of all agents in the economy. In fact, from the definition of the 'tâtonnement' process it is clear that exchange would only take place at equilibrium, within a framework of prices, guaranteed by the auctioneer to balance out all supplies and demands. In such a system of exchange, the receipts and expenses of each agent would be similarly balanced out, which implies that settlements could be effected only through the clearing process. Our interpretation differs from Shackle's[34] in that we do not consider that uncertainty in itself excludes the possibility of such processes, which it is conceptually possible to make complete through the interplay of Arrow-Debreu style conditional and futures markets.

Therefore, the need for money, both to control decentralised exchange and to prevent the occurrence of disequilibria, derives from the absence of such mechanisms of co-ordination and organisation of exchange, in the economies of the real world.

If we can explain the relationship between money and disequilibrium in terms of their common origin, then we might say it represents a notable example of a spurious correlation, to which it would be mistaken to attach a causal interpretation.

Part Three
Growth

Classical dynamic theory advanced the notion of a period of capital accumulation giving way to a stationary state, on meeting the barrier of supply costs. Pre-Keynesian dynamic theory conceived of economic movements principally in terms of cycles. Indeed, the theoretical representation of growth as a continual process of expansion of the volume of activity is recent. Undoubtedly, the context of a high rate of growth of the world economy from 1945 to 1973, an experience unique in history, was favourable to this view. Today, faith in such a pattern of indefinite development is questioned. The barrier of natural resource availability, which an unbounded confidence in the possibilities of technology had encouraged to neglect, has now become apparent. It has cast doubt both on the likelihood of unlimited growth and on the belief that post-Keynesian macroeconomics provided the means to ensure its regulation.

The study of growth assumes several levels of understanding of the phenomenon. In the first place, we will meet the methodological problem of portraying growth in such a way as to permit theoretical identification and empirical measurement of its sources. The contribution made at this level, as much in socialist as in Western countries, derives from a neoclassical approach, which has been the subject of animated attacks from the Cambridge School.

Secondly, we will attempt to understand growth from the point of view of its regulation and stability. Keynesian and neoclassical theoreticians have been pitted against each other on this point, in a stormy debate brilliantly opened by Harrod. It has led to some clarification of the scope and limitations of various conceivable modes of regulation, in particular the level of savings or technology. However, the theories adopted in this debate are ambiguous, as we will demonstrate in questioning the black and white nature of the antagonism between these simplified constructs.

We will then tackle the question of the pattern of growth and assessment of its optimal rate. The theory of optimal growth will be presented only in simplified form in such a way as to illustrate its rationality, before we concern ourselves with the analysis of disturbances arising from the existence of non-renewable resources and other limits to growth.

7 The Representation of Growth and its Sources

Investigating the sources of growth of production and consumption initially comes down to identification of the constraints working upon them at a given moment. In dealing with a long-term context, as we are here, we are forced to agree with Ricardo's conclusion that the limiting factors are to be found in the nature of production possibilities: the endowment of non-produced primary factors; the availability of capital – that is all the means of production which may be produced but which require prior accumulation; and the efficiency with which they are employed. This chapter will be concerned with determinants of the potential level of output, assuming the factors are fully employed. The problem of co-ordinating potential and realised production is related to the regulation of growth, which will be studied further on.

A study of production possibilities has to rely upon production functions[1] and, historically, assessments of the sources of growth have in general been based on the use of this concept. However, there are serious difficulties associated with the transposition of the concept of the production function from the microeconomic to the aggregate level. Similarly, the introduction of technical progress alongside the traditional factors of production has been the subject of some 'caveat clauses'.

The Cambridge School, following J. Robinson, has developed an animated critique of the aggregate production function, directed in particular at the utilisation of the concept of capital at the macro-economic level. This critique is based especially, but not exclusively, on the phenomenon of 'capital re-switching'.

Nevertheless, many studies have endeavoured to measure the contribution of different factors at the empirical level. Their results typically bear witness to the predominant influence of technical progress as measured by a 'residual', which one then strives to explain.

These three levels of development will be considered in turn.

1 MACROECONOMIC PRODUCTION FUNCTIONS AND TECHNICAL PROGRESS

Having already defined the production function as an expression of technological constraints (see chapter 5), technical progress would seem to amount to a shift in these constraints, and hence a distortion of the function. However, it is worth examining first to what extent this definition of the production function can be retained at the macro-economic level. We will then study the ideas on which the introduction of technical progress rests, before recalling the hypotheses adopted for the determination of its rate and character.

A The aggregation conditions for production functions

The difficulties associated with the aggregation of relationships have been mentioned previously, without according them a systematic presentation. The complexity of the problem, in particular at the mathematical level, prevents us from giving a full treatment[2] of them here. Nevertheless, as it is the aggregation of production functions which has been the most controversial, it is worth pointing out the principles of this process and the main results at hand. Beginning with a brief reminder of the nature of the microeconomic production function, we will examine the three types of conditions required for aggregation, that is to say for the derivation of an aggregate function from individual functions. The three types of conditions are formal, economic and empirical respectively.

1 The microeconomic function, a technological relationship
Conceptually, the aim of the production function is to express the technological constraints to which economic decisions are subject.[3] In the strict sense, then, it is defined at the level of the production unit – the firm or, more accurately, the process. Many studies[4] have illustrated its validity and usefulness at this level; and it seems to us that the *a priori* refutation of the concept by certain economists constitutes an unwarranted extension of the Cambridge critique, which might be said to rely more on the techniques of 'mixing' in ideological debate, rather than on scientific argument. On the other hand, it would be equally unwarranted to transpose this relationship to the macroeconomic level without considering what significance it bears. That the existence of stable functions, expressing the technological constraints operative at the microeconomic level, implies the existence of an aggregate production function of the same, purely technical character is not an

evident proposition, but one which would in general, that is to say with the exception of particular cases, prove false.

In order for a macroeconomic production function to be linked to the functions determined at the microeconomic level, it must result from an explicit process of aggregation. Its shape and properties are thus conditioned as much by the characteristics of the aggregation process as by the microeconomic technical constraints. It is necessary to classify the various conceivable methods according to the sets of conditions, which ensure their coherence and determinacy. The conditions may be formal (mathematical), economic or empirical.

2 The formal conditions for aggregation

Let us assume there exist n units of production securing an output y_i of an homogeneous good, by combining m inputs x_{ij} according to a technique described by a set of functions f_i. An aggregated production function $y = f(x_1, \ldots x_j, \ldots)$, if it exists, relates an 'aggregate' y, the measure of the total product, to the aggregate inputs $x_j \ldots$. The natural wish of the economist is to find an aggregation process which satisfies the following two properties:

(a) That the aggregates y and x_j are obtained by direct summation of the individual magnitudes:

$$y = \sum_{i=1}^{n} y_i \, , \, x_j = \sum_{i=1}^{n} x_{i,j}$$

and are thus compatible with the statistical definition of aggregates.

(b) That the aggregation process is valid whatever is the distribution of inputs and outputs between firms (though the f_i functions must obviously be satisfied), that is to say they must form a system with $n(m + 1) - n$ or mn degrees of freedom.

We may show that such a process imposes extremely severe restrictions on the microeconomic production functions, which must be linear and with identical coefficients[5] for each firm. Thus:

$$y_i = a_{io} + \sum_{j=1}^{m} a_j \, x_{ij} \, .$$

The principle of the proof is easy to grasp.[6] This property ensures that the aggregate is invariant to the distribution of microeconomic variables. Furthermore, note the symmetry established in this case: it is unimportant whether the inputs are first aggregated and the sum of their productive contributions then taken, or if individual contributions are calculated first and then aggregated. This observation suggests that there exists a general relationship between the aggregation of functions between microeconomic units and the separability of these functions, that is to say the possibility of breaking down factor contributions in an additive manner.

Seeing the drastic nature of these formal conditions, one may well seek to weaken them. But the possibilities of doing so are limited and not without their disadvantages.

Firstly, it is possible to lessen the exactingness of the requirement for identical coefficients, by accepting systematic differences in factor efficiency between firms. It is sufficient to define the aggregated inputs in terms of efficiency and calculate them as weighted sums. This solution is equally applicable where there coexist factors of different ages and therefore different degrees of efficiency.[7]

A linear production function implies, as we have seen,[8] an infinite elasticity of substitution, which is a very rare case. Can we contemplate using other typical functions, such as the Cobb-Douglas? We can, but only within very strict formal conditions. In fact, if we consider the logarithms of the variables, the Cobb-Douglas function is linear and can satisfy the above conditions. However, the indices of output and of the inputs associated with the aggregate function must then be defined as geometric not arithmetic means and clearly do not coincide with aggregates currently in use.

More generally, the theory of aggregation shows that an aggregation is formally possible when the production function embodies properties of both homogeneity and separability. It remains true that interpretation is difficult and that one might conclude that the severity of the required conditions precludes the possibility of development of a purely formal solution to the problem of aggregation. One must thus reduce the bound of the problem by restricting the number of possible distributions of outputs or inputs to be aggregated.

3 The economic conditions for aggregation

Outside of the above conditions on the nature of the individual production functions, the indeterminacy of the aggregate function is more clearly apparent. For given quantities of factors, there are in general as many possible associated values of output as there are distributions of these factors between production units. Certainly, we may speak of an aggregation over a given factor distribution, but the result is so unstable that it is likely to be of no use whatsoever. One obvious solution consists of adopting the maximum value of output given the set of possible factor distributions.[9] Such a solution always exists and may be specified if returns are decreasing. Let us take as a definition:

$$y = \text{Max } \Sigma_i f_i (x_{i1}, ..., x_{ij}, ...)$$

under the condition that for all values of j, $\Sigma_i x_{ij} = x_j$. This maximisation problem may be easily resolved by the Lagrange method. The necessary conditions for maximisation are that the marginal productivities of each input should be the same in every enterprise employing that input. This situation would correspond in particular to the case of an equilibrium in all factor markets, in which factor prices (in real terms) would be equal to their marginal productivities.

Thus, the economic condition for aggregation – equalisation of marginal productivities between firms – is ensured by the attainment of competitive equilibrium. It is worth noting that it is only in this 'equilibrium' case that aggregation permits the interpretation of the production function as the technological frontier of the economy to be preserved, as only here is it possible to classify it by the definition established at the microeconomic level.

It may seem surprising that a set of formal conditions (linearity and identity of coefficients) may be replaced by a theoretical condition relating to allocation. The equivalence of these conditions results from the fact that in the vicinity of an equilibrium allocation, the balance of productive contributions between factors and between firms is 'locally' equal. Instead of reasoning in terms of isoquants – surfaces which are parallel as a result of identical techniques – equilibrium is approached on surfaces which are parallel to each other, because they represent the same price system.

While being a good deal more satisfactory, this second aggregation condition presents a serious limitation. By definition, it justifies aggregation only in equilibrium and the question of the determination of aggregates out of equilibrium is left open. So let us also consider alternative conditions which might be more broadly applicable.

4 The empirical conditions for aggregation
When neither the formal nor economic conditions for aggregation are satisfied, the result obtained is a function of the distribution of variables across the data sample. Therefore, certain general results to be obtained require specific assumptions on the stability of this distribution.

The simplest assumption is that of an invariance in the structure of prices, or alternatively quantities. The former case was explored by Hicks, whose theory of composite commodities established that one could always aggregate commodities whose relative prices remained constant. The latter case might also be pertinent for particular studies. We will see later that disequilibrium theory relies largely on fixed-price models. Hicks's theorem ensures that aggregates may be defined in such models.[10] An equivalent condition was proposed by Leontief, among others. It relies on the stability of quantity ratios and may be applied in fixed-proportion models, such as 'circuit' models often are.

Though it may not be rigidly fixed or obey an equilibrium condition, the distribution of determinant variables may obey a set of rules conducive to stability in aggregate relationships. One example is the case of non-competitive equilibrium, or at the purely empirical level, when variables obey a stable statistical pattern. Thus, several studies have shown that the microeconomic distribution of income or capital conforms either to a log-linear distribution or to Pareto's law. J. Tobin and K. Borch[11] have shown how an aggregate consumption function could be constructed in the former case, while H. Houthakker[12] has deduced an aggregate production function for the latter case. A very important aspect of these results is that they have established that aggregate relationships therefore depend as much on the observed or assumed pattern of distribution as on the actual form of the micro-economic relationship. Thus, a macroeconomic variable frequently depends on the degree of deviation in microeconomic variables and not only on their mean level.

The nature of these aggregations seems at first sight paradoxical, but on reflection explicable. In fact the resultant macroeconomic relation-ships are often more regular than microeconomic relationships. Thus, Houthakker, in the work quoted above, assumed that firms had individual production functions with constant coefficients and that capital was distributed empirically according to Pareto's law. Upon aggregation, he obtained a function for total production of the Cobb-Douglas form.[13] More generally, the diversity of the situations of different firms introduces a continuity in the function for total production, which the individual functions do not possess.

Thus, the conditions under which stable aggregate relationships may be obtained from individual production functions are in fact quite varied, but the aggregation process has as much bearing on the information expressed as the individual technical constraints.[14] More precisely, it is only the general equilibrium assumption of an optimal allocation of resources which allows a macroeconomic production function to be defined as a purely technical concept. In every other case, the function derived embodies in addition to technical determinants factors linked to empirical regularities such as distribution of inputs and their efficiency.

Aggregation conditions are severe, but they do not apply any more strongly to the production function or the capital stock than to any other aggregate.[15] The reader might reflect on the current interpretation of *per capita* income in terms of welfare or standard of living: there is no basis for this interpretation outside of the equilibrium which justifies the price system utilised. It is certainly possible, outside of equilibrium, to aggregate on a cost basis, but who is coherent or purist enough to give a discourse on 'national costs *per capita*'?

Over and above the uncertainties arising from the conditions for consistent aggregation, the use of aggregate production functions in the evaluation of sources of growth relies on essentially empirical justifications. Thus, current forms of production function appear in the form of indices measuring factor quantities or their rates of growth.

B The introduction of technical progress

In the context of an analysis taking production functions as the description of the technological frontier of the economy at a given moment, technical progress appears as a synthetic concept denoting all the transformations undergone over time by this frontier. Thus, the integration of technical progress into the production function arises from the analytical (in the etymological sense of the word) desire to break down an aggregate effect into rigorously defined components. In this way, variations in factor productivity, especially in labour productivity, are broken down into one part, which may be explained by the increase in capital per head, a second component derived from economies of scale and therefore linked to variations in the volume of production and a third attributable to technical progress, which intervenes over time as a mere trend. Decomposition of this kind has sometimes been criticised, in particular by Kaldor, who proposed to take account of these effects through a single 'technical progress function', without distinguishing between them.

Following common practice, we will illustrate the introduction of technical progress by relating to a production function defined with reference to the indices of factor volumes, K_t and N_t. The notion of technical progress which implies a trend shift in production possibilities, leads to the following format:

$$Y_t = F(K_t, N_t, t).$$

In this very general unrestricted form, the effect of technical progress remains indeterminate. So, in addition we are compelled to introduce a more precise formula, of a conventional character. However, we will find that this conventional formula is rather narrowly linked to the typical properties of technical progress, in particular with regard to the question of how it is apportioned when the distribution of incomes is

competitive. So, we will deal with conventional formulae for technical
progress, and then with the economic interpretation of them in terms of
neutrality.

1 The conventional formulae for technical progress

In seeking a more precise format for the incorporation of technical
progress, one initial solution consists of assigning its effect directly to
output, or to all or some of the factors of production.

In the first case technical progress is defined as 'product-augmenting'
according to the following relationship (with factor quantities unchanged):

$$Y_t = A(t) \, F(K_t, N_t) \text{ with } \frac{dA}{dt} > 0$$

and thus:

$$\left. \frac{\partial Y}{\partial t} \right|_{K_t, N_t} > 0.$$

Effectively, this formula suggests most directly that the effect of
technical progress is separable from factor contributions.

$$\frac{dy}{dt} = \frac{\partial A}{\partial t} \cdot F(K_t, N_t) + A(t) \cdot \frac{\partial F}{\partial K} \frac{dK}{dt} + A(t) \frac{\partial F}{\partial N} \frac{dN}{dt}.$$

It leads one to conceive of technical change as 'factor neutral' – as a
shift rather than a real deformation of the technological frontier.

An alternative approach consists of treating technical progress as
synonymous with an expansion of factor volumes, in other words,
'factor-augmenting':

$$Y_t = F(A_t N_t, B_t K_t)$$

The particular cases of 'labour-increasing' and 'capital-increasing'
technical progress are obtained when the coefficients B_t and A_t
respectively are constant.

It is intuitively obvious that this definition entails only simple changes
in production frontiers, and that the economic effects of technical
progress, as introduced here in these conventional ways, will not prove
very general.

2 The implications of 'product-augmenting' technical progress

The definitive equation for 'product-augmenting' technical progress
implies that the marginal productivities of factors should be multiples of

A(t). In calculating marginal rates of substitution, the factor *A(t)* consequently disappears and the economic properties of a mode of technical progress obeying this convention derive from this result.

Ceteris paribus, product-augmenting technical progress will leave unchanged the marginal rate of substitution and, above all, the proportions of factors. Therefore, it possesses a certain form of neutrality highlighted by Hicks, which bears his name as a result.

Hicks neutrality was conceived in the context of a study on value and distribution. It corresponds to a situation where factor shares are left unchanged by technical progress. It is worth pointing out that distinguishing between this type of technical progress and the notion of increasing returns to scale may prove tricky. In general, one assumes that technical progress follows a regular trend, the factor *A(t)* growing at an exponential rate. Even in this case, disassociating the two concepts will be tricky if output is growing regularly. In an extreme case, with output growing at a constant rate, the distinction between the concepts of increasing returns to scale and Hicks-neutral technical progress has no operational purpose, which explains why in numerous theoretical and empirical applications the assumption of a production function homogeneous of degree one is adopted, thus presenting constant returns to scale.

Some textbooks advocate simple graphical representations of Hicks neutrality. One must not forget that they are useless unless the production function is homogeneous (i.e. it may be illustrated in terms of isoquants) of degree one (i.e. with a graph in terms of output per head). We will study these representations further on.

3 The implications of 'factor-augmenting' technical progress

Interpreting $A_t N_t$ and $B_t K_t$ as factor measures denoted in efficiency units is the basis for a direct interpretation of this type. As long as their outputs are unchanged, and the volume of production thus remains constant, factor shares are unaffected. If, in addition, the production function is homogeneous, this invariance in factor shares is preserved provided that the ratio $A_t N_t / B_t K_t$ itself remains constant. Let us consider the particular cases where, in the absence of economies of scale, technical progress 'augments' only one factor, labour, for example (thus let B_t be constant, and by convention equal to one).

In these conditions, to assume $A_t N_t / K_t$ is constant implies continuous substitution, with the ratio of factor volumes N_t / K_t falling at the same rate at which the efficiency of labour A_t improves. The marginal productivity of capital which depends only on the ratio $A_t N_t / K_t$,[16] is unchanged. Similarly, the proportional expansion of factors (by assumption) and of output (as a result of constant returns) ensures that the capital-output ratio is unchanged. This combination of effects is characteristic of Harrod neutrality, which under the assumptions we have made (and only in this case), thus coincides with the notion of 'labour-augmenting' technical progress. In fact, in Harrod's view, technical progress is neutral if it leaves the capital-output ratio unchanged at a given rate of interest. Note that this definition again implies an invariance in factor shares, but, in contrast to Hicks, account has here been taken of adjustment in factor proportions.[17] Thus, unlike Hicksian neutrality, Harrodian neutrality is not a purely technical phenomenon.

We may demonstrate that the corresponding case of 'capital-augmenting' technical progress ensures the invariance of output per head for a given wage rate, all of technical progress being 'absorbed' by the rise in the remuneration per unit of capital. This property is called Solow neutrality.

The importance of Harrodian neutrality is inescapable. It denotes a type of technical progress, which, by regularly increasing wages and labour productivity, permits a mode of capital accumulation which is quite opposed to the Classical and, above all, Marxist law of the tendency of the rate of profit to fall. Harrodian neutrality depicts a situation in which, through technical development, trend stability in the rate of profit is rendered compatible with the pursuit of capital accumulation.

Solow neutrality has sometimes been seen as the expression of a purely formal problem, whenever it is of special significance in the two following cases. In the first place, F. Fisher has demonstrated the importance of this assumption as a requirement for aggregation in the context of capital-theoretic models. Secondly and most importantly, when reference is made to economies with surplus manpower, the concept of Solow neutrality assumes a historical and theoretical significance. The development theorists J. Fei and G. Ranis developed the same concept, under the name of U-neutrality, to show the logical evolution of an economy, in which all technological effort was directed towards economising capital, with the remuneration of labour remaining constant.[18]

Economic interpretation of the more general case, in which there is simultaneous improvement in the different factors is more tricky. Note, however, that incorporating technical progress in the form of a coefficient affects both marginal and average productivity, and thus implies proportional variations in the marginal rate of substitution and in factor proportions.

4 Diagrammatic representation

The different forms of neutral technical progress correspond to particular changes in the shape of the technological frontier. These may easily be represented in graph form in terms of isoquants or output per head functions.

Taking first the case of a production function, homogeneous of degree h, the following representation in terms of isoquants is possible, where A_0, A'_0, B_0 and A_1, A'_1, B_1 designate the initial values of the coefficients of overall and factor efficiency.

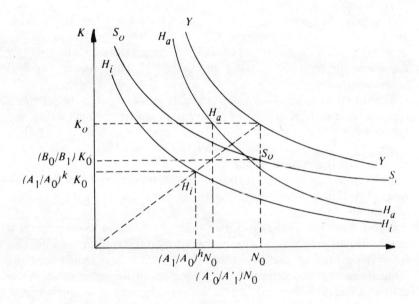

Figure 7.1

Take a point (K_0, N_0) on the initial isoquant Y. We denote by H_i, H_a and S_0 respectively the isoquants resulting from neutral technical progress in the sense of Hicks, Harrod and Solow. Neutral technical change in the Hicks sense reduces use of each factor by the ratio $(A_0/A_1)^{1/h}$. Harrod-neutral technical progress combines an unchanged K_0 with a required level of employment of $A'_0/A'_1 N_0$.[19]

Representation in terms of magnitudes per head (or equivalently, per unit of capital) is possible if the degree of homogeneity, h, is equal to one, in which case the following archetypes are obtained (Fig. 7.2).

In the case of Hicksian neutrality, average product (Y/N) and marginal product [the slope of a tangent to the curve $F(K/N)$] grow

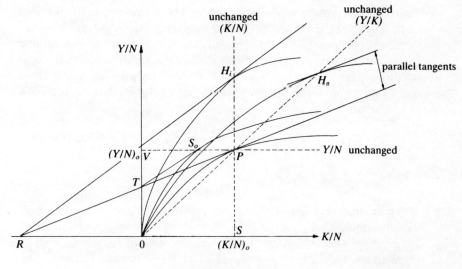

Figure 7.2

in the same proportions. Indeed, at the point H_i we obtain by construction:

$$\frac{\tan (SRH_i)}{\tan (SRP)} = \frac{SH_i}{SP}$$

The ratio RO/OS shows the unchanged relationship between wages and profits. Harrodian neutrality is represented by a shift PH_a, which preserves both the capital-output ratio, and therefore is situated on the ray OP, and the marginal productivity of capital, shown by the slope of the tangent to the curve at P.

We may obtain a representation of neutrality in the Solow-sense by marking the distribution of output per head on the y-axis. TV measures profit per head, while OT represents the wage rate. Technical progress which is neutral in this sense must preserve both output per head (Y_0/N_0) and the wage rate OT. This corresponds to the situation illustrated by the point S_0.

5 The conditions for equivalence

It has been noted that the Hicksian and Harrodian concepts of neutrality refer to different stages in the process of technical change. So one may well ask if they can coincide and be simultaneously satisfied by certain types of production functions. The answer to this question is trite. In fact, if a production function implies changed factor shares, it is clear that distribution would be unchanged both *a priori*, all other things being equal, as Hicksian neutrality requires, and *a posteriori*, once factor proportions had been changed, as indicated by the Harrod and Solow concepts of neutrality. Such is the case with the Cobb-Douglas function, where as a result of its functional separability these three specifications and the general notion of factor-increasing technical progress coincide:

$$Y_t = (A_t N_t)^\alpha (B_t K_t)^\beta = (A_t{}^{\alpha/\beta} B_t K_t)^\beta N_t{}^\alpha = (A_t B_t{}^{\beta/\alpha} N_t)^\alpha K_t$$

$$= A_t{}^\alpha B_t{}^\beta N_t{}^\alpha K_t{}^\beta$$

We may here recognise 'factor-augmenting',[20] 'capital-augmenting', 'labour-augmenting' (neutral in the Harrod sense) and 'product-augmenting' (neutral in the Hicks sense) forms of technical progress respectively. Similarly, it was shown by M. Beckman and R. Sato[21] that the CES function corresponded to an equivalent class of generalised definitions of neutrality, which preserved the elasticity of substitution.

With regard to these conventional formulae for the introduction of technical progress, it is worth pointing out how inappropriate is the oft-used expression 'the dynamisation of the production function'. The introduction of a variable *t* into a relationship is not a criterion of dynamic analysis. The term 'dynamised production function' would correspond more to the sort of formula associated with the notion of internal adjustment costs,[22] something of the form $Y_t = F(K_t, N_t, \dot{K}_t, \dot{N}_t)$, where factor quantities and factor variations are combined in the determination of efficient output.

C The determinants of technical progress

The conventions which govern the formal introduction of technical progress involve very specific implications, particularly in the field of factor distribution. But they are not linked with the hypotheses adopted on how technical progress is itself determined. We will pick out various of these in turn: firstly the hypothesis that it is purely exogenous; then the hypothesis that it is embodied in one of the factors of production and lastly the view that both the rate and direction of technical progress are endogenously determined.

The pure exogeneity approach amounts to treating technical progress as independent of every economic variable in the system and related only to time, generally following an exponential trend of the form:

$$Y_t = e^{\gamma t} F(K_t, N_t) \quad \text{or} \quad Y_t = F(e^{\mu t} K_t, e^{\nu t} N_t)$$

to quote only the cases of 'output-augmenting' and 'factor-augmenting' technical progress. We can see to what extent such a concept of exogeneity might be unsatisfactory, since technical progress is, if not produced, at least channelled, by economic activity.

1 The embodiment hypothesis

It has been assumed up to now that the increase in productivity due to technical progress applied to all factor units in use at a given date, regardless of the initial date of utilisation of the process and, thus, of its age. A definition of this kind does not allow any account to be taken of the fact that technical progress frequently implies a modification of productive equipment, or relies on the improved training of new generations of workers.

Therefore, the alternative assumption was proposed of technical progress being 'embodied' in a factor of production, generally productive capital. In the models constructed to expound this hypothesis, a distinction is made between different generations (or 'vintages') of factors. Although the notion of manpower generations is pertinent in taking account of the advance of basic education, we will here develop essentially the idea of capital vintages.

In this approach, two time subscripts have to be introduced, the first which denotes the date of the original investment in the cycle K_v, and the second t, which relates to the current period of use. The general formula for embodied technical progress considers total output as the sum of the contributions of these vintages, thus:

$$Y_t = \sum_{v=t-\theta}^{t} Y_{t,v} = \sum_{v=t-\theta}^{t} F(K_{v,t}, N_{v,t}, v),$$

where θ denotes the number of vintages in operation. Technical progress as embodied in an input may take any form: 'augmenting' output, this input or even another input. Far from being paradoxical, this latter eventuality merely illustrates the degree of freedom this approach permits by comparison with the conventional presentations studied above. Typically, technical progress might be assumed to be embodied in capital, for example, yet labour-increasing.

$$Y_t = \sum_{v=t-\theta}^{t} F(K_{v,t}, A(v) N_{v,t})$$

The reader may note that in our presentation the quantity of labour is measured at v, although it refers to a homogeneous group. The fact is that, in general, it does matter with which generation, of the factor embodying technical progress a homogeneous factor is combined. More generally, in the context of capital vintage models, it is important to specify in full the degree of substitution permitted between factors.

In these models an additional distinction is introduced over and above the conventional case. Effectively, substitution can be studied either at the time of the investment decision or in relation to an already established generation of capital.[23] Adopting the hallowed terminology, we will speak of a 'putty-putty' model when substitution is possible both before and after investment, of a 'clay-clay' model when factor proportions are fixed in both cases,[24] and lastly of a 'putty-clay' model when we assume that factor proportions may be altered at the time of the investment decision, but cannot later be modified, once machinery is installed.

From the point of view of the consequences, the essential distinction relates to the possibility of substitution of installed equipment. Thus the 'putty-putty' model is pitted against the two others. In this case, first studied by R. Solow,[25] it is possible to continuously reduce the quantity of the homogeneous factor relative to the quantity of the factor embodying technical progress, so that the marginal productivity of this factor will be the same with every generation. Then, one may take a weighted aggregate of the heterogeneous factor, capital for example, constructing what is equivalent to an aggregate production function.

In the example studied by Solow, the production function for each cycle is a Cobb-Douglas function of the form:

$$Y_v = A e^{m v} K_{v,t}^{\alpha} N_{vv}^{1-\alpha}$$

We may show that total output is itself determined by a Cobb-Douglas function:

$$Y_t = A J_t^{\alpha} N_t^{1-\alpha},$$

where N_t is total employment and J_t an index of 'effective capital' obtained by a weighted aggregation of the investment cycles I_v; thus, assuming the rate of physical depreciation of equipment to be zero:

$$J_t = \sum_{v=-\infty}^{t} e^{m/\alpha} I_v$$

In the case of the 'putty-clay' and 'clay-clay' models, factor aggregation of this kind is impossible, as the productivity of the homogeneous factor itself varies according to the generation with which it is combined. Thus, the only aggregate concept which has any meaning is that of total productive capacity – the direct sum of the productive capacities of each cycle. Let us express this concept in detail, taking the case of an '*ex ante*' production function; homogeneous of degree one. The average production of capital for a generation v depends on its capital-intensity and on the technical progress it embodies (assumed, for simplicity of exposition to be 'product-augmenting'):

$$\frac{Y_{t,v}}{K_{t,v}} = \frac{A(t)\,F(K_{t,v}\,N_{t,v})}{K_{t,v}} = A(t)f\left(\frac{N_{t,v}}{K_{t,v}}\right).$$

Total output attributable to this vintage is obtained by multiplying this term by I_v the level of investment at v,[26] and macroeconomic productive capacity by summing over the generations:

$$Y_t = \sum_{v=t-\theta}^{t} A(v)f\left(\frac{N_{t,v}}{K_{t,v}}\right)I_v$$

Clearly, the assumption of embodied technical progress may be combined with a non-embodied trend. Its specific characteristic is that it ties the integration of technical change to the rate of investment. Statistical studies have endeavoured to evaluate the rate of capital replacement, which reduces the margin between the most recently available techniques and the mean of the techniques in operation in the economy at a given moment.

2 The determination of the direction of technical progress
Conventional representations have been associated with specific properties of technical progress, particularly in the matter of factor shares. However, we may accept that the form of technical progress is not naturally given but may be adapted in response to economic objectives. In particular, innovatory effort may be devoted to economising a certain factor of production as a matter of priority.

The simplest formula for induced technical progress lies in the general realm of 'factor-augmenting' change. It is considered that there exists *a priori* a continuum of innovations each characterised by a co-ordinate *(dA/dt, dB/dt)* measuring the 'increase' in labour and capital. By analogy with the notion of the production technique, we will define an efficient innovation as a feasible innovation not dominated by any other – that is to say an innovation such that no other feasible innovation permits greater economies in labour (or capital respectively) while economising at least as much capital (labour). The set of efficient innovations forms the innovation possibility frontier,[27] which is analogous to a transformation curve in the theory of production.

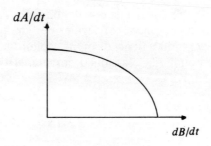

Figure 7.3

The selection of a point on this frontier is determined as a function of the constraints weighing on factor endowments. Thus, an economy with surplus manpower would be situated on the y-axis *(dA/dt = 0)* and would adopt capital-augmenting innovations; an economy constrained by the natural rate of population growth would confine itself to labour-augmenting innovations *(dB/dt = 0)*. The 'product-augmenting' case (Hicksian neutrality) is obtained where *dA/dt = dB/dt*, at least in the case of homogeneous production functions.

3 Determination of the rate of technical progress
In the previous section, we considered the direction of technical change as an endogenous variable, taking the rate of innovation as exogenously given. In fact, it may be useful to consider the creation of knowledge and new techniques as the result of an economic process. We then have two options: either we consider technical progress as the by-product of productive activity in general, and we have the theory of learning by doing, or we take technical change as the result of a specific process of production of innovations, through the application of research and development effort.

(a) *Learning by doing* – Learning by doing is, quintessentially a concept of a technological nature. In the American aircraft industry, for example, 'progress ratios' have been estimated showing the reduction in labour time expected per plant as a function of the length of the production series.[28] Similarly, the observed growth of productivity in a Swedish steelworks, at a rate close to 2.5 per cent even in the absence of investment, gave birth to the expression the 'Horndall effect'. An article by K. Arrow[29] proposed a method of formalising this effect, based on the idea that the productivity of labour would grow as a function of gross cumulated investment – denoted by *G*. Assuming the capital-output ratio is constant, the process of learning leads to a regular decrease in the coefficient of labour required per unit of output:

$$\lambda(G) = bG^{-n} \qquad \text{with the rate} \qquad n > 0.$$

Thus output Y is expressed as a function of employment N and cumulated investment according to the following relationship:

$$Y = aG \left[\frac{1 - (1 - N)}{cG^{1-n}} \; 1/1 - n \right]$$

Although this relationship looks very different from a production function, Arrow demonstrates that it is possible to attach to it a notion of marginal productivity of labour and capital. The point remains that learning by doing introduces a divergence between the private rate of return on investment and the social return, as the contribution of investment in raising the future level of factor productivity is not expressed in terms of any gain or factor saving at the level of the firm.

(b) *The theory of innovation* – Schumpeter's work constitutes the main historical reference in this field. Yet, in his view, innovation is better described as the adoption of new factor combinations rather than the creation of new knowledge. In *Capitalism, Socialism and Democracy*, J. Schumpeter underlined how the continuous and organised effort in research and development, which characterised large corporations, differed from the activity of the innovating entrepreneur, which it had superseded. Given this fact, a theory of innovation in the modern sense of the term still remained to be constructed. Work in this field has tended to concentrate on the microeconomic foundations[30] of this type, both with regard to the effect of research and development effort and the determinants of that effort. Thus, Nordhaus[31] has proposed a model in which the 'output-increasing' parameter dA/dt is a function of the number of innovations N_t and the level of technological development reached:

$$\frac{dA}{dt} = k_0 + k_1 \, N^\beta A^\alpha \quad \text{with } \beta \text{ and } \alpha \in [0,1],$$

while the number of innovations is explained by the balance between their cost D and the discounted quasi-rents, to which they give rise:

$$N_t = \left(\frac{i^\beta \, Q_t}{A^\alpha D_t} \right) \; 1/1 - \beta.$$

The rate of innovation is an increasing function of the size of the market Q_t, the rate of interest i and the elasticity of the 'product-augmenting' factor; it is a decreasing function of the cost of innovation and the level of technological development achieved. An econometric study based on time-series data relating to the agricultural sector and the railways sector proved unfavourable to the first equation but confirmed the latter, thus supporting the hypothesis of an 'innovation equilibrium'.

2 THE CAMBRIDGE CRITIQUE

The representation of growth in terms of an aggregate production function incorporating technical progress is subject to very strict aggregation conditions. It is difficult to determine directly what limitations follow from this. It was the Cambridge School who took it upon themselves to evaluate them, being a group of writers based around Joan Robinson and Piero Sraffa.

Since 1953, J. Robinson had issued a number of objections to the notion of the macroeconomic production function, and in particular to its use in the theory of income distribution. The main thrust of this criticism lay in the impossibility of undertaking a purely physical measure of the stock of capital, hence in the impossibility of considering a relationship embodying this aggregate as purely technological. P. Sraffa developed this critique in 1960, and, confirming J. Robinson's proposition, established the impossibility, under his assumptions, of classifying techniques according to their capital intensity in such a way as to derive from them a relationship between the wage rate and the rate of return which evolves in a monotonic manner as in the case of the neoclassical production function. Since then the debate has widened, and, while a number of results have now been established, a large divide exists between 'Cambridgians' and neoclassicists over the significance which should be accorded to them.

We will first consider the problem of 'capital re-switching', then certain questions associated with the evaluation of capital, in order to attempt finally to draw some conclusions from the controversy.

A The representation of techniques, and capital re-switching

It is first convenient to state the assumptions common to the type of models around which the discussion is centred. In the first place, the reasoning is in terms of discreet linear techniques – thus ruling out non-constant returns, and the possibility of a continuous technological frontier but not necessarily factor substitution, which takes the form of switching from one technique to another. Secondly, the analysis relates to long-period equilibrium states in which classical 'normal prices' or

Marxist 'prices of production' prevail. Thirdly, a distinction is drawn between goods used exclusively for production and goods used exclusively for consumption, where these goods are characterised by their production conditions. Under these assumptions, a set of equilibrium positions may be presented from which there arises the possibility of the phenomenon of 'capital re-switching'.

1 The factor price frontier

A 'technique' A, in the two-sector model, may be illustrated by a technological matrix indicating the respective quantities of capital and labour required for the production of each good:

$$[A] = \begin{bmatrix} a_{KC} & a_{LC} \\ a_{KM} & a_{LM} \end{bmatrix}$$

where a_{KC} denotes the number of machines required to produce a unit of consumer goods, a_{LM} the number of workers necessary in the manufacture of a machine, etc. . . . From this, equations may be derived both for the factor quantities employed and for prices. Let p be the price of a machine in terms of consumption good, w the real wage rate (in terms of consumption good) and r the rate of profit. The assumption of a long-period equilibrium ('normal prices') enables us to write, for consumption goods:

$$1 = a_{LC} w + a_{KC} pr$$

and:

$$p = a_{LM} w + a_{KM} pr$$

for the price of machines, whose life-time is here presumed to be infinite.

This system of two equations has three unknowns: p, w and r. Thus, it permits one degree of freedom, so we may express the set of solutions in terms of the feasible (w, r) pairs for example. From the first equation, we may derive:

$$p = \frac{1 - a_{LC} w}{a_{KC} r} ,$$

which is equal in value to the right-hand side of the second equation. Resolving for w the expression thus obtained gives:

$$w = \frac{1 - a_{KM} r}{a_{LC} + (a_{KC} a_{LM} - a_{KM} a_{LC}) r} ,$$

where, if D is the determinant $(A) = (a_{KC} a_{LM} - a_{KM} a_{LC})$ of the technological matrix A:

$$w = \frac{1}{a_{LC} + Dr} - \frac{a_{KM}}{a_{LC} + Dr} r.$$

The above equation, which expresses the maximum rates of remuneration possible, is called the factor price frontier (f.p.f.) for the technique A. The presence of r in the denominator shows that it is in general a non-linear relationship. The ratio:

$$\frac{dw}{dr} = \frac{a_{KM} a_{LC} + D}{(a_{LC} + Dr)^2} = -\frac{a_{LM} a_{KC}}{(a_{LC} + Dr)^2}$$

is always negative as the technological coefficients are necessarily positive. As a result, the f.p.f. always shows w as a decreasing function of r.

It is interesting to consider the case where the f.p.f. is linear. An examination of the equation reveals that a necessary and sufficient condition for that is that the determinant D should be zero, that is to say that the technological matrix should be singular or otherwise that its rows (alternatively its columns) should be proportional to each other:

$$D = 0 \Leftrightarrow \frac{a_{LM}}{a_{KM}} = \frac{a_{LC}}{a_{KC}}.$$

Capital intensity, that is the number of workers per machine, is then the same in both sectors and the factor price frontier becomes:

$$w = \frac{1}{a_{LC}} - \frac{a_{KM}}{a_{LC}} r.$$

On the other hand, the determinant D is positive if the machine sector is more labour intensive:

$$\frac{a_{LM}}{a_{KM}} > \frac{a_{LC}}{a_{KC}},$$

and negative if the consumer goods sector is the more labour intensive. We may show that the convexity of the f.p.f. is governed by the sign of this determinant. In fact, the term:

$$\frac{d^2 w}{dr^2} = \frac{2 D(a_{LC} + Dr) a_{LM} a_{KC}}{(a_{LC} + Dr)^4} = \frac{2 D a_{LM} a_{KC}}{(a_{LC} + Dr)^3}$$

shows the sign of D. So the f.p.f. is convex if D is positive, that is to say if the machine sector employs more labour, and concave if the consumer goods sector is relatively less capital-intensive (more labour-intensive). From which the following graphic representation of the f.p.f. is derived:

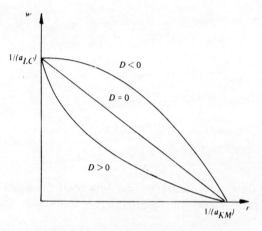

Figure 7.4

In this way, the concept of the factor price frontier permits us to associate a representation of the technology with an illustration of feasible factor remunerations, without any recourse to a production function. It remains to be seen whether they both lead to the same results.

2 Capital re-switching
Let us now introduce the possibility of the economy having access to various techniques other than A. Each one has an associated factor price frontier. Let B be one of these techniques. There are three possibilities now open: either B is superior to A, that is to say it will always permit the economy to reach higher (w, r) pairs, or A is superior to B, or otherwise A allows higher wage rates at certain rates of profit but lower wage rates than B at other rates of profit. If one can choose freely between techniques, the set of possible (w, r) pairs comprises all the possibilities offered by each technique. Its frontier – the factor price frontier of the economy (F.P.F.) – is the envelope of the factor price frontiers (f.p.f.) of the techniques.

The outline of this frontier depends on the shape of factor price frontiers of the individual techniques. In the very particular case in which all techniques showed the same capital-labour ratio in each sector, the f.p.f.s would all be straight lines and their envelope could be found as follows:

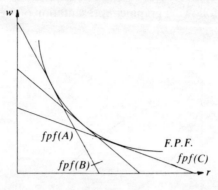

Figure 7.5

In this case, the points of intersection between techniques are unique. As the rate of profit r falls, the technique A is abandoned for B, then C, etc. . . .

Thus, there is a monotonic ordering of techniques uniquely associated with a regular decrease in the ratio w/r. This priority does not hold in the general case as the following example shows:

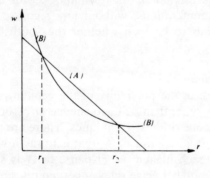

Figure 7.6

In fact, we can see that at the rate of profit r_2 one 're-switches' to the technique B, which was abandoned at the rate of profit r_1. Thus, B is preferred to the technique A both at a higher and a lower rate of profit: no monotonic ordering of the techniques is possible.

This is the phenomenon of 'capital re-switching', which undermines the belief of earlier neoclassical theory that a technique A, abandoned at a rate of profit lower than r_1, would be less capital-intensive than the technique B preferred to it at that point and so could not later be re-adopted at a still lower rate r_2. In fact, capital re-switching is only one aspect of the Cambridge critique, though it is true it is without doubt the easiest to grasp.

Underlying this phenomenon is the role of the relative price of capital. In fact, the capital being remunerated is a value. The same technique physically defined, will appear more or less capital-intensive according to the price system, but the price system itself depends on technology and factor costs. The example shown above illustrates this interpretation.

No re-switching is possible where factor proportions are the same in each sector. That is precisely because, the structure of costs being the same, the relative price of machines is not altered when factor remunerations are modified. In a model where goods are differentiated essentially by their method of manufacture, this case of equal factor intensity would in fact correspond to an economy with a single good, which is at the same time both a capital good and a consumer good. Such is the true significance of this key case in which capital re-switching is impossible.

B The classification of techniques and the evaluation of capital

The phenomenon of re-switching brings us back to the more general question of the evaluation of capital, which comes to interfere with the choice of techniques. In examining this matter, we will first deal with the notion of Wicksell effects as compared with neoclassical hypotheses, then we shall show that these evaluation problems have a more general application than the phenomenon of re-switching. Lastly, we will describe the particular solution to the evaluation problem proposed by Piero Sraffa.

1 Wicksell effects
In his attempt to analyse the impact of changing factor costs on the value of capital employed in production, Wicksell had pinpointed the factors involved in capital revaluation, in the idea that a wage increase entailed not only a lengthening of the production process (increasing its degree of 'roundaboutness') but also an 'unproductive absorption of capital'.[32] Whence the term 'Wicksell effect' attributed to this phenomenon since J. Robinson.

Let us express as follows the breakdown, between wages and profits, of output per head q, evaluated in terms of consumer goods:

$$q = rk + w.$$

Comparing long-period equilibria, a variation in rates of profit entails a simultaneous adjustment of the wage rate, output and capital per head. Thus, the variation in the value of capital is measured by the differential:

$$dk = 1/r \, [dq - kdr - dw] \, .$$

A direct consequence of this is that the marginal productivity of capital, in the sense of the present argument, is not equal to the rate of profit:

$$\frac{dq}{dk} = r + k \, \frac{dr}{dk} + \frac{dw}{dk} \, .$$

J. Robinson saw this as a crucial point of criticism[33] against the neo-classical theory of distribution, interpreted in simple models as signifying the equality of the marginal productivity of capital and the rate of profit. In terms of the variation in the value of capital, the following breakdown is obtained:

$$dk = \frac{1}{r} \, dq - \frac{k}{r} \, dr - \frac{1}{r} \, dw \, .$$

Of these three terms, the first may be interpreted as the capitalised value of physical productivity and corresponds to a real effect known as the Ricardo effect or the real Wicksell effect; the other two correspond to capital revaluation effects and make up the Wicksell price effect, or the Wicksell effect in the strict sense. According to the sign of dk/dw (i.e. contrary to the sign of dk/dr) Wicksell effect will be positive or negative. Thus a positive Wicksell effect is 'normal' and a negative effect appears to be 'perverse' with respect to neoclassical standard effects. The value of Wicksell effects may be examined by looking at the graph of the f.p.f.

The output per head q is also the maximum wage w_x attainable with the given technique. So capital per head $k = (q - w)/r$ is always equal to the tangent of the angle β. Now, this tangent increases with r, as long as the f.p.f. remains concave, that is as long as the determinant of the technological matrix is negative $(D < 0)$, as in the present case. In this case, the Wicksell effect is negative, or 'perverse', because the value of capital rises when the rate of profit increases. On the other hand, if D is positive and the f.p.f. concave, that is to say if the machine sector employs more labour, the value of capital falls as r rises, then the price

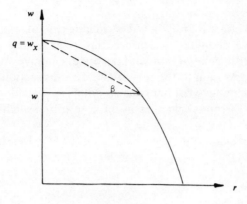

Figure 7.7

effect is positive or 'normal' and reinforces the real effect. So we may see that, while not actually excluding the possibility of re-switching, the case of a convex f.p.f. corroborates neoclassical results as far as one unique technique is concerned.

There remains the case of a linear frontier, that is to say when the technical coefficients are identical in both sectors. The price effect is cancelled out, and the rate of profit is equal to the marginal physical productivity of capital. Thus, we have:

$$k \, dr + dw = 0, \qquad \text{or} \qquad -\frac{dw}{dr} = k.$$

In other words, the value of capital per head is equal to the slope of the f.p.f. (in absolute value terms). If there are many techniques of this kind, the envelope of the f.p.f.s will display the standard neoclassical properties, with the value of capital falling steadily as the rate of interest increases. P. Samuelson[34] has demonstrated that in this case there could be defined a surrogate production function $S(J, N)$, homogeneous of degree one, which determined total output from the level of employment and an index of the 'quantity of capital' J.

The capital surrogate J is evaluated simply by multiplying employment by the absolute value of the slope of the factor price frontier $k = dw/dr = J/N$. In fact it comes to $J = [dw/dr]N$.

$$k = |dw/dr| = J/N \qquad\qquad J = |dw/dr|.N$$

We have seen how particular this case is: it essentially describes a one-good economy. We must also turn our attention to cases which do not come from the neoclassical drawing board.

2 *Capital re-switching revisited*

If the Wicksell effect is null, then re-switching cannot appear. However, for all that we should not confuse this re-switching anomaly with Wicksell effects in general, nor with perverse, negative, Wicksell effects which act in opposition to the real effect. This distinction may be made clearer by examining 'what happens' at points of switching and studying how the value of capital changes in the case of re-switching.

(a) *A reinterpretation of 're-switching'* – Let us take the simplest case of a technique (*A*) with a linear frontier, and a technique (*B*) with a concave frontier.[35]

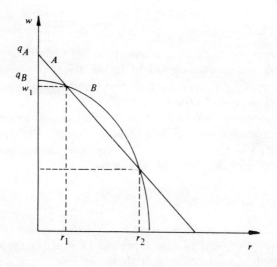

Figure 7.8

As r_1 is a point of switching, the techniques *A* and *B* are equally profitable at that point. Now, at every point $K_A = (q_A - w_1)/r_1$ is greater than K_B $(q_B - w_1)/r_1$, that is to say the value of the capital associated with technique *A* exceeds that of technique *B*. As the Wicksell effect for *B* is negative, the value of its capital increases as r grows, whereas K_A remains constant as the Wicksell effect is zero for this technique. So at r_1, the intersection entails switching to a less capital-intensive technique in response to a rise in the rate of profit. There is thus a positive real Wicksell effect, conforming to neoclassical predictions. On the other hand, at r_2 the intersection entails switching to a more capital-intensive technique in response to a rise in the rate of profit.[36] So the real Wicksell effect is negative or, in the context of neoclassical beliefs, 'perverse'. How can we explain this paradox? The technique *A* is always more productive physically. So logically it should always have a higher associated capital value.[37] But there is no steady relationship between this productivity margin and the difference in values. At certain rates of profit the handicap of having a greater amount of capital to be remunerated may outweigh the advantage of greater productivity; at other values, the advantage of physical productivity may more than compensate for this handicap. The fact that there should be several equilibrium positions arises from the non-linearity of the expression from which the value of capital is derived. Indeed, we may show that if several machines were utilised, there would be as many different points of intersection as there were different sectors associated with each technique.

At this stage, the analogy with microeconomic problems of investment choice is quite apparent. Two projects, exhibiting different profiles of returns over time, will each appear more profitable at some stage according to the discount rate chosen. There may be as many values of the rate of interest which render them equivalent as there are periods in the time allowed for maturity. Thus we could have said that re-switching is an analogous problem at the macroeconomic level to that of the multiple rates of return associated with microeconomic investment projects.

(b) *Re-switching of techniques and the value of capital* – The value of capital per worker as a function of the rate of profit remains to be deduced from the previous example.

In the new quadrant we have added to Fig. 7.9, we express the movement of the value of capital per technique, k_A and k_B, and for the economy as a whole (bold frontier). For a given technique, the movement of the value of capital is determined by the Wicksell (price) effect, thus with *B* it increased regularly and with *A* it remains stationary. It is at points of intersection, and only at these points, that the real effects – the effects of switching techniques – occur. In the example above, the value of capital for the economy as a whole evolves by stages, with discontinuities at the points of intersection, and in any case in a manner very different from the regular pattern observed in the neoclassical case.

Thus, under the model's assumptions of linear techniques, long-period equilibrium and goods defined by their methods of production, the value of capital per worker may increase with the rate of interest, even if we disregard the points where re-switching of techniques takes place, as we may observe above between r_1 and r_2. On the other hand, we can see that where frontiers are convex *(D > 0)*, it is only the

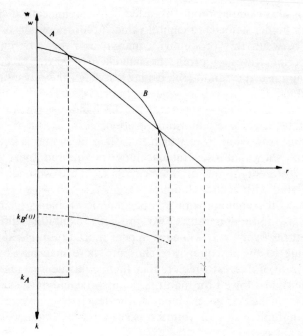

Figure 7.9

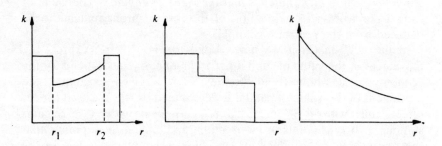

Figure 7.10   The above case
The Samuelson case
The continuous neoclassical case

phenomenon of 're-switching' which casts doubt on the verisimilitude of the neoclassical case.

(c) *The Sraffa problem* – The Cambridge critique of the neoclassical treatment of capital relies on the dependence of the normal prices for distribution on given technical conditions, thus placing itself firmly within a neo-Ricardian perspective. In fact, one finds in Ricardo a preoccupation with the search for a standard of value, equivalent or superior to the labour theory of value. Piero Sraffa undertook to resolve this problem, basing a critique of neoclassical political economy upon its resolution.[38] The best-known part of his work is the notion of the standard commodity, a composite commodity capable of providing the solution to Ricardo's preoccupation.

We have seen above that the relative prices of goods are affected by the cost of factors to the extent that these factors are embodied in different proportions. Furthermore, the prices of goods employed in each other's production processes are clearly interdependent. So under what conditions can we provide a determinate solution to the problem of finding a system of values or prices independent of the distribution of wages and profits?

Sraffa considers a set of n commodities within an economy which are necessary for their own production and that of all others (basic commodities). In his preliminary model, they are incorporated in the production process in the form of circulating capital, according to the already determined technical coefficients a_{ij}.[39] In addition, wage-earners, their relative number determined by a vector of coefficients a_{lj}, receive a wage w. For each commodity we have a price equation:

$$p_j = a_{ej} w + (a_{lj}\, p_1 + a_{2j} p_2 + \ldots + a_{nj} p_n)\,(1 + r)$$

Or in matrix notation:

$$P = a_i w + AP(1 + r)$$

In this model wages are not advanced, but paid from the surplus. So in general, the structure of prices depends on the wage and profit rates. However, let us assume that there exists a commodity – simple or composite – which is itself the only commodity required for its own reproduction. Any alteration of the pattern of distribution alters the value of the input and the output, and therefore of the surplus which is the difference between them, in the same proportion. Let Z be the weighted vector, which defines a composite commodity possessing this property, that is to say a commodity whose input and output vectors Z_I and Z_o are collinear:

$$Z_o = \lambda Z_I.$$

But Z_I is expressed according to Leontief equations:

$$Z_I = A^t z_o \quad \text{whence} \quad \frac{1}{\lambda} z_o = A^t z_o.$$

This expression defines Z_o as an eigenvector of the technological matrix and $1/\lambda$ as its eigen value. Since A is a non-negative matrix,[40] by Frobenius' Theorem, there exists a positive vector Z_o associated with a positive number $1/\lambda$, the solution of this equation. Furthermore, if surplus production is possible, the number λ must be greater than one. We will say that the vector Z defines the standard commodity and the number $\lambda = 1 + R$ the standard ratio of net production to means of production. R is the rate of surplus – the maximum rate of profit which can be attained in a system where wages are nil.

Taking the value of the total output of the standard system as the numeraire, it may itself be broken down into the value of the surplus $R/(1 + R)$ and the value of the means of production employed $1/(1 + R)$. If w, the wage rate, is defined as a proportion of the surplus of the standard system, the volume of profits is $(1 - w)R/(1 + R)$ and the rate of profit r is the ratio of this sum to the value of the means of production:

$$r = R(1 - w)$$

Sraffa demonstrated that this linear relationship between the wage rate and the rate of profit was actually applicable in the real system, as long as wages and profits were defined in terms of the standard commodity.

We have seen, in the foregoing analysis, the controversial significance of the Sraffrian model. At the technical level, we may extend it to encompass the case of fixed capital by considering the output of a process and the capital remaining as joint products.[41] Sraffa applied it to the resolution of the Marxist problem of transforming values into 'prices of production', to the determination of values in terms of quantities of dated labour and also as a testimony to the impossibility of classifying techniques in the way neoclassical theory assumed.

As a critique of the neoclassical economy, Sraffa illustrates a model in which normal prices are determined from technological and distributional conditions quite independently of demand. In that he is only repeating a result established by Samuelson and other neoclassical writers under the name of the non-substitution theorem. The connection between this theorem and the conversion of values into quantities of dated labour has been pointed out, notably by N. Georgescu-Roegen who showed that these two theories both depended on the assumption of there being a single scarce resource in the economy – labour. Introducing scarce natural resources ('land') into the analysis for example, destroys these results.

Sraffa's system raises other problems. In it, wages are paid from the surplus, but the standard surplus consists only of producer goods. There reappears the Ricardian belief that the rate of profit depends only on the conditions of producton of 'basic' goods, but here no wage-good is 'basic'. Formally it is part of the family of linear models, yet Sraffa and his disciples maintain that they make no assumptions about returns as they reason in terms of a given product. This solution is formally possible, but it is bold indeed to propose a reconstruction of the whole science of political economy on the basis of such a restrictive assumption. Undoubtedly, one of the essential contributions of Sraffa has been in reviving and revitalising methodologically a forgotten field of analysis.

C Some developments and conclusions

The controversy over capital re-switching and the impossibility of classifying techniques according to their capital intensity erupted again in the context of an alternative approach formulated by Solow, which placed emphasis on defining the rate of return directly rather than in relation to the value of a stock of capital, and hence assuming a production function. L. Pasinetti, however, among others was to show, that this approach ran up against the same objections[42] as the traditional neoclassical 'parables'.

Thus the four 'tenets' refuted by the Cambridge School are as follows:[43]

1 The rate of profit is a decreasing function of capital per head.
2 The rate of profit is a decreasing function of the capital-output ratio.
3 The rate of profit is a decreasing function of the attainable rate of regular growth in *per capita* consumption.
4 The distribution of profits and wages may be explained in terms of the marginal products of capital and labour.

While it is true that neoclassical writers established various conditions under which 'perverse phenomena' (such as re-switching) would not occur, these conditions seem excessively restrictive when seen in the light of the Cambridgian assumptions.[44] We must, then, assess the significance of their critique.

The Cambridge critique established beyond question that the traditional neoclassical model, attributed to Ramsey and Clark, which relied on the notion of a macroeconomically stable technical relationship between physical output and a volume of aggregate capital, was, in general, an inaccurate approximation, in particular: as the basis for a theory of distribution, and for a comparison of long-period equilibria.

On the other hand, the claim of certain Cambridgians that the recent debate has shown the impossibility of any neoclassical theory of production and distribution seems quite excessive. The objections they have formulated are not in fact applicable to a general equilibrium approach, nor to a case in which there exists a reasonable degree of substitutability, and outside of the static framework in which they have been formulated their validity is debatable.

In particular, the very common 'circularity' argument, which objects that in neoclassical theory the value of capital must be known to determine the rate of profit, yet this rate of profit is assumed given in measuring the value of capital, is based on false conceptions. In fact, neoclassical theory assumes only co-determination – a simultaneous determination of these two variables. So, in practice, the 'circularity' criticism is only acceptable with regard to simplified aggregate constructs, such as those from which the four traditional tenets were derived.

At the disaggregated level adopted in general equilibrium analysis, this objection is not tenable and the physical productivity of capital goods can indeed be defined.[45] In this sense, we might consider, along with M. Brown, that 're-switching' is essentially an aggregation problem.

Certainly, some Cambridgians (like Garegnani) have questioned the determinacy of general equilibrium itself, but they have not always been supported in this field. Thus, G. Harcourt[46] is careful to specify that the critique is directed at the aggregated version of neoclassical theory, explicitly excluding modern general equilibrium theory. Similarly, he shows that Pasinetti's criticism of Solow is directed at the latter's use of the rate of return at the aggregate level, and not at Fisher's theory in general.[47] In Harcourt's eyes, the pure neoclassical theory of the rate of interest is valid but relates to a concept distinct from the capitalist rate of profit.[48] This brings the basis of the debate to the problem of realism – the moulding of concepts to reality.

Secondly, once the assumption of fixed coefficients is abandoned and a certain degree of substitutability introduced, we will again perceive a stable ordering of techniques and a regular movement of the value of capital. At the technical level, total rigidity may be no more realistic than the perfect substitutability found in the most idealised neoclassical models. Neoclassical writers believe further research is necessary to assess the significance of this point.

Lastly, it is worth noting that the debate has been conducted entirely in terms of comparisons of long-period equilibria, that is to say in terms of comparative statics or comparative steady state dynamics. That leaves wide open the debate on the incidence of capital re-switching and 'perverse' effects at the dynamic level. Now, such phenomena are less likely in a dynamic context, as M. Bruno's[49] model shows. There are two factors leading to this result. On the one hand, a really dynamic model takes account of the interdependence of decisions over time and brings into play the phenomena of depreciation and expectations. On the other hand, such a model will show a detailed system of shadow prices, associated with the constraints of the model, not 'historic' prices.[50] The counter example of this model shows that the Cambridgian arguments do not arise, as much as their authors suggest, from an internal critique of neoclassical theory. Indeed, to define prices and rates of return in terms of historic costs is quite alien to the spirit of neo-classical analysis.[51]

While the importance of the Cambridge critique would justify this attempt at an appreciation, it remains true that we are still far from having drawn all the conclusions from the debate. For a long time yet, the theory of growth will, for want of rigorous proofs of the validity of its analytical instruments, have to content itself with more pragmatic justifications of them. The debate has, at least, illustrated the limitations of this field and revealed the fallacy of viewing the macroeconomy purely as a network of aggregate quantities.

3 THE FACTORS CONTRIBUTING TO GROWTH

The acceleration of growth in the aftermath of the Second World War must be explained at several levels. One of these consists of identifying and evaluating the contribution of various factors to the trend growth in output. The evidence of the numerous studies which were undertaken on this point suggested that quantitative growth in traditional factors accounted for only a limited part of growth. There was, instead, a large 'residual' element in these studies which was interpreted as showing the influence of changing techniques.

A second series of studies was therefore undertaken to break down this residual, reducing to a minimum the part of growth which remained unexplained. These studies achieved only partial success and sometimes only through adopting some rather peculiar conventions. A third stage of research, notable in particular for a contribution by Jorgenson and Griliches, witnessed the assertion, at the theoretical and empirical levels, of the absence of a residual, considering it as the result of a statistical illusion attributable to errors of measurement.

A The evaluation of the residual

The incorporation of technical progress in the production function, proposed by J. Tinbergen as early as 1942, forms the basis of the methods adopted by M. Abramovitz and Schmookler in 1952 and above all by R. Solow in his famous study of 1957,[52] in their researches on the contribution of technical progress to economic growth. The method and the results are now well known.

1 The method

The method generally followed in placing a value on the contribution of technical progress – a contribution which is residual to that of the traditional factors – relies on the use of neoclassical production functions and indices measuring the volumes of the quantities of labour and capital. While we may relax the former assumption, it is difficult to see how research could be conducted independently of the latter.

Let us begin with the method adopted by Solow. Production possibilities are assumed to be representable by an aggregate production function, homogeneous of degree one in K_t and N_t:

$$Y_t = A(t) \, F(K_t \, N_t).$$

Increments in output over time are expressed from the total differential of production:

$$\frac{\partial Y}{\partial t} = \frac{\partial A}{\partial t} \, F(K_t, N_t) + A(t) \, \frac{\partial F}{\partial K} \, \frac{\partial K}{\partial t} + A(t) \, \frac{\partial F}{\partial N} \, \frac{\partial N}{\partial t}.$$

We divide each term by Y_t and denote by g_A, g_Y, g_K and g_N the proportional rates of growth in efficiency $A(t)$, output, capital and employment, which take the form $(1/Y)(\partial Y/\partial t)$. We then have:

$$g_{Y,t} = g_{A,t} + \frac{A_t}{Y_t} \, \frac{\partial F}{\partial K} \, K_t \, g_{K,t} + \frac{A_t}{Y_t} \, \frac{\partial F}{\partial N} \, N_t \, g_{N,t}.$$

If factors are remunerated according to their marginal productivities, ω_t, the share of wages at time t, is equal to:

$$\frac{N_t \, w_t}{Y_t} = \frac{N_t \, A_t}{Y_t} \, \frac{\partial F}{\partial N} = w_t.$$

while the complementary term $(1 - \omega_t)$ is equal to the share of profits, hence the expression:

$$g_Y = g_A + \omega_t \, g_N + (1 - \omega_t) g_K.$$

As the terms g_Y, g_N and g_K are measurable, as is the weight ω_t, the above equation enables the contribution of technical progress to be calculated by subtraction, as the residual element unexplained by traditional factors:

$$g_{A,t} = g_{Y,t} - \omega_t\, g_{N,t} - (1 - \omega_t)\, g_{K,t}\,.$$

It is worth noting that, up to now, this derivation has been carried out at a given moment. However, the problem of the sources of growth must be assessed within a relatively long period, and in terms of the average values of the weight ω and the rates of growth of factors and output. Thus, the empirical model corresponds to an image of an economy which grows regularly with the share of wages remaining constant.[53] The same empirical result may, therefore, be obtained either on the basis of a much stricter hypothesis – a Cobb-Douglas function – or a much more general hypothesis, without assuming any type of production function.

Take first a Cobb-Douglas function in which technical progress occurs at the trend rate g_A:

$$Y_t = e^{g_A t}\, A_o\, N_t^{\omega}\, K_t^{1-\omega}\,.$$

Transcribing this relationship into logarithmic form and then taking the total differential, we have:

$$\frac{dY_t}{dt} = g_A + \omega\,\frac{dN_t}{N_t} + (1 - \omega)\,\frac{dK_t}{K_t}\,,$$

an expression which, when taken at a single moment in time, coincides with the Solow breakdown.

On the other hand, we will see further on that the same relationship can be obtained under very general conditions, quite independently of any reference to a neoclassical production function, by resorting to Divisia indices.

Thus, breaking down the rate of growth of output in an additive manner into the rates of growth of factors and a residual, attributed to technical progress, constitutes a robust method, little influenced by the nature or even the existence of the production function, though nevertheless requiring, for its own stability, a stable distribution of income between wages and profits.

2 The results
Practical application of the method described above may encompass

several forms. In particular, one could carry out the estimation of the coefficients ω and g_A from the equation:

$$g_{Y,t} = \omega \, g_{N,t} + (1 - \omega) \, g_{K,t} + g_A + \epsilon_t \, .$$

As the coefficients of the rates of growth of labour and capital sum to one, we could subtract the rate of growth of employment from each side of the equation, hence:

$$g_{Y,t} - g_{N,t} = (1 - \omega) \, (g_{K,t} - g_{N,t}) + g_A + \epsilon_t \, .$$

This amounts to explaining the growth of output per head in terms of the growth of capital per head. We note that in this econometric equation, the most common one, it is the constant term coefficient which is estimated as the contribution of technical progress, so the term 'residual', which has been attached to it, is methodologically rather unfortunate, as the econometric residual is the term ϵ_t, whose mean contribution is by assumption zero.

Solow's first study yielded estimates for the annual contribution of technical progress to the growth of the United States of 1% for the period 1909 to 1929 and 2% for the period 1929 to 1949. Estimates for France are significantly higher (of the order of 4% since 1945).

The method of treating technical progress as a trend variable independent of increments in factor volumes leads to it being attributed 50% to 75% of the responsibility for growth in industrialised countries, depending on the period and country under consideration. Given this fact, it is distinctly embarrassing that the principal explanatory factor should be measured as a residual.

In fact, under these conditions 'the importance of the residual can be taken as a measure of our ignorance of the causes of economic growth'.[54] It is, therefore, not surprising that subsequent studies have endeavoured to analyse this residual and reduce the unexplained element in growth.

B The analysis of the residual

The steps undertaken to 'decompose' the residual followed two distinct paths: specification of the qualitative aspects of factor efficiency and clarification of the economic processes leading to an interaction between factor growth and technical progress. But one had to be resigned to the fact that there remained a new residual, which could not be broken down into specific elements contributing to the rise in productivity.

(a) *Qualitative factors* – Solow's method involved only quantitative development of productive factors. Subsequent researches endeavoured to evaluate the impact of an improvement in the quality of the factors of production. In the case of manpower, the principal factor studied with regard to increased productivity has been education. Certain conventions based more or less explicitly on the neoclassical theories of distribution and human capital permit the evaluation of this factor by reference to the structure of incomes. Among the other causes of the rise in labour productivity per hour, one must mention the reduction in the length of the working day.

No objective reference of this type is possible with regard to the improvement in the quality of equipment. It is necessary to resort to the formalism of capital vintage models, which permit evaluation of the contribution of 'capital renewal' to the average productivity of labour. Let us assume that the rate of technical progress embodied in capital, in 'product-augmenting' form for example, is of the order of 1.5% per year. The efficiency of a given stock of capital then depends on its average age. A level of gross investment which reduces by a year the mean age of capital will result in an increase in productivity of approximately 1.5%. So from the observed variations in the mean age of capital and an estimate of the trend rate of technical progress embodied in capital, it is possible to derive a measure of this effect.

(b) *Interactive factors* – The concept of improvement in the quality of factors is reminiscent of models of embodied technical progress, but maintains the theoretical possibility of dissociating the input of technology from the material accumulation of the means of production. In fact, there is a whole series of causes leading to the intervention of economic factors in the process of technological change. Biased technical progress, allocation and re-allocation effects and economies of scale are typical examples of this phenomenon.

Whereas the incorporation of technical progress leaves open the possibility of isolating the input of technology where there is a regular trend, non-neutrality introduces an essential interaction between the growth of factor inputs and the development of their productivity – an interaction which cannot be eliminated by formal manipulation. Among the more interesting studies of this type, we must mention the contribution of David and Van de Klundert.[55] Clearly, one can only take account of non-neutrality in a production function with an elasticity of substitution different from one. In data for the United States over the

period 1899–1960, the aforementioned authors obtained an estimate for
σ of 0.316 and a rate of 'labour-augmentation' consistently in excess of the
rate of 'capital-augmentation'[56] (finding rates of 2.3% and 1.58%
respectively). This calculation resulted in a significant reappraisal of the
contribution of labour to growth. However, the more general effect of
these models of non-neutral technical progress is to put into question
the practice of breaking down in an additive manner the contributions of
technology and of factor inputs.

Average factor productivity at the macroeconomic level does, indeed,
develop as a result of increased productivity in the different productive
sectors, but in reality the different levels of productivity achieved in
each sector are not equal, and so at the aggregate level productivity is as
much dependent on the distribution of employment between sectors
with different degrees of efficiency. In this way, inter-sectoral reallocations of factors, especially labour, have come to be considered
among the elements contributing to growth. Massel,[57] in particular, has
given a theoretical underpinning to this factor. Estimation of technical
progress and the efficiency margins between sectors or firms is
conducted by pooling cross-sectional data relating to different periods.
Technical progress, from inter-firm transfers, may be found by weighing
up the factor reallocations against the efficiency margins.

In the statistical studies actually undertaken, this factor was foreseen
in the case of rural migration, which is a regular flow of manpower,
leaving agriculture where its productivity is only low, to work in industry
or services.

Economies of scale are the source of productivity gains not attributable to individual factors. We have pointed out the conceptual and
practical difficulties involved in distinguishing them from a 'product-
augmenting' technical progress trend, in particular if growth is regular.[58]
Certain writers, notably E. Denison,[59] have nevertheless attempted an
evaluation of them. In particular, this writer reduces the notion of the
expansion of markets into a measure of expansion in terms of national
prices, a measure of expansion in terms of a reference price system (US
prices) and the growth in units of production or distribution which
occurs independently of the total growth of markets. Despite this
analytical effort, numerical evaluation remains essentially arbitrary.

C The persistence of a residual

The purpose of undertaking fuller studies, such as those of E. Denison,
was to reduce the part of growth implicit in the residual by evaluating

effects linked, on the one hand, to the quality of factors and, on the other, to the efficiency with which factors are employed. The results achieved have proved inconclusive, as they are highly dependent on the conventions adopted, and only partially successful, as they leave a significant remaining residual.

We will quote three studies typical of work in this field. The first, due to Carré, Dubois and Malinvaud, relates to France, the second by Denison and Poullier similarly relates to the French case, while the third, by the same authors, relates to the United States and is here given for reference (see Table 7.1)

Comparison of the three columns illustrates, firstly, how Denison reduces the residual by placing a significant weight on economies of scale and on the contribution of resource reallocation in France (essentially rural migration) and, secondly, that the difference in the rates of growth of France and the United States cannot be explained simply in terms of factor utilisation.

It is interesting to test the hypothesis that the difference in the rates of growth since the end of the Second World War might correspond to a 'catching-up' effect. Carré, Dubois and Malinvaud discuss this factor, and Denison attempts to evaluate it in terms of two specific factors: firstly 'a modification of the delay in the application of new knowledge', that is to say a speedier alignment with American technology, and secondly, exploitation of certain economies of scale arising specifically from a movement of the national structure of consumption towards the American norm – a movement measured by the degree of convergence of the price systems.

A more recent study by Abramovitz seems to confirm the importance of the 'catching-up' effect. The difference in the average rates of growth of the United States and a group of three European countries over the period 1950–1962 amounted to 2.18%.[60] Growth of inputs, inclusive of the quality of labour, would explain 0.29%. Improved allocation of resources would account for 0.79%. Thus, the gross residual (or 'Solow residual') would explain 1.10%. Analysis of this residual reveals that economies of scale would account for 0.89% of which 0.23% comes from exploitation of economies under the existing structure (relative to American prices) and 0.66% is associated with the restructuring of expenditure, but there remains a second residual (the 'Denison residual') of 0.21%, interpreted as the 'reduced delay in the application of new knowledge'.

The sum of the effects connected with the 'catching-up' effect would therefore explain nearly three-quarters of the difference in growth between the United States and these European countries. This fact would lead us to expect a reduction of this margin in the future.

Table 7.1 *The analysis of the rate of growth of output*

	France[i]	France[ii]	USA[iii]	
Country				
Writers	Carré, Dubois, Malinvaud	Denison and Poullier	Denison and Poullier	
Period	1951–1969	1950–1969	1950–1962	
Rate of Growth (GNP) %	5	4.7	3.36	Rate of growth (Nat. Inc.)
Employment (in sectors)	0	0.08	0.9	Employment (total)
Length of working year	− 0.1	− 0.02	− 0.17	Length of working year
Quality of workers	0.4	0.39	0.39	Quality of workers (Composition by age, sex and education)
Volume of capital	1.1	0.79	0.83	Volume of capital
Capital replacement	0.4	0	0	Capital replacement
Reallocation of manpower	0.6	0.95	0.29	Improved resource allocation
Intensity of demand	0.1	1	0.36	Economies of scale
		0.75	0	Modification of the delay in application of new knowledge
Residual	2.5	0.76	0.76	Development of knowledge[61]

Sources: Column i Carré, Dubois and Malinvaud, 'La croissance française', p. 275
          ii Denison and Poullier, 'Why Growth Rates Differ', p. 306
          iii *Ibid*, p. 298.

3 The validity of the residual

In addition to the attempts to reduce the amount of the residual, it is worth mentioning two approaches, which question the whole principle. The first considers that the sum of the contributions of inputs, when correctly measured, must necessarily account for the growth of output, the residual – Solow's or Denison's – being only a reflection of errors in measurement. The second lays down in principle the impossibility of separating technical progress, economies of scale and the accumulation of capital.

The theory that output growth must be equivalent to a certain balance of factor growth, if the latter is correctly measured, has been championed in particular by D. Jorgenson and Z. Griliches.[62] These authors take as their starting point the basic identity between the value of output and the total cost of factors, which may be expressed as follows, aggregating m products at price q_i and n factors at price p_j:

$$\sum_{i=1}^{m} q_i Y_i = \sum_{j=1}^{m} p_j X_j$$

Total factor productivity A is expressed as the ratio of an index of the volume of output Y and an index of the volume of factors X. Instead of laying down arbitrarily fixed weights for the construction of these indices, the authors adopt the Divisia index,[63] which gives a weight, for each period, to the relative variations in the basic variables. Thus:

$$\frac{dY_t}{Y_t} = \sum_{i=1}^{m} u_{it} \frac{dY_{it}}{Y_{it}} \quad \text{where} \quad u_{it} = \frac{q_{it} Y_{it}}{\Sigma_i q_{it} Y_{it}}$$

and,

$$\frac{dX_t}{X_t} = \sum_{j=1}^{n} v_{it} \frac{dX_{jt}}{X_{jt}} \quad \text{where} \quad v_{jt} = \frac{p_{jt} X_{jt}}{\Sigma_j p_{jt} X_{jt}}$$

are the weights for outputs and inputs respectively. Variations in total productivity are therefore measured as follows:

$$\frac{dA_t}{A_t} = \frac{dY_t}{Y_t} - \frac{dX_t}{X_t} = \sum_{i=1}^{m} u_{it} \frac{dY_{it}}{Y_{it}} - \sum_{j=1}^{n} v_{jt} \frac{dX_{jt}}{X_{jt}} .$$

Note that the formula for Divisia indices provides a justification for the standard equation for the definition of the residual, which is dependent neither on the existence and properties of the production function. nor on the assumption of a system of distribution according to the marginal productivity of factors. It is the desire to attach to this notion of total productivity the usual interpretation of the neoclassical theory of production and not to be content with a conventional definition derived from the application of an 'index calculation' type of formula, which leads to the introduction of the assumptions of a production function homogeneous of degree one and a system of distribution according to marginal productivities. But Jorgenson and Griliches themselves recall that constant returns to scale may result from the convention of measuring inputs in terms of efficiency units.

In this way, these writers endeavour to show that the residuals of Solow and Denison reflect a series of errors in measurement, which have led in particular to an underestimation of the contribution of capital. The principal amendments they make are as follows:

- capital is measured as a flow of productive services rather than as a stock;
- capital price series are reconstructed in terms of Divisia indices of elementary series assumed to be more reliable;
- the use of capital is taken into consideration and measured from the consumption of electricity;
- the weighting for capital services is calculated on the basis of user cost[64] and incorporates interest rates, tax rates, capital gains and rates of depreciation.

This set of corrections permits Jorgenson and Griliches to obtain empirical confirmation of their theory. The term residual to the increase in total factor productivity becomes reduced to 0.1%. However, it is to be noted that this first contribution was itself the subject of criticism, in particular with regard to the indicator adopted for capital utilisation. A subsequent study by Jorgenson and Christensen[65] intended as a reply to these criticisms, led to an increased estimate of the 'residual' from total productivity growth of 0.31% for United States data in the period 1929–67. Even so, it remains true that, by lending a greater degree of rigour to the methodological debate over evaluation of the residual, these studies revealed more clearly the influence of the conventions adopted in the measurement of factors and the sensitivity of the results to these conventions.

A notion akin to the rigorously neoclassical approach of Jorgenson in Kendrick's[66] idea that total output Y should be expressed as a flow of returns R_k from the different components of total capital K_k. Thus:

$$Y = \sum_{k=1}^{s} R_k K_k .$$

the five components of capital being the tangible (equipment) and non-tangible (research and development) elements of non-human capital, the tangible (food) and non-tangible (education, health, safety) elements of human capital and lastly foreign investment. The capital-output ratio measured at constant prices is interpreted as the level of productivity. The breakdown finally obtained from a rate of growth of 3.4% in the private sector of the domestic economy of the United States between 1929 and 1969, was a 2.4% growth in total capital (of which 1.7% was due to tangible capital) and a 1% 'residual' increase in total capital productivity.

In contrast to these neoclassical approaches, the Cambridge stance, maintained by N. Kaldor, is to refuse to integrate technical progress in a modified production function, adopting only a 'technical progress function', which incorporates the effects of economies of scale, investment per worker, and technical progress.[67] In fact, he considers it both artificial and arbitrary to distinguish between a shift in the production function and a movement along this function. Kaldor proposes a direct relationship between the rate of growth of output per worker g_y and the rate of growth of capital per worker g_k. The 'technical progress function' thus obtained, $g_y = f(g_k)$, is concave and incorporates a positive intercept on the y-axis, which expresses that part of technical progress not embodied in capital.

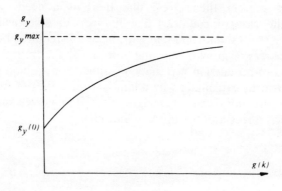

Figure 7.11

In fact, under certain conditions Kaldor's formula does not really differ from a specification in terms of a production function embodying technical progress, as Black and Kregel have demonstrated.

At the empirical level, Kaldor is in other respects tied to the idea of an explanation of productivity in terms of output growth, according to a relationship known by the name of 'Verdoorn's law'. This law establishes two symmetrical relationships between the rate of growth of output and the rates of growth of, on the one hand, productivity and, on the other hand, employment. Kaldor quotes the following results obtained from the average rates observed for different OECD countries.[68]

For manufacturing industry:

$$g_y = 1,035 + \underset{(0,07)}{0,484} \ g_Y \qquad R^2 = 0,826$$

$$g_N = -1,028 + \underset{(0,04)}{0,516} \ g_Y \qquad R^2 = 0,844.$$

A similar distribution between productivity and employment is obtained for different industrial sectors. On the other hand, in the primary sector the coefficient for productivity is the higher one (1 in agriculture, 0.67 in industry) to the detriment of employment growth, while in transport this coefficient is weak, the principal influence being on employment. The fact remains that this 'law' of Verdoorn's gives only a very fragmented picture of the factors which govern the development of productivity.

To conclude, the debate on the sources of growth leaves uncleared a number of uncertainties relating both to the theoretical backing required, and to the accounting conventions adopted. Two obvious conclusions present themselves: that there is a need, particularly acute in the case of countries like France, for statistical work on improving historical data and that a distinction is required between the study of *sources* of growth, showing how an expansion in the material possibilities of production was made possible, and an inquiry into the *cause* of growth, explaining why additional quantities of factors have been put to use and technical changes adopted in a given society[69] and telling which forces are driving economic change.

8 The Stability and Regulation of Growth

Whether we are concerned with problems of aggregation, valuation of capital or with measuring technical progress, we have been able to appraise the importance of the special case in which the economy grows evenly. More generally, the theory of growth centres around the concept of balanced growth just as traditional macroeconomic theory used the notion of equilibrium as a reference-point. For an equilibrium framework has been substituted one of balanced growth, obtained by a simple transposition of the concepts. This shift in the problem framework corresponds to the distinction between statics and dynamics in Harrod's sense;[1] for whom indeed dynamics does not mainly represent a change in the method of analysis, but 'a new method of approach – indeed, a mental revolution.'

By contrast, the distinction between statics and dynamics in Samuelson's sense is internal to an equilibrium problem set-up, but it is reproduced in the problem of balanced growth, in which the opposition between equilibrium and disequilibrium dynamics precisely corresponds to it. The transition is made in effect by substituting into the determination of the variables of a model, variables from a model of rules of adjustment to certain equilibrium conditions, assumed not to be realised. The same process of conceptual transition enables us properly to distinguish the idea of balanced growth from that of an economy which grows smoothly, following a steady-state growth process. Balanced growth, in fact, corresponds to a growth-path satisfying either a classical market equilibrium, or else an aggregative Keynesian equilibrium. A steady state corresponds to a growth path satisfying a stationary solution of a properly defined differential system and thus exhibiting certain conditions of constant growth rate in a single-sector model, constant proportions in a model with several sectors. In practice, balanced growth paths will often be steady states, but this of course cannot justify a confusion of the two ideas. The comparison of balanced growth-paths, which may also be steady states, is the object of comparative dynamics, analogous to comparative statics. Comparison of adjustment paths comes from comparative dynamics of disequilibrium. Meanwhile, the shift from equilibrium paradigm to balanced growth has preserved the order of questions we want to ask about equilibrium: existence, uniqueness, stability, optimality.

The developments in this chapter will be devoted to the properties of existence and of stability, optimality being studied in the next chapter. Historically, these problems have been marked by a controversy between the Keynesian and neoclassical traditions. As early as 1939, in the aftermath of the *General Theory*, Harrod proposed the principle of the instability of balanced growth. An early series of studies discussed this principle in the framework of highly simplified models with a single good, or single category of agent and no money. These pieces of work will be dealt with first.

Further work has dealt with the possible mechanisms for regulating growth through the intermediary of production structure, or of the savings rate. In the first case, models have been developed which include several sectors, or several generations of capital. In the second case, regulation through the savings rate is made possible by distinguishing two types of income, two social classes or by introducing money and financial assets.

1 THE PROBLEM OF INSTABILITY

The Keynesian debate over the issue of short-period equilibrium sought to show up the instability of full employment general equilibrium and also, but with less evidence, the stability of global underemployment equilibrium. Harrod shifted the debate to the sphere of long-period growth paths. In each case, the central issue is the suitability of market mechanisms for assuring the regulation of a decentralised, capitalistic economy.

In fact, economic analysis distinguishes two main stability concepts and several secondary qualifications. The central distinction leads the following definitions to be formulated.

An equilibrium point P_o in a system of economic variables is said to be *stable in the static sense* in a neighbourhood: N_o of the point P_o if, starting from any point in N_o, the system *tends to return to* the point of equilibrium.

An equilibrium point P_o in a system of economic variables is said to be *stable in the dynamic sense* in a neighbourhood N_o of the point P_o if any path starting from a point in N_o *converges towards* the point of equilibrium.

Static stability depends on the existence of appropriately aligned corrective mechanisms. Dynamic stability further requires that these mechanisms act at a rate and a rhythm which are not excessive.

In general, stability is established for a given interval N_o. When the region of stability includes all the possible states of the system, the equilibrium will be described as globally stable, which implies the uniqueness of the equilibrium position. If on the other hand stability is only established in a neighbourhood of P_o small enough that all the relevant functions could be replaced by their first-order approximations, the stability will be referred to as local. Finally, the term relative stability denotes the restoration of a certain set of proportions regardless of the levels of the variables considered. It is typically applied to the stability of input-output systems satisfying the Hawkins-Simon conditions.[2]

With these definitions in mind, we may now examine the stability of growth-paths. Historically, the problem was first set by Harrod with his demonstration of unstable balanced growth. The neoclassicals replied by presenting models illustrating the theory of stability. It is now possible to show that these results conflict only very marginally since, from the beginning, they did not set out to solve the same problem.

A The Harrodian theory of instability

Harrod's model set out to apply to growth the fundamental concepts of the *General Theory*. However, its formal specification was primitive in its first published form; its essential properties followed afterwards from additional indications, whose importance was revealed by subsequent formalisation and interpretation.

1 The Harrod model
A highly simplified model is dealt with, in which there is a single good whose longevity as a capital good is infinite. The effective rate of growth of output is denoted by g. Harrod defines the warranted rate g_w as 'the rate which, if it occurs, will leave all parties satisfied that they have produced neither more nor less than the right amount.' (Harrod, 1939, p. 16.) Here we recognise a definition in the Marshallian tradition, though Harrod himself refuses to speak of an equilibrium rate, which seems to him incompatible with the instability of the warranted rate.

The 'fundamental equation' determines the value of the warranted rate as a function of the propensity to save ss and of the state of technology as expressed by the required capital-output ratio c:

$$g_w = s/c.$$

In effect, the definition of the warranted growth rate implies that at each point in time, the investment desired by firms is equal to the normal savings of the economy. Desired investment is obtained by multiplying the required capital-output ratio c by the increase in output:

$$I^* = c \Delta Y.$$

Normal savings are proportional to the current level of income:

$$S_N^* = sY.$$

From this equality we get the condition:

$$\frac{\Delta Y}{Y} = \frac{s}{c} = g_w \ .$$

However, the equality of realised savings and investment is, in Keynesian theory, an accounting identity.[3] This leads to the formulation of a similar equation, this time in terms of the actual growth-rate g, the actual ratio between capital produced and variation in income v, and the ratio s_m between actual observed savings and income:

$$\frac{s_m}{v} = g \ .$$

This second equation is now a tautology:

$$I = S$$

In fact, it is often held that the propensity to save is relatively stable $(s_m \approx s)$, the ratio between the actual rate and warranted rate being found exactly in the ratio v/c between the actual capital coefficient and the required one.

If now the labour force is assumed to grow at a constant rate, given exogenously, then the rate of economic growth needed to maintain full employment if the latter is realised initially is called the natural rate of growth, g_n.

At this point, it is interesting to think of Harrod's ideas as the result of a transference of Keynesian concepts. The natural growth rate corresponds to full-employment income; the actual rate g to actual income; the warranted rate g_w to the equilibrium level of income. Two distinct adjustment problems therefore arise. Full employment income and equilibrium income may differ persistently depending on the behaviour of savings and of investment, and the same will apply to the natural and warranted rates. Actual and equilibrium income differ in the case of errors of foresight on the part of entrepreneurs; this point was not enlarged upon in the *General Theory*. Harrod by contrast expands on the analysis of divergences between the actual and warranted growth rates.

Since the fundamental equation $g_w = s/c$ fully determines the warranted rate, it is clear that the latter has no reason in general to coincide with the natural rate, given elsewhere in the system. Only their coincidence, purely fortuitous in Harrod's analysis, would allow regular full employment, or 'golden age' to use Joan Robinson's expression, growth. If the natural rate is lower than the warranted rate, a lasting balanced growth régime will not be possible, for want of sufficient resources. If on the other hand the natural rate exceeds the warranted rate, growth in Keynesian equilibrium is possible *a priori*, but is accompanied by an increasing rate of unemployment.

Hence, the first problem found by Harrod, the non-coincidence of the natural rate and the actual rate, follows from a formal 'over-determination' of the model, the rate of growth being determined separately by the fundamental equation and by the datum of the natural rate. Solution of this problem requires the removal of this over-determinacy, an additional variable being endogenised in the model. Thus, the capital-output ratio could be considered as a variable given factor substitution or the savings rate through the bias of changes in distribution, or the natural rate by postulating that population or technical progress adapt to the warranted rate. In the first two cases, the warranted rate adjusts to the value of the natural rate, while the adaptation is reversed in the last case. These formal solutions lead to the examination of possible regulatory mechanisms which might lead the equilibrium growth towards the steady-state golden age which sees a lasting full employment of factors.

This is an important problem and one to which we shall return, but which differs from the question of the stability of balanced growth which will now be considered.

2 Harrod's conception of instability

It has been noted, by reference to the static Keynesian case, that the warranted and actual rates may differ in the case of entrepreneurial errors in foresight. For Harrod, such a divergence is cumulative, generating a fundamental instability of balanced growth.

Let us suppose for example that entrepreneurs have underestimated the increase in effective demand resulting from their investment. They observe an actual growth in their revenue g greater than the warranted rate g_w and therefore a capital-output ratio v between the warranted ratio c. They are then induced to increase their investment and hence to accelerate the growth of income, which will have the effect of widening the gap $g - g_w$ between the actual and warranted rate. An error on the other side, through overestimation of demand, would lead to a symmetrical process of progressive reduction in growth. This is the line of argument followed by Harrod,[4] and the many attempts since made to formalise it have pointed to problems with it.[5]

Let us now consider a model which illustrates the theory of instability. Through the action of the multiplier, the rate of growth of output, g, and that of investment coincide. Entrepreneurs tend to increase investment if the marginal capital/output ratio v_t is lower than the average ratio c, and vice versa. So we have, in discrete time:

$$g_t \, (I) = g_{t-1} \, (I) + \beta(c - v_t) \text{ where } \beta > 0$$

and hence in continuous time (the limiting expression)

$$\frac{dg}{dt} = \beta \, (c - v_t) = \beta_s \Big(\frac{1}{g_w} - \frac{1}{g_t} \Big) = \beta_s \frac{(g_t - g_w)}{g_w g_t}$$

Measuring the divergence from equilibrium growth by the distance $D_t = (g_t - g_w)^2$, this result implies

$$\frac{dD}{dt} = \frac{2\beta s}{g_w g_t} \, (g_t - g_w)^2 > 0 \text{ where } g_w g_t > 0$$

Any divergence of the growth rate from the warranted rate increases cumulatively as illustrated in Figure 8.1.

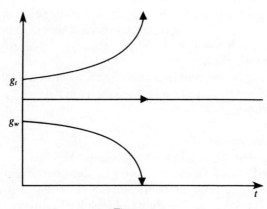

Figure 8.1

Negative growth rates are excluded by assumption, as they would imply a negative level of income. This simple model captures Harrod's main point well, that a disequilibrium observed at a point in time is translated into modification of the growth *rates* themselves, rather than just of *levels*. We shall see later, by means of a counter-example of a formalisation leading to stability, the importance of this distinction.

B The theory of automatic regulation

Paralleling discussions of the results of the short-period Keynesian model, writers such as Tobin (1955, pp. 103–15), Swan (1956, pp. 334–61) and Solow (1956, pp. 65–94) sought to develop models of growth, introducing some neoclassical assumptions. Their work, particularly that of Solow, was perceived as establishing, in opposition to Harrod, the stability of balanced growth. To this end, Solow's model integrates a description of mechanisms regulating economic growth.

1 The Solow model
The model proposed by Solow in 1956 describes in an idealised manner the workings of a market economy with a single good. Like Harrod's model, it retains the Keynesian identity of investment of savings, and the determination of savings from current income. But unlike Harrod, Solow introduces a production function with substitutable factors, and only considers situations of full employment. These assumptions underlie the model:

$$Y_t = F(K_t, N_t)$$

$$I_t = dK/dt = sY_t$$

$$N_t = N_o e^{nt}$$

Employment increases at the constant rate n, comparable with Harrod's natural rate. The production function is homogeneous of degree one and 'well-behaved'.[6] It is then possible to work in terms of relative magnitudes, all variables being expressed in values *per capita*. Thus, the following relationship is established between output *per capita* $y_t = Y_t/N_t$ and capital *per capita* $k_t = K_t/N_t$:

$$Y_t = F(k_t, 1) = f(k_t).$$

The rate of growth of capital *per capita*, k_t, is equal to the difference between the rate of growth of capital:

$$\frac{1}{K_t} \frac{dK}{dt} = \frac{sY_t}{K_t} = \frac{sY_t/N_t}{K_t/N_t} = sf(k_t)/k_t$$

and the rate of growth of population, n, so that:

$$\frac{1}{k_t}\frac{dk}{dt} = \frac{s}{k_t} f(k_t) - n \, .$$

Among the growth paths thus defined, there exist some which leave capital *per capita* k_t unchanged, so that they correspond to a stationary solution of the differential equation:

$$\frac{1}{k_t}\frac{dk}{dt} = \frac{s}{k} f(k) - n = 0$$

If $f(k)$ increases monotonically from zero, there exists a unique value of k, k^* for which this function takes on the required value $n f(k^*)/s$, as in Figure 8.2:

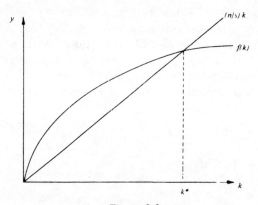

Figure 8.2

Notice that k^*n represents investment *per capita*, so that nk^*/s is effective demand per head resulting from the action of the multiplier, $f(k^*)$ denoting the output per head attainable as a function of the production possibilities. Solow's equilibrium condition may be interpreted in terms of equalisation of aggregate supply and demand, or of savings and investment. It constitutes a special case of Harrod's model in which the capital-output ratio c takes the value $k^*/f(k^*)$ and the warranted rate the value $sf(k^*)/k^*$.

At this stage, we have an answer to the first problem set by Harrod: there exists a steady-state balanced-growth regime at the natural rate which ensures the maintenance of full employment: the flexibility of the capital-output ratio enables the warranted rate to take on any value, and in particular to adapt itself to the value of the natural rate.

2 The stability of the Solow model

Solow inquires into the stability of golden age growth (steady-state full employment equilibrium) whose possibility he established. This stability may be understood in terms of restoration of the natural rate of growth, of the capital-output ratio or of capital per person. These indicators being equivalent, let us retain the last, which leads to the most convenient expressions to deal with.

Under the assumptions of the model, the behaviour of capital per person is governed by the differential equation:

$$dk/dt = s f(k) - nk,$$

which of course is zero for k^*, the golden age solution. For a lower value of capital per person, $k < k^*$, dk/dt is positive because of the concavity of the production function. Similarly for $k > k^*$, capital per person is decreasing. The behaviour of an economy subject to the assumptions of Solow's model may then be represented as in Figure 8.3

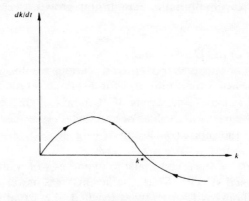

Figure 8.3

This stability is global in the sense that convergence is found starting from any state of the economy representable by the model. The mechanism ensuring this stability is the flexibility of the capital-output ratio. If the latter is too low, the effective growth of capital per person $sf(k)$ exceeds the investment warranted by growth at the natural rate nk. Such an adjustment assumes the action of relative prices guiding the decisions of entrepreneurs to coincide with this movement. Yet, in this first formulation, prices are not explicitly introduced. Implicitly, it is allowed that they adjust instantly so as to realise everywhere equilibrium in markets for labour, goods and services.

C The debate over stability: unreal problem and real question

Following Solow's contribution, the conventional presentation of the problem of the stability of balanced growth rested on the conflict between a 'neoclassical' theory favouring stability and a Keynesian theory hostile to it, apart from long-term regulation through the savings rate. Similarly, it was held that this qualitative difference could be explained by the respective assumptions of factor substitution, made by Solow, and of fixed proportions, adopted by Harrod. Belief in a technological regularity tended to mark out two distinct schools and the basic issue – that of the capacity of a capitalist economy for self-regulation – found itself confined to this very particular aspect.

In fact, it is not exactly correct to oppose the Harrod and Solow models as leading to conflicting conclusions regarding the stability of growth. Harrod's case for instability may be contested, while in a certain sense, Solow's model may be shown to be unstable. From this study it will emerge that the two models possess fundamentally the same stability, in equilibrium dynamics, and share the same instability, in dynamics out of equilibrium: equilibrium growth occurs 'along the razor's edge'.

1 The stability of the Harrod model

Formalisations of Harrod's model led to various results. Some, such as that outlined above, support the case for instability.[7] Others end up with a complicated typology, the types of evolution of the economy being governed by the particular values of parameters (see Allen, 1967). Still others (such as the subtle conclusion of Jorgenson, 1960) conclude that equilibrium is stable.

It should first be observed that the hypothesis of a macroeconomic production function with fixed coefficients was never proposed by Harrod, for whom, as Eisner (1958) recalled, the actual rigidity of the capital-output ratio resulted from monetary factors, from the downward rigidity of the rate of interest. The argument is probably best adapted to a Keynesian situation of persistent unemployment. It remains true, however, that on the first point, the usual presentation should be corrected.

The reappraisal of the Harrodian conception of instability stems from the following idea: the Keynesian vision of an economy motivated by investment decisions, and therefore based on the expectations of entrepreneurs, does not in itself imply this instability, which Harrod introduced by a particular specification of these expectations, at the price of some confusion between a line of reasoning in magnitudes and one in terms of rates.

Like Harrod, this writer has growth determined unilaterally by entrepreneurs, and desired investment always realised. However, he assumes the expected rate of growth to be equal to the warranted rate: this is clearly an assumption excessively favourable to stability but not contradictory with Keynesian theory which made no systematic distinction between the equilibrium level of income and effective demand, the concepts analogous to the warranted rate and expected rate.

More generally, in the absence of this assumption of perfect expectations, it is very Keynesian to propose that the expected rate of growth corresponds to some *a priori* idea of the normal long-term rate of growth and is not sensitive to current variations in the actual rates.[8] Harrod by contrast connects the expected rate to current disequilibria, and reinforces this link with a confusion in his reasoning between level and rate. Indeed, Harrod's original article mentioned above showed that the gap between the desired and actual capital stocks must increase in absolute value, but that is not sufficient to show that this gap need grow in relative size, and that the actual and warranted growth rates must diverge. The stability at issue, christened by Jorgenson as 'stability in the sense of Harrod', is in fact a case of relative stability and requires the convergence of rates, not of magnitudes. The following model, compared with that set out in the first paragraph, will illustrate its special characteristics by showing the possibility of a stable Harrodian model.

The investment function is now derived from levels alone, with growth expectations held static

$$I_t = \Delta K_t = \beta(K_t^* - K_t) + c \, \widetilde{\Delta Y} = [\beta(c - V_t) + c \, \widetilde{g}_{t+1}] \, Y_t \, ; \, 0 < \beta < 1$$

where V_t is the average capital-output ratio, and $\widetilde{\Delta Y}$ and $\widetilde{g}_{t+1}$ are respectively the increase in and expected rate of growth of output. Thus the investment function includes a correction factor for the gap between desired and actual capital stock together with a term for expected growth. We can derive:

$$\frac{\Delta V}{V_t} = \frac{\Delta K}{K_t} - \frac{\Delta Y}{Y_t} = \frac{\beta \, (c - V_t)}{V_t} + \frac{c}{V_t} \, \widetilde{g}_{t+1} - g_t$$

and hence, assuming static expectations ($\widetilde{g}_{t+1} = g_t$)

$$\frac{\Delta V}{V_t} = \frac{(c - V_t)}{V_t} \, (\beta + g_t)$$

If the departure from equilibrium is given by the (squared) distance $D_t = (c - V_t)^2$ we have

$$\frac{dD}{dt} = -2(c - V_t)\frac{dV}{dt} = -2\frac{(c - V_t)^2}{V_t}(\beta + g_t) < 0$$

which proves convergence towards the warranted growth-path.

In the model expressed in terms of levels, it is clear that the assumption of static expectations is not necessary for stability. The same result would hold in general for perfect or self-fulfilling expectations. It would equally be possible to suppose that entrepreneurs anticipate growth at the warranted rate, as Rose (1959) suggested.

The convention in the model of Hahn and Matthews, seems to correspond in spirit with Harrod's ideas, and serves to illustrate this idea that an adjustment towards the desired level of the capital stock is treated by entrepreneurs as a variation in the anticipated rate of growth. The resulting overadaptation becomes the mechanism generating instability. By trying to adjust their capital stock, insufficient in relation to demand, too quickly, entrepreneurs will cause via the multiplier a more than proportionate growth in income and in demand which will amplify the initial imbalance. It is accepted that assumptions of slower adjustment, of wiser expectations or of a multiplier effect strung out in time could suppress this overadaptation and ensure stability. It is accepted that thinking in terms of rates leads to the coming into prominence of an overadjustment which is certainly possible, but only in a particular configuration of the parameters expressing the sensitivity of expectations.

It therefore seems possible to conclude that the stability of growth at the warranted rate is likely in the case where long-term expectations are 'close' to the warranted rate and relatively insensitive to current variations in the pattern of growth, as well as the adjustment of capital stock being moderate in its rate. Stability becomes problematical when one departs from these conditions, and instability prevails in the Harrodian world in which expectations magnify current disequilibria affecting rates of growth.

2 Instability of neoclassical growth

To the assertion of the stability of balanced growth which seems to follow immediately from the 'neoclassical' assumption of factor substitutability, three objections are raised: firstly, only a relative stability, or stability in the Harrod sense, has been established; secondly, dynamic stability in equilibrium only has been established, hence not opposable to Harrod's system; lastly and above all, it actually appears that in disequilibrium dynamics neoclassical growth is unstable.

Going back to the first part, Deardorff (1970) has shown that Solow's model, although it produced asymptotic convergence of the rates of growth of output, capital and employment, did not exclude a gap increasing in absolute size between actual and equilibrium values. Thus, starting from an actual ratio k below the desired level k^*, the ratio of increments in capital to increments in labour, dK/dN, remains below the equilibrium ratio, which casts new doubt on the adjustment paths conceived by Solow in terms of isoquants (Figure 8.4).

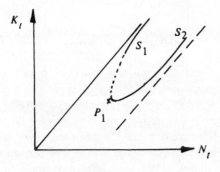

Figure 8.4

The paths S_1 postulated by Solow, which would imply perfect stability, are not feasible. Only paths of the type S_2, along which the incremental ratio $(dK/dt)/(dN/dt)$ moves towards the equilibrium ratio k^* and thus by the same token the average ratio K_t/N_t, are possible. Such paths S_2 run asymptotically to a time parallel to the ray $K_t = k^*N_t$, not to this ray itself, and the distance $K_t - K^*_t$, as K^*_t is measured right along k^*N_t, never decreases.

In the second case, it should be noted that the Solow model only deals with situations of equilibrium, albeit temporary, but featuring none the less an equality of supply and demand in current prices in all markets. In this respect, as Hahn and Matthews observe (loc. cit.), it clearly derives from equilibrium dynamics, being concerned with the possible convergence of equilibrium paths towards particular steady states such as the golden age. One particularly strong condition is that this model assumes realisation of full employment at all points. We can therefore see that these results cannot be opposed to those of Harrod, whose analytical approach differs on more fundamental matters than the properties of the production function.

It is essentially this fact which underlies the property of razor's-edge growth obtained by Harrod, then for the Solow model by Kurz.

The two models differ, however, in the definitions of the domain of stability which they incorporate. This domain is defined in terms of a configuration of the implicit prices of capital, capital per person for Solow in terms of rates of correction of expectations and, for Harrod, of adjustment of capital. This serves well to show that the essential difference between the models lies in the locus of operation of the assumed regulation, which for Solow is in market and price mechanisms, and for Harrod in the internal logic of entrepreneurial behaviour. Having thus refined the analysis, we are brought to the heart of the debate between Keynesians and neoclassicals.

2 REGULATION THROUGH THE STRUCTURE OF PRODUCTION

The traditional discussion of the Harrod model brought out the possibilities for regulation which flexibility of the capital-output ratio represents for an economy. The neoclassical assumptions of substitutability in response to changes in factor prices illustrate one type of flexibility of the structure of production at the aggregate level.

It might be held, however, that this is but an initial impression of production which needs to be expanded by taking account of a plurality of productive sectors and, in addition, of a range of generations of capital incorporating the technology of successive periods.

In each case, models have been constructed to enable exploration of the main implications of the means of adjustment of the productive structure being considered.

A Growth and stability in a two-sector economy

The distinction between two sectors, one producing investment goods[9] and the other consumption goods, puts in doubt the possibility of a global production function possessing the properties usually assumed by neoclassical writers. However, paralleling work on the Samuelson pseudo-production function, the two-sector assumption has been used in the construction of growth models, in particular by H. Uzawa (1961, p. 40).

It should incidentally be noted that the schemes of reproduction presented by Marx, with their two productive sections, already derived from a bisectoral model, also developed in this century by Feldman (Domar, 1957, chapter IX) and Mahalonobis (1953).[10]

In addition, pre-Keynesian theories of fluctuations often had recourse to a bisectoral logic of analysis, for example by insisting on the uneven progress of prices over the cycle.

Modern two-sector models appear as extensions of the neoclassical model as much in their assumptions as in their view of balanced growth and its stability.

1 Representation of the economy

Following Uzawa, ideas have been focused on a model which directly generalises Solow's own model and so retains the main neoclassical assumptions.

Thus, in the 'machines' sector, as in that of consumption goods, production occurs through smooth neoclassical production functions,

$$Y_M = F_M(K_m, N_m) \text{ and } Y_C = F_C(K_C, N_C).$$

These functions, being homogeneous of degree one, can be rewritten in terms of output per head $(y = Y/N)$ and capital per head $(k = K/N)$:

$$y_m = f_m(k_m) \quad \text{and} \quad y_c = f_c(k_c).$$

A virtual assumption here is that of perfect mobility of factors, in particular capital, between the productive sectors. Given this, it may be conceded that competitive prices lead to a continuing reallocation of factors so as to hold equal the values of marginal product in the two sectors.[11] At full employment, there being equilibrium in factor markets, incomes equal the respective marginal productivities. Taking the consumption good as numéraire and writing P for the price of the capital good, this gives, for the rate of profit r:

$$r = \partial F_c/\partial K_c = \partial f_c/\partial k_c = (P\partial F_m/\partial K_m) = (P\partial f_m/\partial k_m);$$

and for the wage w:

$$w = \partial F_c/\partial N_c = P\partial F_m/\partial N_m.$$

But given the assumption of constant returns to scale, wages may equally well be found as the difference between output per head and profits per head,

$$w = y_c - k_c \ \partial f_c/\partial k_c = [P y_m - k_m \ \partial f_m/\partial k_c].$$

The physical depreciation of capital follows the same rule in each sector, say a constant rate δ.

These assumptions regarding technology and distribution must be completed by making explicit the behaviour of savings and of investment. Several examples could be explored regarding savings behaviour; in any case, that most frequently found in this context is the case called 'extreme classical' of total saving of profits and total consumption of wages. Investment is taken as in Solow's model to be determined by the total available savings. The identity $I = S$ is hence assumed always to be satisfied in the model. So:

$$Y_c = w(N_c + N_M)$$
$$Y_M = I = r(K_c + K_M).$$

The nature of this model may therefore be clearly seen. Like Solow's basic neoclassical model, equilibrium on the goods and factor markets is presupposed and as a result we are squarely and deliberately placed in a methodological context of equilibrium dynamics.

2 Balanced growth and steady state

The assumptions set out above determine each state of the economy as a situation of equilibrium in different markets. The model therefore represents growth as a succession of temporary equilibria, that is, equilibria at a point of time dependent on the conditions bequeathed by the previous period, in particular the capital stock.

When this evolution is connected over time, it constitutes a balanced growth path. Under unchanged exogenous conditions, this continuity is manifest in the invariance of characteristic variables, and a steady state.

In the context of a multi-sector model, we discussed the notion, of wide applicability, of a causal explanation of economic growth. Application of the principle of causality stipulates that the behaviour of the economy would be entirely determined, starting from given initial conditions, by its operational rules as described by a system of equations.[12]

Since the pre-existing conditions and the operational rules are translated at each instant into a temporary equilibrium, the following result can be seen intuitively:[13]

The uniqueness of temporary equilibrium is a necessary and sufficient condition for causal determinacy.

The assumptions outlined above allow a more precise description of steady state growth which, as in Solow's model, is characterised by the constancy of capital *per capita*.

The rate of growth of capital dK/dt is equal to net savings:

$$dK/dt = Y_M - \delta K.$$

Incorporating the assumptions governing savings and distribution,

$$dK/dt = r K/p - dK = K \cdot \partial f_m/\partial k_m - \delta K,$$

In getting to the rate of growth, and deducting the rate of growth of the population n, we obtain the expression for the rate of growth of capital *per capita*:

$$(1/k)(dk/dt) = (1/K)(dK/dt) - n = (\partial f_m/\partial k_m) - (d + n).$$

The growth of capital *per capita* is equal to the difference between the marginal physical productivity of capital in the machines sector and the sum of the natural rate of growth of the population and the depreciation rate. When this expression becomes zero, capital per head and consequently marginal productivities themselves remain constant, thus defining a steady state growth régime.

The condition for steady state growth is written:

$$dk/k\,dt = 0 \quad \Rightarrow \quad \partial f_m/\partial k_m = n + d$$

$$\text{or} \quad \partial f_m/\partial k_m - d = n.$$

The net marginal productivity of capital in the capital goods sector is equal to the natural rate of growth.

It might seem surprising that technical progress does not figure explicitly in this model of growth. In fact, this factor may be introduced without modification, if it takes the 'labour-augmenting', or Harrod-neutral, form. It then occurs as an increase in the efficiency of the labour-force, and the natural rate must then be viewed as the sum of the physical increase of the population and the rate of increase in its efficiency.

3 The stability of growth
The similarity of these assumptions with those of the Solow model suggests that the problem of stability may be set in the same terms, that is by distinguishing an equilibrium dynamics – concerned with the convergence of a sequence of temporary equilibria towards the steady state – and a disequilibrium dynamics, concerned with the stability of the equilibrium paths themselves. The first problem is less complicated and has been more fully studied. In respect of the second, only general indications will be given.

As compared with the single-sector model, the distinction of two sectors introduces an element of flexibility tending to facilitate regulation through greater pliability of the structure of production. At the same time, though, this distinction complicates the operation of the regulatory mechanisms. In effect, a new variable is introduced, the relative price of capital goods in terms of consumption, whose movements lead not only, as in the 're-switching' model, to perverse revaluing effects, but also to factor reallocations between the two sectors which can overcompensate for an initial disturbance and turn out as a result to be disequilibrating.

The best known, sufficient but not necessary, condition for stability of the steady state is that the consumption goods sector be more capital-intensive than the capital goods sector (in our notation, $k_c > k_m$). This condition may be justified by the following line of reasoning:

Starting from a steady state growth at the rate n, where capital per person k is constant in the two sectors, let us suppose that one exogenous shock destroys part of the capital in each sector: k_c and k_m are then below their steady-state values and so $\delta f_m / \delta k_m$ is greater than $n + d$. k will increase globally, which in the single-sector model would suffice to bring the system back to equilibrium. Here, it is necessary to be sure that the rise in k actually increases capital per person in the capital goods sector k_m, so that $\delta f_m / \delta k_m$ falls and growth slows down to rejoin the natural rate n.

It would be conceivable that new investment could go entirely into the consumption goods sector, or even be accompanied by a relative transfer of capital to this sector which made k_m fall. However, since the equality of values of marginal productivity must be preserved, such a transfer can only occur if the price of capital goods, P, falls so as to maintain the condition:

$$r = \partial f_c / \partial k_c = P \, \partial f_m / \partial k_m \, ,$$

with k_m decreasing and k_c increasing. In order to exclude this perverse case, it is sufficient that the capital goods sector be less capital-intensive $(k_c > k_m)$. Indeed, in this case, the increase in k and hence in the ratio of factor costs w/r, raises the price of labour-intensive capital goods relative to the price of capital-intensive consumption goods. It is then certain that acceleration of investment increasing k, and hence w/r, increases P, which excludes a transfer of capital towards the consumption-goods sector. Hence k_m also rises, $\delta f_m / \delta k_m$ falls and the rate of growth of capital converges towards the natural rate.

It is clear from the arguments just set out that this is merely a sufficient condition. Solow (1961) remarked that it would be most surprising if stability were to depend on the chance satisfaction of a technological condition.[14] Further conditions, indeed, were eventually established, ruled by the principle that there should exist a sufficient degree of substitutability between the two sectors.

Analysis of dynamic stability out of equilibrium is more complicated. Inada (1964) did study the cyclical properties of two-sector models, and

synthetic models have been presented by Stiglitz and Uzawa (1969), as
well as by Hahn and Matthews (1972).

The most interesting studies of disequilibrium have, however,
been performed in the context of multisectoral models, notably by
D. Jorgenson and F. Hahn. The fecundity of these approaches results
from integrating the dynamics of prices and quantities.

Working in the framework of dynamic Leontief models, Solow (1953)
was to assert and Jorgenson (1960) to demonstrate a property of dual
instability of prices and quantities.

Prices being defined as dual variables associated with a system of
quantities, Jorgenson shows that stability of the quantity system implies
instability of the price system, and conversely (see also Burmeister and
Dobell, op. cit.). Roughly speaking, one could say that this result
integrates as alternative solutions of a general model the Harrodian case
of quantity instability and the Wicksellian case of instability of the price
system. Of course, this result requires more restrictive assumptions in
an open model, or in one including factor substitution, but it shows the
general impossibility of a 'causal', or deterministic, balanced evolution
starting from arbitrary initial conditions.

Stability requires either very special initial conditions or, more
relevant to analysis of reality, more flexible, non-deterministic modes of
regulation.

F. Hahn's analysis again rests on the relationship between dual
variables and competitive prices. It points up the very general risk
of instability of growth of a multisectoral economy with myopic
expectations. His analysis was later transposed by Kurz to the single-
sector case, to show up the instability of Solow's model.

Thus, discussion of the complications introduced by considering two
or more sectors, by leading to a better integration of price and quantity
dynamics, allowed a more detailed investigation of the instability of
competitive balanced growth paths, contradicting the belief that the
neoclassical approach would offer only analysis supporting the hypothesis of stability.

B Models with generations of capital

The inclusion of technical progress leads to differentiation of generations of capital by age and hence by productive efficiency. In fact,
this assumption has very different implications depending whether
substitution for existing equipment is (putty-putty models) or is not
(clay-clay or putty-putty models) allowed. In the putty-putty case, it is
possible to compensate fully for obsolescence by reducing the quantity

of labour applied to the older generations of capital. Thus, each generation remains in use indefinitely, with a lower and lower amount of employment and output associated with it. In this model, no fundamental modification is made relative to Solow's neoclassical model.

On the other hand, in the case of fixed coefficients on the generations already in use, it is impossible to compensate for obsolescence and equipment has a finite longevity T. A new sort of problem is then introduced. Domar (1957) had already suggested the possibility of regulating growth by making capital redundant. Models with generations of capital allow this idea to be made precise.

The exposition will relate mainly to the 'clay-clay' assumptions, for which a model will be set out with its mechanisms and properties. The special features of a 'putty-clay' model will then be set out.

1 The clay-clay model

The clay-clay specification corresponds to the case of fixed coefficients both at the time of installation of the equipment and during its utilisation. It was studied initially by Solow, Tobin, Weiszacker and Yaari (1966) in a piece of work one of whose objectives was to show that factor substitution was not a necessary condition for the construction of a neoclassical model of growth.

We shall present the components of a model of this type in sequence.

(a) *Employment and productive capacity* – The average productivity at time t of the labour applied to a vintage installed at time v will be denoted $A(v,t)$. Also, the number of labour units at work on that generation's equipment will be written $B(v,t)$. Total employment is found by summing over generations of capital:

$$N_t = \sum_{v=t-T}^{t} B(v,t) I_v,$$

as is productive capacity

$$Y_t = \sum_{t=t-T}^{t} A(v,t) \; B(v,t) \; I_v.$$

(b) *The rule for capital retirements* – For a wage-rate in terms of output W_t, each unit of working equipment brings in a quasi-rent, the excess of its average productivity per unit of labour over the real wage

$$R(v,t) = A(v,t) - w_t \, B(v,t).$$

As the sequence of $A(v,t)$ terms increases monotonically, this quasi-rent falls as the age of the vintage increases (Figure 8.5).

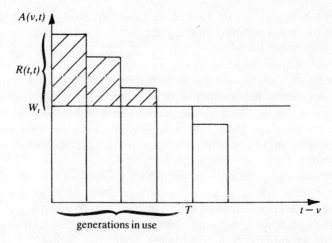

Figure 8.5

It is then clear that equipment must be retired when $A(v,t) \leq w_t B(v,t)$, the condition which determines the economic life of capital, T. Alternatively, if T is known, this condition determines the wage.

(c) The rule for savings and investment – As in the Solow model, investment is determined by the available savings:

$$I_t = S_t = s Y_t .$$

However, this model does include an investment decision rule. The discounted value of the quasi-rents must equal the supply price of capital goods (identically equal to one, since there is only one good in the economy).

$$\sum_{t=v}^{v+T} R(v,t)/(1+r)^{v-t} = p_k(v) = 1.$$

Since it is assumed that the investment thus determined is in equilibrium $(I = S)$, this equation defines an actuarial rate of return, or interest rate of the system, which replaces the rate of profit, which in itself would have no meaning here as no single stock of capital can be defined. Since $R(t,v)$ decreases with W_t increasing, so does the rate of return r. Hence we can define a decreasing function $r(W)$, the factor price frontier in the clay-clay model.

We shall further assume that the labour force grows at an exogenous, 'natural' rate n, so $L_t = L_o (1 + n)^t$, and that there exists an autonomous demand which generates a total demand D_t, to be compared in each period with the productive capacity Y_t.

2 The workings of the model

As the rigidity of technical combinations prevents adjustments by capital *per capita k*, the model may incorporate various modes of operation, according to the exact constraint prevailing in the period under consideration. Three regimes are to be considered: the cases of excess labour supply, of full employment and of Keynesian under-employment.

(*a*) *Under excess labour supply* – The accumulated generations of capital remaining operational do not offer enough jobs to employ the whole working population. The wage, given exogenously according to the Ricardian hypothesis of a subsistence wage, lies below the average productivity of the last surviving generation. Such a system of operation may be illustrated by the diagram, Figure 8.6

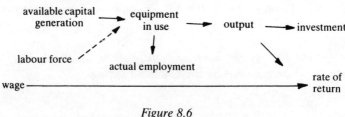

Figure 8.6

This regime will terminate if the rate of growth of the number of jobs created by investment exceeds persistently the growth of the population.

(*b*) *Under full employment* – Under this regime, the number of jobs still warranted by the capital bequests exceeds the labour supply available. Actual employment is then equal to this supply, which determines the number of jobs actually provided, and so the economic life of capital and the wage rate, equal to the mean productivity of labour applied to the generation at the margin. Longevity of capital and wage-rate finally determine the rate of return.

The diagram for the causal relationship between the variables of the model is then as in Figure 8.7.

(*c*) *Under Keynesian underemployment* – Under this regime, full employment cannot be attained because of the insufficiency of demand.

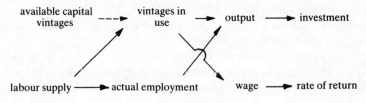

Figure 8.7

Autonomous demand then determines output through the Keynesian multiplier mechanism; the productive capacity required determines the number of generations of capital in use and so the economic life of capital, the volume of employment and wages, as the following schematic diagram (Figure 8.8) indicates:

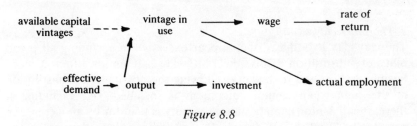

Figure 8.8

The clay-clay vintage model thus offers a logical framework in which to analyse very different régimes.

3 Properties of the growth paths
The dynamic analysis of an economy represented by the clay-clay model is complicated. None the less, Solow, Tobin, Yaari and Weiszacker found out various properties of existence, stability and comparative dynamics of the model.

In the first place, the existence of at least one full-employment steady-state growth path, given that technical progress is labour-augmenting (Harrod-neutral), was shown. The rate of growth of output and of investment is then equal to the natural rate $n + \mu$, where n denotes the rate of growth of the labour force and μ the rate of growth of labour productivity. All along the path, the longevity of capital is constant, as is the rate of return, and the wage increases at the rate along with labour productivity.

The stability of this steady state is guaranteed in dynamic equilibrium. The authors just cited, indeed, showed that for $1 > s > (n + \mu) \, K/Y$, the growth-paths considered, in equilibrium by assumption, converge asymptotically towards the steady state. We do not have precise enough results for disequilibrium dynamics, but it may be taken for granted that the model exhibits a saddle point property and is then unstable in the sense discussed above (p. 230).

The comparative dynamic analysis consists in comparing steady-state paths with each other. It can be shown that $\delta T/\delta s < 0$, $\delta T/\delta r > 0$ and $\delta T/\delta w_t < 0$; the economic (or) profitable life of capital falls when the propensity to save s increases, since the reallocation of the labour force towards newer vintages is hastened. If the rate of interest increases, and therefore also the equilibrium rate of return to maintain the equality of supply price and demand price for investment, the quasi-rents must be higher, so that the number T of vintages yielding positive quasi-rents is increased. Finally, if the wage-rate increases, all other things being equal, the opposite effect is obtained; the quasi-rents are reduced, and T falls.

4 The putty-clay assumption

The clay-clay hypothesis may appear excessive in excluding all possibility of substitution. Thus, the putty-clay assumption offers a more flexible and general framework, allowing the possibility of substitution at the time when capital equipment is installed, but excluding it thereafter.[15] Unfortunately, this generality is paid for by an increase in complexity. Two points are worth developing, since they mark the principal differences with the clay-clay case: they are the choice of techniques, and a less precise determination of the properties of the model.

The capital-intensity of new capital goods is determined by the maximisation of quasi-rents with respect to capital *per capita* and to the expected optimal life-span of capital.[16] Indeed, the more capital-intensive a generation is, the greater the average productivity of labour applied to it and so the longer that productivity will continue to exceed the wage-rate.

It can be shown that the result of this optimisation depends not only on the current wage-rate and rate of interest, but also on the expected increase in wages over the life-cycle of capital goods. The marginal productivity of capital must be equal to a user cost defined as follows:

$$u_t = (r + d + \beta - \gamma) P_K / (1 - \tau)$$

where d is the rate of depreciation of capital goods; β the rate of labour-augmenting technical progress (non-embodied); γ the rate of growth of wages, and τ the net tax-rate.

The putty-clay model brings out the two forms of capital-labour substitution occurring during growth: substitution at the extensive margin through replacement of old equipment by newer, more capital-intensive generations; and substitution at the intensive margin by increasing the capital-output ratio when new generations are installed. This model therefore constitutes an irreplaceable tool for a comprehensive study of substitution in the long run.

One must guard against the intuitive reasoning, that an increase in wages should lead to a greater degree of substitution and shortening of capital life-span in the putty-clay model. On the contrary, if the rise in wages is anticipated, substitution at the extensive margin will be reduced and retirement of capital slowed down.

While much of econometric work on the putty-clay hypothesis tests for indirect implication, an attempt at direct estimation carried out for France in the period 1952–75 gives some idea of the order of magnitude of the various substitution effects: for every 2.5 jobs which would have been created with unchanged 1952 technology, only one actually was created, one disappearing through substitution at the extensive margin and 0.5 at the intensive margin (shortening of longevity) (Hénin, p. 93).

In view of its technical complexity, it is not possible to deduce *a priori* all the properties of growth paths in the putty-clay model. Thus the effect of variations in the interest rate remains indeterminate. The stability of the model depends on assumptions made about expectations: Bliss (1968) has them perfect, while Kemp and Thanh (1966) use stationary expectations. For dynamic disequilibrium, it would seem in vain to hope for analytical results, and preferable to proceed by simulation.

3 REGULATION THROUGH THE SAVINGS RATE

The Harrodian equation $g = s/v$, suggests that an element of adaptability may reside in flexibility of the aggregate savings rate s, an increase in s raising the warranted rate g_w, and conversely. In the spirit of neoclassical theory, this flexibility would be obtained directly through the medium of the rate of interest, but we have seen that Solow's model includes the assumption of a given constant propensity to consume. Flexibility of the savings rate has in fact been discussed in the context of two very different sorts of model: 'Cambridge' models in which the behaviour of savings differs according to the type of income or social class; and growth models incorporating money, constructed in a neoclassical framework.

A Cambridge-type models with differential savings behaviour

The idea of a savings rate flexible in response to changes in the distribution of income was considered by Hobson, by Kalecki and by Keynes himself.[17] It was developed by post-Keynesian writers in the Cambridge mould, in particular by Kaldor and Pasinetti. From this viewpoint, it is important still to distinguish clearly two principles of differentiating: according to type of income – wages and profits – and according to social class.

1 Savings behaviour differentiated by type of income
The implications for a growth model of a propensity to consume different for profits and for wages were principally explored by Kaldor in a series of studies presented between 1957 and 1962. Kaldor's approach proposes short-run dynamics based on the relationship between profits and accumulation, while long-term dynamics are dominated by technological factors.

(a) The relationship between profits and accumulation – We know that one way of looking at the Keynesian multiplier is to consider how this mechanism generates the levels of income and savings needed to realise the condition $I = S$. Kaldor transposes this method to show how a given rate of accumulation requires a certain rate of profit to finance it. Let s_w and s_π be the propensities to save respectively from wages and from profits, with $0 < s_w < s_\pi < 1$.

$$S = s_w Y + (s_\pi - s_w) \pi$$

which gives for $I = S$, bringing in the rate of profit

$$\pi/K = [I/K - s_w Y/K] /(s_\pi - s_w)$$

Kaldor assumes that I/K and Y/K can be taken as given exogenously in this equation, which therefore would determine the rate of profit. A special case, assumed notably by Joan Robinson, is that in which s_w is zero, with all savings made out of profits:

$$\pi/K = (1/s_\pi) I/K.$$

Mrs Robinson also integrates this relationship into a system of interaction between accumulation and distribution. To achieve this, she assumes that the rate of accumulation is itself a function of the rate of profit, tracing the curve φ in Figure 8.9:

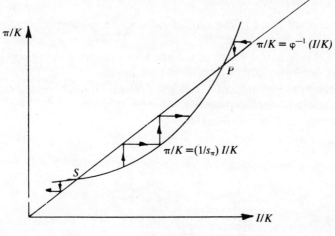

Figure 8.9

The points of intersection S and P correspond respectively to an unstable and a stable equilibrium. Between S and P the actual rate of profit is greater than that required, and accumulation accelerates, while the opposite occurs outside the segment SP.

Mrs Robinson completes these basic results by investigating the choices of techniques and, more originally, showing two boundaries to the possible evolutions: a subsistence constraint representing a minimal supply of consumption goods and an inflationary boundary beyond which any increase in the desired rate of accumulation degenerates into inflation because of resistance by wage-earners to any increase in the share of profits. Nevertheless, Mrs Robinson declines to construct a closed model leading to a unique solution. By contrast, Kaldor does determine the long-term growth path as a function of technological constraints.

(*b*) *Existence and stability of a steady state* – We have already seen how Kaldor, rejecting the neoclassical method of integrating technical progress into a production function, had aimed to provide a more general representation with his technical progress function, whose equation is, to a linear approximation:

$$g_y = a + b g_k.$$

From this, a steady state growth path is obtained for $g_y = g_k$, so that:

$$g_y = a/(1-b), \text{ the rate of growth of output per head}$$

and

$g_Y = n + a/(1 - b)$, the rate of growth of total output or of capital

where n denotes the growth in volume terms of the working population and $a/(1 - b)$ the rate of growth of productivity.

Accumulation introduces a multiplier effect, $1/(1 - b)$ on the rate a of non-embodied technical progress. Figure 8.10 illustrates the long-period equilibrium, and its possible stability.

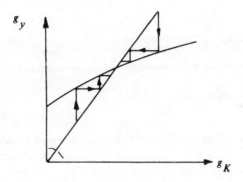

Figure 8.10   Dynamics of the Kaldor model

The stability of the steady state in Kaldor's model appeals to the accumulation-distribution relationship examined above. Kaldor includes an investment function of the form:

$$g_K = g_Y + 1 / (\alpha + \beta\pi/K) \qquad d(\pi/K)/dt$$

The first term leads to a 'stepwise' pattern of adjustment along the technical progress function represented in Figure 8.10. The second term stands for the indirect effect occurring through variations in the rate of profit. This effect exerts a stabilising influence if it tends to increase the rate of growth of capital when this lies below g_y, and vice versa. Convergence towards the steady state is then assured.

Even if the indirect effect is destabilising, convergence may still be maintained if the direct effect dominates. Furthermore Kaldor, in response to a paper by Kubota (1970) challenging the stability of his model, asserted that under his assumptions, the indirect effect is always stabilising. The stability of steady states in Kaldor's model would then be assured.

Notice that Kaldor's model preserves the Harrod duality in growth rates. The steady-state rate of growth, $n + a/(1 - b)$, corresponds to the definition of the natural rate, while changes in distribution allow the warranted rate to be brought to this level, the only one compatible with long-run balanced growth. In Kaldor's (1955) words,

> Hence the 'warranted' and the 'natural' rates of growth are not independent of one another; if profit margins are flexible the former will adjust itself to the latter through a consequential change in π/Y.

2 Savings behaviour differentiated by social class: the Pasinetti model

The drawback with Kaldor's models, which postulate a differentiation of savings rates by source of income, is that they ignore the fact that some capital is held by wage-earners, resulting from their contribution to savings. Accordingly, Pasinetti has explored the assumption of savings behaviour differentiated by social class rather than by source of income, introducing it into a model which otherwise retains all the features of that of Solow (Pasinetti, 1962).

Total capital $K = K_c + K_w$ is held by the capitalists and wage-earners. By dividing each term through the whole population, one gets $k = k_w + k_c$. Capital is paid its marginal productivity $r = f'_k$, hence the value for the wage rate:

$$w = f(k) - kf'_k$$

The total savings of each class is then

$$S_c = s_c f' K_c$$

$$S_w = s_w N[f(k) - k_c f'_k]$$

from which we obtain the differential equations describing the growth of the stock of capital held by each class:

$$d k_c/dt = [s_c f'_k - n] k_c \, ,$$

$$dk_w/dt = s_w [f(k) - f'_k k_c] - nk_w \, .$$

A long run steady state equilibrium is obtained for k^*_c and k^*_w constant, so that by setting the above equations to zero and regrouping terms,

$$k^*_c f'_k = n/s_c \ k^*_c \, ,$$

$$f(k^*) = k^*_c f'_k + k^*_w \ n/s_w = n(k^*_c/s_c + k^*_w/s_w).$$

Solving these equations leads to two distinct solutions. The first may be satisfied for $f'_k = n/s_c$ or for $k^*_c = 0$.

This first case was the only one studied by Pasinetti, while Samuelson and Modigliani (1966) explored the second solution.

(a) *Pasinetti's solution* – The fundamental equation in this case is

$$f'_k \text{ or } r = n/s_c$$

meaning that in the final analysis, the rate of profit is determined by the rate of growth and the savings behaviour of capitalists only. This is a traditional proposition of the Cambridge School, since Kalecki, but now deduced in the framework of a model which retains most of the neoclassical assumptions.

(b) *The 'anti-Pasinetti' solution* – In this case, $k^*_c = 0$, and all the variables of the system are determined by the second equation. The logic of this solution is simple. Asymptotically, the share of the capitalists disappears and all capital is held by wage-earners. We then return to a model with a single class – in effect, to Solow's model. The second equation becomes:

$$f'(k^*) = n\, k^*_w / s_w .$$

Thus there exist two long-term solutions for the economy described by the model. Either the two classes coexist and each own capital (the Pasinetti case), but then only the savings behaviour of capitalists affects distribution and growth; or wage-earners gradually acquire all capital (the anti-Pasinetti case) and their behaviour governs the evolution of the economy which, in consequence, contains only a single class.

The anti-Pasinetti case occurs if the rate of increase of K_w begins to exceed that of K_c, the capital held by the capitalists, since K_w then becomes infinitely large relative to K_c in the long term. It can be shown that the critical condition for this result is that:

$$s_w \geq s_c\, rk / f(k) .$$

The maximum savings of wage-earners (occurring if they received all of the income) then exceeds the maximum savings of the capitalists (if they held all capital and received the whole of profits).

B Introduction of money and financial assets

The models of growth so far considered dealt only with the real aspects of the economy. Reference to monetary factors therein is implicit only, as in the Harrod case. Construction of a model involving money was achieved by J. Tobin in 1965. However, the restrictive character of this first model quickly became apparent and further work attempted either to incorporate more fully the functions of money, or to adopt a dynamic disequilibrium approach akin to a Keynesian or Wicksellian framework.

1 Tobin's model

Tobin's 1965 model was limited in its objectives. It was mainly concerned with exploring the implications of the introduction of a monetary asset into a growth model which otherwise retained the central Solow assumptions.

The assumptions made are of a single real good, used both for consumption and investment, produced by a constant returns technology which can be represented by a regular (in the neoclassical sense) production function. The labour-force grows at an exogenous, so-called natural rate, n. Prices and wages are flexible and allow for instantaneous adjustments of the different, assumedly competitive, markets.

The single monetary asset is a government debt: it is therefore an 'outside' money. An interest rate i, which may be zero, is payable for holding it. Agents' behaviour is affected in two ways by the introduction of money:

(a) Firstly, the wealth held is composed of real balances M/p for a proportion b and of the physical asset K for a proportion $(1 - b)$. In Tobin's model, this proportion b is endogenous and results from a portfolio equilibrium. Agents adjust their portfolios to take account of their preferences and of the difference between the return on money, or real rate of interest $i - g_p$ where g_p stands for the rate of inflation, and the rate of return on the physical asset, or marginal productivity of capital denoted by $\partial f/\partial k$ or f'_k. Hence we get the expression for the proportion held of the monetary asset:

$$b = b(i - g_p - f'_k).$$

b increases with the rate of interest, but decreases as the return on the real asset and the rate of inflation increase.

(b) Secondly, the split between consumption and savings pertains to a total income which now has two sources: aggregate output $F(K,N)$ or $f(k)$ per consumer, and the growth in the real value of money balances.

Thus we get, for income of the individual,

$$y = f(k) + (1/N) \, d\,(M/p)\,/\,dt$$

and for aggregate savings

$$S = s Y = s [F(K) + d(M/p)/dt]$$

Under these assumptions, the state of the economy at any given moment will be determined by two stock variables: capital per person k, and real balances per person $m = M/pN$. In order to give a description of growth, it is therefore necessary to write down the differential equations giving the evolution of these variables.

The growth of real balances per head dm/dt can be decomposed as follows as a function of nominal monetary growth g_M, the rate of inflation g_p and the rate of population increase n.

$$dm/dt = m \ (g_M - g_p - n).$$

The corresponding savings contribution, a function b of total savings, has to be related to the rate of growth of real balances $d(M/p)dt$ divided by the existing population, that is, to just the first two bracketed terms in the previous expression:

$$(1/N) \ d(M/p)/dt = m (g_M - g_p)$$

or, since m is the fraction b of total wealth, $K/N + m$,

$$(1/N) \ d(M/p)/dt = (g_M - g_p) \ bk/(1 - b),$$

which is substituted into the expression for total income *per capita* y:

$$y = f(k) + (1/N) \ d(M/p)/dt$$
$$= f(k) + b/(1 - b)(g_M - g_p) \ k.$$

Net aggregate investment may then be written:

$$dK/dt = Nsy - d(M/p)/dt = N[sf(k) + (s-1)b/(1-b)(g_M - g_p)k].$$

which gives, via the relationship for capital per person:

$$dk/dt = g_k \ k = (g_K - n) \ k = (dK/Kdt - n) \ k$$

and by rearranging

$$dk/dt = sf(k) - n \ k - b[(1 - s)/(1 - b)](g_M - g_p) \ k$$

The differential equations giving dm/dt and dk/dt enable us to study the progress of the economy. In particular, a steady state will be obtained when capital per person and real balances per person are stationary, hence for $dk/dt = 0$ and $dm/dt = 0$, which implies:

$$g_p = g_M - n,$$

and

$$sf(k) - nk = b\,[(1 - s)/(1 - b)]\,n\,k,$$

or by combining the conditions,

$$sf(k) = nk\,[(1 - sb)/(1 - b)]\,.$$

The steady state condition illustrates well how Tobin's model generalises that of Solow. Indeed, if the share of savings earmarked for holding monetary balances, b, becomes zero, we are back at the Solow condition.

2 Implications of the model

From here we may derive the qualitative implications of introducing money through the assumptions of the model:

(a) the introduction of money does not affect the steady-state rate of growth, since this rate is exogenous at the natural value n.

(b) The introduction of money reduces capital intensity k along the steady-state path, and therefore also reduces output per head $f(k)$. Indeed, savings per head and so investment per head y are lower for all values of k:

$$nk = sf(k)\,[(1 - b)/(1 - sb)]\,,$$

since the term in square brackets is less than one for any positive value of b. Thus each term of the equation is less than $sf(k)$, the value of savings or investment per head in the absence of money. Figure 8.11 illustrates this properly.

The introduction of money reduces the steady-state capital per person, k_s, Solow's solution, to k_M. Output per person is reduced by the same amount. In order to understand this result (which might seem paradoxical) money has to be viewed in this model as an unproductive absorbent of savings. It therefore reduces, *ceteris paribus*, the capacity for accumulation of the economy.

Because it leads to these real effects, money is not neutral in Tobin's model.

(c) The capital per person, k^*_M, is a decreasing function of the

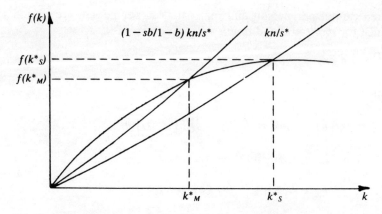

Figure 8.11   Tobin's versus Solow's steady state

proportion of wealth held in the form of money, b. It is therefore a decreasing function of the nominal rate of interest i, and an increasing function of the steady-state inflation rate, $g_M - n$.

Under the assumptions of this model, the government has at its disposal two instruments of monetary policy: the nominal rate of growth of the monetary aggregate, g_M, and the nominal interest rate i. A policy adjusting g_M, but maintaining the real rate of return $i - g_p$, or $i - g_M + n$ adapting i, would determine some rate of inflation g_p without affecting the real characteristics of the economy.

Thus, in Tobin's model, monetary policy can only influence real magnitudes when it affects the relative return on the monetary asset and on productive capital.

3 Neoclassical critiques and further developments

The very special implications of Tobin's model underline its theoretical nature as a representation of a monetary economy. In particular, it seems to imply an inferiority in the working of an economy with money as compared with a barter economy. As a result, various critiques and developments have been set out; some neoclassical, others Keynesian in inspiration; the former usually derived from equilibrium dynamics, the latter more often from disequilibrium dynamics.

According to neoclassical critics, such as Levhari and Patinkin (1968), the appearance of money in the basic model as merely an unproductive absorption of savings reflects Tobin's failure to incorporate its capacity to render particular services. In order to take account of these positive contributions, it is necessary in this framework to introduce money services as a consumption good – formally, as an argument in the utility function – and as a producer's good – formally as an argument for the production function. Including these modifications, Levhari and Patinkin show that growth paths with money can dominate those of a barter-economy.

The introduction of money directly into the production function is highly debatable. On the other hand, various studies have set out in greater detail the position of money in accumulation over time. Cass and Yaari (1967) introduced a sequence of generations of savers with fixed lifetimes.

In a more recent model, Tobin (1969) has explored the consequences of the coexistence of money with other financial assets.

4 Developments in a disequilibrium framework

Tobin's basic model, which retains all the assumptions of the Solow model regarding the functioning of markets, possesses the same type of stability also. It is stable in dynamic equilibrium (balanced growth paths return to the steady state in the long run), but this stability is no longer guaranteed in dynamic disequilibrium.

Nagatani (1970) established that Tobin's model presents the saddle point properly, and then convergence towards a steady state is guaranteed only for certain given initial values for capital, money balances and prices. For other initial values, paths in which expectations are continually fulfilled lead to a cumulative divergence of the economy from its long period equilibrium.[18]

Similarly qualified results have been obtained by Sidrauski (1967), who showed that under adaptive expectations over the rate of inflation, stability of the steady-state growth requires the coefficient of revision of expectations to be small.

While, therefore, these pieces of work hold true to a methodology based on neoclassical equilibrium, they make apparent the risks of instability of growth in a monetary economy. A different look at this point is given by analyses which break explicitly with the approach in terms of equilibrium.

Effectively, from Solow to Tobin and the developments considered hitherto, it is assumed *a priori* that investment is equal to savings. In fact, this assumed identity determines the behaviour of aggregate investment, and there is no specific investment function to represent autonomous behaviour of capitalists, in relation to the trade-off between physical and monetary assets.

5 'Keynes-Wicksell' models

Several attempts have been made to formulate a representation of growth out of equilibrium in a monetary economy, notably by F. Hahn,

H. Rose and H. Stein. These efforts spawned a family of so-called 'Keynes-Wicksell' models, of which two variants will be set out here:

(*a*) *The first Keynes-Wicksell model* – In the neoclassical model, the general price level adjusted fully in each period. Thus a portfolio equilibrium, keeping real balances held in proportion with the capital stock, was attained in each period. When the price level fails to adjust completely, growth is accompanied by a portfolio disequilibrium, represented by a gap between real balances per head, m, and the demand for them l^* $(k, \widetilde{g}_p)$ as a function of capital per person and anticipated inflation. This gap governs the behaviour of the general price level.

$$g_p = \lambda \, [m - l^*(k, \widetilde{g}_p)]$$

It can be shown that the behaviour of capital per person in this model obeys the equation:

$$dk/dt = f(k) - nk - c(k + m).$$

where the term cm represents consumption induced by the level of real balances. In this model, an acceleration of monetary growth, raising the level of m, consequently reduces the level of capital per person k^* and hence the level of output per head. This conclusion is the opposite of that which prevails in Tobin's model, in which an acceleration of monetary growth raises k^*.

(*b*) *The second Keynes-Wicksell model* – This model substitutes for the idea of a portfolio disequilibrium the assumption of a disequilibrium in the goods market. It allows for the possibility of a divergence between savings and investment in each period, this divergence determining the rate of inflation:

$$g_p = \lambda \, (I - S) / K,$$

where *ex ante* investment I is an increasing function of the rate of return on the physical asset K and a decreasing function of the real rate of interest. The investment actually realised must lie between I and S, so that:

$$g_K = a \, I/K + (1 - a) \, S/K,$$

with $0 < a < 1$ in a period of excess demand. Given a shortfall of demand, *ex ante* investment is fully realised ($a = 0$). Combining these two equations, we obtain:

$$g_K = a\, g_p \,/\, \lambda + S/K.$$

Thus, the rate of growth of capital equals S/K under deflation or in equilibrium, but lies above it in inflationary conditions. The term $a\, g_p/\lambda$ then represents the contribution of forced savings towards the financing of investment.

It can be shown that in such a model, an acceleration of the money supply and of the rate of inflation increases the capital per person k^*.

The framework of Keynes-Wicksell models is appropriate for exploring other types of disequilibrium and other adjustment processes. Thus, if savings plans are fully realised ($a = 0$), the disequilibrium in the goods market fully persists and is balanced by an opposite disequilibrium between money supplied and demand for money balances. J. Stein (1970) has shown that in this case an acceleration of inflation lowers k^*.

It is of interest to examine the effects of these varied assumptions on the stability of the models under consideration. This analysis does, however, turn out to be technically involved, and will not be pursued here.

6 A comparison of models of monetary growth

The impact of growth of the monetary aggregate may therefore differ according to the model being considered. These models may be compared among themselves and in relation to the Solow model by reference to the fundamental equation determining the stationarity of capital (Table 8.1).

Table 8.1 *Comparative properties of monetary growth models*

	steady state condition $(dk/dt = 0)$	dk^*/dg_p
Solow's Model	$sf(k) - nk = 0$	undefined
Tobin's Model	$sf(k) - nk = b\,nk(1 - s)\,/\,(1 - b)$	> 0
Keynes-Wicksell Model – 1	$sf(k) - nk = (k + m)$	< 0
– 2	$sf(k) - nk = -\,a\, g_p\, k/\lambda$	> 0

This comparison is illustrated in Figure 8.12:

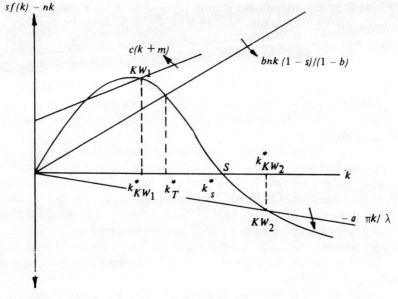

Figure 8.12

The arrows indicate the direction of the shifts caused by an acceleration of inflation.

Thus an examination of models of monetary growth illustrates a means of adjusting the Harrodian warranted rate through flexibility of the savings rate, *s*.

It is possible to reduce the rate of investment by increasing stocks of money, as Tobin's model demonstrates, but equally, the rate of investment may be raised by means of enforced savings which add to the *a priori* savings rate *s*.

9 Growth: Trends and Limits

Historically, research on optimal growth-paths preceded the Harrodian concern with the search for conditions of stability of equilibrium growth. The theory of optimal growth has seen interesting extensions, some of them connected with the theory of decentralised planning. Consideration of optimal growth has needed to allow for the problems created by the existence of natural exhaustible resources, allowance for which has been a feature of the recent development of economic research on growth. The limited availability of natural resources does not, however, appear to be the only limit to growth.

Optimal growth, exhaustible resources as limits to growth: each of these matters will be dealt with in its own section.

1 OPTIMAL GROWTH

The abundant literature and powerful techniques of optimal growth theory in fact cover several levels of analysis.

Firstly, in comparative dynamics, the comparison of steady states enables the optimal rate of accumulation to be studied. Secondly, in an economy with several goods and several techniques, the problem of the optimal combination of activities presents itself. Finally, one can investigate paths not expected to be smooth, to discern their asymptotic properties. For simplicity, we shall now return essentially to a single-good economy.

A Optimal steady-state growth: the golden rule

We know that to solve the optimal growth problem we must consider paths which maximise certain criteria independently of the operational laws which can lead to realisation of these paths. In order to approach this problem of the optimality of growth, we shall consider the simplest case of a single-good economy equipped with a 'Solow' technology, which may be represented by a production function homogeneous of degree one (i.e. CRS), whose development is constrained by the exogenous growth of the labour input at a natural rate n. We further restrict comparison by assumption to steady states only, these being characterised by a constant capital-labour ratio k^*. Solow's model has shown us that the rate of growth in such economies is independent of this ratio, as it is of the savings rate, since it coincides with the natural rate.

Since we wish to compare steady states growth at the natural rate, what variable remains which might provide a means of comparison? Consumption *per capita* is not invariant, differing as it does among the paths. Given this, the problem becomes that of determining the steady-state growth-rate characterised by a savings-rate and a capital-output ratio which maximises consumption at each point of time. Indeed, since the growth rates are identical, a comparison at one point of time is valid for all points, along the path.

Let $k^*(s)$ denote the steady-state capital-output ratio, associated with a given savings ratio s, and let $f(k^*)$ be the *per capita* output which it allows. The value of consumption per head, c, is then:

$$c = (1 - s) f(k^*(s)).$$

From the equality of savings and investment per head nk we have:

$$c = [1 - nk^*(s) / f(k^*(s))] f(k^*(s)) = f(k^*(s)) - nk^*(s).$$

A rise in the savings rate raises capital and therefore output per head, but reduces the proportion of this output which is consumed. The optimal savings rate must balance these two effects and satisfy the equation

$$dc/ds = (\partial f/\partial k^* - n) \, dk^*/ds = 0.$$

Under the model's assumptions,[1] dk^*/ds is always positive, and $\delta f/\delta k^*$ decreases monotonically. The above equation therefore has a unique solution $\hat{s}$ and constitutes a sufficient condition for maximisation of consumption per head. This solution implies

$$\partial f/\partial k^* = n.$$

In other words, the marginal productivity of capital equals the rate of growth, exogenously given at the natural rate.[2] Moreover, substituting this rate into the equality (of identity) of the savings ratio and investment rate, we obtain:

$$\hat{s} = \frac{nk^*(\hat{s})}{f(k^*(\hat{s}))} = \frac{k^*(\hat{s})}{f(k^*(\hat{s}))} \frac{\partial f}{\partial k^*},$$

an expression equal to the share of profits in total income, if factors are remunerated according to their marginal productivity.

This double result due to Phelps[3] constitutes 'the golden rule of accumulation'. Among steady-state paths of growth at the 'natural rate', the path maximising consumption per head at each point obeys the following rules:

(a) The marginal productivity of capital is equal to the rate of growth.
(b) The savings rate equals the share of profits under a competitive régime, in which factor payments correspond to marginal products.

The simplicity of this result should come as no surprise, given the very special assumptions of the optimisation undertaken.

B The von Neumann model

Initially presented as a general equilibrium model,[4] the von Neumann model has allowed clarification of the conditions for effective and optimal growth in an economy with many goods and many activities. Its exposition will be made as simple as possible.

1 Representation of the economy

The economy consists of m goods produced by, and utilising, n fixed-coefficient processes. Each technique j produces good i in quantity b_{ij} and consumes it in quantity a_{ij}. Additionally, the intensity of utilisation of technique is measured by a non-negative number z_j. In matrix notation, the vector of inputs is $X = AZ$ and the vector of outputs $Y = BZ$. The net product of the economy is thus $(B - A)Z$.

Let $\alpha = 1 + g$ denote the growth factor. For a rate of growth to be feasible, it must satisfy the system of inequalities:

$$BZ_t \geqslant AZ_{t+1} = \alpha AZ_t$$

Each good must be produced in a quantity sufficient to allow for its use as an input in the following period. We shall call a system of proportions z_j which maximises the growth factor α, a *von Neumann* path.

To establish the existence of this path, and to characterise it, it is necessary to introduce further conditions:[5]

(a) $\displaystyle\sum_{i=1}^{m} a_{ij} > 0$ for all techniques j

(b) $\sum_{j=1}^{n} b_{ij} > 0$ for all goods i

which is equivalent to the statements that each technique has positive output (is productive) and that each good is consumed within the system. The maximisation problem is:

maximise α such that

$$(B - \alpha A)\,Z \geqslant 0 \quad \text{(availability of inputs)}$$

$$SAZ - 1 \geqslant 0 \quad \text{(normalisation of activities)}$$

$$z \geqslant 0 \quad \text{(non-negativity of activities)}$$

$$\alpha \geqslant 0 \quad \text{(non-negativity of expansion coefficients)}$$

The constrained maximisation of α is equivalent to maximisation of the following Lagrangian, where P is an m-vector of multipliers associated to the goods availability constraints; and u, V and w are multipliers associated with the normalisation and non-negativity constraints:

$$\mathcal{L}\,(\alpha\,Z) = \alpha + P\,(B - \alpha\,A)\,Z + u\,(SAZ - 1) + VZ + w\,\alpha\,.$$

It can be shown that the maximisation problem has a unique solution, which defines the von Neumann growth rate associated with an activity vector z^*_j invariant through time. The maximum growth rate is a proportional (balanced) one. We proceed to interpret this result further:

2 Interpretation of optimal growth
The growth path, or maximum rate, is characterised by the following set of Kuhn-Tucker conditions:

$$\partial\mathcal{L}/\partial z_i = 0 \Rightarrow \nabla \quad \Sigma_i\, p_i\,(b_{ij} - \alpha\,a_{ij}) + v_j = 0$$

Interpreting the multiplier p_i as shadow prices, these conditions imply that wherever a particular technique is employed, the value of its outputs is equal to that of its inputs multiplied by the growth coefficient; that is, it produces zero profit if α is taken as the interest rate. If any technique would produce negative profits in this sense, it is not utilised.

$$\partial y/\partial \alpha = 0 \Rightarrow 1 + w = \Sigma_i\, \Sigma_j\, p_i\, a_{ij}\, z_j\,.$$

If the coefficient of expansion is positive, w is zero and the value of inputs consumed is positive. Here it is arbitrarily assigned the value unity, which corresponds to a normalisation of the price-vector. If the value of inputs were zero, then no positive level of activity would be feasible *(w ≠ 0, so α = 0)*.

$$\Sigma_i \; \Sigma_j \; p_i \, (b_{ij} - \alpha \, a_{ij}) \, z_j \; = \; 0$$

The value of output equals the value of inputs: put otherwise, national product equals national income.

$$\forall \; j, \; V_j \, z_j \; = \; 0$$

If a technique is utilised, the imputed cost V_j is zero.

$$w \, \alpha \; = \; 0$$

If the growth coefficient is positive, the multiplier w is zero. The point to emphasise is that these conditions define an equilibrium associated with the von Neumann maximum growth path. This equilibrium is characterised as follows:

(a) $BZ^* \geq \alpha^* \, AZ^*$; the rate of growth is feasible.

(b) Since each of the terms in (3) is non-negative, the sum can be zero only if each term is zero:

$$p_i \cdot \Sigma_j \, (b_{ij} - \alpha a_{ij}) \, z_j = 0.$$

Any good produced in excess of the required quantity has zero price. In market terms: the value of excess demands is zero.

(c) From (1) it follows that no technique can yield a positive profit at the rate of interest $i = \alpha^* - 1$.

(d) (1) and (3) ensure that a technique which cannot be hired at the rate $\alpha^* - 1$ will remain unused.

(e) From (2), if not all techniques are unused, the value of the product is positive.

The connection of an equilibrium with optimal growth is justified through the interpretation of the multiplier p_i as competitive prices and of $\alpha - 1$ as rate of interest. This interpretation is reinforced by consideration of the following problem, the dual of the optimal growth problem.

Minimise the interest coefficient α with respect to β and to prices p_i

such that $P(B - \beta A) \leq 0$ for all techniques

$$\Sigma_i\, p_j\, (b_{ij} - \beta\, a_{ij}) \leqslant 0 \qquad \text{non-positive profits}$$

$$\beta \geqslant 0,\ \ P \geqslant 0 \qquad\quad \text{interest coefficient and prices are non-negative}$$

For this problem a vector of multiplier Z is introduced; these will be interpreted as intensities of use of techniques. This comparison enables us to establish that the von Neumann growth-rate is at once the maximum feasible rate given the constraints on the availability of goods and the minimum rate of interest which leaves profits non-positive.

$$\text{Max}\ \alpha\ =\ \text{Min}\ \beta$$

Notice that the equality of the rate of growth and the rate of interest in von Neumann's case is reminiscent of the Golden Rule. In fact, this result applies equally to the particular assumptions of that model: wage earners' consumption is treated as intermediate consumption and profits are automatically reinvested. The model has been enlarged to accommodate alternative assumptions about these matters.

The von Neumann model deals with optimal growth in terms of steady state proportionality. When the problem is treated more generally, we find that the von Neumann path represents a particular point of reference. An optimal growth-path over a finite time horizon between a given starting point and predetermined final conditions will consist of three periods: the first tending towards the von Neumann path, the second in the vicinity of balanced growth at the maximum rate, the third moving to satisfy the final conditions. This result, christened the 'turnpike theorem', is often derived in the context of multi-vector models.[6] We shall confine ourselves to examining a comparable result in the simpler context of optimal growth in a single-good economy.

C Optimal growth in a single-good economy

'What proportion of its income ought a nation to save?' – this is the question which Ramsey asked in 1928. To this question the Golden Rule provides a partial answer limited to comparison of steady states. Considered more generally, investigation of this problem involves the use of dynamic optimisation techniques such as the calculus of variations, which Ramsey used,[7] or the principle of the maximum, or control theory which today's theoreticians use and which enable additional constraints to be dealt with.

1 A basic model
Let us remain in a 'Solow economy' with a production function

homogeneous of degree one, which allows us to write output per head as a function of capital per head, $y = f(k)$. Consumption per head c and gross investment per head h_t must satisfy the condition

$$c_t + h_t = f(k_t) \quad \text{or} \quad h_t = f(k_t) - c_t$$

The utility obtained from consumption per head obeys an increasing concave function $u(c)$. The cumulation of utility from consumption over a given time-horizon, which we will take here as infinite, leads us to define an objective function V defined over utility in each period, whose simplest form is given by a constant discount rate γ:

$$V = \int_{t=0}^{\infty} u(c_t) e^{-\gamma t} dt$$

The problem is that of determining the optimal consumption régime, as a value of c_t for each point of time which maximises this objective given the constraint defining the evolution of k_t. If capital depreciates at a rate δ, and if the labour force grows at a rate n,[8] growth of capital per head will be equal to investment per head h_t, less the investment required to equip the addition to the labour force with capital, and less replacement investment. The growth of capital per head must thus be:

$$dk/dt = \dot{k}_t = f(k_t) - c_t - (\delta + n)k.$$

Optimal control theory[9] has shown that optimisation of a dynamic system of this type is achieved by a consumption schedule which maximises at each point the following auxiliary function, which is called the Hamiltonian of the system:[10]

$$H(c_t/k_t, q_t) = u(c_t) + q_t [f(k_t) - c_t - (\delta + n)\dot{k}_t],$$

where q_t is a co state variable or shadow price associated with the equation of change of capital per head, the co-state variable of the system. The Hamiltonian is easy to interpret. It shows that the total contribution in one period to the maximand V consists of a direct contribution, measured by the utility of the consumption of that period; and of an indirect contribution in the form of capital accumulation allowing the level of consumption in succeeding periods to be maintained and increased. Maximisation of the Hamiltonian for given values of capital per head k_t and of the auxiliary variable q_t implies the following condition

$$\partial H/\partial c_t = \partial U/\partial c_t - q_t = 0$$

giving the optimal value of consumption c_t^* (k_t, q_t), which equalises marginal utility with the given value of capital q_t.

To complete the solution of the problem of optimal growth, the equation of change of the capital stock being given above, we need to know the laws governing movement over time of the co state variable q_t. A fundamental theorem of optimal control theory states that:

$$d\varphi /dt = \varphi_t = - \partial \mathcal{H}/\partial k$$

where φ_t is the discounted price $q_t e^{-\gamma}$ and $\mathcal{H}$ the discounted Hamiltonian $He^{-\gamma}$.

The variation in the shadow price of a state variable is the negative of the derivative of the Hamiltonian with respect to this variable, in this case capital. In economic terms, this variable measures the impact of a relaxation of the constraint constituted by the historically given value of the state variable on the criterion function to be maximised. In the present model, this property justifies the interpretation of q_t as the shadow price of capital and allows the following calculation of variations in q_t:

$$dq/dt = d(\varphi e^{\gamma t})/dt = e^{\gamma t} d\varphi /dt + \gamma q_t$$

Since $\quad d\varphi /dt = \partial (H e^{-\gamma t})/\partial k_t = -e^{-\gamma t} q_t (\partial f/\partial k_t - \delta - n),$

it follows that $\quad dq/dt = q_t (\gamma + \delta + n - \partial f/\partial k_t).$

When the price q^*_t and the capital stock k^*_t resulting from this evolution are introduced into the calculation of the optimal consumption $^{-H}$a period, $c^*_t (k_t, q_t)$, the consumption plan c^*_t maximising the criterion V over an infinite time horizon, and therefore the solution to our optimal growth problem is obtained.[11]

Since the shadow price of capital is at all points equal to the marginal utility of consumption, these variables therefore have identical rates of growth. The rule governing price behaviour therefore implies,

$$\partial f/\partial k_t = (1/u'_c) du'_c/dt = \alpha + \delta + n = (1/q_t)dq_t/dt$$

which means in effect that the marginal productivity of capital in terms of utility is equal to the subjective rate of time-preference increased by the rate of depreciation, and by the rate of growth of population. This fundamental condition for optimal growth clearly generalises the rule which Ramsay (1928) established.

An optimal growth-path therefore satisfies the conditions for the evolution of the stock of capital, and of its price:

$$\dot{q}_t = q_t \left(\gamma + \delta + n - \partial f / \partial k^*_t \right)$$

$$\dot{k}_t = f(k^*_t) - c^*_t - (\delta + n) k^*_t$$

These differential equations do not depend essentially on time: that would imply a distortion of the relationship between the variables under consideration. They are referred to as 'autonomous'. In consequence they possess a stationary solution, characterised by a constant amount of capital per person and a constant price. This solution is defined by the conditions:

$$\dot{q}_t = 0 \text{ and then } \partial f / \partial k = \gamma + \delta + n.$$

$$\dot{k}_t = 0 \text{ and then } \hat{k}^*_t = [f(\hat{k}^*_t) - c^*_t] / (\delta + n)$$

which implies that savings per head, $f(k^*_t) - c^*_t$ are equal to the level of investment required for replacement and to equip new workers. The stationary values of capital per person and of price in this steady-state solution, generalising the Golden Rule, will be denoted $\hat{k}_t$ and $\hat{p}_t$. It will be shown that this particular solution plays an important part in classifying the possible paths of the economy.

2 The 'consumption turnpike'
In the context of the von Neumann model, the 'turnpike theorem' denotes the tendency of optimal growth paths to move towards the path of even growth at the maximum rate. A comparable result appears in this simpler model where the only proportion to be determined is the ratio c_t/h_t, of consumption per head to investment per head. For this reason the label 'consumption turnpike' is sometimes attached to it (e.g. Burmeister and Dobell, 1970, p. 400).

In order to establish this, it is necessary to represent the possible paths of the economy in the (k_t, p_2) space.[12] Let us first, in Figure 9.1, draw in the loci of the stationarity of price ($\dot{p} = 0$) and of capital ($\dot{k} = 0$). Capital per person falls below the curve $\dot{k} = 0$ and increases above it, since a smaller p is associated with a higher level of consumption. The price increases for a capital stock in excess of its stationary solution $\hat{k}$ and falls for a lower value, as $\dot{p}$ depends negatively on marginal productivity, which is decreasing; hence the graphical treatment in Figure 9.1.

In each quadrant, the convected arrows indicate the behaviour of the characteristic variables, while the dotted arrows indicate movements of the economy. The paths located in quadrant (1) show a continual fall in

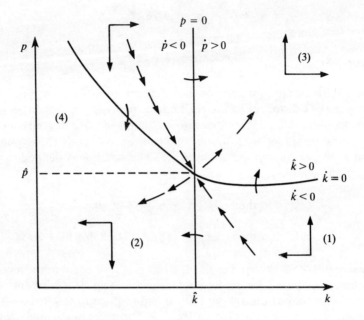

Figure 9.1   The optimal growth path

k and an increase in price. The only one lying continually in the interior of the quadrant, tends towards optimal steady state, or golden rule, growth $(\hat{q}, \hat{k})$. If, on the other hand, they reach a boundary of the quadrant, they must leave the quadrant and enter (2) or (3). Quadrant (4) has symmetrical properties. In contrast, from any point in quadrant (2) or symmetrically, in quadrant (3), any path diverges increasingly from the stationary solution.[13]

However, it can be shown that any path entering quadrants (2) or (3), and failing to escape, cannot be optimal.[14] Let us start in quadrant (3). There, capital always exceeds $\hat{k}$, and price eventually exceeds $\hat{p}$ since it is always increasing. Hence, $c(q_t)$ lies below its steady-state value. Under these conditions a preferable path could be obtained by reducing the quantity of capital in order to consume more, and thus moving in towards $(\hat{q}, \hat{k})$. Such a path cannot be optimal since it is possible to describe a trajectory which dominates it at all points.

It follows that the only optimal paths of the economy are those which converge towards the steady state satisfying the Golden Rule. The 'consumption turnpike' property is thus established.[15] In particular, if one considers a maximisation problem over a given horizon T, this subject to terminal conditions acting as constraints, one finds again the three phases of approaching the turnpike, evolution in the neighbourhood of the stationary solution, and a deflection of the path towards the imposed final point.

Moreover, the Golden Rule solution is here a saddle-point, which may be interpreted as implying a knife-edge instability of optimal path. However, as it was seen when discussing the stability of equilibrium growth, the instability implications of saddle-point solutions have to be interpreted cautiously.[16]

Indeed, the essential contribution of optimal growth theory is probably to obtain the possibility of, and conditions for, an inter-temporal decentralisation. For a global optimisation over an infinite time horizon to reduce to a sequence of optimisations in each period, it is necessary and, under certain conditions, sufficient that agents correctly evaluate the shadow-price of capital q^*_t – that is, the contribution of current investment to the utility of future consumption stream.

Thus, the theory of optimal growth brings an ambiguous message concerning the suitability of market mechanisms for the efficient long-term guidance of the economy. While it demonstrates rigorously the possibility of such guidances, it reveals at the same time its lack of robustness, and underlies the need for more detailed study of the modes of regulation operating in such an economy.

2 EXHAUSTIBLE RESOURCES

Ricardian dynamics expected industrial growth to come up against the barrier of limited supplies of raw materials and requiring increasing costs for their increase. The intellectual influence of Marx, of the neoclassical economists, and of Keynes, combined to divert the attention of economists from this problem. Along with the factor 'land', all reference to natural resources disappeared from theoretical models, and in 1965 once more, L. Pasinetti criticised the neoclassical economists for seeking to base their theory of growth upon the principle of scarcity. Whilst the rebirth of theoretical concern with scarce resources barely preceded the crisis of 1973, it must be acknowledged that it did precede it, to do justice to the instigators of this train of analysis.

A fundamental result, appearing in the pioneering article of H. Hotelling (1931), establishes the narrow connection which exists between a policy of intertemporal utilisation of scarce resources and the evolution of their shadow prices, which would be translated by the evolution over time of their actual price on perfectly competitive markets. After an examination of the basic solution given, we must move on to study the implications of scarce resources for growth under various assumptions, particularly regarding their substitutability as well as the ability of technical progress to compensate for these effects.

A Rules for evaluating exhaustible resources

The theory of scarce resources at first proposed a microeconomic treatment of the appreciation of these resources, applicable to the competitive or to the monopolistic case. However, the equilibrium assumptions which underlie these analyses may not appear to be those best suited to reality, which has led to less simplistic approaches, for example in terms of game theory.

1 The competitive case

Analysis of the competitive case starts from the idea that given a resource existing in a given quantity s_o, its equilibrium price should equalise the discounted benefit accruing to its owner from its current or future exploitation. In any two consecutive periods, the owner has the choice between an immediate exploitation bringing a rent R_t equal to the difference between the current price P_t and the extraction cost C_t

$$R_t = P_t - C_t$$

and a future exploitation bringing in a rent which has to be discounted at the rate of interest i:

$$R_{t+1} / (1 + i) = (P_{t+1} - C_{t+1}) / (1 + i)$$

A pair of equilibrium prices P_t, P_{t+1}, must equalise the discounted benefit of these two solutions.

$$R_t = \frac{R_{t+1}}{1+i} \Rightarrow \frac{P_{t+1} - C_{t+1}}{P_t - C_t} = 1 + i.$$

or, denoting the respective changes in rent, price and extraction costs by ΔR_t, ΔP_t, and ΔC_t,

$$\frac{\Delta R_t}{R_t} = \frac{\Delta P_t - \Delta C_t}{P_t - C_t} = i.$$

The rate of increase of profit must thus be equal to the rate of interest.

To derive the sequence of prices from this, let us obtain a term for this sequence by multiplying each side by $(P - C)/P$. We obtain:

$$\frac{\Delta P_t}{P_t} = \frac{P_t - C_t}{P_t} \; i \; , \; \frac{C_t}{P_t}\frac{\Delta C_t}{C_t} = \frac{R_t}{P_t} \; i \; + \; \frac{C_t}{P_t}\frac{\Delta C_t}{C_t}$$

So we see that the price of a scarce resource realising a stock equilibrium (implying indifference of the owner between present and future exploitation) increases at a rate equal to the sum of the rate of interest weighted by the share of rents in the price, and the rate of increase in extraction costs, weighted by the relative size of those costs. In the limit, where the cost of extraction is negligible, as is the case for some Middle-Eastern crude oil, the theoretical equilibrium price itself evolves at a rate equal to the rate of interest.

This line of reasoning certainly determines a possible pattern over time for the price of exhaustible resources, but not the level of that price. To determine the latter, a reference element must be introduced: opportunity cost, or costs of substitution. In a simple case, the reasoning proceeds as follows.

Let us consider a commodity substitutable for our scarce resource when it runs out, say after T periods. It might be a resource at present very expensive, or requiring technology yet to be developed. At the date of substitution T, the two resources must have the same price $\bar{P}$, evaluated on the basis of the expected cost of output of the substitution. Let C_T be the expected cost of extraction of the last units of the exhaustible resource. The equality just mentioned can be written, in terms of current prices (P_o) and cost (C_o):

$$\bar{P} = P_T = (P_o - C_o) \; e^{iT} + C_t \, ,$$

from which we get the expression for the current price-level of the exhaustible resource from its production cost and expectations of the price $\bar{P}$ of the substitutable resource at date T and of the extraction cost at this date, C_T :

$$P_o = (\bar{P} - C_T) \; e^{-iT} + C_o \, .$$

This relationship is not affected if substitution occurs in several periods. It is sufficient to evaluate $\bar{P}$ and C_T at one of the dates of substitution, T. We shall see an interesting application of this equation. Starting from an estimation of the date and cost of development of an energy source generally substitutable for oil, the producer states must determine their supply price as a function of their discount rate, i, a price which they must seek to establish through the cartel constituted by OPEC. However, some of the oil-producing countries, such as Venezuela, Algeria and Iran, possess limited reserves in relation to their potential for development, and must therefore apply a higher discount rate, while the others, having plentiful reserves relative to their potential for development and their opportunities for re-investment, must apply a low discount rate, limited to the real rate of return available in international capital markets. Thus the former countries will pursue a rapid price increase, the latter favouring a slower progression; a pattern not belied by observation.

2 The case of monopoly

The example of oil underlines the extent to which the assumption of competitiveness may prove ill-suited to the case of markets for non-renewable resources, whence the interest of a study incorporating the alternative assumption of a monopoly market.

The problem in this case is quite simple to set up. The monopolist, the sole owner of the resource, will seek to maximise his discounted profits under the constraint of a selling price as a function of the rate of exploitation X_t:

$$V_o = \int_o^T [X_t\, p(X_t) - C_t\, (X_t)]e^{-it}\, dt$$

subject to $\int_o^T X_t\, dt = S_o$,

S_o being the total endowment of the resource. The monopolist must choose a rate of exploitation and a price profile such that the marginal rate of profit increases at a rate equal to the rate of interest, so that:

$$\frac{dr_t}{dt} = [\frac{dp}{dX_t} - \frac{dC}{dX_t}]\, \frac{dX}{dt} = ir_t$$

It is of particular interest to ask whether this rule leads the monopolist to set higher prices and so to restrict the exploitation of the resource in comparison with the competitive case, or on the contrary to accelerate exploitation. Unfortunately, there does not appear to be a general solution to this complex problem – which notably depends on the autonomous movement of costs and of demand. Some writers believe themselves to have shown that monopoly would slow down extraction, others that, contrariwise, it would increase the rate of exploitation of the resource. G. Heal (1977) proposes a rather more subtle answer, a function of the evaluation of the elasticity of demand. If the elasticity of demand increases with the scale of the market and therefore with the rate of exploitation, the monopoly solution involves a faster increase of prices than the competitive solution, and so a slower rate of extraction (cf. Stiglitz, 1976) (Figure 9.2).

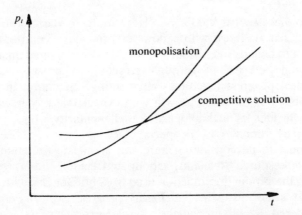

Figure 9.2 Alternative path for the price of resources

Conversely, the assumption of an elasticity decreasing with the rate of exploitation makes the monopoly path produce a slower price increase than the competitive solution.

The assumption of monopoly may itself seem inappropriate, which justifies approaches in terms of sellers' oligopoly, or bilateral oligopoly. Game theory has enabled some of the cases linked to these assumptions to be dealt with, and the resulting evolutions to be identified (Heal, ibid.).

It remains true that such models may underestimate the importance of variables influencing prices in the short term, and in particular of stocks. It is well known that prices of, for example, non-ferrous metals exhibit substantial variability, speculative in origin, behind which it is difficult to discern any trend connected with interest-rates. It is, notwithstanding, more helpful to bypass a viewpoint of partial study of markets for exhaustible resources in order to integrate them into a full growth model.

B Balanced growth and exhaustible resources

The difficulties raised by the introduction of exhaustible resources into a model of balanced growth go far beyond the formal complexity introduced by a third factor. They are principally linked to the specific constraints to which this additional factor is subject. Intuition, agreeing with many received ideas, considers the possibility of balanced growth to be incompatible with the existence of exhaustible resources or it may suggest that at best one can achieve convergence towards a stationary state.

In fact, the classical model is related more to the case of limited resources, that is, those whose flows of productive contributions are finite, than to exhaustible resources, which exist in limited quantity and are not renewed except through recycling, a process viewed as technological progress 'resources augmenting'. Similarly, the idea of incompatibility of balanced growth with exhaustible resources is often based on an idea of technological complementarity whose realism is limited, apart from some very special cases.

The model to be considered here will allow substitutability of the exhaustible resource R against labour and capital.[17] For reasons of simplicity, the production function used is Cobb-Douglas with constant returns to scale, in which technical progress will by convention be considered as labour augmenting (Harrod-neutral), giving the expression:

$$Y_t = K_t^{\alpha} (A_t N_t)^{\beta} R_t^{1-\alpha-\beta}$$

From this expression it follows that the rate of growth of output is a weighted average of the respective rates of growth of capital g_k, of labour measured in efficiency units (natural rate n) and of the quantity of the exhaustible resource used up g_R:

$$g_y = \alpha g_k + \beta n + (1 - \alpha - \beta) g_R .$$

Growth of capital, which is assumed to have an infinite lifetime, occurs through investment from savings:

$$dk/dt = sY_t, \text{ and hence } g_{K,t} = s\, Y_t/K_t = s/v_t.$$

The evolution of the utilisation R_t of the exhaustible resource is constrained by the condition:

$$\int_{t=0}^{\infty} R_t \, dt = S_o .$$

By assumption, we are concerned here with equilibrium paths along which the price p_t of this resource must increase at the rate of interest. But equilibrium implies simultaneously the equalisation in each period of, on the one hand, this price, measured in terms of output with the marginal productivity of the resource:

$$P_t = \partial F/\partial R_t = (1 - \alpha - \beta) \, Y_t/R_t ,$$

and on the other hand of the marginal productivity of capital with the rate of interest:[18]

$$\partial F / \partial K_t = \alpha \ Y_t / K_t = \alpha / v_t = i.$$

Combining these three conditions, it follows that the rate of growth of the marginal productivity of the scarce resource must be equal to that of capital and so, given the value of these marginal productivities,

$$g_{Y,t} - g_{R,t} = \alpha \ Y_t / K_t = \alpha / v_t \ .$$

The time-path of the capital stock and of the utilisation of the exhaustible resource having thus been identified, it is possible to make explicit the expression for the rate of growth, which gives, by substituting,

$$g_{Y,t} = [n + \alpha \ (s - \gamma)/v_t]/(\alpha + \beta) \ .$$

It is worth noting that the equilibrium rate of growth does not explicitly depend on the rate of resource utilisation, but only indirectly through the intermediary of the capital-output ratio. With a given savings rate and rate of increase of the labour force in terms of efficiency units, the growth rate will be greater, the smaller the capital-output ratio.

It is interesting to characterise the equilibrium growth-paths in terms of economically meaningful relationships: the capital-output ratio v_t, and the rate of depletion of scarce resources $d_t = R_t/S_t$, where S_t represents the unused part of the resource:

$$S_t = S_o - \int_{\theta=0}^{t} R_\theta \ d_\theta \ .$$

The rate of growth of the capital-output ratio is obtained from the growth of output and of capital, giving

$$g_v = \frac{\beta_s + \alpha(1 - \alpha - \beta)}{v(\alpha + \beta)} - \frac{n}{\alpha + \beta} \ ,$$

while the rate of growth of the ratio R_t/S_t is the difference between the rate of growth of the numerator, g_R as determined earlier, and of the denominator, which by definition is simply $- d$, minus the rate of depletion of the stock of resource. Hence finally:

$$g_d = d + (n - \alpha(1 - s)/v) / (\alpha + \beta).$$

It remains for us to investigate the shapes of such equilibrium paths,

which we shall do according to the now familiar method of representing
the loci of stationarity of the capital-output ratio, and of the rate of
resource utilization. The condition $g_v = 0$ depends only on v and is
therefore represented by a horizontal line in the (d, v) space (Figure
9.3). It corresponds to the stationary value for v:

$$\hat{v} = [\beta_s + \alpha (1 - \alpha - \beta)] / n.$$

The condition $g_d = 0$ does however depend on v. The curve which
represents it, whose equation is

$$d(v) = \frac{\alpha (1 - s)}{v(\alpha + \beta)} - \frac{n}{\alpha + \beta},$$

is decreasing in v, and the stationary value of the rate of resource
utilisation is obtained by substituting the value $\hat{v}$ in the previous
expression which gives:

$$\hat{d} = \frac{n(\alpha - s)}{\beta_s + \alpha (1 - \alpha - \beta)}.$$

The signs of the growth rates are determined, completing the 'phase
diagram' in Figure 9.3.

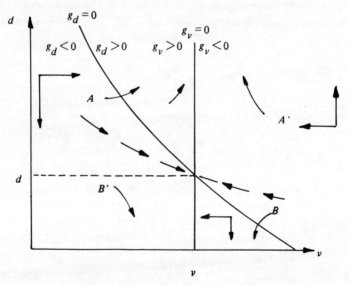

Figure 9.3   Equilibrium growth path in a resource-using economy

Analysis of this diagram yields a good deal of information about balanced growth-paths with exhaustible resources, under the particular assumptions of this model.

There exists a unique steady-state balanced growth-path, fully defined by the rate of resource utilisation, the capital-output ratio $\hat{v}$ and the growth-rate which results. Moreover, this path has a meaning only if $\alpha > s$, that is, if the share of profits exceeds the savings rate; otherwise, the rate of resource utilisation would be negative.

The steady-state solution is a saddle-point, which means that only one balanced growth trajectory leads to A, represented in Figure 9.3 by broken arrows.

Any other equilibrium path diverges cumulatively from the steady-state and from the constant rate of resource utilisation $\hat{d}$. Thus for example a path A starts from a situation characterised by a deficiency of capital and an excessive rate of depletion. Since by assumption this path satisfies the conditions at a point in time for equilibrium, the process of the exhaustible resource is too low at points on the path. It tends at first to increase, but at a decreasing rate since v is increasing.[19]

Thus resource utilisation, after correctly slowing down, picks up again and tends towards infinity. The paths A' have resource depletion accelerating continuously, having started from an already excessive level. Resources will in consequence be exhausted in finite time. Symmetrically, the paths B after a period of self-correction, and B' from the beginning, represent a slowing of the rate of depletion, starting from an inadequate level and therefore leading to an abandonment of use before the stock runs out.

It therefore is clearly apparent that the rule for valuing resources in a competitive, even idealised market may not be sufficient to lead the economy towards a coherent policy of utilisation of those resources. Any divergence from the unique path leading to the steady state will effectively, if this rule is applied, increase cumulatively. No doubt such a rigid conclusion reveals as much the highly simplified character of the model as the limitations of market mechanisms, but it nonetheless has the virtue of demonstrating once again that the attainment of a temporary equilibrium does not guarantee the 'correct' movement of the economy in the long term.

C The costs of growth

The controversial simulation exercise of 'World Dynamics' initiated by J.Forrester and developed by the so-called 'Club of Rome' illustrates the explanation of the limits to feasible growth. The limits to desirable growth depend on the advantages of and problems raised by this process, and therefore call initially for a consideration of the costs of growth. Once the most important of these costs, direct or indirect, have been identified, they will be related to the objectives of growth.

1 The direct costs
Although pragmatic, the distinction between the direct costs of growth and the indirect costs, arising from related mechanisms, is entirely a relative one. All we shall attempt here is a brief survey which, without pretending to be exhaustive, will simply aim to bring to mind some factors which ought to be considered in any reflections on the desirability of growth. The destruction of free goods will thus be mentioned, along with the intensification of effort and transitional costs.

Growth, taking place through extension of the sphere of industrial processes and reduction of the domain left for the natural environment, brings with it the disappearance of free goods and services disposed of in this natural sphere. When this happens, either the corresponding goods and services are not replaced, at the cost of a reduction in the real quality of life, or more realistically, they are replaced by produced goods and services which are then incorrectly taken as elements of national income. Pollution represents a limiting case of this process, influencing negatively first the utilities obtained from a given real output, but also in the longer term, the development of the population and its economic activity.

Growth seems to require a certain intensification of effort, a certain increased mobilisation of human resources. The intensification of work, a corollary of the forms of work organisation adopted since the beginning of the twentieth century, is well known. It has notably been emphasised that the transition from physical to nervous exhaustion seems to mark an increase in the human costs of work. This factor should be assessed with caution, for fear of underestimating the unpleasantness of the jobs of many workers in earlier societies.

Similarly, the renewed increase of work-associated illnesses has been accompanied by a falling incidence of some afflictions traditionally linked with certain lines of work.

An aspect of this factor worth maintaining is the idea that the increase of labour productivity is not a net gain, as it partly includes a process of intensification. However, unless it is reduced to a mere tautology by appropriate definitions, it is difficult to see how all increases in labour productivity could be reduced to such a process.

A third type of costs is associated with changes which necessarily accompany the growth process. Firstly, there are human costs associated with mobility of labour, with the risks of de-skilling, the costs of retraining and the disruption of lifestyles which accompany it. There are also tangible costs to the change, such as those resulting from accelerated obsolescence, or from the discarding of disused infrastructures.

2 Indirect costs

Other costs of growth, though not resulting directly from the development of production, arise widely as consequences of the forms which it assumes in industrialised capitalist economies.

Under this head, we shall mention inequalities, costs of mobilising demand, and costs stemming from relative degrees of frustration and satisfaction. These elements have in common the nature of costs of mobilising resources in a decentralised economy.

Historical experience does not in any way indicate that the degree of inequality in industrialised societies exceeds that of traditional less-developed societies: the evidence rather suggests the reverse. However, there is no doubt that a period of rapid growth, of necessity unbalanced, generates new inequalities linked to occupational mobility to the profits therefrom, and to the need to develop financial incentives for industrial enterprise. A social cost might be assigned to an increase in status inequalities.

The cost due to systems for mobilising demand lies firstly in the resources required for this end, and the increase in 'selling costs'. But it also finds expression in an increased dependence on patterns of consumption, the loss of autonomy illustrated by the 'channel reversal' image in which modelling of demand as a function of the requirements of production replaces the consumer sovereignty dear to the liberal heart. Here again, the image of a reciprocal relation between the structures of production and consumption is probably nearer the truth than one or other channel alone, representing a single direction of causality.

It is widely agreed that the satisfaction derived from a collection of goods and services is relative at the same time to personal experience of consumption and to the perception of a common norm or to a peer group's standards. As a result, the systems for mobilising demand which seek to preserve a tension between perceived needs and their satisfaction generates psychological costs in terms of frustration arising from exclusion from some forms of consumption presented as a norm to be followed. Once again, inequalities of socio-economic status are at work.

The common factor in these indirect forms is that they constitute costs of mobilising resources towards the goal of growth, while the direct costs correspond to the consumption of these human or natural resources. The form taken by these mobilisation costs is doubtless specific to the decentralised capitalist economies, but their existence itself is not. Comparison of them with political or ideological procedures adopted in the centralised economies remains, however, eminently subjective.

3 Taking account of the costs of growth

The point is not, perhaps, merely to identify the costs of growth, but most importantly to see how far they are taken into account in the mechanisms or analyses of market economies. Two weaknesses, moreover complementary, should be mentioned.

Firstly at the level of national accounts, the accepted conventions do not allow for inclusion of freely provided services, nor therefore of their possible elimination. By the same token, there exist cases in which inclusion of a good or service in final consumption where it has replaced a free good or service, or one counteracting pollution, is obviously a source of overestimation of the benefits of growth. Efforts to increase, in this respect, the number of variables included in national accounts may contribute usefully to the measurement and reduction of this bias.

But the main problem raised by the costs of growth is that usually they take the form of externalities, or external disutilities in the case of consumption; that is, the variables which cause the costs are not under the control of those who suffer them. It is well known that in the presence of externalities, the equilibrium allocation to which market forces lead is not optimal. Public intervention becomes necessary to balance social and private costs, though it is surely naive to expect it perfectly to perform that function.

The evolution of objectives raises still greater difficulties. It is easier to observe the myopia of expressed individual preferences than to appraise its importance. The rationality of collective decisions which can make up for that myopia may be assessed according to the trust placed by each person in the bodies charged with these decisions and which doubtlessly leads to a more cohesive view of society.

If one takes the view that growth has been too rapid, or at least too intensive, weighted towards an excessive consumption of energy and of raw materials, the reasons for this misallocation must still be identified. The most frequent explanation offered is that large organisations – private firms in capitalist countries, state bodies in socialist ones – have caused their own growth objectives to overrule the preferences of the people at large. Whilst it is difficult to assess the soundness of this theory in so far as policy-making bodies and consumer behaviour have legitimated these growth options, it does nevertheless have the virtue of reminding us that preferences as to the rhythm and direction of growth cannot be considered independently of the power associated with their fulfilment.

Part Four
Instability in the Short Term: Disequilibria, Inflation, Unemployment

Whilst the old distinction between growth and fluctuations came into doubt at the same time as did the inevitability of a regular cycle, it remains convenient to group together analyses of a series of problems which belong in the field of short-period analysis. The short term is the special domain of disequilibria which are resolved in the long term through various regulatory mechanisms.

Throughout the post-Keynesian period, unemployment was the most conspicuous form of disequilibrium at the macroeconomic level; more recently, inflation came to be perceived as the manifestation of an opposite disequilibrium. When, at the end of the 1960s, these conditions appeared simultaneously, the notion of 'stagflation' was introduced to describe a state of affairs perceived, in the standard macroeconomics of the time, as an abnormality.

Methodologically, the study of short-period instability harks back initially to the analysis of fluctuations, which will be the subject of chapter 10. The real or imagined need to choose between inflation and unemployment, which crystallises the disagreements of various theoretical approaches, will be dealt with in chapter 11. Finally, the last chapter will look at present-day disequilibria, both as empirical observation of the progressive rise of various indicators over the past twenty years or so, and as central concept of a theoretical reformulation which may supersede the aggregative and static Keynesian texts, if not the very kernel of their arguments, to set out the problem of dynamic regulation of a decentralised economy in its fullest generality.

10 The Analysis of Fluctuations

Keynesian theory signified a departure from traditional business cycle theories,[1] especially by stimulating the construction of a series of models. It seems to the present author, however, that the analysis of fluctuations should begin from a more fundamental reappraisal of the concept of stability, and its meaning in various contexts (Section 1). The approach in terms of models of fluctuations will then be considered, starting from an example and its subsequent developments (Section 2). We shall then set out to explain fluctuations which arise from today's large-scale macroeconomic models, with special emphasis on the respective roles of the internal dynamics of an economic system, of partly endogenous and of wholly exogenous factors (Section 3). Finally, the possibility of controlling fluctuations, in the context of modern methodology based on these models, will be investigated.

1 THE STABILITY OF DYNAMIC MODELS

Theoretical analysis of models of economic cycles pays much attention to problems of stability. We have encountered such problems with regard to balanced growth and steady states. We shall now return to simple cases to reinforce the theoretical tools with which we are equipped to analyse instability. To this end, we shall consider in turn the problem of stability of global equilibrium for price adjustments and for quantity adjustments, in order ultimately to derive conditions for the stability of general equilibrium.

A The stability of equilibrium for price adjustments

The basic system of a market in which a supply and a demand schedule meet to determine price and quantity traded may be extended to the case of macroeconomic equilibrium, viewed in terms of aggregate demand and supply.[2] Though this is a great simplification, it remains useful as an example to help introduce widely ranging concepts, as here for the specification of different degrees of stability of an economic model.

An initial distinction, above,[3] contrasted static and dynamic notions of stability: that is, the presence of stabilising forces, as against the existence of paths by which the economy could return to equilibrium. However, even within the problem of dynamic stability, there are two sorts of process to be considered. In the case of price movements in an adjustment process prior to exchange, as in a stock exchange or auction sale, the outcome of the process does not essentially[4] depend on the quantities demanded or supplied at each stage. This is true of the Walrasian tâtonnement. If, on the other hand, transactions occur at each stage of the process, agents' environments are changed and so, in general, the outcome of the process is affected. We therefore shall consider three distinct problems of stability.

1 Static stability
In the case of a single market, the 'stabilising force' on which depends the possibility of returning to equilibrium is the response of prices to excess of demand over supply in a given situation. When equilibrium is defined by the elimination of this excess demand, as in Walras's theory as opposed to that of Marshall, this equilibrium is stable if and only if the excess demand $E(P)$ is a decreasing function of price in the domain considered:[5]

$$\frac{dE}{dP} = \frac{dD}{dP} - \frac{dO}{dP} < 0.$$

Indeed, the condition ensures that a positive excess demand corresponds to a price below that of equilibrium; and conversely.

In the Marshallian tradition, equilibrium is defined by the equality of supply price and demand price. Stability now requires that the excess of demand price over supply price $e(Y)$ be a decreasing function of the quantity supplied in the relevant domain:

$$\frac{de}{dy} = \frac{dP_d}{dy} - \frac{dP_s}{dy} < 0.$$

It is easily verified that these conditions for static stability coincide if the demand and supply curves have gradients of opposite signs, but conflict where these signs are the same.

2 The dynamic stability of a tatonnement process

Instead of noting the existence or otherwise, at a given time, of equilibrating forces duly taking effect, we now move on to specify the behaviour of these forces over time; in this case not only their direction but also their intensity and the lags in their effect must be considered. The results we have seen are consequently affected.

If aggregate supply and demand are represented by linear functions, a linear excess demand function is naturally obtained:[6]

$$Y_d (P_t) = a P_t + b$$

$$Y_s (P_t) = c P_t + d$$

$$E (P_t) = (a - c) P_t + b - d$$

We consider an adjustment process in the general price level, throughout which market conditions are unchanged. This case corresponds, in particular, to a Walrasian tatonnement process. The price response function takes the following very simple form, k being a positive coefficient:

$$P_{t+1} = P_t + k E (P_t)$$

The movement of price over logical time is now given by a first-order difference equation:

$$P_{t+1} - [1 + k (a - c)] P_t - k (b - d) = 0.$$

The rules of mathematics tell us that the general solution to such an equation is the sum of a general solution to the homogeneous equation (without the constant term) and a particular solution of the whole equation.[7] In our present case, the general solution of the homogeneous equation is of the form:

$$P_t = A [1 + k (a - c)]^t P_o ,$$

where P_o stands for the initial price level. A constant term B must be added, and must be determined along with A from a particular solution of the whole equation. We shall take as a particular solution the case in which the initial price level has led to equilibrium. Prices being now static, the coefficient A must cancel to leave P_o, hence $A = P_o - P^*$. The equilibrium level P^* for which $E(P)$ is zero is itself equal to $(b - d)/(a - c)$. It is also equal to the constant term B of the difference equation. Hence the final form of the solution is:

$$p_t = [P_o - \frac{b-d}{a-c}][1 + k(a-c)]^t P_o + \frac{b-d}{a-c}.$$

The price path is governed by the sign and size of the term $[1 + k(a - c)]$ which will be denoted R. Four types of path are possible:

1 If R lies between 0 and 1 exclusive, the term R^t decreases smoothly and the price tends to an equilibrium level P^* evenly, without oscillating.

2 If R is strictly greater than unity,[8] R^t tends smoothly towards infinity and the price diverges from its equilibrium value monotonically, tending towards infinity if it started too high, and towards minus infinity if it was too low.

3 If R lies strictly between -1 and 0, R^t decreases smoothly in absolute value, but takes positive and negative values alternately. The general price level converges to equilibrium by discrete damped oscillations.[9]

4 If R is strictly less than -1, R^t increases steadily in absolute value[10] but again alternately changes sign. The price therefore diverges from its equilibrium value in explosive discrete oscillations.

These four cases are illustrated in Figure 10.1, in which the price-paths are represented in relation to two lines: the 45° line, and the price revision function, $P_{t+1} = P_t + kE(P_t)$:

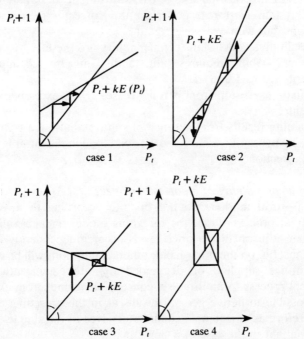

Figure 10.1 A discrete tâtonnement process of price adjustment

The corresponding time-paths are shown in Figure 10.2:

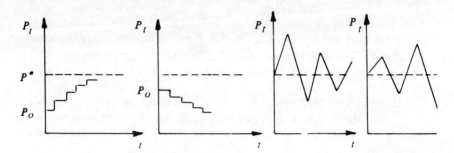

Figure 10.2

The condition for stability, $-1 < R < 1$, implies the restriction $-2 < k(a - c) < 0$ on the parameters of our model. k being positive by definition, it is necessary that $(a - c)$ be negative and, at the same time, that k be not too large $[k < 2/(a - c)]$. In the first inequality we recognise the condition for static stability, which therefore turns out to be necessary but not sufficient for dynamic stability. The second requirement expresses the risk of overadjustment: destabilisation of a dynamic system by forces acting in the correct direction, towards equilibrium, but with excessive vigour.

The qualitative conclusions of this inquiry are these:

1 Dynamic stability requires static stability and a limited amplitude of adjustments (cases 1 and 3).

2 Oscillations result from strong (case 3) or excessive (case 4) adjustments.

3 Instability results from absence of static stability (case 2) or from destabilising overadjustment (case 4), even though the latter is acting in the right direction.

3 The dynamic stability of a non-tatonnement process
Most real-world markets do not operate according to a Walrasian tatonnement process. True, the foregoing model remains valid to the extent that adjustments to price levels occur independently of actual transactions; but on the other hand, other assumptions will be needed if the quantities supplied or demanded operate significantly in the adjustment process. A multitude of conceivable formulations exists, and it is impossible to derive general results as in the preceding case. We shall therefore as an example confine ourselves to the simple 'cobweb' model, familiar in the case of a single market.

Non-tatonnement models are distinguished from one another by the manner in which they specify the transactions outside equilibrium. The 'cobweb' assumes that the quantity supplied is always taken up, at a price satisfying the buyers. Producers adapt their behaviour to the price thus established, to determine the quantity supplied in the following period. Lags in supply, and the impossibility – or at least the high cost – of storage, are circumstances in which these hypotheses are particularly justified.

Using the same notation as before, the general price level is determined along the whole of the aggregate demand curve, say

$$P_t = (Y_t - b)/a ,$$

and output, measured on the aggregate supply curve, depends on the price in the previous period:

$$Y_t = cP_{t-1} + d,$$

whence the difference equation defining price over time:

$$P_{t+1} - (c/a)P_t + b - d/a = 0,$$

to which we may apply the same techniques as before. In particular, the general solution for the price at time t is:

$$P_t = (P_o - \frac{b-d}{a-c})(\frac{c}{a})^t + \frac{b-d}{a-c} .$$

If the aggregate demand and supply functions have different slopes, the time-path of the price-level is described by discrete oscillations in the form of a cobweb, whence the name of the model.[11]

The stability condition here is that the absolute value of c/a be less than one; that is, the coefficient of response of supply must be less than that of demand, as the following cases illustrate.[12]

By considering each case illustrated (Figure 10.3) we can verify that static stability is always a precondition for dynamic stability, so long as the Marshallian condition $(1/a)-(1/c)<0$ is retained. But this condition is not always sufficient, since the assumptions of the model imply a considerable adjustment of price and of quantity supplied. It can be shown that if suppliers restrict their output adjustments, for example by basing their decisions on an expected price imperfectly elastic to current variations – as is the case with adaptive expectations – the zone of stability of aggregate equilibrium is substantially enlarged.

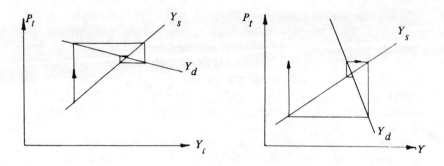

Figure 10.3

It remains true that, non-tatonnement situations being the most general, specification of adjustment processes within them cannot be accomplished *a priori*, and that the range of hypotheses which might be constructed to complete this specification is large. In any case, manipulation of aggregates, like analysis at the level of a single market, deals with only a few of the implications of the distinction between a tatonnement process and a process of adjustment with transactions, a distinction which can fully be seen from the perspective of general equilibrium, due to the inter-market effects which there become apparent.

B The stability of aggregate equilibrium for quantity adjustments

The problem of short-term macroeconomic stability was considered firstly with regard to price adjustments, under conditions formally identical to those of a single market. However, post-Keynesian debates have led to consideration of the possibility of adjustment paths throughout which prices and wages are rigid whilst quantities produced and the rate of interest adjust.

Two alternative hypotheses will be considered here, in order to specify the state of the economy at points along the adjustment path. Firstly, we shall consider a model in 'real time', without tatonnement, supposing a temporary flow equilibrium to occur at each point in time. The dynamics of the model then follow from stock adjustments from period to period. Afterwards, we shall consider paths through which equilibrium conditions are not met, and in which adjustments of income and of the rate of interest occur simultaneously.

Given fixed prices, we shall proceed from the following version of the full Keynesian *IS-LM* model:

$$I = I_o - ai + bY$$

$$S = sY, \quad S = I \qquad \text{from where follows the } IS \text{ curve}$$

$$i = (b - s) Y/a + I_o/a \quad \text{and}$$

$$M_d = L_o - Li + mY \quad ; \quad M_d = M_o$$

giving the *LM* curve

$$i = m Y/l + (l_o - M_o)/l.$$

We must now make explicit the two specifications of the dynamics of the system outlined above.

1 Adjustments ordered in real time

Following a piece of work by Hicks (1951, chapter XI 'The Monetary Factor') it is possible to link to the *IS-LM* framework a dynamic model in which the feedback of the goods market onto the money side, instead of occurring instantaneously, operates with a lag. Current income is then determined along the *IS* curve, which describes a temporary flow equilibrium.

$$Y_t = I_o - a \, i_t/(b - s).$$

On the other hand, the *LM* curve dictates the lagged reaction of money balances and of the interest rate:

$$i_{t+1} = mY_t/l + (L_o - M_o)/l.$$

This process implies that all markets clear at each moment of time, but not that equilibrium is attained on the monetary side, since agents only adapt their savings decisions after a lag.

The time-path of income is now governed by the difference equation:

$$Y_{t+1} + \frac{am}{(b - s)l} Y_t + Y_o = 0$$

$$\text{where} \quad Y_o = \frac{I_o}{(b - s)} - L_o - M_o.$$

The sign and the absolute value of the coefficient of Y_t determine the features of this time-path. This term will have the same sign as $(b - s)$: that is, negative in the usual case where the propensity to invest b is lower than the average propensity to save.[13] In this case, income progresses by discrete oscillations.

Dynamic stability requires that the absolute value $|am/(b - s)l|$ be less than one; in other words, the gradient of the *LM* curve, m/l, must be less in absolute value than $|(b - s)/a|$, the modulus of the slope of the *IS* curve. Here we see again the formal conditions of the cobweb model, which was applied earlier to the general price level, and is illustrated in Figure 10.4

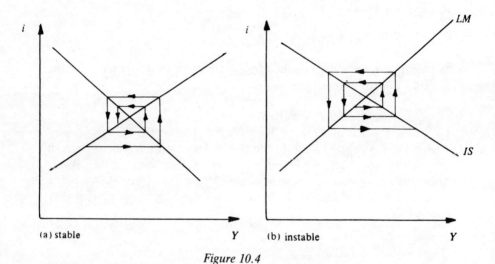

Figure 10.4

2 Simultaneous adjustment of income and the rate of interest

The latter formulation specified a full adjustment of the income level enabling a temporary equilibrium to be attained. One might propose that, on the contrary, income and interest rates adjust simultaneously. Markets are now no longer in equilibrium along the adjustment path and so, lacking at this stage a theory of the economy in disequilibrium, it may be convenient to imagine the process we are about to study unfolding in notional time, in a tatonnement framework. We shall assume that income grows as a function of excess of investment over saving and that the interest rate adjust as a function of excess demand for money. Denoting the differences between actual income and the interest rate and their equilibrium levels by $\hat{Y}$ and $\hat{i}$ respectively we have:

$$dY/dt \ = \ k(b - s)\,Y - a\,k\,\hat{i} \qquad \text{and}$$
$$di/dt \ = \ k'\,m\,\hat{Y} - k'\,\hat{i}$$

where k and k' denote the coefficients of adjustment to excess demand of income and of the rate of interest, respectively.

This dynamic system differs from those set out above in that it comprises two equations, and is set in continuous time. By substitution of variables it can readily be reduced to a single second-order differential equation. Stability now depends on the roots of the characteristic equation:

$$\lambda^2 - [k(b - s) - k'l]\lambda + kk'[am - (b - s)l] = 0.$$

But the same equation may be obtained by a method of direct solution of the two-equation system, as the determinant of the matrix:

$$
\begin{matrix}
k(b - s) - \lambda & -ak \\
k'm & -k'l - \lambda.
\end{matrix}
$$

In a dynamic system in discrete time, it was necessary for convergence of the terms of the form $A\lambda^t$ that the roots λ were of absolute value less than unity. The solutions of a dynamic system in continuous time consist of terms of the form $A \exp(\lambda t)$ which converge if and only if the roots λ are negative, or complex with negative real component.

In the case of a second-order system, a necessary and sufficient condition for stability is that the trace T of the matrix of partial derivatives be negative and its determinant D positive,[14] which ensures that the roots have a negative sum and a positive product.

The first condition now becomes:

$$T = k(b - s) - k'l < 0 \qquad \text{and the second:}$$
$$D = k'k[am - (b - s)l] > 0$$

Given *a priori* the sign of the coefficients, these conditions reduce to the inequality

$$b < \text{Min}\ (am/l + s,\ l\,k'/k + s)$$

from which we see immediately that the condition $b - s < 0$, the condition for convergence of the generalised multiplier, is sufficient without being necessary for stability.[15] Indeed, monetary adjustments through the rate of interest can compensate for any possible instability in the process of income adjustment. The condition $D > 0$ implies that $m/l > (b - s)/a$, that is, that the gradient of the *LM* curve exceeds in algebraic value that of the *IS* curve. The condition that trace $T < 0$ requires $b - s < k'/kl$; the speed of adjustment of the rate of interest must be correspondingly greater relative to that of income to the extent that the propensity to invest, b, is increased.

A graphical treatment may help in the interpretation of these results. The sign of the adjustments dY/dt and di/dt depends on the sign of the excess demand for goods and services $I - S$ and for money $M_d - M_o$, from which we get the directions of evolution shown in Figure 10.5.

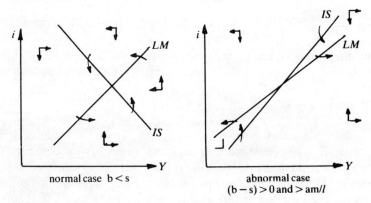

Figure 10.5

The 'abnormal' case above is one of the two cases of unstable equilibrium. It corresponds, in terms of the partial effect of income adjustment, to an absence of static stability. The second case of instability, since it violates the condition $b - s < k'/kl$, corresponds again to an upward-sloping *IS* curve, but not necessarily one of steeper gradient than that of the *LM* curve, with a speed of adjustment of income 'excessive' in relation to that of the rate of interest, as Figure 10.6 illustrates:

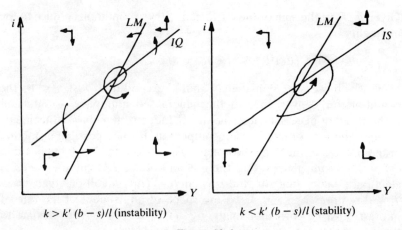

Figure 10.6

It is worth noticing that only the relative speed of adjustment kl/k', and not the absolute speeds, is relevant here. On this point, models in continuous time differ fundamentally from those in discrete time,[16] which serves to warn the reader that two apparently closely related formalisations can lead to different conclusions if they include distinct implicit assumptions.

3 A digression on the correspondence principle

The dynamic case study set out above presents an opportunity to explain the principle of correspondence between static and dynamic analysis, formulated by Samuelson (1947). This principle asserts that the comparative static properties of a model may depend on its dynamic properties. In comparative statics, for a rigorous derivation of the multipliers, one searches in the neighbourhood of an initial macro-economic equilibrium for the shifts $\hat{Y}$ and $\hat{\imath}$ to a new equilibrium taking account of changes $\hat{I}_o$ and $\hat{M}_o$ in the exogenous variables, here autonomous investment and the money supply.

These changes must satisfy the equation system:

$$\begin{pmatrix} b - s & -a \\ m & -l \end{pmatrix} \begin{pmatrix} \hat{y} \\ \hat{\imath} \end{pmatrix} = \begin{pmatrix} -\hat{I}_o \\ \hat{M}_o \end{pmatrix}$$

whose solution by Cramer's rule gives expressions of the form

$$\hat{y} = \frac{\begin{vmatrix} -\hat{I}_o & -a \\ \hat{M}_o & -l \end{vmatrix}}{\Delta}$$

and

$$\hat{\imath} = \frac{\begin{vmatrix} b - s & -\hat{I}_o \\ m & \hat{M}_o \end{vmatrix}}{\Delta}$$

in which the determinant $\Delta = [a\,m - (b - s)\,l]$, whose sign is critical for the dynamic stability of the model, appears in the denominator. The investment multiplier, for example, is positive if and only if $\Delta > 0$, which holds when macroeconomic equilibrium is stable. To speak of a negative multiplier is therefore a meaningless comparative static proposition as a shock $\hat{I}_o$ in I will lead the economy to cumulative divergence and not to a new equilibrium position to be compared with the initial one.

This, then, is the gist of the correspondence principle, and it warns us to be careful in studying the comparative statics of a model whose dynamic properties are unknown.

C The stability of general equilibrium

The logical consistency of the general equilibrium model makes that framework appropriate for analysis of the role of certain adjustment processes in a market economy. Once again, a primary distinction enables us to distinguish two sorts of approach, in terms of tatonnement and of non-tatonnement processes.

1 Tatonnement processes

The first investigations of stability of general equilibrium were carried out by Hicks (1939) in terms of static stability. Samuelson (1947) was to provide the earliest treatment of the problem of local dynamic stability, by specifying a tatonnement process in which price revision takes place in the light of excess demands observed in the various markets. For each good j,

$$dp_j/dt = a_h \, E(p_1, ..., p_j, ..., p_n) \, .$$

With this type of price adjustment, Arrow and Hurwicz followed by others such as Quirk and Saposnik (1968 pp. 191–8) were subsequently able to demonstrate the global stability of general equilibrium under various alternative assumptions, in particular that all goods are gross substitutes (meaning that the demand for any one good is an increasing function of the price of any other).[17]

2 Non-tatonnement processes

In the absence of tatonnement, it is necessary to specify how exchange takes place outside general equilibrium. Among the many conceivable processes, particular attention has been given to two, respectively labelled the Edgeworth process and the Hahn process.[18]

The Edgeworth process, developed by Uzawa, assumes that exchange takes place whenever there exists a group – a coalition of agents – for which exchange is mutually beneficial. A sequence of situations, in which the utility of agents progressively increases for a given set of prices, is therefore considered. This process assumes that agents are fully informed of exchange possibilities and is not easily extended to include production.

The Hahn process assumes that markets are sufficiently well

organised that in each either a net excess supply or excess demand remains, with all agents on the 'short' side being satisfied. From one period to the next, the non-satisfied agents see their theoretically attainable utility level fall, due to the price rise if they are buyers in an excess demand situation or to the fall if they are sellers in the case of excess supply.

The Hahn process requires less information to be known to agents, and is more readily generalised than the Edgeworth process.[19]

Demonstrations of stability proceed by showing, in the Edgeworth process, that the sequence of attained utilities converges to an upper limit, or in the Hahn process, that the sequence of theoretically attainable utilities tends to a lower limit.

It is clear that the study of stability in non-tatonnement processes directly raises the problem of the workings of an economy out of equilibrium and, therefore, takes us back towards the mainstream of modern disequilibrium theory.

2 BUSINESS CYCLES

While, in the pre-Keynesian period, a profusion of theories purporting to explain business cycles existed, the explanations advanced at best rested only on a partial formulation. They thus left unspecified certain of the hypotheses which dictate the evolution of the economy. The post-Keynesian reconstruction of analysis of fluctuations, in contrast, moves on to the specification of dynamic models which, for all their simplicity, have the advantage of defining fully the mechanisms on which they are based. These models in general begin with a multiplier-accelerator combination, and introduce lags in the effects of the variables considered. One typical example, which we shall look at first, is due to Samuelson. Extensions of the analysis in various directions have been proposed and will be mentioned subsequently, while we shall end by considering the matter of the formal integration of the analysis of fluctuations and of growth.

A Samuelson's oscillator

In this very well-known model, first suggested in 1939, Samuelson considers an aggregated economy in which investment is determined by the action of the accelerator in the consumer goods sector, and consumption is determined by the income level with a one-period lag, called the 'Robertsonian lag'. Government expenditure G_t is also included. Total income may therefore be written:

$$Y_t = C_t + I_t + G_t ,$$

Substituting for the components we have:

$$C_t = \alpha Y_{t-1}$$

$$I_t = \beta [C_t - C_{t-1}] = \alpha \beta Y_{t-1} - \alpha \beta Y_{t-2}$$

$$Y_t - \alpha (1 + \beta) Y_{t-1} + \alpha \beta Y_{t-2} - G = 0.$$

The path of income is therefore given by a second-order difference equation. Its stationary solution Y is easily determined by setting $Y_t = Y_{t-1} = Y$:

$$\hat{Y} = G/(1 - \alpha).$$

Since G is here the only remaining form of autonomous expenditure, the general solution of the homogeneous equation includes the roots λ_1 and λ_2 of the characteristic equation:

$$\lambda^2 - \alpha (1 + \beta) \lambda + \alpha \beta = 0$$

and takes the following form:

$$Y_t = A_1 \lambda_1^t + A_2 \lambda_2^t + G/(1 - \alpha) .$$

The roots may be real or complex, and they take the values

$$\lambda_1, \lambda_2 = [\alpha(1 + \beta) \pm \sqrt{ \alpha^2(1 + \beta)^2 - 4.\alpha \beta }] / 2.$$

Real roots are obtained if the discriminant $\alpha^2 (1 + \beta)^2 - 4 \alpha \beta$ is positive, that is if $\alpha > 4 \beta/(1 + \beta)^2$. Otherwise, we obtain complex roots of the form:

$$\lambda_1, \lambda_2 = [\alpha(1 + \beta) \pm i \sqrt{ 4 \alpha \beta - \alpha^2 (1 + \beta)^2 }] / 2.$$

To understand the behaviour of the system we consider the modulus of the roots, $\mu(\lambda)$; this includes the absolute value for the complex numbers:

$$\mu(\lambda)^2 = [\alpha^2 (1 + \beta)^2 + 4 \alpha \beta - \alpha^2 (1 + \beta)^2] / 4 = \alpha \beta .$$

When writing out the general solution, it is convenient to substitute for complex roots involving the imaginary term i their expression in terms of polar co-ordinates involving trigonometric functions. Simplifying the general solution and using the particular solution of the stationary case, the following expression is obtained:

$$Y_t = (\alpha \beta)^{t/2} (Y_t - G/(1-\alpha)) (\cos \theta_t + \epsilon) + G/(1-\alpha)$$

where θ is an angle (an argument of the complex variable) and ϵ an arbitrary constant appearing in the transformation.

The interesting feature of this expression is that it shows that the case of complex roots leads to oscillatory solutions, since the cosine function is periodic.

Unlike the 'discrete' oscillations of the cobweb type, associated with the negative roots of a first order equation, the cyclical fluctuations in income here have a fixed period, whose length depends inversely on the size of θ. The amplitude of these fluctuations is governed by the modulus of the roots, $\sqrt{\alpha \beta}$. If this number is greater than one, the amplitude increases and the system diverges from its equilibrium. Vice versa, the fluctuations are damped if $\alpha \beta$ is less than one[20] and income tends towards its equilibrium value, while the amplitude is constant for $\alpha \beta = 1$.

Returning to the several conditions we have found, we can locate four types of behaviour of the system in the parameter space (Fig. 10.7).

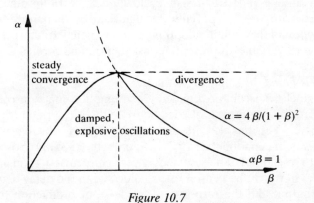

Figure 10.7

Since real roots cannot be negative, they lead to a regular exponential movement towards equilibrium for $\alpha \beta < 1$, or diverging from it, for $\alpha \beta > 1$. The two areas of the diagram characterised by complex roots give rise to damped, explosive, or, on the boundary, sustained oscillations.

This model above all retains an endogenous mechanism generating regular cycles. This mechanism depends not so much upon the combination of accelerator and multiplier as on the influence of lags introduced into this interaction. Several objections to this may be advanced. Firstly, the assumption that investment is induced solely by variations in the demand for consumption goods is a very special one. It may be replaced by the more usual accelerator specification involving changes in total income Y_t. The model thus obtained, as examined by Hicks in particular, is expressed in the following difference equation:[21]

$$Y_t - (1 + \beta - \alpha) Y_{t-1} + \beta Y_{t-2} + G = 0,$$

whose solution leads to conditions analogous to the preceding case. Also, the Samuelson oscillator gives the case of sustained fluctuations as a consequence of very special values of the parameters, whose empirical probability is very small and which are anyway incompatible with the pursuit of growth.

This, then, within the narrow bounds of its mechanical description of the economy, is the true prototype for models of fluctuations.

B The development of models of fluctuations

While the Hansen-Samuelson oscillator undeniably occupies a central position among post-Keynesian cycle models, various other models have been proposed, especially distinguished by their introduction of other types of lag, their adoption of non-linear structures, or their inclusion of variables representing distribution and profits.

1 Models based on Lundbergian lags

The Samuelson oscillator retained a consumption function conforming to Robertson's hypothesis of a lag between the receipt and expenditure of income. Yet this is but one of the delays which arise within movements in economic activity. E. Lundberg (1937) proposed a cycle model by means of tables of sequences, constructed from numerical examples in which the central role is allocated to the delay between the sale of output and the response of the level of production to income from sales. His theory was taken up notaby by L. A. Metzler in the context of a systematic exploration of the inventory cycles under various hypotheses relating to the stocking and destocking behaviour of firms. The cases so distinguished are where:
(a) stocks adapt passively;
(b) firms seek to maintain the level of inventories by altering

production by the change in stock level observed in the previous period;

(c) firms try to anticipate the change in stocks;

(d) firms seek to keep stocks in proportion to their output (inventory accelerator);

(e) firms seek to keep stocks in proportion to their expected output (a combination of cases (c) and (d)).

Each case leads to determination of the behaviour of income through a difference equation whose stability is found as a function of the coefficients. The results obtained highlight the destabilising role of stock adjustments, especially in the case of accelerator-type behaviour. In particular, the combination of the accelerator with expectations based on extrapolation may lead to explosive oscillations if the expectations coefficient is not small. Empirical evidence on the role of stocks in variously caused fluctuations seems to accord with the results obtained by Metzler, though with the reservation that an accelerator relationship probably overestimates inventory adjustment, and hence the likelihood of instability.

2 Non-linear models

An explanation of fluctuations based on the complex solutions of a difference equation, such as Samuelson's oscillator, leads one to expect a perfect symmetry between periods of expansion and of contraction, and implies that the same mechanisms operate in different phases of the cycle. Non-linear models enable these assumptions to be weakened. R. Goodwin (1951) proposed a formalisation in which the response of investment to variations in demand is neither symmetrical nor proportionate. (See also Allen (1967).) Investigation of the model constructed on this basis reveals limit cycles, periodic but not symmetrical, as they significantly involve longer phases of expansion than of contraction.

A better-known, though less formalised, example is provided by Hicks's (1951) analysis, in which fluctuations stem from the recurrent impacts of an explosive path lying between a ceiling related to the maximum output allowed by disposable resources, and a floor formed by the level of activity justified by autonomous expenditures.

In Figure 10.8, the line *FF* represents the path of the full employment level of income; line *AA* is the path of autonomous expenditure, so that *LL* is the income path in the absence of induced investment, and *EE* the path of equilibrium income growing at a rate g, through the action of the multiplier combined with the accelerator coefficient v. The economy is subjected to cumulative disequilibrium, as in the view of Harrod; however, the slowing down of expansion near full employment leads to a reversal, through the accelerator effect, just as the slowing down of

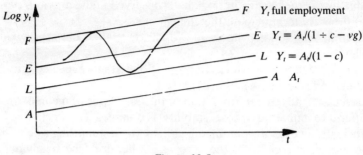

Figure 10.8

recession in the neighbourhood of the lower bound leads to an upturn.[22] It should further be noted that, for Hicks, autonomous expenditures are themselves susceptible to exogenous shocks, further reinforcing the instability of the economy between its guide rails.

Hicks's analysis is of interest as an example of the influence of non-linearities. It remains limited, however, in as much as it takes them as exogenous rather than as a result of the internal regulation of the system.

3 Introduction of variables relating to distribution

The models outlined above took national income as an homogeneous flow in its role of allowing some level of consumption and of stimulating investment through its variations. Considerations of distribution and of profitability are therefore excluded. Kalecki *per contra*, in a series of contributions dating back to 1935, proposed a family of cycle models based on a division of society into two classes: capitalists who receive profits, and wage-earning workers.

Kalecki's models may be distinguished from those set out above, firstly by the relationships between distribution and growth which they incorporate, and secondly by their particular specification of an investment function which introduces a relationship between current investment I_t and distributed lags on investment decisions D_t.

The formal relationship between income formation and distribution is obtained by making investment decisions D_t dependent, not on variations in total income, but on the level of – or variations in – profits, together with the capital stock inherited from the last period, as for example:

$$D_t = a P_t - b K_{t-1} ,$$

while savings behaviour differs as between the capitalists, who have a

Keynesian consumption function with low propensity to consume, c:

$$C_t^k = c P_t + C_o^k \ ,$$

and the workers, whose propensity to consume is high or even, in the simplified model, unity, in which case:

$$C_t^w = W_t \ .$$

National income may be written in terms of income or of expenditure:

$$Y_t = P_t + W_t = C_t^k + C_t^w + I_t = C_t^w + c P_t + C_o^k + I_t \ .$$

Given the share of wages, the multiplier can be found:

$$Y_t = (C_o^k + I_t) / (1 - c) + C_t^w \quad \text{where} \quad P_t = (C_o^k + I_t)/(1 - c).$$

Profits are found by applying the multiplier to the autonomous expenditure of the capitalists alone. The multiplier for wage-earners' consumption is equal to one, which seems reasonable by analogy to the case of a balanced budget, or of fully self-financed investment.[23] Distribution is determined by the degree of monopoly, which Kalecki takes as an increasing function of income, from which:

$$W_t/Y_t = w_1 + w_2/Y_t \ .$$

Substituting this value for the share of workers' consumption, the final expression for income is obtained:

$$Y_t = \frac{C_o^k + w_2 + I_t}{(1 - c)(1 - w_1)} \ .$$

Here we find the usual form of the multiplier, noticing that $c_0^k + w_2$ represents total autonomous consumption, and that the marginal social propensity to save is the product of the propensity to save out of profits $(1 - c)$ and the marginal share of profits in income $(1 - w_1)$.

Analogous to this static expression for income, the dynamics of the model result mainly from the sequencing of investment decisions; in the notation of chapter 5:

$$I_t = \sum_{\theta = 0}^{T} a_{t - \theta} D_{t - \theta} = A (L) D_t \ .$$

However, through the intermediary of realised profits and price variations, past investment affects current investment decisions, leading to a dynamic interaction for which Kalecki proposed the representation in Figure 10.9:

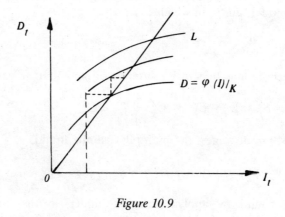

Figure 10.9

There exists a family of curves $D_t = \varphi(I_t)$, each associated with an existing level of capacity and therefore with a given level of investment needed to maintain it. Displacement above OL leads to a process of expansion; below OL, a process of contraction, and hence we obtain the cyclical pattern (Fig. 10.10):

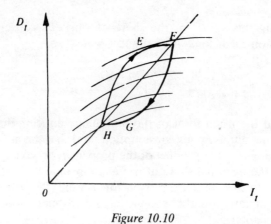

Figure 10.10

At the points of inflexion E and G, the investment path is tangential to the curves $D = \varphi(I)$, which explains the fact that the slowing down of expansion and of contraction respectively begins at these points.

A precise analytical solution of this dynamic model can be obtained, and enables us to define the ranges and values of the parameters for which this cyclical evolution is obtained. The solution is complicated, however, by the fact that Kalecki's specification combines discrete-time (difference equations) and continuous-time (differential equations) formulae.[24]

Of these distribution-based models of fluctuations it is worthwhile to mention both the formulations put forward by Goodwin in Feinstein (1967) from a 'Cambridge' perspective, and by Eagly (1972) and Desai (1973) from a Marxian one.[25]

C Growth and fluctuations

Models of fluctuations in general depict a cyclical movement of income about a stationary equilibrium obtained by applying the multiplier to a constant sum of autonomous expenditures. In this case, cycle analysis cannot be integrated with that of growth. Several means of achieving this integration can be conceived. In the first place, one might assume that autonomous expenditure grows steadily. This is essentially the solution offered by Hicks's model above. The problem with it is, that it fails properly to treat growth as endogenous to the model. A second possibility, explored by Smithies,[26] is to take growth as resulting from ratchet effects, due to downward rigidity in the recession phase. This makes growth a by-product of the cycle and of its regulation, and as such is not really satisfactory.

From the various contributions which have sought a more symmetrical treatment, we shall select a model of Duesenberry's, developed by Pasinetti (1960, p. 215).

To begin with, the Duesenberry-Pasinetti model is set up as a limited generalisation of the Samuelson and Hicks oscillators, obtained by rendering the investment function more flexible. The accelerator gives way to a capital stock adjustment process. The following relationships are assumed:

$$K_t = K_{t-1} + I_t \qquad\qquad Y_t = C_t + I_t$$

$$C_t = a\, Y_{t-1}$$

$$I_t = \alpha\, Y_{t-1} - \beta\, K_{t-1}.$$

From these we obtain expressions for income and capital stock:

$$Y_t = (\alpha + a) Y_{t-1} - \beta K_{t-1}$$

$$K_t = \alpha Y_{t-1} + (1 - \beta) K_{t-1}.$$

Eliminating K_{t-1} from the expression for income, we obtain a second-order difference equation:

$$Y_t = (\alpha + a - 1 - \beta) Y_{t-1} + (\alpha + a - \alpha \ \beta) Y_{t-2}.$$

This expression is of a sort with that found in Samuelson's model, with the simplification that the constant term is zero. The pattern of its solutions is therefore identical to that of the Samuelson oscillator, and can be studied in the space of the parameters a, α and β. We shall at first confine our study of the solutions to the region in which positive growth is possible, that is, where the propensity to invest α is greater than the propensity to save $(1 - a)$, and where the initial capital stock is not excessive in a sense shortly to be defined. In the region thus constrained, then, examination of the roots of the characteristic equation associated with the difference equation which governs the behaviour of Y_t enables the following cases to be distinguished for different values of the capital stock adjustment coefficient (see Table 10.1)

Thus, the formal solution of the model in Y_t demonstrates the possibility of steady growth. We find the behaviour of capital to be similar to that of income, with just a phase-shift in the case of cyclical behaviour. We may also illustrate the results in relation to the capital-output ratio V_t. From our original expressions for income and capital we obtain the following formulae for their respective rates of growth g_y and g_k:

$$g_{y,t} = \alpha + a - 1 - \beta v$$

$$g_{k,t} = \alpha/v - \beta,$$

which may be drawn as in Figure 10.11.

If positive growth is feasible $(\alpha > 1 - a)$, and if the response of capital is not too rapid relative to that of consumption $(\beta < \alpha + a - 1)$, there exist two equilibrium values of the capital-output ratio v_1 and v_2. However, only v_1 represents a stable equilibrium, since for $v_t > v_1$ growth is slowed and v_1 tends to increase, and vice versa for $v_1 < v_t < v_2$. v_2, on the other hand, represents an unstable equilibrium since for $v_t > v_2$ – the case where the initial stock of capital is excessive relative to output – growth tends to fall.

The behaviour of the Duesenberry-Pasinetti model may therefore be

Table 10.1

Case	Value of β	Type of roots	Time-paths of Y_t and K_t
1	$0 \leqslant \beta(\alpha + 1 - a) - 2\sqrt{\alpha(1 - a)}$	Real, positive, greater than 1	Exponential growth
2	$(\alpha + 1 - a) - 2\sqrt{\alpha(1 - a)} < \beta < (\beta + a - 1)/a$	Complex, with modules greater than 1	Explosive cycles
3	$(\alpha + a - 1)/a < \beta < (\beta + 1 - a) + 2\sqrt{\alpha(1 - a)}$	Complex, with modules less than 1	Damped cycles
4	$(\alpha + 1 - a) + 2\sqrt{\beta(1 - a)} \leqslant \beta < \alpha + a - 1$	Real, one of them less than 1 in absolute value	Steady contraction

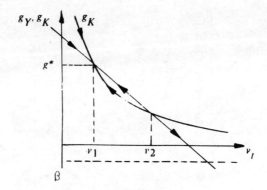

Figure 10.11

analysed in two ways. Firstly, in terms of initial conditions: a necessary condition for stability of equilibrium growth is that the initial capital-output ratio be less than v_2. Secondly, this potential stability will be realised for certain values of the adjustment coefficients, while if these values do not apply, stability will give way to a regular contraction or to explosive oscillations.

Pasinetti's article outlines his thoughts on the links between growth and fluctuations beyond the development of his model. He points out that sustained cycles, which could arise only from a particular set of parameters as an historical accident, must be taken as exogenous, in terms of 'shocks' and 'barriers'; or else as a result of a force acting on endogenous cycles. These, in Pasinetti's view, constitute intrinsic limitations on a purely macroeconomic approach. In fact, one cannot justifiably assume global parameters to be constant since they are associated with aggregates changing over time. If the evolution of the economy affected all goods proportionately, entrepreneurs could indeed make mistakes to begin with, but they would quickly learn the true values of the parameters of the system which, as a result, would converge to equilibrium. In fact, however, growth is in general accompanied by a non-homothetic movement in demand, requiring continuing adaptation of the structure of output. This leads to changes in parameters and, at the same time, to variations in the rhythm of investment, giving growth its inherent cyclical character (Pasinetti, 1960, p. 231).

3 CYCLICAL PROPERTIES OF MACROECONOMIC MODELS

The three cycle models presented above are highly simplified for illustrative and expository purposes. Applied macroeconomists have developed much more elaborate models, for the purpose of forecast and of the evaluation of alternative policies. Such models often contain several hundred equations whose coefficients are estimated using econometric techniques. They serve as a more useful basis for understanding the origin of economic fluctuations and their regulatory mechanisms.[27] We shall first set up the problem of explaining fluctuations in this context, and methods of dealing with it, in a much simplified form. We shall then develop the analysis of cases of instability and of recurrent cycles, before turning to the issue of control in these macro-models, and hence to the matter of dynamic stabilisation policy.

A The problem, and a typology of its solutions

Since historical observation shows the existence of recurrent and more or less regular cycles in business activity, macrodynamic analysis must take account of them. Simple models consider persistent fluctuations merely as a particular case, corresponding to special values of the parameters; hence the idea of introducing exogenous elements into the analysis, exemplified by the Hicks approach. Moreover, work on one of the first large global econometric models, that of the Klein and Goldberger, has confirmed the difficulties raised by a completely endogenous explanation of fluctuations in a model of this type.

1 The work of I. and F. Adelman
In 1959, I. and F. Adelman began to study the dynamic properties of the model of the US economy constructed by Klein and Goldberger (Adelman and Adelman, 1959, pp. 596 et seq.). This model, generally regarded as of Keynesian inspiration, includes about twenty-five dynamic equations. After a few modifications, in particular linearisation of the model, the Adelmans calculate the endogenous variables of the model over an horizon of the order of a hundred annual periods, the exogenous variables being assumed to follow linear trends. The results obtained clearly indicate that the endogenous variables themselves follow a linear trend, and that no cycles appear under these conditions. The authors then seek to test the stability of the model with respect to initial shocks. For example, they assume that in a given year, government expenditure falls by almost three quarters of its value in the reference simulation. The results obtained, summarised in Figure 10.12, well illustrate the strong stability of the model to this sizeable shock (ibid. p. 605):

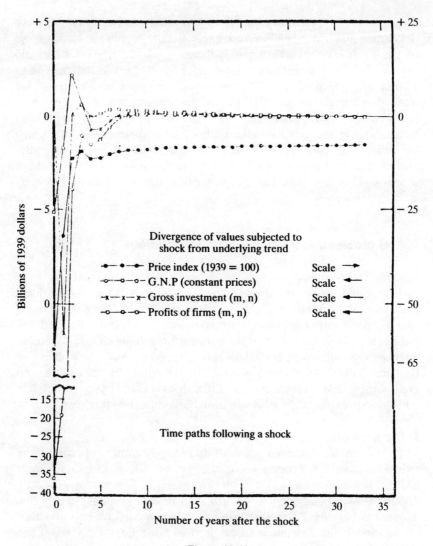

Figure 10.12

The economy undergoes scarcely more than one noticeable disturbance, which lasts about eight years. Fluctuations being highly
damped, the real values of national product, investment and profits,
practically regain their equilibrium values inside twelve years, while
prices move in parallel, without, however, returning to the 'equilibrium'
level of the reference run. This model, therefore, takes account of
recurrent fluctuations only under an assumption of periodic, severe

shocks. The Adelmans' result is typical and parallels the behaviour of the great majority of macroeconomic models.

It should be noted that this study treats the econometric model as deterministic while 'forgetting' the random terms in each equation. Consideration of these random elements is enough to make the model's solutions comparable to the behaviour of the real economy. Before illustrating this diagrammatically, let us consider the problem in its general form.

2 Sources of fluctuations: a typology
Now that we have seen the impossibility of a purely endogenous explanation of fluctuations within a particular model, we must consider some alternative explanations, which may be described as semi-endogenous or as purely exogenous, depending on whether the fluctuations result from non-oscillatory perturbations or from recurrent external shocks. To lend precision to these distinctions, let us consider a general dynamic model and its different levels of solution.

In general, an econometric model explains a set of endogenous variables Y_t by the effects of contemporaneous interactions in these variables, represented by a term $B_o Y_t$; by the effects of lags in these interactions represented $B(L) Y_t$; by a series of exogenous variables whose influence may be lagged, denoted $A(L) X_t$; and finally by a vector of disturbances, representing unspecified variables and considered as random. Hence, the complete 'structural form' of the model is:

$$Y_t = [B_o + B(L)] \ Y_t + A(L) X_t + U_t \ .$$

In general if the elements of B_o are non-zero, we have a system of dynamic simultaneous equations. An initial level of solution consists in eliminating the endogenous variables occurring as explanatory variables in each equation. If this is possible, we obtain the reduced form, expressing the unknown variables as a function of those which are predetermined, the exogenous variables and lagged values of the endogenous variables:

$$Y_t = [I - B_o]^{-1} \ [B(L) Y_t + A(L) X_t + U_t] \ .$$

In this formula, the present state of the economy is found from its past states, the current or lagged values of the exogenous variables and the current values of the random disturbances. We might wish to go further and to obtain an expression for the current state of the economy in terms only of the series of values of the exogenous variables and of the disturbances. In particular, such an expression is required if we wish to discover the final effect of an economic policy measure, or of any other change in an exogenous variable. Such an expression can be found if the adjustment process of the endogenous variables is convergent, enabling us to write:

$$Y_t = [I - B_o - B(L)]^{-1} [A(L) X_t + U_t],$$

called the final form of the model. The exogenous variables occur in the form of a 'rational' lag structure (Jorgenson, 1966), which can be written:

$$[I - B_o - B(L)]^{-1} A(L) X_t = \sum_{\theta = 0}^{\infty} \Pi_\theta X_{t - \theta},$$

where the lag coefficients, elements of the matrices π_θ, are dynamic multipliers measuring the influence of an exogenous variable on an endogenous variable after θ periods.

The Keynesian dynamic multiplier is a very simple special case of this definition, whose applications will be set out later.

Explaining a state of an economy by the final form of a dynamic model amounts to incorporating the whole history of the exogenous variables and assuming that the system has no starting point, which clearly is in general an unrealistic convention. For a complete explanation of the present state of an economy, one must take account explicitly of an initial state, and of a part of the autonomous evolution of the system from this initial state, which is partly autoregressive of the form:

$$Y_t = [I - B_o]^{-1} B(L) Y_t.$$

This term is a generalisation of the homogeneous equation discussed in the context of the Samuelson oscillator. It therefore has a solution of the form:

$$Y_t = D_o R^t,$$

where R is the diagonal matrix of latent roots of the distribution $B(L)$ and D_o is a system of weights dependent on the initial conditions. Furthermore, this solution may be added to the particular solution of the non-homogeneous equation to give the expression for the endogenous variables which corresponds to the full solution of the model. So we may write:

$$Y_t = D_o R^t + D_1(L) X_t + D_2(L) U_t$$

with $D_1 (L) = [I - B(L)]^{-1} A(L)$

and $D_2 (L) = [I - B(L)]^{-1}$.

In this definitive form, then, a state of the economy is explained as the sum of three elements:

(a) An autoregressive expression representing the internal evolution of the system from its initial state. From our discussion of simple models of fluctuations, it follows that this expression will generate fluctuations if some roots r in R are complex. These fluctuations will be damped if the modulus of these roots is less than one, and explosive if it is greater than one.

This form of causal determinacy ·in the strict sense, only when taken alone, allows us to speak of a purely endogenous account of fluctuations.

(b) An expression denoting the cumulative effects of 'purely' exogenous variables (the weather, etc.), or of economic policy instruments. Should the first expression disappear, this second element determines the possible long-term equilibrium state of the economy, giving, if we ignore lags by assuming Y_t and X_t constant:

$$\hat{Y} = [I - B]^{-1} AX.$$

(c) A random element, in the form of a moving average of the random disturbances affecting each endogenous variable in each period. This represents the cumulative effects of the many non-systematic shocks affecting the economy. This term leads to fluctuations even if the values of the random disturbances are not serially correlated – that is, if the value of any U_t is independent of any past value $U_{t-\theta}$. In this case the fluctuations arise from the combination of random disturbances by the moving average operator $d_2 (L)$. This effect known as the 'Slutsky effect' (Slutsky, 1937), gives a *semi-endogenous* explanation of oscillations since the structure of the economy, as represented by the operator $d_2 (L)$, is at the root of the roughly cyclical response to uncorrelated disturbances.

To complete the typology of sources of fluctuations, it is worthwhile to consider the case of a purely exogenous source of oscillations to which the economy adapts passively. From the general expression for Y_t, we see that this can arise either from cyclical behaviour of the exogenous variables X_t, or from a cyclical pattern of the random terms U_t. Autonomous oscillation of the exogenous variables correspond to a set of realistic assumptions. To begin with, it might result from variables outside the economy under consideration: raw materials prices, activity level of major trade partners, and international monetary fluctuations may be sources of imported fluctuations. Turning to internal variables, while there may be no one today who believes in natural cycles, it does seem possible to discern a pattern of economic policy instruments (government expenditure, monetary instruments) which allows us to speak of a political business cycle, linked to stop-go policies, or even to the electoral cycle (Frey, 1978). (On the political business cycle, see also Chapter 12 below.)

Fluctuations of the random disturbances may arise if the latter follows an autoregressive moving average process of order (m, p) of the type:

$$E(L) U_t = 0 \text{ where } u_t = \sum_{\theta=1}^{\infty} \rho_\theta u_{t-\theta} + \varepsilon_t.$$

Experience with econometric models shows such a case to be realistic. Hence, neither of the two possible sources of exogenous fluctuations can be excluded *a priori*.

Having now classified the possible sources of fluctuations, we shall discuss two particularly important types of behaviour: the case of instability, and that of fluctuations induced by the random element of the models.

B Two examples of model behaviour

The discussion of illustrative models with one or two lags taught us to ask in turn the following questions: 'Is the model stable?', and 'Does it have oscillating solutions?' Let us now ask these questions of two contemporary models, taken as examples.

1 An unstable model: STAR

The stability of a model depends on its internal dynamics, starting from an initial situation including a given perturbation. It is entirely governed by the order of size of the roots of the characteristic equation obtained from the homogeneous equation: if at least one of the roots has a modulus (absolute value in the case of real roots) greater than one, the model is unstable; otherwise it converges asymptotically towards a solution given by the exogenous terms. That this condition is a direct extension of the simple cases studied in the previous section can be better understood if one remembers that an nth order linear dynamic system – one with n lags – can always be reduced to a first-order system by bracketing a certain number of these lagged values as functions of their initial values. The homogeneous model:

$$[I - B_o - B(L)] Y_t = 0$$

may thus be written:

$$Z_t = H Z_{t-1} = H_t Z_o .$$

Investigating the convergence of the time-process is equivalent to investigating the iterations of matrix H, and this transformation is normally used to calculate the elements r_j of R.

This method, among others, has been applied by B. Oudet (1975) in a comprehensive study of the dynamic properties of the STAR model of the French economy. STAR, constructed at the Direction de la Prévision,[28] seeks to describe the year-on-year behaviour of the French economy according to a 'theoretical pattern of accumulation and distribution', inspired by the work of Joan Robinson and Marxian approaches. Variables denoting distribution and profits play a major role, and prices in the model are implicitly determined by the interaction between the value of the production needed to 'valorise' capital and the volume of output determined by more traditional methods. After linearisation of the model, calculation of eigenvalues gives the result shown.

Real part	Imaginary part	Modulus	Period
1.03	± 0.19	1.05	25 years
1.20	± 0.03	1.20	25 years
1.19	0	1.19	n/a
1.17	0	1.17	n/a
0.50	± 0.69	0.86	6.65 years
−0.34	± 0.48	0.59	1.53 years

Ten roots have modulus greater than one, some of them real, generating continuous growth; others complex, generating explosive fluctuations with a very long period. The eleventh and twelfth roots, which generate damped cycles with periods more comparable with generally observed behaviour, are also given in the table. Thus, in the short term, STAR is dominated by an explosive and almost monotonic growth pattern, weakly affected by minor fluctuations which are quickly damped, while in the long term it is dominated by explosive oscillations. It is worth noting that numerical simulations run on the full non-linear model confirm this pattern.

The origin of this instability can be traced in the model. Certain equations imply cumulative movements of the variables concerned, in particular corporate debts, the tax-burden of households, social welfare contributions, and incomes and re-investment of the self-employed.

For the purpose of comparison, a similar linearisation of the Wharton, US model reveals five real roots near one (between 0.9379 and 1.0078) from which it can be shown that the autonomous dynamics of the model are dominated by growth of about 3.2%.[29] The first complex solution, having a period of eight years, has a modulus of only 0.0037, implying a very rapid damping of the fluctuations. On the other hand, the behaviour of the Klein-Goldberger model referred to above suggests that its solution values are less than one.

2 Disturbances and fluctuations

Deterministic simulations had not allowed I. and F. Adelman to introduce endogenous fluctuations into the Klein-Goldberger model. Stochastic simulations allowed them to obtain results more in keeping with the historical development of the US economy. Their first specification of random shocks directly affecting the exogenous variables produced only small, quickly damped oscillations. When, however, random shocks were introduced in accordance with the theoretical formulation – additively in each equation except, of course, for accounting identities – the fluctuations obtained show a pattern wholly consistent with observed market movements (loc. cit. p. 609). Moreover, the authors note, using the techniques developed at the National Bureau for Economic Research, that the amplitude and length of the cycles, as well as the leads and lags between variables conform well with observation.

The point is that these results are obtained from serially uncorrelated disturbances. They highlight semi-endogenous fluctuations due to a Slutsky effect. The principle is well illustrated by the following phrase (attributed to Wicksell): 'If you strike a rocking horse with a stick, the movement of the horse will differ a good deal from that of the stick.'

Slutsky tried the following experiment: from sequences of random numbers, he calculated moving averages, for example over ten consecutive terms. He obtained series involving complicated fluctuations whose pattern echoed that of the British price level from 1855 to 1877. It should be understood that the source of these fluctuations, and their features, depend on the type of transformation performed on the disturbances; which transformation is supposed to represent the structure of the economy.

However, the Slutsky effect does not generate regular cyclical fluctuations such as those which can be generated by the internal

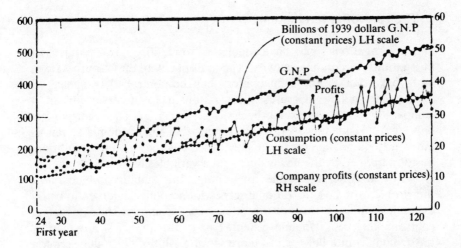

Figure 10.13

dynamics of the economy as given by an oscillator model. It does indeed produce recurrent fluctuations which repeat themselves, but not periodically: that is, they do not follow oscillations of constant, determinate length. In this sense, explanation of cyclical behaviour by the Slutsky effect remains misleading. What really happens is that 'Summation of random numbers generates a cyclical series which tends, over a number of cycles, to imitate a series formed by a small number of sinusoidal curves, but whose structure becomes heavily modified when the length of the simulation series is increased.' (Hernad, Mouillart and Strauss-Kahn, 1976).

This important point could in fact be held to reinforce the empirical importance of the Slutsky effect in so far as the regular cycle is a mirage observation suggesting rather approximately periodic cycles only within given historical sub-periods. Furthermore, the Slutsky effect underlies the so-called 'equilibrium business cycle' approach which will be discussed later (pp. 341–3).

Be that as it may, the Slutsky effect shows the danger in dynamic analysis of using numerical simulation while neglecting the random terms. Howrey and Kelejian (in Naylor, 1971) have shown that the retrospective predictive power of a model is not a correct method of validation, and that non-stochastic simulations could give a misleading account of the dynamic properties of a model, and therefore of the trends of the economy which it represents.

C The control of fluctuations

Our investigations so far have enabled us to identify various sources of fluctuations in economic activity. The multiplicity of these sources leads us to ask whether these fluctuations can be controlled by means of appropriate policy measures. The rationale for intervention in a comparative static context has been discussed earlier. This framework is only appropriate, however, to the extent that the economic system is inherently stable, and moves quickly to the macroeconomic equilibrium position implied by the new values of the variables used as instruments. It is not in general possible to prejudge this stability, which raises the problem of how to rationalise economic policy intervention in a dynamic setting.[30] The first question raised concerns the concept of controllability of a dynamic system. Part of the answer is provided by the dynamic multipliers, whilst more specific solutions introduce criteria for optimisation of public intervention.

1 The controllability of a dynamic system
The possibility of controlling the time-path of an economic system by means of one or more regulatory variables is intuitively apparent in the case of a stable system. If, on the other hand, the system is unstable, controllability is no longer assured.

A dynamic system is said to be controllable or commandable 'if, by acting on its inputs, it can be taken from an arbitrary state $Y(t_o)$ at time t_o to another arbitrary state $Y(t_1)$ at the instant t'_1.[31] J. Tinbergen has shown that, in a comparative static framework, a necessary condition for efficacy of economic policy is that this policy makes use of at least as many instruments as there are objectives to be achieved. A condition of this type remains necessary in the dynamic set-up, but it is certainly not sufficient to the extent that lags in the response of the system to changes in the policy variables must be taken into consideration.

Some experience, using simulation techniques to test for controllability of actual models, prompts the following remarks:

(i) Dynamic instability does not necessarily preclude controllability.

(ii) Formal controllability may be illusory, because the required range of variations of instruments are not politically feasible.

So we find that appraisal of the potential for controlling fluctuations in a given economy must depend on the nature of the model adopted to represent that economy.

2 Dynamic multipliers
The concept of a dynamic multiplier, which appeared with the introduction of Robertsonian lags in the effect of the Keynesian

multiplier, was generalised by the coefficients of the final form of the model, from which its values could be found. The multipliers can in principle be found analytically if the model is linear; they can also be evaluated by means of simulations, especially if it is non-linear. The use of simulations enables a systematic comparison of, on the one hand, the immediate and lagged effects of various economic policy measures; and, on the other, of the evaluations of a given measure implied by different models.

Our first examples, taken from a model of the Australian economy, will look first at the comparison of effects of one measure on several variables, then of the effects of various measures on a single variable (V. W. Fitzgerald, 'Dynamic properties of a non-linear econometric model' in A. A. Powell and R. A. Williams, 1973).

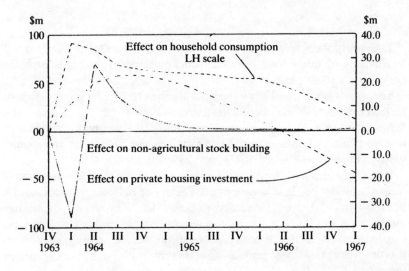

Figure 10.14

Figure 10.14 illustrates the responses of household consumption, investment in dwellings and firms' inventory accumulation to a one-off increase in public expenditure. Figure 10.15 illustrates, for the same model over the same period, the effects on non-agricultural output, of various economic policy instruments put into effect in the first quarter of 1964: increases in personal income tax, in indirect taxes on motor vehicles and in interest rates.

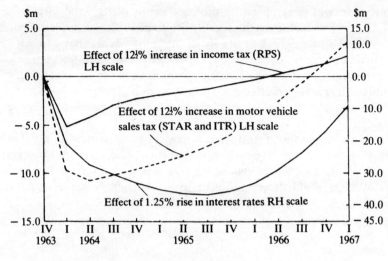

Figure 10.15

The multipliers represent an evolution in the form of damped oscillations of fairly long periods. Stockbuilding experiences a single cycle with a short period.

The use of the multipliers in comparing the effects of a given measure on different models may be illustrated as in Figures 10.16 and 10.17, the first relating to a change in public expenditure, the second to variation in reserve assets of banks, a variable which acts significantly on the money supply (Fromm and Klein, 1973, pp. 385–93).

From this series of American models, we notice that the monetarist St Louis model predicts a very limited effect of budgetary policy, and a limited effect also of monetary policy. The 'Keynesian' Brookings model gives the highest estimate of the public expenditure multiplier. Finally, two cases of non-convergence in the period arise, in Fig. 10.16 for the Hickman-Coen annual government multiplier model and in Figure 10.17 for the MPS (MIT/Pennsylvania) model of the monetary multiplier.

3 Optimal control of fluctuations
A model is controllable when there exists a combination of policy variables allowing a given objective to be attained. In such a case there will in general exist a range of policies which enable this goal to be reached in varying times and by different paths. How then may these policies be classified amongst themselves? Must the quickest always be preferred? Intuitively, the answer is no: thus, the desire quickly to restore equilibrium in the balance of payments after the oil crisis of

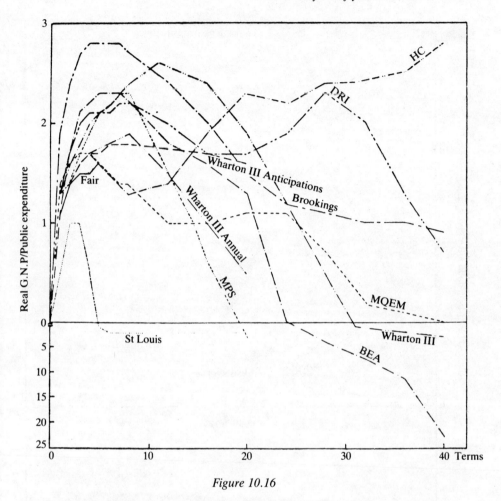

Figure 10.16

November 1973 clearly led the industrialised countries to adopt overly deflationary measures, sacrificing other objectives in the process.

The idea of an optimal stabilisation policy therefore implies a double trade-off: among various objectives, such as consumption, employment and external balance, at a given time; and over time, among possible timing schedules. It therefore requires an objective function balancing these criteria and schedules. A solution often used is to adopt a quadratic function of the divergences from desired levels of the criteria: hence for T periods and m criteria,

$$V = \sum_{t=1}^{T} \sum_{i=1}^{m} \alpha_i \left[O_i(t) - O_i^* \right]^2.$$

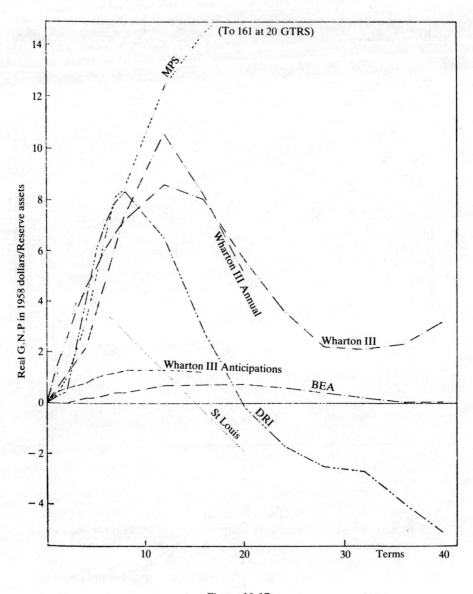

(To 161 at 20 GTRS)

MPS

Wharton III Annual

Wharton III

Wharton III Anticipations

BEA

St Louis

DRI

Real G.N.P in 1953 dollars/Reserve assets

Terms

Figure 10.17

Such a specification may be augmented by the introduction of asymmetric weighting of divergences, a region of indifference or of the adjustment costs of these instruments. It should be noted that the appearance of random disturbances in the system to be stabilised gives rise to formal complications which may appreciably alter the nature of the optimal policies.

The theory of optimal stabilization policy, as developed by B. Friedman[32] or Aoki[33] is then the logical outcome of investigation into the sources and control of fluctuations.

11   Inflation and Unemployment

Keynes's theory, developed under the circumstances of depression in Britain and of the international crisis of the 1930s opposed *a priori* inflation and unemployment as alternative forms of disequilibrium. In 1958 Phillips, in his famous article, was to give a new expression to the dilemma by presenting it as a possible trade-off, a feasible substitution between two 'evils' according to economic policy preferences. The appearance in 1956 in the USA, then in several European countries, of rising inflation in a period of underemployment of resources dealt an early blow to this image of a symmetry between inflation and unemployment, but not until these disequilibria took on a new order of magnitude after 1970, and especially in 1974, did the adoption of the term 'stagflation' to denote the coexistence of stagnation and inflation, signal the abandonment of that image.

And so, after a survey of theories of inflation since the *General Theory* (Section 1), we shall examine the empirical relationship called the 'Phillips Curve' (Section 2), and then its critique by the modern monetarist school (Section 3). Finally, we shall consider the school of labour market analysis which, starting from a consideration of information costs, proceeds to a rehabilitation of the concept of voluntary unemployment from a liberal standpoint (Section 4).

1 THEORIES OF INFLATION

Historically, the first theory of inflation consisted in attributing a general rise in nominal prices to the debasement of coinage – to a reduction in its precious metal content. Credit must be given to Jean Bodin, who in proposing one of the first formulations of the quantity theory (1568), observed that the inflation of the sixteenth century departed from this traditional pattern.

The role of supply and demand factors, introduced with reference to market mechanisms, was developed next. So in this vein, explanations of inflation proposed around 1960 divided into three main categories:

demand-pull, cost-push, and a quantity theory in the process of rehabilitation.

A Demand-pull inflation

The idea of inflation resulting from an excess of aggregate demand has exerted – and continues to exert – a considerable influence on all analyses of inflationary situations. In particular, it underlies the image of a symmetrical opposition between inflation and depression, resting on a functional symmetry between 'inflationary and deflationary gaps'.

The 45° line diagram provides the simplest illustration of this concept.[1] When the level of autonomous expenditure is excessive with regard to the propensity to consume, the multiplier tends to generate a nominal income greater than the value of output at full employment at current prices. Macroeconomic equilibrium can only be reached at a higher price level.

Much has been written on the subject of the mechanism of demand-led inflation. The most famous of these contributions were those of Keynes himself (1972); and of Smithies (1942) who (following the former's influence in the US) investigates the formal conditions for stable full employment in inflationary conditions.

Keynes's article considers the case where a fixed level of public expenditure towards the war effort, added to private demand, exceeds the current value of full employment output. Macroeconomic equilibrium will require a contraction of private demand through enforced savings, to be achieved either by fiscal measures or, if the maximum revenue thereby obtainable has already been reached, by a rise in prices.

Until then, in common with many analysts, Keynes had only explained a given rise in prices by comparative statics, and had not explained a sustained inflationary process. In chapter 9 of *How to Pay for the War*, Keynes proposed a mechanism through which a self-sustained movement of prices could arise. Wage-earners successfully oppose a reduction in real wages by securing, with a lag, an increase in nominal income. This leads to an increase in nominal demand for consumer goods and hence to a shift in the aggregate demand curve (Figure 11.1) from D_1 to D_2, magnifying the effect of the initial shift from D_0 to D_1 due to the increase in government expenditure.

The difference, obviously is that the shift from D_1 to D_2, due to the attempts of wage-earners to catch up, may recur in successive periods so long as the reduction in living standards required by the war effort is not accepted; and the price rise P_1P_2 then leads to further rises. In contrast,

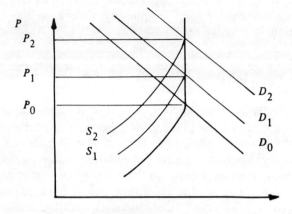

Figure 11.1

the shift from D_0 to D_1 directly implies only a once-for-all price increase P_0P_1.[2]

Despite the decisive role played here by the process of real wage resistance, the process described in *How to Pay for the War* does involve a purely demand-led mechanism of inflation, since shifts in the supply curve, from S through S_1 to S_2, play no role in the inflationary process and would only become important in blocking any subsequent attempt at deflation of the sort criticised by Keynes in *The Economic Consequences of Mr Churchill*.[3]

B Cost-push inflation

The idea of cost-push inflation arises, and is reinforced, with every historical experience of the coincidence of rising prices and under-employment of factors of production. Formally, it may be reduced to the idea of a shift in the supply curve due to an autonomous increase in costs, resulting perhaps from a rise in the supply-price of labour, or from a rise in the price of raw materials.

In general the response to a rise in costs affects both prices (P_0P_1 in Figure 11.2) and the level of output (Y_1Y_0). For prices alone to be affected, the demand curve needs to shift from D_0 to D_1, which will tend to occur if wages rise, leading to an increase in consumers' demand; or if the government reacts with measures aimed at counteracting the fall in production of Y_0 to Y_1.

However, if there is no accommodation of this sort, the rate of price-increase diminishes steadily until it satisfies:

$$P_t = P_t \, \bar{w}/F'_N, \, \bar{N} \; ; \; \bar{N} = F^{-1} \, [Y(P_t)]$$

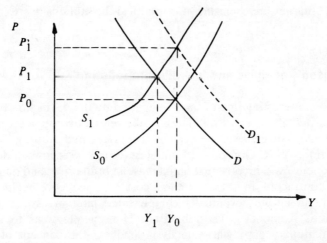

Figure 11.2

that is, where the level of employment $\bar{N}$ for which the marginal productivity of labour F'_N is equal to the aspiration level of real wages $\bar{w}$, is just the level required to produce equilibrium output.

Thus, even when demand for a rise in nominal costs is sustained, cost-push inflation cannot continue indefinitely if it is not fed by a demand response.

For this reason, among others, the distinction between cost- and demand-led inflation in present-day analysis no longer plays more than a minor role. Ackley (1959) had already proposed a model of interacting supply and demand factors, while other writers have taken the view that the distinction comes down to an intertemporal ordering of shocks (Gordon, in Lundberg ed., 1977), or to relative speeds of adjustment.

The theory of cost-push inflation is nevertheless at the root of a wider theory according to which inflation results from the struggle between social groups over shares in national income. This approach has been developed in France notably by F. Perroux (in Dunlop, 1957) and H. Aujac in the 1950s and in the US by Holzman, see also Bronfenbrenner and Holzman, 1965, while Kaldor (1959) stressed the effects of differential savings behaviour, from a Cambridge standpoint.

This approach in particular seemed to go some way towards explaining the rising inflation of the 1960s, and to suggesting the notion of inflation as a regulatory device.[4] There can be no doubt that the rapid inflation of 1974–5 and 1979–80 served to appropriate and to transfer the necessary resources to the profits of OPEC, and to determine *a posteriori* the allocation of this transfer among its providers, which neither market mechanisms nor political institutions were able to achieve *a priori*.

C Hansen's analysis and 'equilibrium inflation'

The most interesting line of inquiry opened by the distinction between demand-pull and cost-push inflation is the search over time for positive or negative correlations between rising prices and slowing down of production. As R. Gordon (in Lundberg (ed), 1977) shows, a demand-pull sequence will involve first an increase in both prices and quantities, then a contraction in output; while a cost-push sequence begins with a decrease in output, eventually compensated later in case of accommodation. A model devised by Bent Hansen allows us to identify two inflationary gaps whose analysis leads to the concept of quasi-equilibrium inflation.

In the space (W, Y) defined by real wages and output (Figure 11.3), an increasing aggregate demand curve, and a decreasing aggregate supply curve are drawn, the former allowing for distributive effects, the latter taking capacity as given. The full equilibrium (a) at full capacity output Y_0 is disturbed by a rise in autonomous demand (b) or in non-wage costs (c).

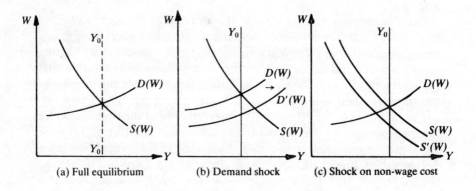

(a) Full equilibrium   (b) Demand shock   (c) Shock on non-wage cost

Figure 11.3

The transition from a once-for-all price rise to sustained inflation occurs if the price level response to P_1 or P'_1 stimulates a recurrence of the initial shock, for example if wage-earners can combat the reduction in the real value of their initial incomes. The process is easily formalised. Let $w_o = F'_N (N_o)$ be the real wage at full employment, and

$\bar{w}$ be the aspiration real wage which leads workers to demand and – let us assume – to obtain in each period a nominal wage $W_t = \bar{w}P_{t-1}$.

The supply-price of firms is now:

$$P_t = W_t/F'_N \ [F^{-1}(Y)]$$

being the price which just ensures the viability of the level of production Y. Macroeconomic equilibrium requires a third equation to be satisfied:

$$Y = Y_D \ (P_t, Z_t)$$

to take account of aggregate demand as a function of the price level P_t and of the government policy parameters Z_t.

This model facilitates the study of various forms of wage inflation as functions of accommodatory government policy: a policy of validating wage increases. It will be sufficient here to examine the limiting cases of full adaptation, where Z_t is such that $Y_D \ (P_t, Z_t) = Y_o$ the full employment output; and of zero adaptation where $Z_t = Z_o$.[5]

In the case of full adaptation:

$$P_t = W_t/F'_N \ [F^{-1}(Y_o)] = \bar{w} \ P_{t-1}/F'_N \ [F^{-1}(Y_o)] = \bar{w}P_{t-1}/w_o$$

with general solution

$$P_t = P_o \ [w/w_o]^t$$

Prices increase steadily at the rate $(w - w_o)/w_o$ which measures the relative excess of aspiration real wages over their full employment level.

Out of equilibrium, prices and wages respond to two disparities, one being $[D(w) - Y_o]$, a measure of excess demand in the goods market; the other being $[S(w) - Y_o]$ a measure of excess demand in the labour market. Thus:

$$dP/dt \ = \ k \ [D(w) - Y_o]$$

$$dW/dt \ = \ k' \ [S(w) - Y_o]$$

implying $\quad dW/dt = k'[S(w) - Y_o]/P - k[D(w) - Y_o] \, w/P$

Under these assumptions, a rise in non-wage costs leads to a excess supply of labour, and thus at first only a fall in wages. An inflationary process could only be set off if the government sought to counteract the fall in revenue by increasing autonomous demand.

If there is such an increase, there is a range of real wage levels for which the excess demands are positive simultaneously and at which a process of generalised inflation arises. Throughout this process, real wages are increasing or decreasing depending which sort of adjustment is taking place. In particular there exists, for any given capacity level Y_o, a real wage level w^* which remains stationary, prices and wages increasing in proportion with each other. This situation was styled 'quasi-equilibrium' by Bent Hansen, and it involves stationarity of the real magnitudes, employment, output and relative prices, accompanied by a proportionate increase in prices. w^* is obtained by:

$$\overline{w}(Y_o) = k' \, [S(\overline{w}) - Y_o] / k \, [D(\overline{w}) - Y_o]$$

Only in the special case of equal rates of adjustment $k = k'$ is the real wage in quasi-equilibrium independent of Y_o and equal to the full equilibrium real wage.

Hansen's analysis, while introducing an equilibrium concept for inflation, also raises the interesting matter of disequilibrium conditions associated with lasting inflation. In this respect, it anticipates the approach of the modern theory of disequilibrium to which we shall return later on.

D Price formation

On the subject of price formation, the first idea which comes to mind is the old 'law of supply and demand', according to which the change in price is an increasing function of excess demand:

$$dp/dt = f(D_t - S_t) \quad \text{with} \quad \partial f / \partial S > 0.$$

Such an idea, however, cannot usually be justified except in the case of a tatonnement process. As Arrow (1959) has remarked, who is in charge of fixing prices in a non-tatonnement economy? Are there competitive demand and supply still relevant to command price adjustments? Furthermore, as we shall see, in disequilibrium situations demand and supply are to be redefined as effective areas which no longer satisfy Walras's law. Once this is allowed, it is no longer certain that revision of prices on this basis will be stabilising. Then, it may be worthwhile to turn our attention to specific studies of price formation.

In this area, our thoughts can first be organised around the confrontation between the traditional neoclassical theory in which price is set at marginal cost, and the criticisms of more empiricist writers such as Hall and Hitch, who found that the most widespread practice was to set a mark-up on average costs or on average variable costs, at a fixed rate aimed at covering fixed costs and allowing normal profits for the firm.[6] Hence, prices are fairly unresponsive to variations in demand. Starting from the observation that certain industrial prices remained stable between 1929 and 1933, while others fell by as much as 60%, G. Means (National Resources Planning Board, 1940, pp. 142–3) suggested a distinction between prices determined by the market, and administered prices. Indeed, for this writer: '. . . while many factors influence price insensitivity, the dominant factor in making for depression insensitivity of prices is the administrative control over prices which results from the relatively small number of concerns dominating particular markets.'

The system of administered prices (which one must take care not to confuse with prices regulated by the state) results in a detachment of price behaviour from variations in effective demand. Firms seek to straighten the path followed by their prices.

Modern neoclassical theory has moved substantially towards this point of view. It assumes that prices are determined through gradual adjustment aimed at profit maximisation in the long run. Three possible justifications are proposed by W. Nordhaus (1972): uncertainty regarding costs and demand; anticipated reactions of competitors in oligopoly; and adjustment costs. As a result it is nowadays common to explain price formation within a framework of models of adjustment, involving distributed lags on cost variables.

Differences remain, however, in the specification of costs and of the required mark-up. The logic of long period adjustments suggests that prices are formed on the basis of normal costs. There is now in many countries much empirical evidence supporting this hypothesis, which is redolent of the idea of administered prices.[7]

On the other hand, several empirical studies would seem to indicate that in the French case, prices depend more on actual than on (standardised) normal costs. The difference has important implications. Taking account of fixed costs, actual costs are higher than normal costs in recession; lower during expansion. Thus, while for the normal cost hypothesis prices are rather insensitive to demand, the actual cost assumption supports the thesis of a perverse flexibility of prices: due to short-term rigidity of cost, a deflationary policy may result in an increase in prices.

In addition, the distinction between these two specifications may prove impossible to separate empirically from a difference in the rate of adjustment of prices: it may be equivalent to adjust quickly to steadily evolving normal costs, or slowly to less stable current costs.

A second question relates to the determination of the mark-up. Should it be regarded as a constant rate, proportional to the capital stock to be 'valorised' in a Marxian view,[8] or as a proportion of self-financing investment in the line advocated by Courbis (1968) in Harcourt and Kenyon (1974), or again as neoclassical user cost of capital?[9] These give, respectively,

$$P_t = ulc + emc + \rho \, M_{t-1}/Y_t$$
$$p_t = ulc + umc + \alpha \, I_t/Y_t$$
$$p_t = ulc + umc + c \, K_{t-1}/Y_t$$

where *ulc* and *umc* are respectively unit labour cost and unit cost of materials; ρ, α and c the required rates of profit – the rate of self-financing, and user cost of capital,[10] M_{t-1} and I_t capital stock and investment in value terms, and K_{t-1} the inherited capital stock in volume terms.

It is therefore possible to introduce an explicit determination of profits into an explicit price equation. It is not necessary, contrary to an approach advocated by French authors (e.g. J. Mazier, 1975), to return for this purpose to an implicit determination of prices. In each case, however, the problem of demand arises.

Applied econometric investigations widely concur in attributing a weak and often insignificant influence of the indicators of pressure of demand, on prices. In some cases, better results are obtained by assuming that a demand proxy variable V (capacity utilisation) is interacting with cost rather than having an additive effect.

This weak response of prices to the 'quantity signals' provided by the indicators of the level of demand can be better understood in the context of a global model of the roles of price and quantity adjustments, like that by M. Bruno (1967) at a theoretical level. On an empirical ground, for Maccini (1977, p. 507), who estimated such a model, 'the results provide support for the proposition that changes in demand-oriented forces are absorbed primarily by changes in output whereas changes in cost-push forces give rise primarily to changes in prices.'

E The Monetarist approach and the quantity theory

In the last two decades, we have seen a revival, propelled by Milton Friedman, of the explanation of inflation by means of the quantity theory of money. In comparison with post-Keynesian analyses bogged down in attempts to separate supply and demand factors, the Monetarist

School seemed to present an alternative at once simple and of great generality. As early as 1948, Friedman (1948) had set himself up as an advocate of a programme of monetary stabilisation opposing Keynesian interventionism with the automatic regulation of the economy through the market mechanism.

At the analytical level, his permanent income hypothesis brought back into question the autonomous expenditure multiplier as justified by the Keynesian consumption function, and implicitly the budgetary policies based thereon. Rejection of the Keynesian theory would leave room for an alternative theory of nominal income determination, whose empirical superiority (Friedman alleged) would allow categorical repudiation of the Keynesian explanation and its economic policy corollaries.

1 The money multiplier
In this new approach, the central relationship is the demand function for money, whose derivation has been studied above[11] and which can be simplified to give

$$M_d = k\,Y$$

Equality of this demand with an exogenous level of supply, provides the second equation of this highly simplified model, whose solution gives the reduced equation of nominal income determination:[12]

$$Y = 1/k \cdot M_o$$

The monetary multiplier determines nominal income. The relative roles of price and quantity adjustments remain undetermined in the short term according to Friedman who, however, offers the opinion that the above equation tends to determine real income in conditions of underemployment, and the general price level in full employment. It is clear, then, that the departure from Keynesian theory has more to do with the mode of determination of nominal income than with its price-quantity composition.

As we have on several occasions observed, the logical validity of the quantity theory stems from supply being inelastic with respect to the price level, which inelasticity arises in the long term (according to the Friedmanites) from absence of money illusion, whereas for the Keynesians it is only to be found in the short term and at full employment.

Monetarist analysis differs from the full Keynesian model in attributing a negligible role to the rate of interest, both in a static (whence a vertical *LM* curve) and in a dynamic setting, while income adjustments respond directly to excess money supply. Figure 11.4 depicts the adjustments at underemployment given by the respective theories to an increase in the money supply, shown by a permanent shift from *LM* to *LM'*.[13]

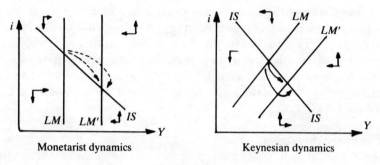

Monetarist dynamics   Keynesian dynamics

Figure 11.4

2 Stability of the money multiplier

The permanent income hypothesis leads one to expect an unstable Keynesian multiplier, but the same line of argument militates against stability of the money multiplier, since the demand for money is also a function of permanent, rather than current, income. The monetarist case then rests upon empirical arguments developed in three separate stages. First, a detailed study of long series led M. Friedman and A. Schwartz (1963) to find better correlations between nominal income (or consumers' expenditure) and the monetary aggregate, than between the former and autonomous expenditure. This study sparked off the controversy referred to as '*MV* versus *C + I*' in which Keynesian protagonists criticised the approach starting from correlation, proposing instead models specifying *a priori* the direction of causality.

In particular, A. Ando and F. Modigliani (1965), in the framework of simple structural models, established results more favourable to Keynesian theory, and J. Tobin (1970), moving on to theoretical simulations of alternative models, showed that an economy with ultra-Keynesian mechanisms could generate a lagged correlation of income and consumption with the monetary base. He did then denounce the 'post hoc ergo propter hoc' argument.

In the second stage, the monetarist argument rested on estimation with a simple framework called the 'St Louis Model', in which the basic relationship is a dynamic equation explaining nominal income by lag distributions for the money stock and autonomous expenditure.[14]

$$Y_t = \sum_{\theta=1}^{T1} \alpha_\theta \, M_{t-\theta} + \sum_{\theta=1}^{T2} \beta_\theta \, A_{t-\theta}$$

This equation has desirable statistical properties, and attributes an essential explanatory power to monetary variables, but a negligible one to autonomous expenditure variables. Once again, criticism centred on the model's specification, which did not explain the underlying transmission mechanism envisaged for the monetary variables.[15]

In 1970–71, Friedman developed a model articulating the main macroeconomic variables in his theoretical set-up. He was led to admit certain concessions to the Keynesian approach, introducing new elements representing inflationary expectations and the real rate of interest.[16]

In fact, monetarists consider the specification of the role of money in Keynesian models, generalising *IS-LM*, to be too restrictive and indirect. Too restrictive, because it allows only substitution between money and other financial assets, while monetarists include substitution with real assets. Too indirect, because it confines money's influence to transmission through interest rates, poorly supported by statistics, and does not make explicit the role of wealth effects. As a matter of fact, Friedman for a long time mulled over the ambiguity between the idea of a direct and general money-goods substitution as suggested by the monetarists' econometric formulations, and a process more theoretically coherent with the neoclassical approach espoused by him.

What, then, remains in this theory of an integration of money more complete than in the Keynesian case? The substitution of money against real assets? This introduces nothing new if it represents merely a traditional substitution effect in terms of relative returns, and to give it a more powerful interpretation in terms of a spillover, or quantity adjustment effect, one must break completely with Friedman and turn to a disequilibrium approach. Wealth effects? We have discussed the limitations of the Pigou effect. If the Keynes effect is invoked, we are brought back to the Keynesian schema of transmission through interest rates.[17]

The contradiction of monetarism is to extol, on the basis of direct statistical time-series relationships, a view of the immediate effectiveness of money supply changes incompatible with the reduction of money to the status of an asset among others in an equilibrium framework, a reduction which implies that rates of interest are the only essential variables. There is some contradiction between main thesis of monetarism and the logic of the neoclassical framework to which it appeals.

Moreover, monetarist theory assumes that the quantity of money in circulation may be determined by its exogenous supply. Only if this is true can the money multiplier be given a causal interpretation, and assume the mantle of a policy instrument. If the correlations, even lagged ones, can be demonstrated to be erroneous, judgment as to causality by reference to the structure of a model remains contingent on the model itself. Recent developments have therefore concentrated on the application of statistical techniques for identifying and testing for any possible asymmetry between two variables held to be obeying a random process through time, this asymmetry having a causal interpretation.

While an early application of methods of this sort by C.Sims (1972) proved somewhat favourable to the monetarist theory of a causal influence of money supply on national income, subsequent investigations have given more mitigated results (e.g. Goodhart, 1975, p. 191).

The techniques for detecting intertemporal causality consist of finding lagged correlations between series which have been 'prefiltered'; that is, stripped of their systematic components such as autoregressive processes. The output of this filtering may be termed the 'innovation' in the series, the information unattributable to its past evolution. Causality, in the Granger-Sims sense, runs from money stock to income, when the 'innovations' as defined above in the money stock are explained by later values of income, while those in the income series are explained by lagged values of the monetary series. The monetarist thesis of a causal influence of money stock on nominal income, received uncertain support, empirical studies, unearthing sometimes reciprocal causality, sometimes statistical independence, and sometimes an opposite direction of causality (see Feige and Pearce, 1976).

2 THE PHILLIPS CURVE AND ITS DEVELOPMENTS

Starting from causal empirical observation, the inverse statistical relationship between the inflation rate and the rate of unemployment has led to various developments, some of which relate to the introduction of analysis invoking the structural consequences of a fragmented set of 'micro-markets' for labour.

A Phillips's approach and its interpretation

In 1958, A. W. H. Phillips undertook to estimate a relationship explaining the variations in the money wage-rate in terms of unemployment rates observed in Great Britain in the period 1861–1957. To be more precise, he set out four propositions:

(1) The relationship between growth of money wages and unemployment is an inverse one.

(2) This relationship is highly non-linear because the wage-rate, while highly elastic in the upswing when employers are bidding competitively for the available labour, becomes rigid in a depression as workers resist wage cuts.

(3) The rate of increase in unemployment inversely affects the rate of increase in wages.

(4) The rate of increase in retail prices, since it depends on import prices, partially carries through into an increase in money wages.

Phillips's statistical study is divided into sub-periods. The best fit, found for the period 1861–1913, is of the following form:

$$g_w + 0{,}9 = 9{,}64 \ U_t^{-1,39} .$$

A cyclical movement around this curve was also observed, giving rise to 'loops': counter-clockwise in the period 1861–1913, clockwise since 1945, and alternating in direction in the period 1919–39 (Figure 11.5).

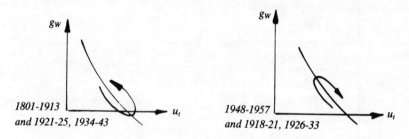

Figure 11.5

It is tempting to look for a theoretical basis for the Phillips curve conforming to the general principle of price adjustment as an increasing function of excess demand in a given market. Strictly speaking, this principle was laid down by Walras only in the context of the tatonnement process, a hypothetical process connecting two actual equilibria – but its extension to a disequilibrium situation is intuitive. On this basis, R. G. Lipsey developed the first interpretation of the Phillips curve. Let us suppose that wage adjustments are an increasing function of the excess demand for labour (or equivalently, of the excess supply of jobs):

$$g_w = \frac{1}{w} \ \frac{dw}{dt} = f\left(\frac{N_d - N_s}{N_s}\right) = f(N_E) .$$

Lipsey further assumes that unemployment is a stable function, and therefore a valid indicator of excess demand:

$$u = g(N_E) \quad \text{and thus} \quad N_E = g^{-1}(u).$$

The Phillips curve may then be derived as a function of a function:

$$g_w = (f g^{-1}(u)) = h(u),$$

whose properties are illustrated in Figure 11.6.

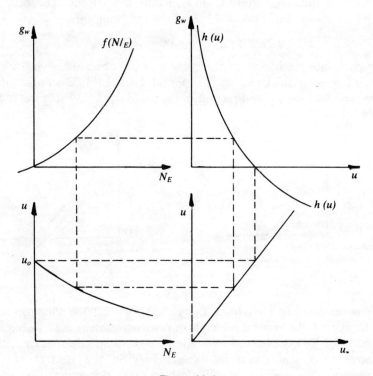

Figure 11.6

The value of this demonstration lies in the interpretation provided of the rate of unemployment u_o for which the rate of wage increase becomes zero. This value corresponds to the elimination of excess demand N_E on the labour market; yet, the equilibrium thus obtained is apparent only. It in fact corresponds, not to the elimination of unsatisfied demands and supplies, but merely to their equality.

It is therefore problematical to consider u_o as an 'equilibrium' level of unemployment, without resorting to a supplementary line of argument. But under these conditions, there is no reason to suppose that changes in the wage-rate cease for zero excess demand N_E (i.e. when the number of unemployed given by u equals the number of vacancies V). In terms of market forces acting on wages, the assumption that a man unemployed exerts a force equal and opposite to an unfilled vacancy is entirely arbitrary.

It follows that g_w does not necessarily pass through the origin, and therefore not only that wages may be static when the number of unemployed differs from the number of vacancies, but most importantly, that theory does not necessarily predict the Phillips curve's stability, as subsequent experience was to prove.

The interpretation of the Phillips curve in terms of excess demands gave some support to its use as a 'trade-off' curve, a locus of feasible combinations of inflation and unemployment. To see this, it is sufficient to note that, for fluctuations about the short-term configuration, the rate of increase of wages can be expressed as the sum of the rate of inflation π and the rate of growth of labour productivity γ:

$$g_w = \pi + \gamma ,$$

whence the expression for the rate of inflation:

$$\pi = h(u) - \gamma .$$

'This (modified Phillips curve) shows the menu of choice between different degrees of unemployment and price stability', stated Samuelson and Solow (1960), and it shows in particular the rate of unemployment needed for price stability.

B Introduction of complementary variables

Our discussion of Lipsey's thesis has illustrated the difficulty of explaining the Phillips curve in terms of market forces. Moreover, wage determination on the labour market involves processes of negotiation and confrontation in which excess demands vie with other factors. Reference to wage bargaining processes firstly offers an alternative explanation of the Phillips curve, in so far as the importance attached to unemployment weakens workers' bargaining power.[18] Secondly, it suggests a set of additional explanatory variables: the inflation rate, the rate of productivity growth, the rate of profit or change therein, and the rate of growth of unemployment itself.

1 The rate of inflation
The introduction of the inflation rate, with a positive multiplier b, into the Phillips curve equation, represents the hypothesis that wage-earners are sensitive to the effect of inflation on their purchasing power. The limiting case, $b = 1$, represents a full carry-through of inflation onto wages and hence a static real wage for the 'pseudo-equilibrium' rate of unemployment u_o on the labour market. A variant of this hypothesis, taking an anticipated rather than an observed inflation rate, has been defended by the monetarists, and will be explained in due course.

2 The rate of profit
Two justifications may be proposed for the introduction of the rate of profit, with a positive coefficient, as a complementary variable in the Phillips relationship. First in terms of market fluctuations: a high rate of profit will most often be followed by a fall, generally through the intermediary of a redistribution in favour of workers. Second, and most importantly, in a period of high profitability, the opportunity cost of strikes is higher for employers, who will therefore be inclined to concede more to wage demands.

   The influence of the rate of profit on the position of the Phillips curve was investigated notably by Perry (1964) in the USA.

3 Growth of productivity
From the point of view of wage negotiations, growth of productivity tends both to strengthen union demands and, especially, to increase the ability and willingness of firms to satisfy those demands. It must therefore appear with a positive coefficient, with a limiting value of unity in the case of a full transmission of productivity improvements. We can see that the simultaneous introduction of the inflation rate and of productivity growth leads to all intents and purposes to a trivial model in that the overall distribution of income varies only slightly in the short run.

   Just such an impact of productivity is established (*inter alia*) in the study done by N. J. Simler and A. Tella (1968, pp. 32–49). On the other hand, E. Kuh (1967) uses productivity as the foundation for an alternative explanation of wage inflation, from a neoclassical perspective.

4 Some specific indicators of demand expectations
Lipsey's original interpretation took unemployment as an indicator of excess demand in the labour market, in which we could see one constituent of workers' bargaining power. More generally, this bargaining power is increased whenever firms face increased demand for their

output. In fact, 'Okun's Law' establishes a functional relationship between unemployment and the gap between actual and potential GNP, the latter corresponding to a full utilisation of resources. In this sense, two solutions are available. The introduction of an indicator of aggregate resource utilisation such as the shortfall below potential GNP is clearly a substitute for the rate of unemployment in a Phillips curve, plotted against the rate of wage increase or of price inflation. On the other hand, it is conceivable that a specific indicator of the rate of capital utilisation such as those derived from business surveys data could be introduced besides unemployment in a Phillips relationship.

5 Direct indicators of union strength

The determinants of union bargaining power may be used to justify inclusion of supplementary variables in the Phillips equation. One might consider introducing variables measuring more directly union pressure and the 'fighting spirit' of employees. In this vein, Hines (1964) considered changes in the unionisation rate to be more sensitive as indicators of union power than the level of this rate. Another indication of the same effects are the number of working days lost due to strikes or the number of labour disputes settled during the year; this enters into the equation of variation of real wages.

6 Variations in the rate of unemployment and in the Phillips loop

It is worth remembering that, in Phillips's original article, it was shown that the variation in the rate of unemployment exerted a significant influence over the determination of money wages. This variable was also interpreted as a factor in the diminution of workers' bargaining power.

The following expression is eventually obtained:

$$dw/dt = a + b/u_t + c \, du/dt \qquad c < 0.$$

Thus the position of the Phillips curve is a decreasing function of the rate of change of unemployment. Since the latter rate often follows an approximately cyclical pattern, the evolution of money wages is described by a Phillips loop (Figure 11.7).

In an expansionary phase (point E), unemployment is decreasing and the level of the curve (in three dimensions) increasing. Conversely, in a period of rising unemployment (point R), the growth of money wages is slowed down for the same level of unemployment as before. This argument supports the existence of a Phillips loop operating anti-clockwise.

Clearly, the same loop effect might be observed in the relevant variables, though it might be quite unstable, from any cyclically

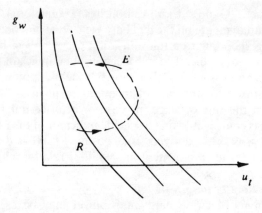

Figure 11.7

fluctuating complementary variable. The loop will be anticlockwise if the additional variable is considered as pro-cyclical, and clockwise if it is contracyclical.[19]

The same additional variables may be invoked to explain the apparent upward and rightward shift of the Phillips curve over the past twenty years or so.

C The 'structural' hypothesis

The observed instability of the Phillips curve, along with the problems of interpreting it in terms of excess demand, led Lipsey to ask whether there might be a relation between the global Phillips curve and a possible similar relationship at the level of 'micromarkets' for labour by region, sector and skills. The instability, and the loop effect, can then be explained by the distortion introduced by the process of aggregation through time.[20]

For ease of exposition, we shall consider identical and stable Phillips curves for each micromarket.

The application of aggregation conditions set out earlier suggests that, in order to obtain an identical curve at the aggregate level, we would need either linear functions at the micro level, or an even distribution of unemployment among these markets. In general, however, the aggregative curve will differ from those pertaining to the micromarkets, and will be above them if the latter are convex; that is, if their slope decreases in absolute value as unemployment increases. The gap between the global curve and those of the micromarkets depends on the dispersion of unemployment rates. Now, this dispersion can be affected by market variables tending perhaps to increase in a period of expansion (or to fall); or to fall in a recession: we then have once more a Phillips loop, displaced towards the right.

Taking this into account, the macro Phillips curve can be moved downwards by policies to encourage mobility, favouring adjustments through movement of the work force among micromarkets: geographical mobility, professional training, better dissemination of information, etc.

Lipsey's 'structural' theory may be tested by introducing an indicator of the dispersion of unemployment, such as its variance, into the econometric estimation of the classical Phillips curve (Archibald, 1969). It may be extended by taking account more explicitly of asymmetries in adjustment, as J. P. Fitoussi has systematically done.[21]

D Instability of the Phillips curve

The large number of extensions proposed to Phillips's initial relationship between unemployment and the rate of growth of money wages, has coincided with the observation of the increasing empirical instability of this relationship, as is, for example, shown in Figure 11.8.

3 THE ACCELERATIONIST CRITIQUE AND RATIONAL EXPECTATIONS

Amongst the theoretical critiques of the Phillips curve seeking to take account of its instability, the most important one rests on inclusion of expectations over the inflation rate. This gave way to the so called 'accelerationist' or 'natural rate' hypothesis, and provided a considerable range of application to the concept of rational expectations.

A The accelerationist theory

When expected inflation is introduced into the Phillips curve, the short-term instability of the latter can be explained and its existence in the long-term questioned, whilst a 'monetarist' theory of stagflation emerges.

1 The 'expectations-augmented' Phillips curve
This relationship may be written:

$$g_p = h(u_t) + \alpha \tilde{g}_p \qquad \text{with} \qquad 0 < \alpha \leqslant 1$$

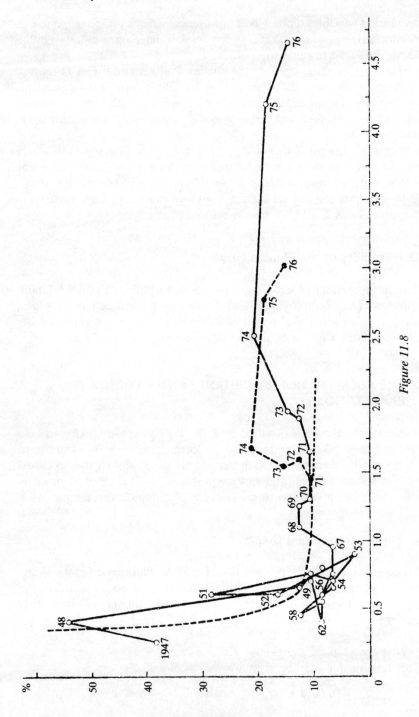

Figure 11.8

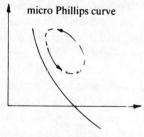

Figure 11.9

where $\widetilde{g}_p$ denotes the anticipated rate of inflation and g_p the current rate.[22] The coefficient α expresses the proportion of anticipated inflation incorporated into the current rate of growth of prices and wages. A more comprehensive analysis of the 'expectations-augmented' Phillips curve requires some explanation of the process of expectations formation. The above expression is valid in the short term for a given anticipated inflation rate, while in the long term it is assumed that expectations are realised, so that

$$\widetilde{g}_p = g_p,$$

$$g_p = h(u_t)/(1 - \alpha)$$

The gradient of the long-run Phillips curve is greater than that for the short run, which implies that the cost in terms of inflation of reducing unemployment is increased. In the limit, with absence of money illusion and full carry-through of anticipated inflation, the coefficient α equals one, and the Phillips curve is vertical. It is then no longer possible to obtain a permanent reduction in unemployment by allowing a higher level of inflation.

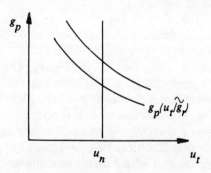

Figure 11.10

There exists a family of short-run Phillips curves, whose level is a function of anticipated inflation and which in the long term, with $\widetilde{g}_p$ endogenous, equal to the actual inflation rate, gives way to a vertical line. The unemployment rate u_n is then compatible with any rate of inflation. If it be allowed that anticipated inflation follows actual inflation with some degree of inertia, the accelerationist theory may be established. The simplest expectations formation process which includes such inertia is the static process $\widetilde{g}_p = g_{p,\,t-1}$, for which the augmented Phillips curve, while maintaining the assumption of absence of money illusion, becomes:

$$g_{p,t} = h(u_t) - g_{p,t-1} \quad \text{giving} \quad \Delta g_p = h(u_t)$$

The trade-off is now no longer between unemployment and inflation, but between unemployment and the acceleration of inflation, whence the name 'accelerationist' given to this theoretical approach.[23]

The only rate of unemployment consistent with a constant inflation rate is u_n, called by Friedman the 'natural rate' of unemployment. Defining a function h over the gaps $\hat{u}_t = u_n - u_n$, between the current unemployment rate and the natural rate, we have:

$$\hat{u}_t = h^{-1} (g_p - \widetilde{g}_p)$$

and $\quad \hat{u}_t = h^{-1} (\Delta g_p)$

The first expression, general for $\alpha = 1$, indicates that the departures of unemployment from its natural rate are a function only of errors in forecasting prices. The second expression, which further assumes static expectations, indicates that these departures are linked to the acceleration or deceleration of inflation.

2 The explanation of stagflation

The foregoing critique of the Phillips curve enabled Friedman to present an explanation of stagflation based on the role of inflationary expectations.

Suppose an initial situation, A in Figure 11.11, of long-term equilibrium with a stable inflation rate. Now impose a force tending to increase the number in employment – for example a Keynesian policy aimed at reducing unemployment below the natural rate u_n. The economy then moves along the short-run Phillips curve AB, with an acceleration of inflation accompanying the reduction in unemployment. Now, however, agents will adjust their expectations of inflation to the actual rate, which leads to an upward shift of the short-run Phillips curve. An equilibrium at point C then becomes possible, if monetary policy is compatible with the corresponding rate of inflation; but any attempt to oppose the increase of unemployment between B and C would lead to a renewal of the process and a higher 'floor' for the inflation rate would be reached. Conversely, a reduction of the rate of inflation presupposes a reduction in its anticipated rate, which in general cannot be achieved without confounding the expectations of agents, by taking the economy to the point D by a restrictive policy, and accepting a rate of unemployment higher than the natural rate.[24]

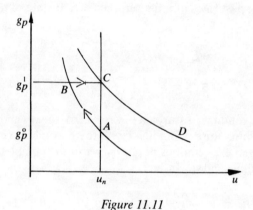

Figure 11.11

It is therefore very likely that stagflation will follow any period of accelerating inflation, due to the inertia of inflationary expectations. It is undoubtedly of interest thus to isolate the role of inflationary expectations, but monetarist theory sees in them the only factor tending to lead to cumulative inflation, and the only form of delaying factor acting on rational behaviour. The concept of permanent income is recalled: only expectations are imperfect, decisions always conforming to the theory of choice. Sluggish adjustments and institutional sources of propagation in no way intervene in the stagflation process; only agents' expectations are at issue. Thus this view too might be described as an excessively reductionist conception of economic reality.

B The rational expectations hypothesis

Friedman's theory marries well with the idea of adaptive expectations, revised in each period by some fraction of the past forecast error.[25] Such a process indeed allows us to see that errors may persist through time and, for example, that divergences of the actual rate of unemployment from its 'natural rate' are not random, but rather cyclical.

However, is it really consistent to assume, as Friedman does, that agents are rational in their choices, but not in their expectations? Indeed it is not; Muth (1961) accordingly proposed the concept of rational expectations to denote the hypothesis that economic agents formulate their expectations to take the best possible account of the information available. One formulation of this hypothesis is to suppose that an agent's anticipated inflation rate for time t is the statistical expectation of the inflation rate, given the information I_{t-1} available to him at $t-1$, including past rates of inflation, the current state of the economy, and so on:

$$\widetilde{g}_{p,\,t} = E(g_{p,\,t} \,/\, I_{t-1})$$

which implies: $g_{p,t} = \tilde{g}_{p,t} + E_t$

where ϵ_t is a random disturbance with zero mean and zero auto-correlation – white noise. Combined with the natural rate equation, the theory of rational expectations implies *a priori* the complete disappearance of the Phillips curve. In fact,

$$\hat{u}_t = h^{-1} (g_t - \tilde{g}_p) \quad \text{becomes} \quad \hat{u}_t = h^{-1} (\epsilon_t) \quad \cdot$$

meaning that departure from the natural rate of unemployment can only result from unforeseeable random shocks experienced by the economy. A very powerful result of this combination of the natural rate and rational expectations hypotheses is to exclude all possible effectiveness of systematic, and hence foreseeable, economic policy.

The rational expectations school thus takes to extremes the Friedmanite programme of questioning anew the rationale for stabilisation policy. Yet this apparently powerful reinforcement is, at the same time, self-destructive, because it destroys the analysis of stagflation outlined above, and appears in its basic form to be incompatible with observed facts as pronounced as the serial correlation of unemployment or cyclical fluctuations in economic activity.

In order to examine these points, without entering into the rapidly growing complexity of macroeconomic models with rational expectations, it is worthwhile considering a simple model.

1 An elementary macromodel with rational expectations

Let our model consist of the following aggregate supply and demand functions, linear in terms of logarithms:[26]

$$y_t^s = y_o + \alpha \, [P_t - \widetilde{P_t}]$$

$$y_t^d = \gamma M_t - \beta P_t + v_t$$

We assume that prices are perfectly flexible, and in each period move to equalise supply and demand. The supply function, which makes production depend upon 'surprises' in prices $(P_t - \widetilde{P_t})$, plays a very important role for the rational expectations school, and will be discussed in due course. In addition, with a view to maximum simplicity, the random shocks are assumed to affect directly demand only, in the form of a white noise term, v_t.

It is instructive to solve the model for different specifications of expectations formation: perfect, static, and rational.

For perfect expectations, $\widetilde{P_t} = P_t$, $y_t = y_o$ and prices follow the quantity equation to within a random error:

$$P_t = [\gamma M_t - y_o]/\beta + v_t/\beta$$

For static expectations, $\widetilde{P_t} = P_{t-1}$, the equation $y_t^s = y_t^d$ gives the price:

$$P_t = [\alpha/(\alpha + \beta)] \, P_{t-1} + [\gamma M_t - y_o + v_t] / (\alpha + \beta)$$

Prices obey a first-order stochastic difference equation, generating for fixed M_t fluctuations converging to or diverging from equilibrium according to the values of the parameters.

To investigate the case of rational expectations, let us again begin from the equilibrium condition $y_t^s = y_t^d$ giving:

$$(\alpha + \beta) \, P_t = \gamma M_t - y_o + \alpha \widehat{P_t} + v_t$$

This equation being linear, conditional expectations can be taken:

$$(\alpha + \beta) \, E(P_t | I_{t-1}) = \gamma E(M_t | I_{t-1}) - y_o + \alpha \widetilde{P_t} + E(v_t | I_{t-1})$$

But the expectation of the disturbance is zero, and that of the price equal to its anticipated value, so that:

$$\beta \, E(P_t | I_{t-1}) = \gamma \, E(M_t | I_{t-1}) - y_o = \beta \widetilde{P_t}$$

while the 'surprise' or departure from the anticipated value is

$$P_t - \widetilde{P_t} = \{ \gamma \, [M_t - E(M_t | I_{t-1})] + v_t \} / (\alpha + \beta)$$

and hence production, determined by the supply function, is

$$y_t = y_o + [\alpha/(\alpha + \beta)] \ \{ \gamma \ [M_t - E(M_t|I_{t-1})] + v_t \ \}$$

This equation clearly underlines the basic message of the rational expectations school: output, in an equilibrium model, only diverges from the natural level as a function of unforeseeable shocks and non-systematic components of economic policy, here represented by the discrepancy between the money stock and its anticipated value.

Thus, any systematic policy is ineffective, while one can show that a non-systematic policy, which would indeed affect y_t, would have in essence the undesirable consequence of increasing its variance about its natural level.[27]

2 Specification of the supply function

It has been pointed out that the supply function, introduced by Lucas, was essential in obtaining the results set out above. To see this in more detail, let us first consider two common alternative specifications:

$$y_t^s = y_o + \alpha \tilde{P}_t$$

and $y_t^s = y_o + \epsilon_t$, (in the absence of money illusion, equal apart from a random disturbance).

The second specification, a formulation of the classical pre-Keynesian theory, trivially implies independence of output from all economic policy, which can result only in nominal effects. The first, on the other hand, requires a non-trivial derivation. From the equilibrium condition,

$$y_o + \alpha \tilde{P}_t = \gamma M_t - \beta P_t + v_t$$

it follows that

$$P_t = E(P_t|I_{t-1}) = [\gamma E(M_t|I_{t-1}) - y_o + v_t]/(\alpha + \beta)$$

and hence,

$$y_t = y_t^s = y_o + [\alpha/(\alpha + \beta)] \ [\beta \ E \ (M_t| I_{t-1}) - y_o + v_t]$$

This time, by contrast, only the foreseen part of the money stock influences output. If there is money illusion among wage-earners, or more generally, if supply is an increasing function of prices anticipated by firms, the rational expectations hypothesis no longer implies the neutrality of money or of any other economic policy instrument.

It clearly seems, therefore, that the theory of rational expectations leads to a revival of the classical hypothesis of absence of money illusion which, as we have seen, implied the neutrality of money and of economic policy in the deterministic macroeconomic model. This accounts for the christening of this school as 'new classical' by J. Tobin and W. Buiter (Buiter, 1980). The result is trivial with a probabilised classical supply function; the interest of Lucas's function lies in obtaining it in a non-trivial way.

To this supply function, whose justification seems open to question as it denies the existence of money illusion in reaching equilibrium only to reintroduce it at the margin in the form of deviations, Lucas nevertheless subjoins an interesting idea. The partial money illusion which his equation represents stems from the difficulty which any agent will experience in dividing the variations which he observes in prices and incomes into variations in the general level of prices which would not justify a change in his decisions, and variations in relative prices. Agents misperceive part of the general variation in prices as relative changes. In order to obtain Lucas's supply function, it is enough to assume that this error in perception affects only the non-anticipated part of price variations.

3 The problem of autocorrelated deviations and the 'equilibrium business cycle' theory

The equilibrium rational expectation model is not only a model of static equilibrium. In the view of 'new classical economists' it gives for economic disturbances and even business cycles an explanation consistent with the neoclassical basic principles of market equilibrium. Then, a fundamental challenge for the theory of rational expectations is the existence in the economy of persistent disequilibria, such as lasting unemployment. To explain these autocorrelated deviations in the basic equilibrium model, we have to assume autocorrelated forecast errors, as said for instance Modigliani (1977).

The instinctive reply, to suggest serial correlation of the process generating the disturbances v_t, is not a solution, since if $v_t = \rho v_{t-1} + e_t$, where e_t is a white noise process, it is clear that the term ρv_{t-1} was experienced in $t-1$ (though not directly observed), and must be included in the formation of rational expectations over the variables of the system. The idea has been put forward that, the gathering and use of information being costly, 'economically rational' expectations (Feige and Pearce, 1976) would correspond to the use of only a part of the available information, so that serial correlation could remain. Similarly, E. S. Phelps (1976) has set out an example in which the discrete character of certain variables is the source of autocorrelated error terms, even in the case of rational expectations. For example, in forecasting the end of a war, the decisions taken must in each period consider a non-zero probability of the conflict ending; which in hindsight appears as a sequence of errors. An alternative explanation of serially correlated disturbances lies in the possible existence of information lags (see Sargent, 1979, pp. 330–1 and p. 378).

In any case, the easiest way to cope with this problem and to get an 'equilibrium business cycle' model is to assume adjustments costs in output changes, leading to a redefinition of the supply function in autoregressive form:

$$y_t^s = \lambda y_o + \lambda \alpha [P_t - \tilde{P}_t] + (1 - \lambda) y_{t-1} \text{ where } 0 < \lambda < 1$$

which leads to the expressions

$$\tilde{P}_t = E(P_t | I_{t-1}) = [\gamma E(M_t | I_{t-1}) - \lambda y_o - (1 - \lambda) y_{t-1} + v_t]$$

$$/[(\lambda - 1) \alpha + \beta]$$

$$y_t = \lambda y_o + \alpha \lambda \{\gamma [M_t - E(M_t | I_{t-1})] + v_t\} / [(\lambda - 1)\alpha + \beta]$$

$$+ (1 - \lambda) y_{t-1}$$

Using μ_t to denote the unanticipated part of the money supply, and substituting successively for y_{t-1}, we obtain the expression:

$$y_t = y_o + \{\alpha\lambda/[(\lambda - 1) \alpha + \beta]\} \sum_{\theta = 0}^{\infty} (1 - \lambda)^\theta (\gamma\mu_{t-\theta} + v_t)$$

The introduction of a term for the partial adjustment of supply does not affect the main conclusion of the invariance of output with respect to foreseeable components of the money supply. However, deviations from the natural rate, $y_t - y_o$, are no longer white noise but a weighted sum of all the shocks; the exogenous random disturbances v_t and the unforeseen variations in money supply μ_t, which the economy has experienced. We have seen above that through the Slutsky effect, such linear combinations of random shocks can generate approximately cyclical patterns of movement in given sub-periods.

While there exist more elaborated 'equilibrium business cycle' models like Lucas's 1975 model introducing the asset market, the basic rationale remains the same as in our single case: cycles are obtained through a Slutsky effect, the model providing a linear moving average operator to apply a random shock. If we remind ourselves that Keynesian econometric models generally fail to produce self-generated cycles, this dependence upon the Slutsky effect to explain cycles is a common feature – and may be a common weakness – of competing business cycle theory.

4 Appraisal of the rational expectations hypothesis

Any appraisal of the rational expectations hypothesis has clearly to distinguish between the different levels on which the hypothesis may be evaluated, from the stringent form of the neutrality-inefficiency proposition of Lucas, Sargent and Wallace to the formal concept of rational expectations.

Within the macromodel with rational expectations, one has to wonder both what is the robustness of the LSW inefficiency proposition on theoretical grounds and how much is supported by empirical evidence as derived from econometric studies.

On the first issue, many objectives have been raised to the LSW proposition, which are related in good surveys, like those of Buiter (1980) and McCallum (1980) whose personal point of view is different. Let us consider the main points of the debate.

(i) Policy ineffectiveness no longer generally holds if the instantaneous price flexibility assumption is discarded. It was shown by Honkapohja (1979) if prices are partially adjusted *ex ante* and by Buiter (1980) if prices are partially adjusted to their *ex post* equilibrium level. If price or wage sluggishness is explained by contraction, the invalidity of the inefficiency proposition results from models by S. Fischer (1977) and Phelps and Taylor (1977).

(ii) Policy can influence the second moment of output and thus reduce its variance, if the model integrates expectations which are formed at different dates and conditioned by different information sets. Such is the case in a model proposed by Turnovsky (1980) which retains a Lucas supply function where the expectation relative to current price is conditioned by the information I_{t-1} while the money demand in the *IS-LM* part of the model depends upon the expectation of future inflation conditioned by I_t.

(iii) Another case for more neutrality includes the existence of differences in information between government and private agents, but also the differences in opportunity set. Similarly, non-neutrality may occur from distributional effect in an overlapping generation model (Muench, 1975).

Owing to the preeminent place taken by 'new classical economists' in recent developments of macroeconomic theory and debate, a growing body of econometric work is devoted to the test of the Natural Rate/Rational Expectations Hypothesis. The core testable implication of the NR/REH is that the deviation of output or unemployment from their natural level is a function of only the unanticipated part of money growth or public expenditure. But M. Hall (1975) shows in US quarterly data for the period 1954–79 that 93 per cent of the variance of the rate of unemployment is explained by its first two lagged values, which means that the basic static form of the NR/REH cannot be maintained. More recent studies are directed towards testing the 'equilibrium business cycle' version of the REH, with an autoregressive supply function. Barro's (1977) study is typical of this approach. Assuming that natural rate depends upon a time trend t, a military draft variable d_t, an indicator of minimum wage regulation w_t, he considers the following regression

$$u_t = \alpha_1 \dot{\mu}_t + \alpha_2 \dot{\mu}_{t-1} + \alpha_3 d_t + \alpha_4 w_t + \alpha_5 t + \alpha_6 + e_t$$

The unexpected money growth rate $\dot{\mu}_t$ and $\dot{\mu}_{t-1}$ are computed from the fitted value of the actual rate of money growth from the auxiliary regression

$$\dot{m}_t = 0.087 + 0.24\,\dot{m}_{t-1} + 0.35\,\dot{m}_{t-2} + 0.082\,g_t + 0.027\,u_{t-1}$$

where g_t is a federal expenditure variable and u_{t-1} the lagged unemployment rate.

Statistical results for Barro's equations are quite good, but several objections have been raised which undermine their reliability.

(i) Barro assumes, inconsistently, that government expenditure is perfectly expected.

(ii) The military draft variable plays an excessive role, likely to be due to its correlation with an omitted explanatory variable (Small, 1979).

(iii) The residuals are uncorrelated, while the equilibrium business cycle model implies a persistent influence of any shock affecting the economy, not only of unanticipated money growth.

(iv) Barro did not really specify the alternative hypothesis subjected to test. Pesaran (1982) showed that, when an alternative Keynesian equation is specified as an alternative, it performs as well as the NR/REH. More recent tests are subject to similar discussion, and the current state of the econometric inquiry on the new classical paradigm is not conclusive.

Having expressed this doubt towards new classical propositions, we do recognise the usefulness of the rational expectation hypothesis. Its main interest is without doubt to have accustomed economists to integrate forward-looking behaviour in their models, even at the price of great technical complexities coming from the multiplicity of solutions or the time-inconsistency problem. The rational expectations assumption is also a source of progress in econometric methodology. So, in our own opinion, it is meaningless to be 'against' rational expectations, 'they are too important to be left to monetarists'.

4 EXTENSION OF THE CONCEPT OF VOLUNTARY UNEMPLOYMENT

Keynesian theory gave centre stage to the idea of involuntary unemployment, taken at the aggregate level. Recent work has stressed a disaggregated view of how the labour market works under limited information. This view is a new way of looking at voluntary unemployment as unemployment of those seeking a new job.

A Imperfect information in the labour market

Interpretation of the Phillips curve in terms of excess demand turned out to be unrobust because it rests in fact upon a confusion. The notion of excess demand in a 'perfect' or 'organised' market is meaningful since in disequilibrium such a market will satisfy all agents on the short side – all suppliers if there is excess demand, and all buyers if excess supply. In the context of the labour market, this would mean that unemployment u_t was equal to the excess supply of labour if this were positive, and zero if it were not. Symmetrically, the number of vacancies would be equal to the excess demand for labour if the latter were positive, and zero otherwise. Reality fails to conform: the labour market is seen to exhibit unemployment and unfilled vacancies simultaneously, an 'imperfection' of this market representing weaker co-ordination of the relevant aspects. Figure 11.12 summarises this difference between the theory and reality. The horizontal axis represents the demand for labour; the vertical, unemployment and unfilled vacancies (A. J. Brown in Worswick, 1976).

In a perfect market, unemployment U^*_t and unfilled vacancies V^*_t would be represented by orthogonal lines at an angle of 45°. In an imperfect market, the curves u_t and v_t intersect at a non-zero vertical co-ordinate. The locus of possible positions in the labour market is then on the short side of the demand and supply curves, and the unemployment-vacancies pairs produce a convex curve called the 'Beveridge curve'.

The existence of an approximately hyperbolic Beveridge curve has also allowed Bent Hansen to propose what remains without doubt the best simple derivation of the Phillips curve. We have the excess demand for labour,

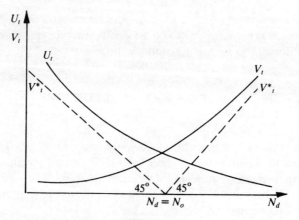

Figure 11.12

$$E(w) = N_d (w) - N_s (w) = [N_d(w) - N)] - [N_s(w) - N] = V - U$$

In general however, equality between unemployment and unfilled vacancies does not coincide with the stability, or non-acceleration, of money wages. One must indeed guard against too readily transposing the Walrasian interpretation of zero excess demands, in which all agents' plans are satisfied, to a non-Walrasian world of markets with friction where such elimination of excess demand means only that the number of plans left unfulfilled is equal on each side of the market. It would be both artificial and naive to imagine that an unemployed person tends as much to 'moderate' wages as a vacancy tends to accelerate them. We

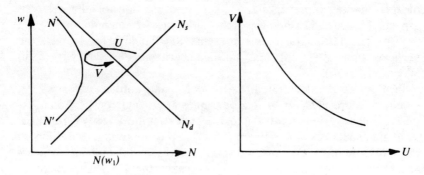

if $UV = h$ and $dw/dt = kE(w)$, we get:
$dw/dt = kh/U - kU$

Figure 11.13

may therefore be sceptical of the Friedmanite concept of the natural rate of unemployment defined as '. . . the level that would be ground out by the Walrasian system of general equilibrium equations, provided there is imbedded in them the actual structural characteristics of the labor and commodity markets, including market imperfections, stochastic variability in demands and supplies, the cost of gathering information about job vacancies and labor availabilities, the costs of mobility, and so on' (Friedman, 1968, p. 8).

As C. C. Holt has shown (in Malinvaud and Fitoussi eds, 1980), the coexistence of unemployment with unfilled vacancies introduces a certain degree of freedom in modelling the labour market rather than a substitute for the classical form of equilibrium, which Friedman's natural rate aspires to be. Because of this degree of freedom, it is appropriate to think of two regulatory variables acting in the labour market, the real wage and the 'job availability', V/U, rather than wages alone.

It is certainly possible to rescue a global Phillips curve with perfect labour markets, so long as wages respond asymmetrically to excess demand, and a certain dispersion of these excess demands exists.

Apart from this case, global imperfections are confined to a lack of mobility among these markets. But casual observation suggests that a stronger result might be sought, namely the coexistence of unemployment and unfilled vacancies in each 'micro-market' for labour. To produce this result, an assumption of uncertainty must be incorporated, to be understood as a situation in which information is costly. The writers mentioned here, such as Alchian, additionally suppose that there is no centralisation of this scarce information within the market, its use being managed only by individual agents, be they wage-earners or employers.[29]

In particular, workers do not know *a priori* the jobs available to them, nor do they know the wages offered with these jobs. Before deciding to accept or reject a job offer, they must accumulate the information necessary for its evaluation. And: 'The key, which, till recently, seems to have been forgotten, is that *collating information about potential exchange opportunities* is costly and can be performed in various ways' (Alchian, 1969, p. 109).

A description of the behaviour of the job-seeking worker ensues.

B Job search

The search for a job entails the exploration of a series of varied offers associated with specific wage-rates. This exploration is analogous to random sampling in order to estimate the (unknown) distribution of wages offered. The expected wage increases with search effort but, in Alchian's view, this 'search productivity' has two distinguishing features:

(1) It is subject to diminishing returns and to increasing costs. There is always the possibility of improving one's remuneration by investigating further opportunities, but this hope diminishes while, the most accessible opportunities being considered first of all, the unit cost of search increases with the number of offers considered.

(2) It may be efficient to specialise in the collection of information, as in any other productive activity. 'If seeking information about other jobs while employed is more costly than while not employed, it can be economic to refuse a wage cut, become unemployed, and look for job information' (Alchian, 1969, pp. 110–11).

From these two principles, it follows that the patterns of returns to search activity over time evolve as in Figure 11.14.

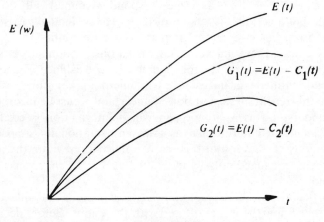

Figure 11.14

The expected wage increases with search time, but at a decreasing rate. Search costs rise at an increasing rate, faster for an employee $c_2(t)$ than for an unemployed man $c_1(t)$. The respective returns to search functions $G_1(t)$ and $G_2(t)$ are found by deducting search costs from expected wages. The maximum point of the returns curve marks the optimal *a priori*, or mean, duration of search.

Since the wage actually obtained is uncertain, the decision whether or not to accept implies a reference rate, an aspiration level or reservation wage W_r. An offer will be accepted if it involves a wage W_i higher than W_r; otherwise, search will continue. The level of the reservation wage represents the expectation of the wage which might be obtained from offers yet to be explored. It is, at least after a certain length of time, a decreasing function of search time, and always a decreasing function of the opportunity cost of search. The reservation wage needed for acceptance of an offer of work therefore increases with the benefits received by the unemployed person (or to be more precise, decreases with the gap between these benefits and the reservation wage itself). Conversely, the higher the reservation wage, the lower is the probability of the unemployed person finding a job satisfactory to him.

The same reasoning may be applied in theory to the voluntary resignation of an employee. To take this decision, he or she must perceive:

(a) an expected wage in alternative employment sufficiently higher than his present wage to cover his search costs; and

(b) an efficiency gain and an economy of search costs if he 'specialises' in search by leaving his job, greater than the opportunity cost of resigning, the gap between his current income and the benefits expected over the search period.

The probability of resignation is clearly a decreasing function of current income, and increasing in expected future wages and unemployment benefits.

C The interaction of labour supply and demand

The firm is in a symmetrical position. It has the choice of announcing an increased wage and rapidly filling its vacancies, or of announcing a relatively lower wage, risking a longer shortage of workers.[30] It is hence possible to represent, as a function of search time, the wages W_o (t) offered by firms, and those demanded by the unemployed, or the reservation wage $W(t)$.

An offer of work announced at t_i may be confronted by a demand for work announced later, in t_j as from that date. In any case, an agreement can only be made after the moment T when the firm's supply exceeds the reservation wage. But, in view of information costs, the coincidence of offers is not guaranteed. Its probability is then an increasing function of time and of the gap $W_o(t) - W(t)$.[31]

The case illustrated in Figure 11.15 corresponds to a duration of unemployment longer than that of job vacancies, and therefore to a somewhat depressed global situation. With buoyant markets, the opposite would prevail $(t_j < t_i)$ and the expected contract wage would be greater, while the duration of vacancies would exceed that of unemployment.

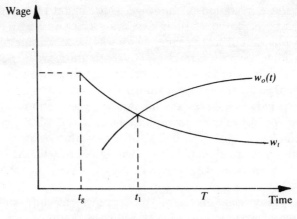

Figure 11.15

Thus, this analysis of the labour market under uncertainty is of considerable interest. Though limited to factors of individual behaviour only, it enables typical relationships at this level to be sought out, to do service at the global level. It has, however, provided a foundation for the theory which states that the greater part of present-day unemployment could be interpreted as search unemployment, and hence as voluntary in nature. Thus Phelps (op. cit. p. 17), wrote in 1980 'Today's unemployment is an investment in a better allocation of a given number of employed workers tomorrow; its opportunity cost, as with any other kind of investment, is a reduction in present consumption.'

This view of unemployment is in accordance with the liberal doctrine, as defended in France by A. Fourcans and J. J. Rosa, for whom present-day unemployment has nothing fundamentally to do with a 'business cycle catastrophe' which drags the supply of jobs down below the demand for them. There is rather '. . . a progressive evolution due to the fact that those demanding jobs can allow themselves longer to make up their minds, insofar as economic circumstances allow.'[32]

To the objection that unemployment today stems from compulsory rather than voluntary redundancies, defenders of the theory reply that compulsory redundancies are no more than substitutes for wage reductions which would have led to voluntary resignations. Thus, sackings merely anticipate resignations which would have followed in their absence.[33]

In fact, far from being a necessary implication of the 'job search' theory, the ultra-liberal case which reduces almost all unemployment to search, and thus voluntary, unemployment, is the specific consequence of two particularly arbitrary hypotheses:

(1) It is more efficient to search for work when unemployed, and the efficiency gain exceeds the opportunity cost of being unemployed.

(2) Dismissals can in general be interpreted as anticipating voluntary departures.

No serious empirical investigation has been advanced in support of these theories. On the contrary, voluntary resignations are negatively correlated with the unemployment rate, and positively with the rate of increase of wages (Eagly, 1965, and Tobin, 1977).

It is noteworthy that a link has appeared between the ultra-liberal interpretation of search unemployment and the monetarist school. Phelps himself, and several contributors to his volume, have suggested justifications for the disappearance of the Phillips curve in the long run. Search unemployment is brought in to reinforce the natural-rate concept and, if unemployment is optimal, then why seek to combat it with activist policies? So, one of the earliest attempts to analyse seriously the problem of behaviour under costly and limited information appear to be connected with a rather doctrinal view.[34]

D Outline of a typology of unemployment

It appears, then, that the labelling of unemployment is an issue of political and intellectual controversy between liberals and interventionists. In particular, the problem arises of the rise of unemployment beyond the excess supply of labour, which will be labelled partly frictional, and partly structural. A Keynesian such as Hines (in Worswick, 1976) considers that the new neoclassical theories have failed to establish a theoretical justification for the coexistence of unemployed workers and unfilled vacancies in each submarket for labour. In contrast to the 'job search' theoreticians, he would therefore view as structural all unemployment not corresponding to excess supply of labour, and therefore in excess of unemployment due to macroeconomic imbalance.

The following definition, however, seems acceptable to both sides: a seeker of work is frictionally unemployed if there exists a job for him in his specialisation or in his region, which he has not yet found and taken up; he is structurally unemployed if there exists a vacancy for him requiring a change of locality or of profession; he is unemployed due to economic circumstances if there exists no possible vacancy for him.

To move on from this concept to a working definition requires the adoption of necessarily arbitrary conventions, of which the following are among the most defensible.[35]

Suppose there are N submarkets for labour indexed i in which supply s_i and demand d_i interact, producing a level of unemployment n_i, so that there are $u_i = s_i - n_i$ unemployed and $v_i = d_i - u_i$ vacancies. It is then possible to define 'macroeconomic' unemployment, or that due to insufficient demand U_d as max $(0, \Sigma_i(u_i - v_i)) = $ max $(0, \Sigma_i(s_i - d_i))$ a measure of the excess supply of labour if positive. Frictional unemployment is measured in conformity with its definition above by $U = \Sigma_i$ min (u_i, v_i). Let us now distinguish supplier submarkets $(u_i > v_i)$ and demanders' submarkets $(v_i > U_i)$. In the former, the total of unemployment is divisible into 'demand-deficient' $(u_i - v_i)$ and frictional unemployment (v_i). The latter, on the other hand, contributes negatively to 'demand-deficient' unemployment $(u_i - v_i < 0)$, frictional unemployment being equal to observed unemployment u_i. The excess of vacancies over unemployment signifies a failure to match supply with demand, and thus a contribution to structural unemployment for which an aggregate measure is obtained by summation,

$$U_s = \Sigma_i \text{ min } (0, u_1 - v_i).$$

This definition has the twin advantages of satisfying immediately the condition $U = U_d + U_f + U_s$ as well as the following property which constitutes a 'weak' definition of structural unemployment: structural unemployment is zero if and only if the excess demands for labour are of the same sign in each submarket, as the reader can easily verify.

12 Disequilibria in the Present Day

Over roughly a century, the industrialised economies developed in a cyclical pattern, marked by the regular alternation of phases of expansion, boom, crisis and slump. After the end of the Second World War, a very different pattern prevailed for some thirty years. Its main characteristics were a considerable acceleration of world growth – a doubling of growth rates compared to previous periods of prosperity – and a damping down of fluctuations, making periods of declining levels of activity unusual, while periods of recession were marked only by a slowing down of growth.

Today, this period appears to have passed. The unusual severity of the depression which followed the 1973 and 1979 oil shocks, marked by a noticeable decline in output and by unemployment rates unknown since pre-war days[1] is certainly a major reason, but so too is the slowness of the recovery which followed, especially in France. This has led some people to believe that the world economy was entering the downward phase of a Kondratieff (long) wave, as in 1870–96 and 1929–45 after the expansionary phases of 1896–1929 and 1945–73. Such a forecast may seem plausible from an empirical point of view, but does not help to explain the process, since no mechanism underlying such cycles has ever been discovered, aside from references to waves of innovations, whose positioning seems arbitrary to say the least.

If the 1974 crisis marked a break with the past, it is more than anything else because of the worldwide inflation which accompanied it and because this new assortment of disequilibria seems to be the result of an accumulation of partial failures of adjustment, whose correction had been deferred during the previous expansionary phase. The determining factor thus seems to be the rise in disequilibria in recent times, which we shall first seek to identify.[2] A mainstream of analysis developed since 1965 will then be studied, under the name of the modern theory of disequilibria, which profoundly reshapes dynamic macroeconomic analysis. Finally, we shall discuss the problem of the genesis, prolongation and resolution of these disequilibria from the points of view of the systemic regulation of today's industrial capitalist economies.

1 THE RISE OF DISEQUILIBRIA

Writing in 1961, N. Kaldor picked out a set of six 'stylised facts', enabling the long-term economic evolution of the associated theoretical equilibrium growth-paths to be compared.[3] If recent economic circumstances were not enough to cast doubt on these observed regularities, it seems possible to add to them a number of features characterising, over a period of about twenty years, an increase in the scale of imbalances, occurring by degrees. These features reveal the irreversibility of certain developments which oppose the cyclical movements observed before the Second World War. They are:

(1) The (disputed) fall in the productivity of, and rate of return on, capital.
(2) The increase, by degrees, in inflation rates.
(3) The increase, by degrees, in unemployment.
(4) Lastly the slowing of trends in labour productivity.

Let us briefly discuss these 'new stylised facts'.

1 The fall in the profitability of capital
Over the period from 1960 to 1980, the rate of return in manufacturing industry exhibits a noticeable decline among the larger OECD countries. This phenomenon was pointed out by Nordhaus (1974) in a pioneering article, and gave rise to much controversy in the US as well as in Europe. The debate is concerned with the factors underlying this pattern as well as with whether it represents a lasting trend or a temporary consequence of the exceptionally severe economic shocks of the 1970s.

The fall in the 'apparent productivity of capital' seems to be a general experience: unsurprisingly, in view of the strong trend of substitution over the period. Was a fall in the rate of returns on capital the inevitable consequence? Some people thought so. In fact, however, the global capital-output relationship does not directly determine the rate of profit. Several forces operated in different directions, the net result being a stabilisation of the rate of profit: changes in the share of value added, and variation in the effective rate of taxation on profits being two. Evidence presented by Mazier, Loiseau and Winter[5] seems to establish a quite noticeable fall, however, a lasting one in the US, Britain and Germany, and at the end of the period only in France.

The more detailed studies by Mairesse and Delestre in France,[6] and Feldstein and Summers in the US[7] lead to more qualified, or even contradictory, conclusions. Mairesse and Delestre found the gross profit rate to be stable up to 1972. It rose from 1968 and 1972 if stock

% rate of return

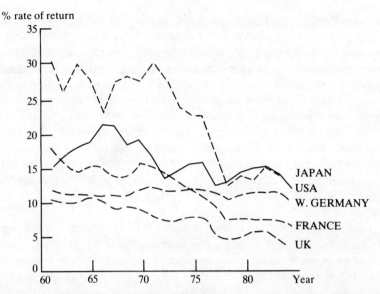

Figure 12.1 Rates of return in manufacturing industry (from CEPII, *The World Economy: Increasing Tensions*, Economica 1983)[4]

appreciation is included, but fell slowly if it is omitted and interest charges are deducted; it then clearly collapsed at the time of the crisis. In the American case, Feldstein and Summers show that there was no real persistent fall in the rate of profit between 1948 and 1976, the variations observed being largely explained by cyclical factors and particularly by rates of capacity utilisation.[8] Noting, however, that the years 1970–6 exhibit an apparent plateau of lower profits, they test their hypothesis by introducing a dummy variable (for those years) in addition to the rate of utilisation. They obtain an estimated gap of 1.6 percentage points for a mean rate of return of the order of 10 per cent which turns out to be only just statistically significant. They consider, however, that, taking account of factors peculiar to this period, there is not sufficient evidence to conclude that there was a permanent fall in the rate of profit.[9]

On the whole, then, while it is clear that profitability collapsed during the crisis, it appears to be difficult to discern in it any medium-term trend.

2 The stepwise increase in inflation rates

From the inflation observed in the depression in the US in 1956–7, through the rising rates of the 1960s to the acute inflation of recent years, we observe an acceleration that has not been regular, but has resulted from the combination of phases of acceleration coinciding until 1974 with expansion of the economy, with phases of deceleration, briefer and less noticeable – generally in periods of recession. For the United States, the investigation by A. Burger reveals an average rate of, for consumer prices, 1.3 per cent from 1952 to 1964, of 3.8 per cent from 1964 to 1972; and of 6.2 per cent from May 1972 to June 1973.[10] Thereafter the rate accelerated, passing the 8 per cent mark in 1974, and 11 per cent in 1975, and then fell back again. Most notably, however, the 1953–4 recession saw an actual fall in the price level; that of 1957–8 a rate of 3.5 per cent followed by a stabilisation of prices; that of 1960–1 saw a rate close to the trend (1.3 per cent); the recession of 1969–70 coincided with a rate of about 4.5 per cent and finally that of 1974–5, a rate in excess of 10 per cent.

From 1945 to 1964 the French inflation rate underwent fairly irregular fluctuations. Since that time, the fluctuations seem to have occurred about three successive plateau levels: of about 2.5 per cent in 1964–7; of 5 to 6 per cent in 1968–73 and of 9 to 11 per cent since. In (West) Germany, starting from a level of about 1 per cent in the early 1960s, the rate moved to 3.5 per cent in 1970, 5.5 per cent in 1971–2, 7 per cent in 1973 and 8 per cent in 1974.[11]

Inflation rates were generally slowing down after the first oil shock, but the second shock in 1979 gave a new impetus to worldwide inflation. For instance, average rates of CPI increase in the 1980–1 period was 10.7 for the US, 12.9 for the UK, 11.7 for France, but only 5.5 for the FRG and 5.1 for Japan. As a consequence of this resurgence, governments became for a time increasingly passive in face of the rise of unemployment.

3 The stepwise increase in unemployment rates

The theme of the deterioration of the trade-off represented by the Phillips curve reflects the parallel movements of unemployment and inflation. The same alternation of pronounced increases in the rates in recession from phase to phase, followed by limited deceleration, may be observed. This pattern was, in particular, found by R. Salais (1977a and 1977b) in the case of France. Following the limited upsurge in unemployment in 1953–4, and the powerful tensions of 1956–7, full employment was more or less maintained until 1965 (under 230,000 unemployed) despite the return of expatriates from Algeria. The phase of stagnation which followed the 'stabilisation plan' (1965–7) saw unemployment reach a new level (350,000) while the oil crisis brought a doubling of unemployment between 1974 and 1976 (from 440,000 to 910,000). What is surprising is not this increase in unemployment at a time of crisis or slump, but that the buoyant activity of 1969–73, although indeed witnessing the creation of many jobs, nevertheless also saw a 'slow drift of unemployment', which rose from 350,000 to 440,000.

As shown in Figure 12.2, much of the increase in unemployment took place during the period following oil shocks, after 1973 and 1979, but the US was the only one of the big OECD countries to experience a reduction in unemployment rate between these two shocks.

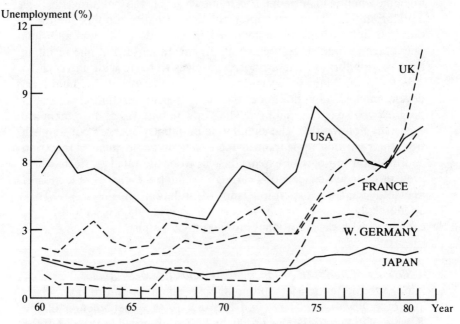

Figure 12.2 Unemployment rates   Source: US Department of Labor

This 'stylised fact' of rising unemployment cannot be understood if the labour supply of households is viewed as an exogenous variable, nor if one abstracts from the structure of employment, of the working population as well as of the dynamics of entry to and exit from the unemployment register. Industrialisation has reached new layers of the population, whose circulation through the labour market is faster, therefore job tenure tends to be briefer and vulnerability to unemployment greater. Thus in the USA during the first oil crisis, a maximal average rate of unemployment of 8.9 per cent at the end of 1975 translates into 6 per cent among male workers but 8 per cent among females and reached 15 per cent among young (16–19-year-old) whites and 40 per cent among young blacks.[12]

We see, therefore, how necessary it is to the understanding of present-day unemployment to guard against two illusions: a globalist illusion, Keynesian in nature, which sees it only as a result of a deficiency of effective demand, is refuted by analysis of the period 1969–73. Stimulating aggregate demand would come up against inflation long before curing the unemployment. But the opposite illusion, seeing only structural unemployment, soon leads one to reduce the essential fact of underemployment to one (a fiction) of voluntary unemployment, in Friedman's framework of the 'natural rate' as equilibrium level of unemployment. In reality understanding is only possible when unemployment is viewed as a disequilibrium phenomenon (and therefore essentially involuntary), but one resulting from disequilibria which are not themselves to begin with universal.

Without wishing to exaggerate the regularity of medium-term developments, they do none the less present an impression of a progressive rise in disequilibria. The stepwise patterns of movement are especially noteworthy. The cumulation of imbalance arises not so much from their periodic appearance – increasing unemployment in recession and inflation in times of expansion – as from the ratchet effects which prevent their self-cancellation through symmetric cycles of reduction of unemployment in expansion and of inflation in recession. This, undoubtedly, is the main feature of present-day disequilibria as compared with the traditional business cycle pattern.

4 Slowing of trends in productivity as a possible determinant

Alongside the tendencies outlined above, the attention of researchers and of policy-makers has been focused on the phenomenon of the slowing of growth of labour productivity first observed at the end of the 1960s, and more pronounced since the break with the past in 1973.

According to a comparative study relating to eleven industrialised countries,[13] the deceleration of labour productivity between the periods 1960–73 and 1973–8 is statistically significant for eight countries, the most important exception being West Germany. The reduction observed in France of 1.2 per cent (from 5.9 to 4.7 per cent) is close to that observed in the United States (from 2.8 to 1.7 per cent or 1.1 per cent) and much less than that seen in the UK (3.8 per cent), Italy (4 per cent) or Japan (6.4 per cent from 9.9 to 3.5 per cent). The lag between this movement and the rather later deceleration of real wage growth is one of the main features of the problems of profitability encountered by the Western industrialised economies.

The most detailed investigations of the causes of this slowing down have been carried out in respect of the US economy.[14] The factors mentioned are several, from the economic effects of very general social phenomena, through deficiency of investment, energy prices, the structure of the labour supply, restrictive legislation and the relaxation of effort in research and development.

A quantification of these factors has been proposed by, among others, Norsworthy, Harper and Kurtz (NHK); and Kendrick, for the periods 1965–73 and 1973–8, in which the slowdown was put at 1.4 per cent followed by 1.1 per cent, or 2.4 per cent below the growth rate by Kendrick (as against 1 per cent then 1.1 per cent by NHK).

The slowdown in investment explains 0.55 per cent percentage points of the fall in productivity growth, occurring mostly after 1974 (NHK) or for 0.2 per cent before 1974 and 6.3 per cent afterwards (Kendrick). Unfavourable effects of redistribution are blamed by Kendrick for 0.5 percentage points (of which 0.4 are said to have occurred after 1973), as against 0.3 according to NHK, resulting from a slowdown of 0.4 per cent after an acceleration of 0.1 per cent between 1965 and 1973.

This slowdown corresponds partly to a fall in the rate of migration from the countryside, and partly to a relative growth of employment in the service sector.

The effect of quality or composition of the labour force was put at 0.3 per cent (Kendrick) or 0.06 per cent (NHK) before 1973, but was said to become favourable thereafter to the tune of 0.2 per cent (Kendrick) or 0.04 per cent (NHK), leaving virtually no net effect between 1965 and 1978. This may be explained by the large-scale entry of young people into the labour market and the female participation rate reaching their peak before 1973.

These effects were reinforced by various mechanisms difficult to illustrate, or of which the impact is more difficult to measure. Thus, according to some writers,[15] the effect of slower capital substitution is underestimated, if account is not taken of the accelerated shifts due to energy prices or regulations introduced for safety and protection of the environment. Research and development expenditure only regained its 1967 level in 1977.

The well-known 'productivity cycle' effect[16] applies to the short run and in principle is of no relevance here. However, in view of the depth of the depression in 1975, it is not clear that the peak of 1978 is comparable with that of 1973 in respect of the adjustment of the employment level. In the longer term, through a Kaldor-Verdoorn effect,[17] the rate of growth may additionally exert a persistent effect on (measured) productivity. Kendrick's study retains a 'volume growth' effect which is said to explain 0.5 percentage points of the slowdown observed between 1965 and 1978, while it attributes 0.6 points to the slowdown in the rate of technical progress.

A commonplace result, though one made clearer by the NHK study, is that the residual, or unexplained, part of the slowdown in observed productivity is most important in the period 1965–73, while in contrast the 1973–8 slowdown is fairly adequately explained. It is then possible to cite some more general social factors, probably linked to a 'generation effect' which profoundly influenced Western societies in this period, and in particular American society with the end of the Vietnam war and French society with the aftermath of the events of 1968.[18]

Can the medium-term trends observed be explained by these social factors or must we, on the contrary, view this cumulation of dis-equilibria as marking the turning-point of a Kondratieff long cycle? Following the 1772–1850, 1850–96 and 1896–1940 cycles, a fourth Kondratieff wave would have seen the expansionary phase 1940–72 come to an end with the crisis of 1973–5.[19] It may be so, but these alternative analyses are of little use without a more detailed investigation of the current situation.

2 THE MARXIST APPROACH: OVERACCUMULATION AND CRISIS

While discussing business cycle models and the cost-push theory of inflation, we met the view that macroeconomic disequilibria were the results of the class struggle over income distribution. Marxist authors generally hold this point but they go beyond, integrating the income distribution disputes in the more general problem of the overaccumulation of capital and of economic crises. Overaccumulation is the central concept of this approach, which interprets as devalorisation of capital most of the adjustment mechanisms occurring during the crisis, in their various historical forms.

A Overaccumulation of capital

The 'overaccumulation' concept was introduced by Marx in *Capital* as one of the explanations of periodic crises. It refers to an 'overproduction of capital', an excess of capital accumulated, not of course with respect to social needs, but instead relatively to the mass or surplus value which can be appropriated by capitalists to ensure its profitability. However, several meanings may be given to the word 'overaccumulation', as we shall see before discussing the very role of this concept.

1 Relative versus absolute overaccumulation
One mechanism of overaccumulation takes effect if the accumulation of extra capital is not on aggregate matched by any increase in the mass of realised profits:

where, therefore, the expanded capital produces only the same mass of surplus value as before, there will be an absolute overproduction of capital; i.e. the expanded $C + \Delta C$ will not produce any more profit, or will even produce less profit, than the capital C did before its increase by ΔC.[20]

The qualification 'absolute' applied to this extreme form assumes the existence of a 'relative form of overaccumulation', occurring when an additional capital does not command an adequate, or proportional extra profit. Formally, absolute overaccumulation refers to a zero elasticity of profit with regard to capital accumulation while the 'relative' form corresponds only to an elasticity value less than one, but the overaccumulation argument ought not to be exclusively related to marginal profit rates. Marxist authors generally do not provide an interpretation of relative overaccumulation more specific than the criterion of an inadequate-profit rate. Three alternative explanations of the initial cause of a decline in the rate of profit are provided, of which the first two are related to an insufficient production of surplus value, and the third are concerned with failures in realisation.

2 Overaccumulation as an insufficient production of surplus-value
An insufficiency of production of surplus value may be related to two different processes: either the argument is narrowly matched with the tendency of the rate of profit to fall, in response to a rising organic composition of capital (ROC), or it refers to a fall in the rate of surplus value, following a rise of the strength of labour (RSL).

The first point is advocated by Marxist 'fundamentalists' as it allows them to relate directly the overaccumulation phenomenon with one of the great 'laws of motion' of the capitalist system. In the context of the ROC argument, 'overaccumulation' means an overproduction of fixed capital with respect to variable capital, i.e. an inner contradiction to the process of capital accumulation.[21] As the ROC induces technological unemployment – the reproduction of the labour reserve army – this first variant of overaccumulation will generally occur together with a rise in the rate of surplus value.

Much different is the RSL argument. It assumes that a successful period of accumulation has brought the economy close to full employment, i.e. has depleted the reserve army of labour. Thus, owing to the competition between capitalists to hire a larger share of the labour force, workers are in a strong position to obtain better wages, and to reduce the ratio of surplus value. The capitalists then suffer from a 'profit squeeze'.

This is exactly the mechanism to which Marx refers in his discussion of absolute overaccumulation. The RSL argument involves implications for employment quite opposed to those derived from the ROC. The rate of profit is falling because employment is too high in the RSL view, but it is falling because employment is too low in the ROC variant of the overaccumulation mechanism. The common point between the two arguments is that the relative lack of profit comes from an insufficiency in the mass of surplus value generated in the production process, due to either a too low rate of surplus value (in RSL) or a too limited amount of variable capital.

3 Overaccumulation due to realisation failure

A third variant of the overaccumulation argument explains the lack of profit not by the insufficiency of the surplus value produced but by the failure of realising it, i.e. transforming it from extra commodity capital to extra money capital by selling commodities at their price of production. Realisation failure appears as a consequence of over-capitalisation, i.e. the disproportionate development of the two departments which respectively produce 'means of production' and 'means of consumption'. As said by M. Aglietta (1979, p. 356) 'there is an overaccumulation of capital when the constraint of the full realization of the value newly created by society can no longer be effected by way of the organic exchanges between the two departments of production.'

In Marxist theory, an excessive development of the department I, 'means of production' is a basic tendency in a capitalist economy because of the contrast between the self-generated dynamism of capital accumulation and the alleged tendency to permanently depressed wages (E. Mandel, 1981, p. 49). Ultimately, the realisation failure does manifest the basic contradiction between the efficiency of the capitalist system to extend its productive potential and its inability to simultaneously develop the consumption potential of society.[22]

According to the RF argument, overaccumulation may occur even while enough surplus value is produced.

4 Overaccumulation: a survey of issues

The existence of three variants of the overaccumulation phenomenon may suggest further discussion of the methodological, political and empirical issues.

(a) The methodological issue – It follows from the above presentation that the 'overaccumulation' concept does not refer unambiguously to a specific phenomenon. This would be a basic failure in standard economic analysis, but for Marxists it is only a feature of dialectics. The overaccumulation concept is polysemic because its role is not to provide

an analysis of specific mechanisms, but to proclaim the basic Marxist postulate of the unity of the various limits to the process of accumulation. The intrinsic limit is not on production in general but on production based on capital accumulation.

(*b*) *The political issue* – The overaccumulation concept does not provide an unambiguous identification of the specific mechanisms underlying a given historic situation. Thus, there is a place left for non-analytical elements to be introduced so as to compensate for the under-determination of the theoretical argument. Such is the role of historical analysis, in conjunction with political praxis. We may quote some sample expositions of this position, typical of the Marxist notion of the impossibility of a scientific research in social science free of political consideration.

For the left-wing fundamentalist (Trotskyist) E. Mandel (1978)

the vulgar theory of crisis as caused by 'insufficient production of surplus value' is obviously dangerous, from the point of view of defending the working class against the capitalist onslaught which always coincides with a crisis of overproduction. . . . 'Profit squeeze' theories involve a similar danger of misuse by the capitalist side in the class struggle.[23]

For the theoretician of the French Communist Party, P. Boccara (1976, op. cit.),

As for an eclectic view, taking the analysis of over-accumulation as complementary to that of the falling rate of profit rather than as the outcome of the latter, without rejecting these distortions out of hand (as revisionist offspring of bourgeois ideology), this view may even lead to their under- or over-consumptionist errors. Such a view tends to confuse analysis in terms of actual prices and in terms of value, without seeing how the theory of over-accumulation/devalorization connects the two, allowing one to avoid needing to distinguish or to confuse, dogmatic and revisionist theories.

(*c*) *The empirical issue* – The preceding quotations do not imply that all Marxist economists rely upon political argument for choosing between the alternative variants of the overaccumulation theory. A good sample of empirical test work is presented by T. E. Weisskopf (1979). Having given a clear analytical content to the three ROC, RSL and RF mechanisms, he statistically measures their negative influence during the post-war US business cycles and concludes (*ibid.*, p. 372):

In brief, the RSL variant received far more empirical support than either the ROF or the RF variants as an explanation of profit rate declines in all of these key periods of time. A rise in the strength of labour vis-à-vis capital as reflected in a suitably adjusted wage share of income accounted fully for the long term decline, partly for the cycle to cycle contraction phases.

Even if it is difficult to infer general conclusions from one particular study, it is amazing to remark that the empirical test supports the RSL variant, judged 'dangerous' by authors favouring political criteria, and seems to refute the ROC version, preferred by the 'fundamentalists'.

B The devalorisation of capital

Devalorisation of capital appears in Marx's writings with a rising rate of surplus-value as one of the main mechanisms through which crises temporarily permit solution of the contradictions of capitalism, which Marxists today call its 'regulation', borrowing this concept from cybernetics:

> Under all circumstances, however, the balance will be restored by capital's lying idle or even by its destruction, to a greater or lesser extent. The major effect here . . . is simply that when these means of production cease to be active as means of production a shorter or longer disruption occurs in their function as a means of production. (*Capital*, Vol. III, p. 362, Penguin, 1981)

This devalorisation takes various forms, destruction of capital by retirement of part of those means of production no longer forthcoming as capital; retirement of part of the stock of money-capital to be frozen or hoarded; depreciating of circulation capital in the form of commodities affected by the slump; closure of factories whether or not followed by their yielding to price reductions.

Contemporary Marxists have developed and generally extended the Marxian concept of devalorisation. The most extreme extension relies upon a broad concept of 'non valorisation', while other writers have developed the idea of 'permissive devalorisation' and the thesis of a permanent devalorisation in the present conditions of capitalism.

1 Devalorisation as a form of non-valorisation

In this first conception, defended in its essence by P. Boccara, devalorisation must be extended from the idea of depreciation, loss of value of capital to include all forms of 'non-transformation of capital'.[24]

The development begins from the theory of absolute overaccumulation (zero additional profit) in which there exists a surplus of capital to be valorised. Three possible solutions then exist: to make fallow part of the capital bringing in zero profit; transformation at a reduced rate of profit; 'negative transformation' or loss of capital.

For Boccara, the most important aspect is the array of institutional and social mechanisms needed for this devalorisation, which characterise a particular historical form of the capitalist mode of production: state monopoly capitalism. On the one hand, the dominant position of monopolies enables them to compel the non-monopolistic private sector (tradesmen, small businesses, etc.) to accept transformation at a reduced rate; on the other, public intervention allows the non-valorisation of the part of capital invested in the nationalised sectors. To these Boccara adds the assumption by the state of control over the 'hidden costs' of capitalist production, particularly in the social sphere, and the means of public financing of private accumulation. All in all, public spending tends to favour realisation of value, while indicative planning contributes to the coordination of decisions in the capitalist system.[25]

This is the sense in which that writer argues that the theory of overaccumulation and devalorisation takes account of state monopoly capitalism as the stage in the evolution of capitalism in which: 'reducing the profit requirement for a part of capital, allows for an increase in the rate of profit for the rest of capital and for the accumulation process to run again' (Boccara, 1976, p. 220). The changes undergone by capitalism are aimed at ensuring the necessary, structural devalorisations of capital.

It does not, however, appear that devalorisation, in the sense intended by Boccara, can lead to the release of the constraint of the surplus-value appropriable as capitalist profit; at most it can 'camouflage' its appropriation. In effect, public investment replacing private accumulation, and financial subsidies, may be viewed as levies on aggregate surplus-value, while social welfare expenditures correspond to a part of variable capital not directly consumed by wage-earners. This set of transfers cannot therefore increase capitalist accumulation at a constant rate of surplus-value: in general it will, on the contrary, reduce it. The main real implication of the devalorisation argument is to suggest that public intervention conceals part of the appropriation of surplus-value, by presenting it as tax levies, thereby reducing workers' resistance to a given rate of appropriation.[26]

Furthermore, one may wonder if it is meaningful to interpret all the structural changes in capitalism as a means to issue proper devalorisation. The alternative interpretation given by P. Baran and P. Sweezy (1966), for instance, refers more directly to these changes as means to avoid realisation failure, either by sustaining effective demand, or by providing an unproductive absorption of surplus, an argument showing some reminiscence of the underconsumptionist view, going back to Malthus.[27]

2 Devalorisation as 'non-validation'

Since goods produced but not sold form a part of capital, any sale below value, or rather below the producer price implied by the general value and rate of profit which prevails, may be analysed as devalorisation of capital. Further, S. de Brunhof has suggested that this non-realisation be viewed as the failure of private labour-time expended on the production of the relevant commodities to be validated as socially useful labour-time. M. Aglietta (1976) connects this interpretation with competition among capitalists through the introduction of new techniques.

> In the originating movement of these new conditions of production, there are always individual capitalists unable to follow the transformation. They make profits below the general rate, or even experience losses. This means that the labour expended under their direction cannot fully count as socially necessary labour.[28]

The particular capitalists thus dominated can only continue to exist autonomously by renewing their means of production and their 'realisation methods', that is by accepting a more or less sharp devalorisation of capital currently lying fallow. 'In all cases, though, there is always the sanction of lack of social validation for private labours.'[29]

This need for social validation of private labour – labour controlled by individual capitalists – enables modern Marxists to combine the constraints of inter-company competitiveness and of specific demand requirements. It relates to Marx's own view of the variables of utility and of demand as no more than preconditions for value-in-exchange, never as causes. However, as an account of devalorisation it is compatible only with a partial or temporary depreciation of capital, since it is difficult to see the meaning of a quantity of socially necessary labour-time from which the economy could generally and lastingly diverge.

3 Devalorisation as accelerated depreciation

One familiar mechanism of devalorisation is the massive depreciation of capital in times of crisis. Boccara's analysis, admittedly in a particular context, described a permanent structural development at the heart of state monopoly capitalism. Aglietta, going back to a more precise conception of devalorisation also believes that it has become permanent due to an acceleration in obsolescence.

Recently, capitalism has followed a path of intensive accumulation – one, that is to say, based on the augmentation of relative surplus-value.[30] With a quickening pace of technical progress, the rate of obsolescence has increased relative to technical depreciation. It thus no longer appears as an exceptional devalorisation. Therefore, to the extent that the structures of oligopolistic or monopolistic markets allow them, firms will anticipate this depreciation by retiring capital more quickly and increasing the mark-up in their selling-prices. This process cannot however proceed unhindered: 'For firms to protect themselves individually from the risks of devalorization, they must be able to predict its scope and tempo',[31] which they will seek to do by diversification and long-term planning.

Aglietta set out to formalise the consequences of this change. He argues that, 'from an analytical point of view, economic depreciation has nothing to do with the transformation of the conditions of production'.[32] From this it follows logically that he views the shortening of the useful life of capital equipment resulting from obsolescence as a waste or material loss, and also that the increase in depreciation for allowances seems to him to be purely imaginary. But this criticism of planned obsolescence has no meaning unless one can find a purely technological definition of economic life-span, independent of the evolution of productive processes. Such a concept has no meaning, either at the level of the firm or of society as a whole. It would be absurd to keep in operation a blast-furnace requiring 30 per cent more energy and labour input than new models, giving as a reason the fact that it is technically still usable. The date at which this blast-furnace should be – or should have been – retired is a function of the progress of material costs and of labour productivity in new furnaces, as well as of the cost of these new units, but certainly not of what the furnace being used cost ten, twenty or fifty years ago. To be more precise, 'vintage' capital models tell us that equipment should be retired as soon as the marginal productivity of labour on new equipment exceeds the average productivity on the old. To behave otherwise would introduce a wastage of labour for society.

True enough, recent history provides numerous examples of recent and technically efficient equipment having to be scrapped. This can be explained either as a result of errors of foresight, or more often by competing firms in the same market embarking on jointly uneconomic projects.

Even if, contrary to Aglietta's view, it is normal for foreseeable obsolescence to lead to an increase in depreciation for allowances and hence in cash-flow also, it is precisely true that this practice leads to an increase in the price level.[33] Can we speak of 'forced savings generated directly by firms'?[34] The answer is yes, only if the level of production is assumed throughout the argument to be constant, but this assumption is perhaps not particularly useful when the effects of acceleration of transformation of the conditions of production, which is not the origin of the obsolescence, are being discussed.

Aglietta takes the view that anticipated devalorisation can explain, at least partially, the coexistence of inflation and unemployment. In effect, increased cash allowances raise prices, but in addition 'they lead to a more and more rapid stream of investment in the future'. Moreover, by including financial reserves in current costs and pushing back their effects into erosion of (the value of) money, firms tend to increase their share of total income while the falling value of money devalorises money wages 'the monetary rights given by wages' (op. cit., p. 315).

The result is a restraint on the growth of effective demand for means of consumption, and then an unequal development of the two production departments, leading to disequilibrium.

So, the increase in depreciation allowances is only inflationary, as is any increase in costs, in the sense that it leads to a once-for-all increase in the price level. In itself it does not cause any increase in the rate of inflation. It may however lie indirectly at the root of such an increase should it lead to a spate of confrontation over the sharing of income, which obviously is a quite likely eventuality.

It appears, therefore, that Aglietta's conclusions are most valid in the case of unforeseen devalorisation, at least at the level of the individual, due to errors in expectations or incompatible investment projects. He has also developed an important and innovative analysis of the persistence of disequilibria, to which we shall return later on.

C The inevitability of crisis and its historical context

While an exploration of the concepts of overaccumulation and of devalorisation has shed some light on various representative aspects of contemporary Marxian crisis theory, it remains for us to consider how these concepts 'operate' in the context of an historical analysis of crises of the capitalist economy.

Since Lenin's assertion, following Hilferding, of a final, monopolistic phase of capitalism, Marxian analysts of crises have distinguished various crucial stages of this development. An important distinction opposes phases of extensive and intensive accumulation in which the issue of the inevitability of crises appears in different forms.

1 The crisis of extensive accumulation and the 1930s

Extensive accumulation is characterised by expanded reproduction of the labour force, in the form of an increase in the working population with labour productivity in terms of commodities more or less constant. It is obvious, as the classic analysis at the beginning of the nineteenth century showed, that such an increase comes up against objective quantitative limits. With productivity held constant, real income is bounded below by a physical reproduction constraint and so the rise in the rate of surplus-value cannot indefinitely make up for the increase in organic composition, itself inevitable in the absence of an increase in productivity in the manufacture of the elements of constant capital.

As an example, we may quote the following view of B. Billaudot (1976, p. 508) which relies upon a standard over-accumulation argument, of the RSL variant:

the inevitability of a phase of accumulation with full realization
leading on to one of over-accumulation with general overproduction
is indeed connected to the fact that the degree of exploitation falls
while under-employment also declines, this reduction in underemployment itself being a consequence of full production and the
tendency for Department I to expand more rapidly. In other words,
this inevitability of crisis is linked to the effects of competition among
capitalists over the formation of real wages.

Formally, it should be noted, the writers cited above only deduce the inevitability of crisis because they reject *a priori* the only long-term equilibrium solution, the only steady state, consistent with their assumption of the absence of technical progress, which is the stationary case.

Their conclusion can only be understood in this framework of a necessarily progressive capitalist system, unable to enter the mature phase envisaged by J. S. Mill or H. Hansen.

Historically it is interesting to ask whether the scenario of a crisis of extensive accumulation is applicable to the nineteenth century, or again in the 1930s. Regarding the crisis of 1930, there seems to be some measure of agreement that the exceptional nature of this crisis can be explained by a partial transition – missed the first time round, into intensive accumulation. Indeed, the growth of workers' consumption did not in the 1920s follow that of productivity, and the expansionary phase ran up against a non-realisation of production of consumer goods as in Department II, temporarily concealed by the unequal development mentioned in Department I.

2 The crisis in intensive accumulation and the 1970s

'Intensive accumulation' is characterised by an increase in the productivity and intensity of work allowing the appropriation of relative surplus-value, obtained without a reduction of the real wage – that is, of the use-values distributed to wage-earners as means of consumption. In this case, it is generally admitted that the traditional 'demonstration' of the law of TRPF no longer holds.[35] Must we conclude from this that the logical inevitability of capitalist crises disappears?

In a preliminary series of analyses, the change introduced into the mechanisms of accumulation does not affect the conclusion regarding the logical inevitability of crises. In particular, on the ROC perspective presented above which emphasises the role of technological determinism and sees the TRPF as merely concealed by the institutions of state monopoly capitalism. From this point of view, from which all past crises appear as the result of long-term trends, the crisis of the 1970s seems especially serious as it occurs at the 'crest of a long wave',[36] as it corresponds 'to a turning point in the "atmosphere" or general economic conditions, that is, in the long period';[37] in other words, because it marks the high point of a Kondratieff cycle.

For other writers, closer to the RSL view, the difference made by the absence of a logical inevitability of overaccumulation (in a regime of intensive accumulation) cannot be neglected. There is no longer a necessity of crisis if the strength of labour may be maintained inside the limits compatible with the development of productive forces.

The logical necessity of crisis is in fact only set aside in order to introduce the idea of a political necessity of crisis.

> Crisis only becomes inevitable when the bourgeoisie can no longer negotiate 'reasonable' (from its own point of view) wage settlements with the labour unions, nor make up for these wage rises by continually altering working conditions (breaks, work structure, night-shifts, etc.) and introducing new industries (or modernizing old ones) at a limited cost.[38]

From this position, it is logical to relate the depth of the crisis of the 1970s to the vigour and extent of workers' wage demands, both regarding wages and working conditions, or even to a weakening of 'capital control over workers in the production process' as written by T. Kawakami (1979, p. 193).

The third approach to crisis – realisation failure, RF – provides the weakest foundations for the idea of a logical or political necessity of crisis. It would instead emphasise the likely occurrence under capitalism of lack of coordination between demand and supply, between production capacity and the distributed income.

Without going into the analysis of these factors here, it is worth noticing the considerable advance made here on traditional Marxist explanations of crisis. A logical inevitability derived by the 'fundamentalists' from an understanding of concepts supposed to grasp the very nature of the capitalist system is replaced by the observation of a lack of regulation, of an unsatisfactory coordination among the advance of productivity, the aspirations of wage-earners and habits of consumption. In this perspective, one is led to consider the actual adjustment mechanisms of the economy, and there is no more reason for an ideological 'bridge' between methodological approaches to this problem.

3 THE MODERN DISEQUILIBRIUM THEORY: THE NON-MARKET CLEARING PARADIGM

In the same period which – since the mid-1960s – witnessed the progressive increase of a set of indicators of disequilibrium, a theoretical effort towards the development of a non-market clearing paradigm began to appear. Some implications of this new approach, which will now be studied for the economy as a whole, have yet been presented when discussing the functions of consumption, investment and demand for money. Based on the explicit formulation of the microeconomic foundations of macroeconomics in a non-Walrasian world, it suggests a taxonomy of macroeconomic non-market clearing situations, and takes as complementary the analysis of dynamic adjustment processes.

A The foundations: a non-Walrasian world

Our study of the economic conditions for consistent aggregation showed how much the problem of moving from micro to macro simplifies in equilibrium, and that highly aggregated growth models (single-sector, for example) seem to suffice for the study of regular evolutions. In contrast, if the market clearing assumption is set aside, the different variables are no longer determined by equilibrium conditions, and the question of proper microfoundations for aggregate relationships arises. Traditional microeconomics are no longer relevant, since they assume, explicitly or not, that the Walrasian tatonnement process works and then that prices provide the whole information which is required for economic coordination. Non-market clearing analysis requires new microeconomic foundations, free of the more extreme Walrasian assumption. Concerning *a priori* coordination of economic activities, we shall consequently need to define this non-Walrasian microeconomic system in order to see its implications at both the levels of individual behavioural relationships and of general systemic coordination of activities.

1 A decentralised economy

As to understand the meaning of the price rigidity – or, more generally – of market failures, considered in the non-market clearing paradigm, one has to discuss the basic issue of the forms of coordination of economic activity working in a decentralised economy. Here, the Walrasian general equilibrium theory presents paradoxical features. While it does indeed rest on the specification and articulation of many individual decisions, it requires at the same time two extremely powerful mechanisms for *a priori* coordination of these decisions, the first being the tatonnement and the second, clearing-house.

The theory of the tatonnement holds each market to be fully organised in the fashion of a stock-market. An auctioneer 'announces' the prices and compares the quantities offered for supply and demand; demanders and suppliers adjust the quantities proposed for exchange, and exchange does not take place until equilibrium between demand and supply is attained. This theory, for Walras, was meant to reinforce the formal proof of the existence of general equilibrium with a concrete image, and to lead on to the investigation of its stability. In fact, it introduces a considerable centralisation of information.

In particular in such a world, agents are constrained only by the value of their endowments at the prices announced. It is sufficient for them to ensure the compatibility of their buying and selling plans with their initial endowments, as they cannot be made to realise one of their offers without all the others also being satisfied. This implies that the output of the price system is enough to ensure that decisions taken at the individual level are coherent and Pareto-efficient. On the other hand, if the coordination by the auctioneer ceases, and the tatonnement is interrupted, an agent can be made to have certain offers of exchange satisfied while others can not. Then the value of endowments at current prices no longer suffices to define the feasible transactions, and additional constraints appear, relating to the quantities which can be exchanged out of equilibrium. In this case, the information to be dealt with is much more considerable, while the hypothetical entity supposed to centralise it has disappeared.

The idea of the general 'clearing-house' in which transactions are regulated is more implicit in Walras's *Éléments d'économie politique pure*. It is, however, the direct corollary of the tatonnement. This hypothesis reduces to the assumption that transactions are not subject to bilateral settlement of the participants but rather to a global clearing of debts and claims. Indeed, to assume that exchange takes place only in equilibrium ensures that such global adjustment is possible, and that balance can be exactly achieved. The point to note is that this assumption is formally sufficient for a Walrasian economy to function, since it implies that in such an economy money does not play an essential role, this perfect substitute for it being conceivable.

If exchange takes place outside equilibrium, a supply offer is no longer a certain revenue available for payment, and problems of solvency do arise. Money must intervene to guarantee the settlements.

The capitalist economy is essentially a decentralised one, and has no mechanism for the *a priori* coordination of exchange, nor for the centralisation of recontracting. The Walrasian model then paradoxically appears as a representation of an economy centralised by powerful coordination mediums. It may be useful for demonstrating the possibility of general equilibrium of the decentralised economy, but it becomes wholly inadequate for analysing the mechanisms for arriving at such equilibrium, or more generally states of the economy outside this particular frame of reference.

Some disequilibrium theorists, following Clower,[39] tend to reduce the necessary reformulation to the opposition between a monetary and a barter economy. The monetary economy is presented as a restricted case of the barter economy, more efficient than the latter nevertheless through the economies in transaction and information costs which it permits. This conception seems to us to confuse the phenomenon and its consequences. Moreover it leads to a mechanistic formulation of the monetary constraint, resulting in a caricature of the theory of disequilibrium.

If we do not assume that tatonnement adjustments are performed by an auctioneer, prices have to be set by the agents, either as a contractual agreement, or as a unilateral decision of sellers or, more rarely, buyers. For instance contractual price agreements are likely to occur in the building industry, but price setting by producer is the rule in the car industry. As Arrow (1959) has pointed out, this will generally involve some departure from the competitive price formation, introducing some monopoly, oligopoly or bilateral monopoly element. The important point is that instantaneous price flexibility becomes an hypothesis difficult to maintain. Actual price-setting processes generally imply some sluggishness, and the econometric studies of price formation give much support to the view of prices adjusting gradually in response to changes in costs and to demand pressures. There is thus some empirical evidence that prices are not continuously clearing markets, which validate a price rigidity assumption in short-run analysis. The non-market clearing paradigm, for the sake of analytical simplicity, rests upon a limit form of the stickyness hypothesis, namely the assumption that prices and wages may be taken as given for the short run, for the Marshallian market period. Thus, modern disequilibrium theory had to purpose build a new concept of equilibrium for a fix-price short-run analysis, to be called equivalently fix-price equilibrium, equilibrium with rationing or even, non-Walrasian equilibrium, which is a less specific denomination.

2 Notional and effective demand

In the absence of the auctioneer and with sluggish price adjustments, it is likely that some markets will have to close out of equilibrium giving rise to transactions which cannot simultaneously satisfy suppliers and demanders. The agents on the long side of the market, unable to satisfy their offers of exchange, will find themselves rationed. It would be inconsistent to assume that they will continue to behave in a manner appropriate to a Walrasian environment. On the contrary, they will adapt their behaviour to the new situation created by this rationing. If they find their resources effectively reduced, they will have to adapt their expenditure to this reduction. If they cannot make desired purchases, they may prefer to retain some of their endowments rather than accumulate savings automatically. This gives rise to what Clower[40] has called a 'dual decision process'. Behaviour is explained at two levels. A first calculation under the Walrasian constraints of the value of endowments, determines the notional supplies and demands. A second, bringing in the additional constraints of the transactions feasible in disequilibrium leads to the formulation of constrained ('effective') supply and demand schedules.

The first calculation enables the cases of rationing to be identified. The second determines the values taken by the decision variables under market disequilibrium. Comparing the two shows how rationing in one or more markets affects all the agent's decisions; for example, how the reduction in money income of the unemployed man results partly in reduced consumption, and partly in reduced savings.

It is important to observe that the constrained behavioural relationships depend not only on prices, but also on the quantities indicating the level of the rationing constraints perceived or anticipated by the economic agent.

(a) *The behaviour of households* – We shall now lend some precision to these ideas by studying consumer household behaviour. Since it is usual in 'Keynesian' formulations to make use of consumption and savings functions forming a linear system, we shall assume for our representative consumer a log linear utility function. Denoting the total volume of consumption C and its price by p; money demand M^*/p as the only form of savings introduced, and leisure time as the difference between a time endowment L_o and the labour supply: $L_o - L$,[41] we have the utility function:

$$U = \alpha_1 \, \text{Log} \, (C) + \alpha_2 \, \text{Log} \, (M^*/p) + \alpha_3 \, \text{Log} \, (L_o - L)$$

Maximisation of this objective under the Walrasian constraint:

$$pC + M^* \leqslant M_o + wL$$

leads to notional demand functions for goods and money and the notional labour supply function; thus for the former:

$$C^* = \frac{\alpha_1}{\alpha_1 + \alpha_2 + \alpha_3} \, \frac{wL_o + M_o}{p}$$

a simple function $C^*(w, p)$, for given endowment (L_o, M_o) and for the latter:

$$L^* = L_o - [\alpha_3/(\alpha_1 + \alpha_2 + \alpha_3)] \, [\, L_o + M_o/w]$$

Notional consumption C^* is (thus) obtained by multiplying the 'notional' propensity to consume, $\alpha_1/(\alpha_1 + \alpha_2 + \alpha_3)$, by the notional income $(wL_o + M_o)/p$, the value of endowments of time L_o and in money balances M_o.

If, due to prices and wage rigidities, the labour market is not clearing, the worker-consumer may be confronted by a constraint of labour saleable in a given time-span (partial or complete unemployment) of the form $L \leqslant \bar{L}$. His constrained consumption and savings functions are then obtained by maximising utility under this extra constraint. For the consumption function, for example, we obtain:

$$\tilde{C} = \frac{\alpha_1}{\alpha_1 + \alpha_2} \, \frac{w\bar{L} + M_o}{p} \qquad \text{of the type} \quad \tilde{C}(\bar{L}),$$

an expression of the same form as the notional consumption function C^* but this time depending on (actual) money balances, initial money balances, and perceived income, rather than hypothetical endowments. Thus, maximisation of utility under the employment constraint produces an expression which can be interpreted as a Keynesian consumption function. Indeed, as soon as income actually realised is an argument of the consumption function, it is possible to obtain the Keynesian multiplier. This is a measure of the reconciliation brought about by Clower between the theory of choice, the core of microeconomics, and the multiplier, the cornerstone of Keynesian macroeconomics which for thirty years had appeared to be totally incompatible approaches.

In symmetry with the rationing occurring in the labour market in the case of unemployment, the consumer may find himself confronted with rationing on the goods market, related to a deficiency in supply. When this happens, actual purchases are constrained by the relation $C < \check{C}$. The limitation of purchases automatically increases savings, here in the form of money, which is the only store of value. Rather than passively allowing these savings to swell, consumers will transfer part of the rationing undergone into a reduction of their labour supply.

The effective labour supply is in this case the solution of the utility maximisation problem under the additional constraint $C < \bar{C}$, which from the example above yields (denoting $\alpha_3/(\alpha_2 + \alpha_3)$ as a_3):

$$\widetilde{L}_s = L_o - a_3 \left[M_o + wL_o - pC \right]/w \quad \text{of the type } L^s(\bar{C}).$$

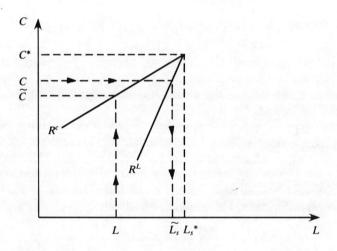

Figure 12.3

It is useful to represent graphically the adjustments which arise from household behaviour in disequilibrium.[42] In the (C, L) space (Figure 12.3) a unique point, (C^*, L^*_s) represents the preferred position of consumers as a function of given prices and wages. In the case of unemployment, a reduction of effective consumer demand

$(C^* - \tilde{C})$ results from a rationing on the labour market $(L_s^* - \tilde{L})$. Analogously, in the case of rationing in the goods market, consumers react by a reduction in their supply of labour $(L_s^* - \tilde{L})$.

The lines R^C and R^L represent the respective loci of adjustments of consumption in the case of unemployment and of labour supply in the case of rationing in the goods market. Their slopes depend on the respective propensities to consume and to modifying available leisure-time. It is useful to look at them as 'reaction curves' by analogy with bilateral monopoly theory.

(b) *The behaviour of firms* – The behaviour of firms is characterised by a supply of goods and a demand for labour. In a Walrasian environment, these functions are derived from profit maximisation, taking account of prices and wages and constrained by the production function. They may thus be written:

$$Q_s^* = Q^s(w, p),$$
$$L_d^* = L^D(w, p).$$

Outside such an environment, firms must include in their economic decisions two possible sorts of additional constraint. In the first place, in the case of deficiency of demand, they may see their sales rationed at a given level, $Q \leqslant \bar{Q} < Q^*_s$. Profit maximisation under this constraint determines the level of effective demand for labour $\tilde{L}_d$ and therefore the amount $(L^*_D - \tilde{L}_d)$,[43] by which the goods market imbalance 'spills over' onto the labour market.

$$\tilde{L}_d = L_d(\bar{Q})$$

Symmetrically, firms may be constrained by labour shortage at the going wage-rate, experiencing a ration $L \leqslant \bar{L} < L_s^*$ on the labour market. Profit maximisation now implies an effective supply function for goods $\tilde{Q}_s = Q_s(\bar{L})$.

As stocks are not introduced into the model, each firm must at all points lie on its production function $Q = F(L)$. This function is therefore the locus of the two sorts of adjustment or spillover envisaged, as in Figure 12.4.

These contributions undoubtedly represent only the first stage in the development of a non-Walrasian economy. Among their limitations, it should be noted that they still possess a static character and that in them the level of rationing is still exogenous. However, the derivation of such functions of constrained behaviour has enabled the problem of

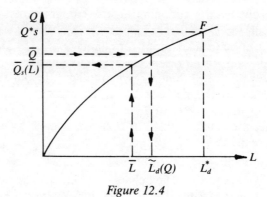

Figure 12.4

coordination of decisions in a non-Walrasian world to be considered in a general form. To achieve this, the notion of constrained behaviour is introduced into models derived from a general equilibrium approach, and then into aggregative equilibrium models.

3 Non-Walrasian general equilibria

Under the assumption of a Walrasian tatonnement process, the interaction of notional supply and demand leads to general equilibrium through price adaptation prior to exchange taking place. One may identically define the Walrasian model by an infinitely rapid adjustment of prices. Marshallian market equilibrium, occurring in the infra-short run, represents the same assumption. As soon as this assumption is relaxed, price adjustments will occur in finite time and will interfere with quantity adjustments. The simplest assumption to probe is then that of a complete reversal of the speed of adjustment: quantities adapt in infinitesimal time, or in the market period during which prices remain fixed. One is then led to investigate the functioning of models formally similar to those of general equilibrium, but in which prices are fixed.

In this setting, what meaning can be attached to 'an instantaneous quantity adjustment'? It certainly cannot be viewed as an adjustment equalising demand and supply since prices are fixed, and in general differ from those which would allow this equalisation. It must therefore in fact be interpreted as ensuring, in some sense, consistency between the demands and supplies announced by agents and the transactions realised.

At the microeconomic level, quantities demanded and supplied were effectively defined for given constraints and rations affecting the agent under consideration. But for the economy as a whole, these rations are endogenous, as the results of interaction between the individual constrained demands and supplies. In essence, the problem is identical with that of the formation of prices in the theory of competitive equilibrium: while taken as given by each individual, they are endogenous to the market.

To speak of a quantity adjustment is, in this context, to label a reciprocal process of adaptation of behaviour and of the arrays of rations faced by agents. The clearest way of looking at this is to reintroduce an explicit tatonnement process, affecting quantities.[44]

(*a*) *A model of quantity tatonnement* – Models of general equilibrium with quantity rationing have been proposed by Drèze (1975) as the outcome of a process of tatonnement over quantities. We shall present the structure of a model of this type less rigorous, but coping with a production economy.

The following model deals with the formation of a quantity tatonnement equilibrium[45] in a competitive economy with fixed prices, where m consumers and s producers are by assumption endowed with utility functions and production possibilities satisfying the necessary conditions for the existence of continuous supply and demand functions. With prices fixed at an arbitrary level, each market generally ends up out of equilibrium, actual transactions being equal to the lesser of the signalled demand and supply levels. Agents on the long side hence experience rationing, which is distributed among them by a given structure of transactions or rationing scheme. These agents then formulate their constrained demand to take account of these rations. The state of each market, and the level of transactions, are determined by these constrained demands and supplies. We may now observe the appearance of a feedback loop effect. A certain degree of cohence is attained when there is identity between the transactions resulting from behaviour subject to constraints and those which determine the rations considered in determining this behaviour.

Figure 12.5 is a flow-chart of the process:

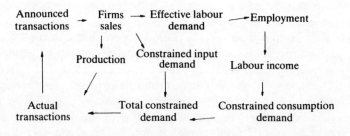

Figure 12.5

Formally, equality between announced and effective transactions constitutes a fixed point of the process, whose existence can be proved under particular conditions. This fixed point describes a state of 'QT-equilibrium' of the economy, a state in which all agents' decisions are realised even though there is general underemployment and disequilibrium in markets. This case precisely corresponds to a Keynesian equilibrium. We may remark that it is only at QT equilibrium that Clower's effective demands are the same, as in Keynes. It would have been more consistent with Keynesian terminology to speak only of 'constrained' demand and supply to indicate the transaction offers expressed during the tatonnement process. In any case, Clower's terminology is by now generally accepted.

The main point of departure from the Keynesian concept is that the latter was associated with the comparison by 'entrepreneurs' of expected aggregate supply and demand, whereas here the structure of supply and demand schedules which can be realised, is itself made explicit. The increase in generality therefore seems considerable. Unfortunately, it must be pointed out that the fiction of the collective entrepreneur has been eliminated only to be replaced by another fiction: the idea of a process of tatonnement in quantities. Thus, one may wonder if the QT equilibrium represents any progress over Walrasian equilibrium in the process of theorising a decentralised economy.

(b) *Non-tatonnement models* – It seems desirable to circumvent this new fiction to provide more general foundations for the concept of fix-price general equilibrium. To this end, J. P. Benassy (1975) has considered a more general model in which the agents derive their constrained offer, demand or supply, not by considering a vector of rations simultaneously announced by an auctioneer, but on the basis of perceived transactions on markets yet visited and of rations rejected on markets to be visited.[46] An equilibrium of the process, which J. P. Benassy calls a K-equilibrium, is a self-reproducing system of effective demand, perceived or expected rations and actual transactions. While formally defined as a fix-point, it corresponds to the convergence of a process involving both learning on rations to be expected and adjusting effective demand. In Benassy's non-tatonnement process, the K-equilibrium is a kind of rational expectation equilibrium characterised by the consistency between the expectation of rations and the actual transactions. While avoiding in principle the fiction of a tatonnement on quantity, the Benassy process appears to be highly information demanding and its outcome is dependent upon the order of markets to be visited. Thus Benassy proposed too a 'systemised' version of his model, which is more similar to a QT model.

Benassy's dynamic model put emphasis on the problem of defining effective demand in a multi-market model, and thus on the proper generalisation of Clower's 'dual decision hypothesis'.

Drèze (1975) considered effective demands as the outcome of a single constrained programme, in which all transaction constraints are simultaneously taken into account. With this definition, effective demands are mutually consistent, but they cannot exceed rations, and thus they do not provide a measure of disequilibrium. The alternative definition of Benassy (1975) and Barro and Grossman (1976) defined the effective demand as the results of $n - 1$ independent programmes, one for each good taking into account the constraints perceived on the $n - 1$ other markets. This definition provides us with a measure of disequilibrium for each market, but the set of effective demand no longer forms a plan consistent with budget constraint. As a consequence, they do not satisfy Walrasian law. This version of 'generalised dual decision hypothesis' has been advocated by Benassy (1982) in another paper, but it remains not fully satisfactory.

B A typology of macroeconomic equilibria with rationing

Aside from the study of non-Walrasian general equilibrium models carried out by Drèze and Benassy, the theory of disequilibria rests on a family of macroeconomic models put forward by Barro and Grossman and developed by Benassy and Malinvaud. Aggregative non-Walrasian equilibrium models in general contain two 'agents', households and firms; and two markets in which goods and labour exchange against money. They retain the assumption of behaviour constrained at the microeconomic level and consider the aggregate relationships which arise from it. The specific problems of aggregation of behavioural relationships when markets do not clear have as yet been little studied, but the aggregation is simplified by the following rules.[47]

If a single consumer is rationed in the goods market, then the market is in global excess demand and no firm is rationed in it. Symmetrically, in the case of excess supply no household is rationed. Similarly on the labour market, households and firms are respectively rationed in the cases of excess supply and demand.

If a single agent is rationed in a market, the global behavioural function relevant to the other markets for the group to which it (that agent) belongs is the constrained function.

From this starting-point it is possible to construct a typology of macroeconomic disequilibria based on the configuration of rations experienced by the different agents.

1 The configuration of constraints

Examination of the state of the different markets and of the configuration of constraints which it generates leads to the identification of four cases, which correspond to situations of Keynesian unemployment, of inflation, of 'classical' unemployment and to a limiting 'anti-classical' case for the economy.

(*a*) *Keynesian unemployment* – This is a situation characterised by simultaneous excess supply on the labour market, so that households are rationed, and on the goods market, so that firms are rationed. Production is equal to effective demand, the sum of constrained consumption and autonomous demand: $Y = C + A$. Assuming that profits are distributed to households the effective demand function given on page 375 becomes:

$$C = \widetilde{C} = a_1 \, (Y + M_o/p) \text{ denoting } a_1 = \alpha_1/(\alpha_1 + \alpha_2)$$
$$\text{and } a_2 = \alpha_2/(\alpha_1 + \alpha_2).$$

Combining these two equations we have:

$$Y = A/a_2 + (a_1/a_2)(M_o/p).$$

Hence the autonomous expenditure multiplier takes the value $1/a_2$ in conformity with Keynesian theory, while a_2 is the 'constrained' propensity to save. The multiplier for initial money holdings takes on a lower value. The level of employment is obtained from the level of effective demand:

$$N = \widetilde{L}_d = F^{-1} (Y).$$

Transposing the reaction curves of firms and households to the macroeconomic level, we obtain the diagram (Figure 12.6).

The similarity of this representation to the Keynesian determination of effective demand is clear. It should not, however, lead one to underestimate the differences in interpretation.

The arrows E_G and E_L measure excess demand signalled for goods and labour according to the principle of the generalised dual decision hypothesis. For instance, excess demand in the labour market is the difference between constrained demand $\widetilde{L}_d$, because firms are rationed on the goods market, and the notional supply L^*_s because households are unconstrained on goods market. 'Keynesian' unemployment is characterised by general excess supply.

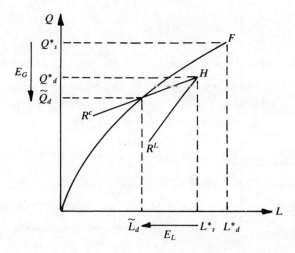

Figure 12.6 Keynesian unemployment equilibrium

(*b*) *Repressed inflation* – Repressed inflation corresponds to the opposite situation, in which excess demand appears in both markets.[48] Firms are then rationed in the labour market and households in the goods market.

Households announce their constrained labour supply $\widetilde{L}_s$, which determines the output offered and actually supplied, $F(\widetilde{L}_s)$. Substituting into the definition of $\widetilde{L}_s$ the expression for value of national income, we obtain the following expression for effective employment:

$$L = L_o - (a_3/a_2)(M_o + pA)/w.$$

Thus the action of rationing on labour supply gives rise to a supply multiplier studied by Barro and Grossman (1973).[49] Under inflation, a rise in autonomous demand or in initial endowments reduces the effective level of employment through a cumulative process.

The graphical representation of the inflationary case makes it apparent that this case corresponds to excess demand in both markets $(E_G, E_L > 0)$. This non-Walrasian equilibrium is then characterised by inflationary pressures, the inflation being 'repressed' as prices are assumed to adjust slowly and to be fixed in the market period.

Thus the analysis of the rationing mechanisms shows how output is reduced in conditions of excess demand relative to the case of market clearing.

(*c*) *Classical unemployment* – A third situation, termed 'stagflation' by

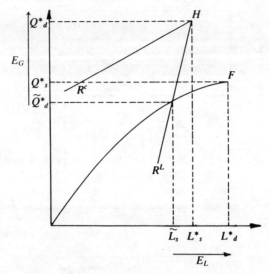

Figure 12.7   Repressed inflation equilibrium

Benassy and 'classical unemployment' by Malinvaud, corresponds to the case of excess supply in the labour market and excess demand in the goods market. Households are then doubly constrained, while firms realise their notional plans.

$$L = L_d\,(w,\,p), \qquad Y = Q^*_s(w,\,p).$$

Households announce their constrained demand $\tilde{Q}_d(L)$ and their constrained offer of labour $\tilde{L}_s(Y)$ but cannot realise these, as Figure 12.8 shows.

The situation of classical unemployment provides an interesting illustration of the implications of the principle of generalised dual decisions: each reaction curve represents a combination of shifts as functions of the constraints perceived in other markets but does not take into account the possible constraint in the market being considered. Thus when an agent is simultaneously constrained in several markets, as are households in this case, that agent can no longer realise his planned constrained supply and demand.

(*d*) *The 'anticlassical' function and underconsumption case* – The converse of the preceding case is that in which firms are constrained in both markets because of excess supply in the goods market and excess demand in the labour market.

In our present model, where firms must be on their production

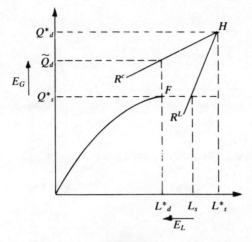

Figure 12.8

function, this case is confined to the following very special situation,[50] we shall call the 'anticlassical frontier'.

For this case to prevail, the wage-price couple must be such that $Q_d^* = F(L_d^*)$. It will become apparent later on that this can happen as the limiting case of either a repressed inflation or a Keynesian unemployment situation.

On Figure 12.9 (b) is represented the 'underconsumption' case which may happen if firms are free to set their production at a level different from their sales, for instance by building up or reducing inventories, as shown for instance by Muellbauer and Portes (1978), a constraint on sales will lead to both a reduction of output and an increase in inventories indicated on reaction curve R^N while firms will respond to a constraint on labour market by reducing sales less than output and reducing inventories as shown on the reaction curve R^S. The fourth case corresponds, then, to a full region, named 'underconsumption'.

Having identified the different types of macroeconomic disequilibria, it remains for us to see how they relate to the exogenous variables.

2 Determination of the regime: a general model
The determination of the macroeconomic rationing equilibrium situation comes from the signs of the excess demand in the goods and labour markets. The effective supply and demand can be expressed, according to the pattern of rationing as a function of the exogenous variables of the model: wages, prices, the real value of money endowments and autonomous expenditure. Graphical representation in two dimensions requires that only two variables be retained. E. Malinvaud chooses

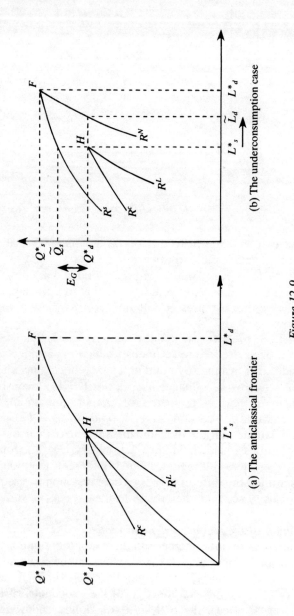

(a) The anticlassical frontier

(b) The underconsumption case

Figure 12.9

wages and prices; J. P. Benassy, whom we shall follow here, takes the real wage and the money balances.

The regions of disequilibrium are demarcated by finding the loci of partial equilibrium which separate them. Thus, partial equilibrium in the goods market may result from the equality of a notional demand with a constrained supply, or of a constrained demand with a notional supply. Equality of notional supply with notional demand implies that no one is constrained on the labour market, and therefore only occurs in general equilibrium. By the same token, it would be meaningful to match a constrained supply with a constrained demand for goods only if firms and households were simultaneously rationed in the labour market, which is excluded by assumption.

The same line of reasoning explains why we will again have two loci of partial equilibrium in the labour market to consider, corresponding to the equality of supply and demand, the one being notional, the other constrained.

Let us use F_1 to denote the equilibrium frontier for the labour market with notional demand and constrained supply. This frontier defines the pairs *(w, m)* satisfying the equation:

$$L^*_d\ (w) - \tilde{L}_s\ (w, m) = 0$$

and hence the differential equation

$$(\partial L^*_d/\partial w - \partial L_s/\partial w)dw - (\partial L_s/\partial m)\,dm = 0;$$
$$\text{of signs } [(-) - (+)]\ dw - (-)\ dm = 0$$

The slope of F_1 is therefore always positive;[51] F_2 will represent the partial equilibrium frontier of the labour market with firms' demand constrained by their markets and the notional supply of households. It satisfies the equation

$$L_d(m) - L^*_s(w, m) = 0$$

where L_d does not depend on *w* if there is no distributional effect. In this case:

$$- (\delta L^*_s/\delta w)\ dw + (\delta \tilde{L}_d/\delta m - \delta L_s/\delta m)\ dm = 0$$

whose coefficients have the following signs:

$$- (+)\ dw + [(+) - (-)]\ dm = 0$$

which implies that F_2 is monotonically increasing in the (w, m) space. The frontier F_3 represents a partial equilibrium with demand constrained in the goods market. In the absence of distributional effects, we have:

$$\tilde{Q}_d(m) - Q^*_s(w) = 0$$

giving a differential equation of the form:

$$(+)\, dm - (-)\, dw = 0$$

F_3 therefore has a negative slope.

The last frontier to be considered, F_4, corresponds to equality of notional demand and constrained supply in the goods market, hence

$$Q^*_d(w,m) - \tilde{Q}_s(w, m) = 0 \qquad \text{and hence}$$

$$(\partial Q^*_d/\partial w - \partial \tilde{Q}_s/\partial w)\, dw + (\partial Q_d/\partial m - \partial \tilde{Q}_s/\partial m)\, dm = 0$$

being of the form $[(+) - (-)]\, dw - [(+) - (-)]\, dm = 0$ giving a positive slope dw/dm.

To obtain these equilibrium loci, it must first be established that the four frontiers have a unique point of intersection, and then on which side of that point each frontier is relevant in characterising the corresponding partial equilibrium.

Let W denote the intersection of F_1 and F_2, thus ensuring full employment with $L^*_d = L^*_s = L_d = L_s$. The equality of L^*_d and L_d implies that the same holds for each firm. W is therefore situated simultaneously on all four frontiers, and corresponds to Walrasian general equilibrium.

To the 'north-east' of W, higher values of m and w generate excess demand for goods. The supply of labour, though not the demand, is then constrained, and F_1 is the relevant partial equilibrium condition; and vice versa for F_2 to the 'south-east' of Walrasian equilibrium. Similarly, if the real wage exceeds its value in Walrasian equilibrium, labour is in positive excess supply, a constrained demand for goods must apply; placing partial equilibrium in the goods market on F_3; and by converse reasoning, the zone of applicability of F_4 is found.

In the general case, where firms possess two distinct reaction functions, the following loci of partial equilibrium may be constructed from a proper combination of functions F_1 to F_4.

It is then possible to superimpose these loci in order to obtain a typology of macroeconomic rationing equilibria, as a function of given wage rate and money stock.

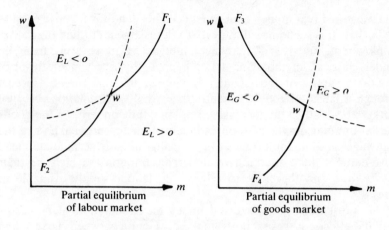

Figure 12.10   Partial equilibrium loci

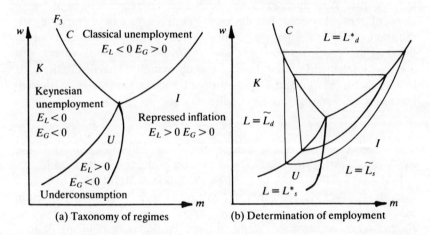

Figure 12.11

An alternative way of constructing the typology and identification of equilibria is to notice that the effective level of employment is the minimum of the four terms of notional and effective supply and demand

$$L = \min\ (L^*_d,\ \widetilde{L}_d,\ L^*_s,\ \widetilde{L}_s)$$

Each regime is characterised by the determination of the level of employment as one of these four functions. This is a valuable indication for the comparative statics of the model, in so far as it permits a simple determination of the levels of employment associated with given levels of the exogenous variables. Iso-employment curves as functions of the real wage and real money endowments have been drawn above (Figure 12.11 (b)). It is seen immediately that Walrasian equilibrium maximises employment, and that employment falls as we move away from W. Under classical unemployment this happens by a- fall in the level of profitable supply of jobs. Under Keynesian unemployment it occurs through a fall in effective demand; under repressed inflation, because workers respond to the increasing rationing they undergo in the goods market by reducing their supply of labour. Finally, the weakness of the real wage, and the importance of the savings already accumulated lead wage-earners, in a situation of underconsumption, to increase their leisure-time and therefore to reduce the labour supply available to firms.

This presentation, constructed under the assumption of no distributional effects, serves to illustrate the distinction between classical and Keynesian unemployment regarding their sensitivity to economic policy instruments. A reduction in the real wage increases employment in classical unemployment, but has no effect in Keynesian unemployment. An increase in real balances or an equivalent increase in autonomous demand increases employment under Keynesian unemployment, but leaves it unchanged under classical unemployment. This distinction was the basis for Malinvaud's suggestion of such a taxonomy of macro-economic underemployment equilibria.

3 A special case
The systems set out above can be fully and simply explained at the expense of particular specifications and simplifications often made.

In the first place, we shall consider the model without stock or capital formation. We have seen that in this case firms have a unique reaction curve – their production function. Partial equilibrium determined at F_2 between constrained demand and notional supply of labour $\tilde{L}_d = L^*_s$, implies that households are not constrained in demand so that $Q = Q^*_d$ and $\tilde{L}_d = F^{-1}(Q^*_d) = L^*_s$. At the same time, F_4 represents a partial equilibrium in the goods market so that no agent is constrained in that market. The constrained supply of goods $\tilde{Q}_s$ is then constrained by the notional supply of labour L^*_s so $\tilde{Q}_s = F(L^*_s)$, that is, the equality $Q^*_d = \tilde{Q}_s$ now implies $L^*_s = F^{-1}(Q^*_d)$, which is precisely the expression derived above for F_2.

We have thus established that, in the absence of stocks, the partial equilibrium function in the labour market with constrained demand – F_2 – and the supply-constrained partial equilibrium frontier in the goods market, F_4, coincide.

Next, the explicit derivation of these frontiers can be simply achieved if particular macroeconomic functions are chosen, for example a constant supply of labour $L^*_s = \tilde{L}_s = \bar{L}$ and a given production function such as $Q = \sqrt{N}N$. In the absence of distributional effects, effective demand is of the form:

$$\tilde{Q}_d = a_2(m + \sqrt{L}) + A$$

F'_L is then $1/2\sqrt{L}$ which gives $L^*_d = 1/4w^2$. The equation for F_1 now becomes $\bar{L} = 1/4w^2$, satisfied by $w = 1(2\sqrt{\bar{L}})$. F_1 is then a horizontal straight line.

F_2, which coincides with F_4, is given by $\sqrt{\bar{L}} = a_2(m + \sqrt{\bar{L}}) + A$ and so is independent of the real wage w, and corresponds to a vertical line (line perpendicular to the m axis)

$$m = [(1 - a_1)\sqrt{\bar{L}} - A]/a_1$$

Finally the frontier F_3 is written

$$a_2(m + \sqrt{L^*}_d) + A = \sqrt{L^*}_d$$

whence as $\sqrt{L^*}_d = 1/2w$

$$w = (1 - a_1)/2(a_2 m + A)$$

the equation of a decreasing hyperbolic curve.

The graphical form of the partition into regions therefore follows immediately.

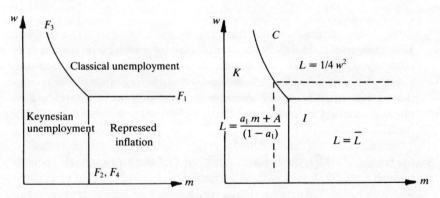

Figure 12.12

A second diagram (Figure 12.12) shows iso-employment loci. In contrast with the general model, employment is now maximised simultaneously at Walrasian equilibrium and in the whole region of repressed inflation.

One implication of the typology suggested by the modern disequilibrium theory is to show, through a comparative static method, that the impact of certain traditional economic policy measures differs according to the configuration of rations at the micro level. Thus, as Malinvaud, among others, has shown, employment can be increased under Keynesian unemployment by increasing money balances, autonomous expenditure or even wages, in case of distributional effects, while such measures will be ineffective, if not perverse, if the unemployment is of the classical type.[52]

These, of course, are only the first results obtained in the framework of a model as central for non-Walrasian macroeconomic analysis as was the *IS-LM* model thirty years before for the Keynesian paradigm.

C The dynamics of disequilibria

The representation of different configurations of rationing equilibria is an important feature of the models outlined. However, one should bear in mind that these are fixed-price models, based on the idea of an infinitely rapid adjustment of quantities relative to prices. It is clear that a more complete system must specify dynamic adjustments of prices as well as adjustment processes for money holdings or productive capacity.

With respect to these adjustment processes to be introduced, it is useful to think of fix-price equilibria as temporary equilibria.

1 The temporary equilibrium approach
Once again, general equilibrium serves as a reference model. The Walrasian model considers the formation of a general equilibrium in N contemporary markets for goods, services, new capital and future claims. Debreu extended this model by considering equilibrium formation simultaneously in NT markets, of which $N(T - 1)$ are futures markets relating to goods and services becoming available in $T - 1$ future periods.[53]

In such a system all decisions are taken simultaneously regardless of the period to which they relate. It is clear that the economy represented by such a model should include a complete system of forward markets in which all agents participate. However, a model seeking to represent the actual economy must take account of the fact that only a limited number of forward markets exists and that current decisions are related to the future essentially through the intermediary of expectations.

The method of temporary equilibria proposed by Hicks in *Value and*

Capital (1938) includes just such an assumption. It investigates the formation of equilibrium in current markets, and in the few existing forward markets, on the basis of agents' behaviour conditional upon the expectations over subsequent periods which they form. These expectations are not necessarily mutually consistent, so that the attainment of a temporary equilibrium in each period does not guarantee that the economy evolves along an intertemporal equilibrium path throughout which expectations are confirmed.

The concept of temporary equilibrium may be applied to general competitive equilibria, or to the non-Walrasian fixed-price equilibria of the preceding paragraphs.[54] It can, however, equally be associated with incomplete *IS-LM* equilibria where adjustment in money holding takes time,[55] or with growth equilibria with myopic expectations.[56]

2 Dynamic adjustments in the aggregated disequilibrium model: money, wages and prices

Despite the drastic simplifications upon which it depends, the aggregated disequilibrium model raises awkward problems when one comes to specify the dynamics of the adjustment process governing the sequencing of K-equilibria through time. Recent studies of this difficulty have initially considered prices and money wages as responding to an excess demand signalled according to equations of the form:

$$dp/dt = f(\tilde{Q}_d - \tilde{Q}_s) \; ; \; dw/dt = g\,(L_d - L_s).$$

It is fairly easy to construct diagrammatically in (w, p) space the evolution of an economy following a sequence of K-equilibria, proceeding through wage and price adjustments.

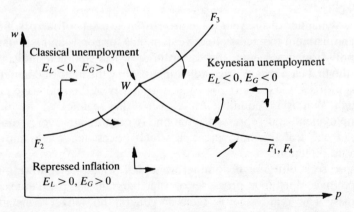

Figure 12.13

The directions of movement result directly from the sign of the effective excess demands. For such a process, the economy converges towards a stationary long-term K-equilibrium, which may be either the Walrasian equilibrium W or some point on the 'anticlassical' frontier, between repressed inflation and Keynesian unemployment.

The analysis is severely complicated by variations between periods in money balances or in productive capital. Some recent contributions have explored the dynamics of disequilibrium in the case of a process of adjustment through prices and money balances.[57]

In this framework, the long-term evolution of the economy is defined from two curves, standing respectively for the loci of stationary real wages and stationary money balances. There is then a tendency for the economy to move towards Walrasian equilibrium if and only if the adjustment processes of these variables possess certain appropriate characteristics.

In the simple models considered here, money creation results from financing government deficit needs, obtained by comparing given public expenditures with endogenous fiscal revenue. The creation of money is thus a decreasing function of the level of employment, all other things being equal. The rate of growth of real money balances is obtained from the money newly created, after deducting the rate of inflation. S. Honkapohja has shown that the loci of stationarity, $g_m = 0$, then becomes a family of increasing curves in the real wage–real money balances space.[58] Only one of these curves passed through the Walrasian equilibrium point W and therefore corresponds to an appropriate level of government expenditure. If government policy is too 'restrictive', the curve $g_m = 0$ passes through the interior of the region of classical unemployment, while one passes directly from Keynesian unemployment to repressed inflation if government policy is too 'lax'.

The dynamics of the real wage arise from two sets of factors: firstly, from adjustment to excess effective demands for goods and labour; and secondly from any secular trends, or more or less complete indexation.

In the first case where price adjustments obey the logic of competitive market forces, the locus ($g_w = 0$) of stationarity of the real wage passes through Walrasian equilibrium, crossing the regimes of Keynesian unemployment and repressed inflation. It cannot, however, cross the area of classical unemployment in which prices and wages move in opposite directions.

The case is different if nominal wage and prices are following non-competitive adjustment processes of wage bargains and price indexation in costs. The real wage is then in general no longer constant at Walrasian equilibrium, where excess demands are all zero. A too high aspiration level in wage bargaining may result, as shown by Pitchford and Turnovsky (1978) in an inflationary bias. Then, the curve g_w will cross the region of classical unemployment.

Starting from these elements of partial dynamics it is possible to categorise the evolutions of the economy. Let us first consider the favourable case, where convergence to Walrasian equilibrium is guaranteed.

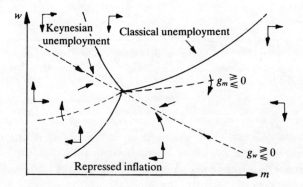

Figure 12.14 Dynamics of real wage and money balances with appropriate fiscal policy

Convergence towards Walrasian equilibrium implies that the curves $g_m = 0$ and $g_w = 0$ pass through this point. Thus government policy is appropriate, and no secular tendency acts against the adjustment of prices and wages as a function of excess demand.

If government expenditure is not appropriate, the economy tends in the long term to a situation of quasi-equilibrium in Hansen's sense,[59] in which nominal magnitudes move in parallel and real magnitudes are constant. If government expenditure is insufficient, a Keynesian quasi-equilibrium is obtained, with steady deflation of prices, wages and the quantity of money (Figure 12.15 (a) below). In relation to the old debate about the persistence of unemployment with flexible prices,[60] this situation corresponds to the case where the stabilising role of the real balance effect is cancelled by a government policy which brings about an equivalent reduction of nominal balances.

Case (b) additionally introduces the assumption of non-competitive adjustments in wage and price, which results in a growth of real wage at Walrasian equilibrium.

The economy then tends in the long term towards a situation of persistent classical unemployment, where the stationarity of the real wage corresponds to the level of unemployment necessary to cancel out

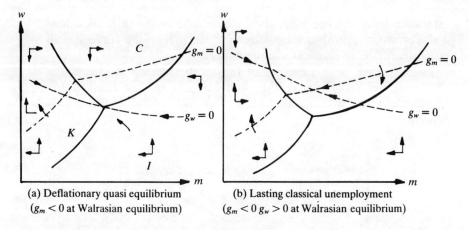

(a) Deflationary quasi equilibrium
($g_m < 0$ at Walrasian equilibrium)

(b) Lasting classical unemployment
($g_m < 0\ g_w > 0$ at Walrasian equilibrium)

Figure 12.15

its inflationary bias. The price level in this case is increasing, as is the nominal money stock. Government policy is not sufficiently expansionary to ensure full employment in a state of repressed inflation, but too much so to ensure the stability of the general price level. Persisting situations analysed in this way provide an interesting approach to stagflation, and illustrate well the analysis suggested above of cost-push inflation, which cannot persist without a certain degree of monetary accommodation, or 'validation'.

These modes of dynamic analysis of disequilibrium have been set out largely for illustrative purposes, in so far as a more detailed study may modify some of its conclusions.

3 Disequilibrium dynamics of capital and growth

A straightforward generalisation of disequilibrium dynamics, beyond the consideration of price and money adjustments, is to exploit the dynamics of inventories which play an important role in absorbing short-run imbalances but also in propagating disequilibria through time. Non-market clearing with inventories have been proposed by Honkapohja and Ito (1979) and by Green and Laffont (1981). We shall not develop their model, in order to cope directly with capital accumulation and growth.

We did emphasise, in chapter 8, that neoclassical growth theory, and the Solow model primarily, assumes instantaneous market clearing and in particular permanent full employment. Assuming wage or price rigidity leads to the occurrence of market imbalances, where alternative disequilibrium regimes have to be considered. A model for this approach was proposed by Ito (1979) and was later extended.

Ito's model retains all Solow's assumptions, except for the wage perfect flexibility and therefore equilibrium on the labour market. Then, he obtains two regimes: the first with full employment and excess demand for labour, and the second with unemployment. As the determination of investment by savings is maintained, the growth of capital stock in the full employment regime is given by the same differential equation as in the Solow model

$$\dot{k}_t = s\, f(k_t) - n\, k_t$$

Unemployment occurs for a notional labour demand L^d_t inferior to exogenous labour force L_t, which happens for a too-high wage rate.

$$w_t > f(k_t) - kf'_k \text{ where notations are straightforward.}$$

Writing k^d_t for the desired capital-labour ratio K_t/L^d_t, and owing to the homogeneity of the first degree of the production functions, we have for the output *per capita*

$$y_t = F(K_t/L^d_t\, ,\, 1)\, (L^d_t/L_t) = f(k^d_t)k_t/k^d_t$$

whence the differential equation for k_t under unemployment

$$\dot{k}_t = k_t\, [s\, f(d^d_t)/k^d_t - n]$$

Assuming that the real wage adjustment is a function of the relative excess demand L^d_t/L_t

$$\dot{w}_t = [k_t/k^d_t\, (W_t) - 1]$$

We have the differential equations for k_t and w_t which enable us to draw the phase diagram (Fig. 12.16).

The equilibrium value $w^*\, (k) = f(k) - kf'_k$ separates the excess demand 'overemployment' region R_o and the unemployment region R_u. The stationarity of capital stock per head k_t is obtained for a critical value $\bar{w}$ of the wage rate in R_u, but in R_o it requires a critical value $\bar{k}$ of k_t. The wage adjustment is straightforward: rising under excess demand for labour, and decreasing under unemployment. Thus, in Ito's model, the growth path converges towards a full employment steady state which is the same as in Solow's equilibrium model.

Retaining the assumption of investment given by saving, the Ito model precludes any disequilibrium in the good market. Extending it as to allow for good market disequilibrium, one obtains a growth model

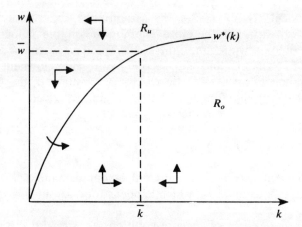

Figure 12.16   Phase diagram for Ito's model

which is the counterpart of the static model with three or four regimes. There are two ways of introducing investment as variable distinct to saving. The first one is to assume an explicit investment function, depending for instance on utilisation rate and profit, as does P. Picard (1982). While his model involves in the short run the three basic regimes of Keynesian or classical unemployment and repressed inflation, Picard is able to show the level stability of long-run Walrasian equilibrium for competitive adjustments in prices and wages. It is interesting to remark that Picard's model looks even more Keynesian because it assumes a fixed coefficient production function, which is however inessential for the disequilibrium issue.

An alternative way of explaining investment is to formalise the optimal accumulation plan for the representative firm. Hénin and Michel (1982) assume firms maximise discounted profits over time and they show that this optimal accumulation programme fully determines the growth path of the economy. This approach gives the following results.

First, rather than defining equilibria with rationing in a static manner, and looking at growth paths as 'sequences of short-run equilibria' linked by more or less *ad hoc* adjustment or expectational processes, this 'optimizing' approach defines directly the disequilibrium growth path, giving the temporary equilibria by mere temporal decentralisation of this path. The essential variable for this decentralisation is the shadow price of capital q_t which, under an assumption of perfect foresight, gives enough information for investment at any point of time to be optimal with respect to all the rationing constraints the firms will be facing in the whole future. Thus q_t is a very specific measure of long-term profitability, the importance of which for current unemployment was emphasized by E. Malinvaud (1980). Hénin and Michel show that the taxonomy of temporary equilibria with rationing may be directly related to both the short term and the long-run profitability, the first commanding the notional labour demand, the second commanding investment and then effective labour demand.

Table 12.1 *Taxonomy of temporary equilibria with respect to profitability*

Short run — Long run		Margin over wage cost	
		Too high ⇒ E.D. for labour	Too low ⇒ E.S. of labour
Investment incentive	Too low ⇒ E.S. of goods	Overcapitalisation	Keynesian unemployment
	Too high ⇒ E.D. for goods	Repressed inflation	Classical unemployment

Table 12.1 is to be interpreted taking into account the given level of capital stock. In classical unemployment, the incentive to invest is high, but marginal productivity of capital is low with respect to real wage: both features are consistent with a relatively low capital stock. In repressed inflation a low wage ensures full employment even if the capital stock appears to be low enough as to justify a high rate of investment. The fourth case is named 'overcapitalisation' because it may correspond to a relatively excessive capital stock, which depresses investment rate and thus explains excess supply of goods, but boosts the marginal productivity of labour and thus justifies full employment.

A third interesting result of the 'optimizing' approach to disequilibrium growth is obtained for the limiting case of a stationary wage rate at a level which may be excessive. In this last case, Figure 12.17 indicates the behaviour of the economy.

The unique optimal path is a saddle path which may involve, for a high initial level of capital stock, an 'overcapitalisation' traverse. When arrived in the Keynesian unemployment regime, the economy follows a warranted path at an endogenous constant rate which is less than the natural rate. Thus, the model provides strong support to the view of a 'warranted growth path', with unemployment if the wage rate is too high. On the other hand, it shows that the economy converges towards a neoclassical full employment path when the wage rate is low enough to allow for a sufficient profitability of capital.

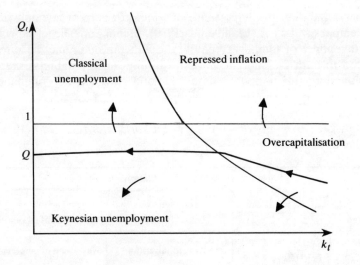

Figure 12.17   Phase diagram for the 'optimizing' model

4 *Behaviour out of equilibrium*

Price adjustments and capital accumulation thus result from the economic decisions of agents, particularly firms, outside equilibrium. To begin with, non-Walrasian microeconomic foundations can be characterised by the introduction of additional constraints in the form of quantity rationing resulting from market disequilibrium. The neoclassical concept of rationality, of maximisation subject to constraints, can certainly be extended to new fields, as it may be to an uncertain environment, but the question arises as to how far the study of disequilibria tends to an extension of the rationality assumed of agents.

Thus, the distance between a theory of administered prices and the neoclassical marginal cost pricing rule is fairly reduced in models which include informational and adjustment costs. Furthermore, in an uncertain and changing environment, one may wonder if rational behaviour implies the solution of formidably complicated optimisation problems, or the adoption of simple rules of behaviour relatively robust to foreseeable changes?

The behaviourist 'school' developed a conception of the firm as organisation, in which internal coordination procedures prevent formal maximisation, giving way to 'satisficing' solutions,[61] by applying simple 'rules of thumb'. Behaviour then responds to a hierarchy of levels of adaptation, from revision of an operational decision to revision of the decision rules or alternation of the goals pursued.[62]

To the neoclassical concept of adjustments resulting from dynamic optimisation we thus find opposed an *a priori* conception of behaviour as a process of adaptation to the environment.[63]

At the level of behaviour of the firm, the idea of a 'satisficing' solution implies that constraints are not always binding. On the contrary, the firm seeks to preserve some freedom of action[64] which, among other things, ensures the availability of an 'organisational slack'. It will thus hold reserves of realisable productivity gains, generating x-inefficiency (Leibenstein) or of unexploited monopoly profits (Galbraith) in order to be able to adapt to disturbances. The problem is how 'to represent the firm as a multidimensional organisation, seeking to survive in the face of constraints and pressures defined by its environment'[65] may help to understand adjustment behaviour relevant at the macro level. Up to now, relatively little work has been done in this area.

If the constraints experienced by economic agents in a situation of disequilibrium represent a decentralisation – a 'micronisation' in Negishi's term – of the global constraints, their perception of these constraints leads to a genuine 'internalisation' of disequilibrium. It may be now helpful to follow F. Perroux[66] or T. W. Schultz[67] in describing their behaviour as an element in a process of equilibration. Schultz's approach remains faithful to neoclassical modes of thought;

> Determining precisely what people do who are not in equilibrium is not one of the notable achievements of economics. What people do is, in general, concealed in the assumption that their optimizing behaviour is such that they regain equilibrium instantaneously. However, it is unlikely that they would be able to do this in fact; but more important, even if they were able, it would not normally be economic for them to make all of the required reallocations of their resources instantaneously. Thus, regaining equilibrium takes time, and how people proceed over time depends on their efficiency in responding to any given disequilibrium and on the cost and returns of the sequence of adjustments available to them.[68]

If for Schultz equilibration reduces to optimal adjustment behaviour, the French economist F. Perroux gave an example of a wider conception, more related to other social or human science approaches, like that of the Swiss psychologist Piaget.

4 DISEQUILIBRIA AND MACROECONOMIC REGULATION

Whilst the formulations of modern disequilibrium theory remain too abstract to constitute an immediate response to the increase in disequilibria observed over the last fifteen years or so, the historical coincidence of this research effort with the challenge of events is striking. It is therefore appropriate to consider more broadly the elements of interpretation which may be suggested. In the process, we shall find some points of contact with the analyses of some Marxist writers, and also some disagreements.

Starting from an identification of the factors creating and propagating disequilibria, we shall first examine the changes which have affected the model of regulation of modern capitalist economies, and then consider the implications which might be suggested for economic policy.

A The impulse factors

In the terminology used by Ragnar Frisch,[69] modern disequilibrium theory undoubtedly appears more as an analysis of propagation than of the 'impulse' factors which underlie disequilibria. Like other approaches such as Marxist analysis of Schumpeter's theory of growth, it does, however, provide a frame of reference enabling certain sources of disequilibrium to be identified – certain features of structural maladjustment, that is to say, which have been of prime importance in recent times.

1 Maladjustment stemming from demand

In the view of L. Pasinetti, it is impossible to understand the mechanisms of growth and fluctuations without taking a disaggregated view of the growth process.[70] Why should growth run into periodical disarray if it was merely a case of producing the same goods with the same techniques? The same author has tried to model this process of non-homothetic growth, in which output and productivity do not grow at the same rate.[71] Under these conditions, the potential equilibrium in each sector between, on the one hand, output and employment and, on the other, productive capacity and demand will always be precarious and will continually be subject to disturbance. The actual growth process involves continuous shift in demand, requiring a continuous reallocation of factors. For this reallocation to be effective in a non-tatonnement world, relative prices have to change frequently and it is not necessary to share a pessimistic view of the market mechanisms to observe that new risks of misadjustment are continuously arising.

2 Maladjustment stemming from production

The evolution of techniques of production is governed by a complex of technical and economic forces which, at the sectoral level, bears very little relation to the assumption of an even trend usually included in macroeconomic models. It in fact proceeds by a succession of phases of acceleration, segregated by pauses. While expectations over technology are possible regarding general trends, they are very fragile as to the time-scale and consequently the expected longevity of equipment is a random variable to which a high degree of uncertainty is attached.

Technical changes include both the renewal of goods and of processes, and the main opportunities of substituting capital for labour, without, however, this latter variable being an automatic corollary of technical progress.[72]

The unequal pace of development of productivity among sectors generates shifts in prices and incomes which are the root of intersectoral disparities and their correction. The concept of 'surplus productivity' is a useful tool for evaluating the scale of these disparities. The 'surplus productivity' in a sector marks the excess of the growth of output in constant prices over the increase in factor incomes calculated in constant prices for the same base period:[73]

$$S = p_o \, \Delta Y - \Sigma_i \, w_i \, \Delta X_i.$$

$$S = - Y_o \, \Delta p + \Sigma_i \, X_i \, \Delta w_i + \Delta \pi .$$

The productivity surplus is necessarily distributed through an increase in factor incomes and profits, and through a fall in the selling price.

We denote current output $Y = Y_o + \Delta Y$, and factors employed in the current period by $X_i = X_{o,i} + \Delta X_i$. In times of acute competition, most of the surplus is redistributed through a fall in prices, and such a solution has from time to time been suggested as a norm in a liberal economy, under the name of the Davidson rule.[74] In this case, nominal incomes remain constant and real incomes increase due to the fall in prices.

In developed capitalist economies, oligopolistic market structures and more developed trade union power lead to the redistribution of the greater part of the surplus in the form of an increase in nominal incomes. Since the movements in productivity are different in the different sectors,[75] and since the patterns of growth of incomes must equalise, the least-productive sectors are compelled to allow increased incomes in line with their more productive brethren, so that these increases, not being matched by increases in their own productivity, are translated into rises in nominal prices. While according to the Davidson rule, a fall in all prices allows real income to be increased correspondingly, the distribution as factor incomes of the major part of the surplus leads to an increase in prices, returning the increased real incomes of the most productive sectors to the mean rate of growth of incomes and productivity. In this process of productivity inflation, notably studied by S. C. Kolm,[76] the rate of inflation is equal to the difference between the rate of growth of nominal incomes in sectors where productivity growth is fastest, and the mean rate of productivity growth.

The important contribution of Aglietta sought to underpin these technical dynamics with a more fundamental evolution of the organisation of labour, which from a Marxian point of view constitutes the specific scene of the appropriation of surplus value, and therefore the 'heart' of the capitalist system. From the beginning of the twentieth century, Taylorism marked a new stage in the process of division of labour by taking to an extreme the compartmentalisation of jobs. At the time of the great crash, Fordism marked a twofold extension of this process, partly by reinforcing the integration of operations into semi-automated production lines, but above all by developing a mode of consumption based on access of the working population to the consumption of goods manufactured by the most advanced processes. Fordism thus enabled sales outlets in these sectors to be guaranteed, particularly in the case of semi-durable consumption goods, while strengthening the integration of the working population – an integration now no longer confined to the labour process, but also in consumption viewed as 'regeneration of the labour force'.[77]

Thus, just as the Great Crash of 1929 seemed to have marked the limitations of Taylorism, being unable as it was to ensure sufficient outlets for the mass of output to which it led, the recent crisis seems to mark the limitations of Fordism, in the face of new technical advances requiring new sorts of process integration,[78] and especially of an increase in the cost of reproduction of the labour force.This cost involves more and more goods which do not benefit from a rapid increase in productivity, such as public goods and health services.[79]

> The stability of the consumption model based on mass consumption of private goods, and of stratification of wage-earners, and increasingly dependent on public goods, is disturbed by the fact that Fordism forces production of these public goods to the fringes of capitalist accumulation. Their cost increases precipitously with rising social demand.

Aglietta's theory certainly identifies an important factor limiting growth and generating divergences in costs. One might however question whether the distinction thus made in terms of trends in productivity does set a group of public goods in opposition to private ones rather than private goods as against the majority of services, whether their mode of production and/or consumption is itself private or collective, and whether it directly obeys capitalist logic or is guaranteed by the state.

3 Maladjustments arising in raw materials markets

The start of the crisis in November 1973 coincided with the 'oil crisis' which took the form, after a temporary embargo, of a quadrupling of the price of crude oil. The role of this shock in the crisis has been much discussed. There is a widespread tendency to minimalise *a priori* the scale of the imbalance thus caused; of the disturbance of cost structures and of the transfers of purchasing power involved. It seems to us that the oil crisis was an essential determinant of the exceptional scale of the wider economic crisis, but was not its primary cause insofar as the progress of the world economy in 1970–73, characterised by a strong inflationary slide, could not so continue indefinitely.

Extending the perspective beyond this particular historical experience, it is possible to identify destabilising factors at the level of commodity markets, generating disequilibrium growth. The pure theory of exhaustible resources, even when developed under an assumption of optimal market allocation, demonstrates the inevitability of trend movements in relative prices.[80] Moreover, since the production and use of these resources depend upon expectations over their exploitation and substitution of other factors of production, the absence of true futures markets for these resources makes regulation by a single market purely hypothetical, more realistic being instability in price movements, which will have effects in other markets.

Lord Kaldor's analysis[81] contrasts the 'primary sector', having flexible prices, with the industrial sector, characterised by administered prices which enable rising costs to be 'passed on'. Arising from this asymmetry, the link between these sectors at world level is seen as a cause of stagflation. Firstly, the burden of price adjustment rests with the primary products alone, so that movements in their prices are amplified. Secondly, this flexibility tends always to depress the level of industrial activity: '. . . *any* large change in commodity prices – irrespective of whether it is in favour or against the primary producers – tends to have a dampening effect on industrial activity; it retards industrial growth in both cases, instead of retarding it in one case and stimulating it in the other.'[82]

Thus, a fall in prices reduces the amount that primary producers can import and hence also the amount that the industrial sector can sell. And this fall in demand does not lead to a fall in prices in the industrial sector, which is insensitive to excess demand.

Kaldor therefore takes the view that stabilisation, through regulatory mechanisms, of trade in these commodities, is necessary in order to moderate disequilibria in the industrialised economies themselves.

4 Other sources of destabilisation

There are several – actual or potential – sources of disequilibrium. But their identification is only meaningful to the extent that they can be considered as relatively exogenous. The problem arises particularly in the case of sources of a political or social nature.

In the case of the political cycle, it is helpful to distinguish cycles caused by alternation of pre- and post-electoral periods – hence exogenous in nature – from those induced by 'stop-go' policies and hence endogenous to the economy.[83]

Certain commentators have pointed out the worldwide phenomenon of spiralling money wages in 1969–70, which contributed to the inflation of the years 1970–73.[84] Was this a by-product of disorder in the international monetary system, or a demographic or cultural phenomenon linked to a 'generation effect', or simply an accumulation of wage claims over the conjuncturally less favourable period of the 1960s?

One sort of historical/political shock certainly plays a determining part: namely, the conflicts in which the dominant economies engaged. The Korean war was followed by a sustained worldwide inflation in 1951–3, then by a prolonged recession in the United States. The Vietnam War, with its inflationary financing by the American administration, contributed powerfully to the increasing disequilibria of 1967–70.[85]

B Propagation of disequilibrium

In order to understand the mechanisms through which disequilibria spread, it is appropriate to start once more from the Walrasian model which supplies the reference-point of contradictory forces brought into balance.

Are we concerned here with shocks affecting autonomous demand? If so, price flexibility will bring us back to full employment by setting in motion a real balance effect. A reduction in supply? If so, the temporary increase in prices will lower demand and tend to encourage an increase in productive capacity. In a non-Walrasian economy however, such mechanisms are only partially effective, and operate with significant lags. Meanwhile, agents adapt their behaviour to disequilibria which have not been resolved, but rather carried over in time to a later period, and in space into other markets where they lead to rationing of other agents. In other words these delays result from incomplete adjustment to equilibrium prices. They must be distinguished from the Walrasian interdependence of markets for which the compensating variations introduced by a local disturbance, tend to compensate for this disturbance and to return the system to a state of general equilibrium.

1 Contemporary spillovers

The effects of contemporaneous spillovers, or those following instantly from a disturbance of some kind, have been shown by Patinkin, who gave them the name 'spillover' effects. They result from Clower's dual decision process: 'As soon as an individual unable to realize his notional supply (or demand) at a given price revises his supplies and demands according to the quantity constraints perceived, spillover effects from one market into the others occur.'[86]

Thus, the unemployed agent carries over the reduction in his actual income into a constrained demand for goods, and therefore into a constraint on firms' selling opportunities. In a model of Keynesian equilibrium in effective demand, these spillovers are assumed to occur instantaneously as in the static interpretation of the multiplier.

2 Temporal, or dynamic, spillovers

The incidence of a disequilibrium constraint modifies not only current decisions, leading to spillovers in the current period; in general it affects subsequent decisions also. Hence a partial adjustment of productive capacity implies investment in later periods. Similarly, price adjustments put into effect at a given time may correspond to the resolution of earlier disequilibria. In many cases, the highest rates of price increase are observed at the end of an inflationary period, while policy had become restrictive but inflationary pressures have been accumulated for several years, due to price regulation. The idea of a temporal spillover may be illustrated in the context of the traditional business cycle models based on the introduction of lags. Thus the introduction of a Robertsonian lag, between receipt and expenditure of income, as into the Samuelson model, generates a consumption (lag) spillover which takes the form of a temporary excess of money balances. The Lundberg lag between sales and production decisions, introduced into Metzler's models, implies a production (lag) spillover which is manifest in fluctuations in inventories of finished products. Furtherance of the study of these spillovers therefore requires stock as well as flow variables to be introduced into fixed-price temporary equilibrium models.

Dynamic spillovers necessarily generate links between successive periods. A postponed investment may be translated into a shortage of capacity; a realised investment by flows of depreciation needing to be accommodated. Above all, borrowing generates future principal and interest repayments bearing our agents' decisions over several periods.

The most fundamental form of spillover is perhaps that which affects agents' behaviour directly. For instance unemployment today means a loss of human capital for tomorrow. Through the action of learning, the formation of habits of consumption, anticipation of wages and of prices, the measures acting to reduce current disequilibria affect the incidence of those in the future.

3 The financial spillover

In the original version due to Leijonhufvud the modern theory of disequilibria replaced the Marshallian adjustment through prices by a quantity adjustment. This is an extreme view, since quantity adjustments are themselves far from being immediate.This is especially true of adjustments to the fall in the level of employment accompanying a fall in output. An important part of the adjustment process remains, therefore, with prices: firms faced with increasing unit wage costs due to the fall in output per employee will, if possible, pass on this increase in costs to their prices, and inflation will be fuelled by the recession, though frequently such an adjustment through prices is limited. What else, other than increased borrowing and credit, offers a solution?[87] At the macroeconomic level, if this credit cannot be fuelled by a sufficient fund of savings, it will be fed by monetary resources. With this in mind the disequilibrium theory, in contrast to monetarism, views the stock of money as endogenous and depending on the partial 'monetarisation' of credit demanded by economic agents.[88]

The financial spillover may certainly be blocked by a restrictive monetary policy, but this results in widespread liquidity problems, especially of firms, and in a prospect of multiple bankruptcies. Historical experience bore witness to this in the United States, when the monetarist-inspired policy followed by the Nixon administration led to the failure of one of the largest American railway companies, the Penn Central (Railroad). Then, and particularly in 1973, the monetary authorities abandoned for some time the idea of seriously opposing the financial spillover, a vital link in the inflationary resolution of present-day disequilibria. The Reagan experience of today seems to make the same difficulties in refusing the monetary accommodation of real disequilibria.

4 International propagation and spillover of disequilibrium

It would be difficult to give an account of present-day disequilibria without bringing out their international dimensions. For medium-sized countries, and for a long time, importation of disequilibria assuredly seems to have occurred. For the world as a whole, it seems more appropriate to view international relations as a factor in the diffusion and amplification of disequilibria.

At the international level, contemporary, temporal and financial spillovers cumulate. Again, it is necessary to start from the idealised automatic adjustment process of the balance of payments. This equilibrating process unfolds at two levels. Firstly, the different rhythms of price variations tend to re-establish the (global) equilibrium of flows of goods, raw materials and capital; and secondly, the international adjustment of relative prices guides choice in each country towards efficient specialisation.[89]

In such a world, persistent disequilibria cannot exist. In the real world, on the contrary, different patterns of adjustment, such as the opposition between real wage rigidity and money wage rigidity (see Branson and Rotenberg, 1979), tend to transform price shock into lasting macroeconomic imbalances.

Due to low adjustment of the structure of a nation's supply of exports to world demand, persistent imbalances arise. Their financing is at the origin of a cumulative development of international lending – largely monetarised under the regime first of the gold exchange standard, then of the dollar-standard – this is the financial spillover at work at the world level. But, since financing through borrowing is insufficient in view of the slowness of adjustments of the strucure of supply of exports and of the share of imports in domestic consumption, the deficits of debtor countries must be held down by an overall check on the level of activity, leading to a fall in domestic effective demand and rationing foreign exporters: these are today's spillovers.

C The characteristics of regulation today

The profound differences of recent development compared with the patterns observed before the Second World War leads one to consider the idea of a change in the mode of regulation of developed capitalist economies. The main features of this change are in the role of automatic stabilisers, downward rigidity of incomes and the 'perverse' flexibility of prices.

1 The role of automatic stabilisers
At the institutional, as well as the behavioural, level modern economies possess a whole range of automatic stabilisers of activity.

This label was first attached to mechanisms of fiscal levies and social (security) contributions sensitive to the state of the economy compared with more rigid expenditures and benefits, which tend to produce a compensatory contracyclical balance; unemployment benefits play the same role, especially if they are not financed from budget funds, since they increase perceived incomes in recession above factor costs.

Stabilisers also appear at the behavioural level. Ratchet effects, consumption habits or permanent income will explain a smoothing of consumer expenditure which tends to limit fluctuations in effective demand. Similarly, the extended economic horizon of large firms makes their investment programmes less dependent on economic circumstances, and is represented by increased average lags in econometric investment functions.

2 Downward rigidity of incomes

Already observable in Keynes's time for nominal incomes, downward rigidity has tended to extend to real incomes. While the index-linking demanded by unions has not been officially instituted in France, the practice of collective bargaining does not appreciably differ from it. In the United States, several sectional collective agreements have included index-linking clauses.

Public intervention tends, moreover, to stabilise agricultural incomes through price policies (in the EEC) or variable subsidies (to some extent in the US), and the collapse of agricultural incomes seen in the 1930s is unthinkable today.

Does such stabilisation of incomes extend to recipients of interest and dividends? Certainly so, if one compares the pre-war years: the impact of expected rates of inflation on rates of interest has been accentuated, though it remains very much a partial effect. At the same time mark-up pricing behaviour tends to reduce the cyclical variability of profits.

3 'Perverse' price flexibility

By studying the dynamics of disequilibria, the rationality of the practice of administered prices, whose movement is relatively autonomous with respect to pressure of demand, has been demonstrated. If in addition these prices incorporate variations in unit costs and a profit margin sufficient to maintain the mass of profits, we obtain not rigidity of prices in recession, but a 'perverse flexibility', characterised by an increase in the margin required per unit of output in depression in order to produce the same overall margin or a reduced quantity. H. M. Wachtel and P. D. Adelsheim (1977) have established the existence of such a mechanism in the most concentrated sectors in the United States. R. Boyer and J. Mistral obtained comparable results for France using a simulation technique.[90]

It is usual to observe that these characteristics lead towards a downward rigidity of incomes and of the level of activity, favouring an inflationary resolution, or at least deferment, of disequilibria. But it is just as important to observe that they are accompanied by an increased rigidity of structures by a blockage or at least a restriction of the reallocations required. In this respect they are the basis rather of a pseudo-regulation, deferring disequilibria as much as resolving them.

4 A new mode of regulation?
To describe a change occurring in the 'mode of regulation' of the developed capitalist economies, some authors have suggested the term 'monopolistic regulation', succeeding a 'competitive regulation'. More specifically R. Boyer and others (1977), within a Marxian framework, distinguish an 'old-fashioned' regulation which prevailed in a society in which pre-capitalist social relations predominated; a 'competitive' regulation characterised by the sensitivity of prices and incomes subject to rapid adjustments to the market situation, and 'monopolistic' regulation, said gradually to have taken over since 1945. This latter form is said to result in essence from three structural changes:[91] the extension of state guarantee for money; the evolution of labour legislation in favour of wage-earners; and the general increase in concentration enabling firms to fix prices. For these authors,[92] 'present-day inflation must necessarily be related to the new form of monopolistic regulation and not to a few incidental phenomena interacting with a still competitive form of regulation.'[93]

The essence of this proposition cannot be denied in so far as it underlines the necessity of understanding the global impact of the structural changes of capitalism on stabilisation policy. This coincides with the view of the American Keynesian Arthur Okun who wrote:[94]

If our economic institutions responded currently to a slump as they did in 1922 or 1938 or 1949, the recession and prolonged slack would not only have stopped inflation in its tracks but created a wave of falling prices.

In fact, the nature of price- and wage-making has been transformed in the modern era. We live in a world dominated by cost-oriented prices and equity-oriented wages (as cited in *Challenge*, November/December 1977, p. 8).

However, despite the undoubted interest of the theory proposed, the interpretation suggested by R. Boyer and his associates may be debated. Proposing a system of global regulation of the capitalist economy certainly offers an enticingly comprehensive framework but one which can lead to the rationalisation *a posteriori* of any sort of economic adjustment. Is there not a risk of replacing the mechanistic view for which, rightly or wrongly, certain Marxists are criticised, with a functionalist determinism? The Marxist conception of the role of the state subordinates it to the regulation of the system, at the cost of a drastic reduction in its autonomy. Economic policy debates are then pushed into the background. If the economic policy pursued is considered as a component of a system of global regulation, there is no longer room for criticism of it, unless it is regarded as a relic from an earlier mode of regulation, not consistent with the currently dominant mode of regulation.

More generally, the very notion of regulation is vague, even though it is a fashionable one. Are we concerned here with a finalised regulation, be it only through the survival of the existing system, the reproduction of the mode of production, or with regulation by a closed loop without an explicit end point? In the latter case we are returned to studies of dynamic stability; in the former, to a mainstream of the theory of economic policy. It therefore appears that the general notion of regulation is not itself without ambiguity.

It therefore seems worthwhile to complete this type of analysis with a train of thought explicitly derived from finalised regulation, and allowing a critique of economic policies.

D Beyond global Keynesianism

If we wish to consider the specific role of economic policy in the regulation of modern Western economies, we must start from the neo-liberal compromise espoused by Keynes in the 'Concluding Notes' of the *General Theory*.[95]

1 The neo-liberal compromise
This compromise rests on a diagnosis: the spontaneous functioning of markets results in a correct allocation of resources, but has shown itself incapable of ensuring their full employment. This leads on to a precept: the government is justified in intervening in order to ensure macro-economic stabilisation, by controlling the level of investment and employment, but should leave to private enterprise the responsibility for allocating resources. This view leads both to the purely aggregative view of the Keynesian tradition and to the exclusively macroeconomic orientation of the policies it inspires.

The fallacy in this reasoning is clearly apparent, and the recent evolution of Western economies further brings it out. Where would it be easier for markets to allocate heterogeneous resources among thousands of alternative uses in a constantly evolving economy than in bringing aggregate investment to the level required for full employment? The aggregative definition of effective demand as equilibrium expected by the 'collective entrepreneur' has enabled Keynesians to avoid asking themselves this question.

The answer is that market mechanisms are incapable of permanently sustaining full employment because they are far from fulfilling the idealised image of Walrasian theory. In the absence of futures markets, of an auctioneer acting in each market, and of a clearing house, they cannot suffice to guarantee *a priori* the coordination of agents' decisions in a decentralised economy. As a result, the attainment of full employment and the efficient allocation of resources are compromised at one and the same time.

2 *The failure of global regulation*

The imbalances perpetually being created by growth and by the non-homothetic development of the world economy occur in the form of many partial disparities between capacity and demand, costs and prices, and between accumulation and the ability to finance it.[96] The price system possesses neither the flexibility nor the efficiency required to absorb these partial disparities instantaneously, so that they persist and tend to spread throughout the economy. Policies of global regulation, whether Keynesian or monetarist in inspiration, deny themselves the possibility of acting directly on these partial maladjustments and seek instead to compensate for them at the aggregate level. In the process, they generate new disequilibria and lead to further spillovers.

These policies were based on an imagined symmetry between inflation and unemployment, between excess and deficient aggregate demand. They lead to an alternation of reflation and deflation, the well-known British 'stop-go cycle', in a rhythm which accelerates when the twin evils coincide. Taking account of the delay in the action of measures of intervention to which the dynamic multipliers give rise, deflationary measures once decided, as for instance in France in September 1974 by M. Fourcade, took full effect one year later, at a time when the same minister introduced reflationary measures of unparalleled magnitude. At its limit, the recent situation in Western Europe could equally well have justified reflationary or deflationary policies, revealing the inadequacy of the conceptual framework vulgarised by the image of the brake and accelerator to be used alternately.

It is, moreover, an illusion to suppose that global intervention measures are neutral in their effects on the allocation and distribution of resources. All stabilisation plans are in fact composed of selective incidences across sectors and firms.[97] These, being neither intended nor controlled, lead in general to new adjustment problems.

414 *Instability in the short term*

3 Some guidelines for a regulation policy

Now that theorising upon the analysis of present-day disequilibria has shown up the failure of global regulation policies, be they Keynesian or monetarist-inspired, it remains for us to outline the guidelines of alternative policies suggested by the modern developments of macro-dynamics.[98]

The converging evidence from historical experience and the criticism of 'new classicals' show how much the programme of 'fine tuning' advocated by the Keynesians in the 1960s did overestimate the efficacy of economic stabilisation policy. Does it mean that we have to adhere to the liberal program? I personally do not think so. New classical and other modern liberals are right in showing how stabilisation policy would interfere with microeconomic behaviour and allocation processes. The modern disequilibrium paradigm considers that policy interventions are needed to compensate for market failures and price rigidities. It cannot ignore the risk that governmental interventions do reinforce these rigidities. To confine policy to aggregate level is not a proper protection against these risks, because interference with allocation processes are not avoidable. Instead, we have to question the dichotomy between the 'allocation bureau' and the 'stabilisation bureau', that Musgrave distinguished.

In concrete terms, stabilisation policies formulated in terms of paths or trajectories must be integrated with some kind of flexible, indicative planning which, in the medium term, guides the allocation of resources and provides a framework for the management of the unavoidable interferences between stabilisation policies and the allocative role of market mechanisms.

Secondly, such a policy has to include prices as well as quantities in its decision variables, price policy aiming not to slow down or conceal inflationary tensions at the cost of introducing new distortions, but rather to render the price structure compatible with the projected development of economic activity. This implies giving emphasis to the impelling informational and signalling role of prices, instead of viewing them as a substitute for the process of financial reallocation which consists in an equalisation of internal rates of return.

Intertemporal consistency, selectivity, and guidance of the necessary reallocations are thus some features of a policy of regulation adapted to an essentially decentralised economy subject to multiple shocks resulting from the uneven development of the world economy.

Conclusion

The destiny of macrodynamic analysis is linked to the vicissitudes which affect its object. The long period of expansion from the end of the war to 1970 had seen its prestige confirmed, and the economist aspire to intellectual supremacy in society. In the climate of crisis which has prevailed since 1973, this prestige at first collapsed, and it was fashionable to pronounce on the crisis of economic science. This reaction was, perhaps, as excessive as the climate of self-satisfaction which had preceded it.

The scale of disequilibria nowadays, the limited success of recent regulation policies must induce modesty. Nevertheless, it cannot be denied that macrodynamic analysis is experiencing a wide and deep period of renewal.

In hindsight, the 1970s will probably appear as a break with the past as profound as the Keynesian revolution. Less visible, because concealed behind complex technical formulations; more diffuse because no new Keynes has appeared to collate the material in a single work; but no less effective if, as forty years ago, it succeeds in stimulating a reformation of action in the sphere of macroeconomic regulation.

Notes

INTRODUCTION

1 Classification was undertaken by J. A. Schumpeter, *Business Cycles*, 1939, following pioneering work by W. C. Mitchell and A. Burns.
2 J. Shiskin, *Indicators of Business Expansions and Contractions*, Columbia University Press, 1967.

CHAPTER 1 GREAT DYNAMIC THEORIES OF THE PAST

1 See Sir Eric Roll, *A History of Economic Thought* (2nd ed.), Faber, 1946, or M. Blaug, *Economic Theory in Retrospect* (3rd ed.), CUP, 1978.
2 Illustrated by the now-famous description of a pin factory which appears in *The Wealth of Nations*.
3 Ricardo, *The Works and Correspondence* (ed. by P. Sraffa), CUP, 1955–62, vol. I, p. 122.
4 A quest which was to be successfully concluded in the twentieth century with the development of P. Sraffa's standard commodity (see Chapter 7).
5 N. Kaldor, 'Alternative Theories of Distribution', *Review of Economic Studies*, 1956.
6 W. J. Baumol, *Economic Dynamics*, Macmillan, 1959.
7 Ricardo, *op. cit.*, p. 390.
8 As do modern theories of growth which will be discussed in the third part of this book.
9 It is with respect to his support for the law of markets that Keynes wrote, 'Ricardo conquered England as completely as the Holy Inquisition conquered Spain', *General Theory*, Macmillan, 1973, p. 32.
10 While still retaining it as a unit of measurement following Smith's theory of the demand for labour.
11 See T. R. Malthus, *The Principles of Political Economy*, New York, Kelley, 1951.
12 This can appear problematic as capitalists pay the production price of labour power and not its value. This is a consequence of the order of exposition followed in *Capital*.
13 Recommended in P. Y. Hénin's thesis, *Capital, production et circulation monétaire*, University of Paris I, 1970, p. 51.
14 In *The Logic of Scientific Discovery*, Popper presents an expanded form of logical empiricism which Joan Robinson for example has long accepted.
15 For direct references to Marx on these points see P. M. Sweezy, *The Theory of Capitalist Development*, Monthly Review Press, 1968, or M. Desai, *Marxian Economics*, Basil Blackwell, 1979.

16 In her work *Economic Philosophy*, Macmillan, 1962.
17 See P. Baran, *The Political Economy of Growth*, Monthly Review Press, 1957, which might be read as a defence of the law. From the opposite viewpoint, P. M. Sweezy, *op. cit.*, highlights a number of defects in Marx's argument in particular with regard to the growth of the organic composition of capital. J. Robinson, *An Essay on Marxian Economics*, Macmillan, 1966, raises similar and other points.
   J. H. Lorenzi, O. Pastré and J. Tolédano maintain that the Marxist case would hold in expanded reproduction but that the rate of profit would be indeterminate in simple reproduction. See *La Crise du XXème siècle*, Economica, 1980, p. 166.
18 In Section 3 of this chapter and more specifically in Chapter 12.
19 The argument is thus very similar to that of the wage fund hypothesis.
20 See M. Blaug, *op. cit.*, 1978, or P. M. Sweezy, *op. cit.*, 1968.
21 In *Imperialism: Highest Stage of Capitalism*, 1st edition, 1916.
22 R. Hilferding, *Finance Capital: A Study of the Latest Phase of Capitalist Development* (ed. by T. Bottomore), Routledge & Kegan Paul, 1981.
23 See P.Baran and P. Sweezy, *Monopoly Capital*, Monthly Review Press, 1966, or M. Djilas, *The New Class: an analysis of the communist system*, Praeger, 1957.
24 We assume a velocity of circulation of capital of one. (Thus capital advanced is equal to capital consumed.) In some ways, it would have been preferable and quite illuminating to have conducted our argument in terms of production prices rather than values, but the above formulation appears in vol. II of *Capital*, whereas the concept of price is not discussed until vol. III.
25 This term can only be rendered meaningful if capitalists buy consumer goods which can be suitably transferred into wages in the following period. On this point, note the controversy between Georgescu-Roegen and Bernard mentioned in Georgescu-Roegen, *Analytical Economics*, Harvard UP, 1967.
26 R. Luxemburg, *The Accumulation of Capital*, 1st edition, 1913.
27 H. Denis, *Histoire de la pensée économique*, PUF, 1966.
28 On this work see Chapter 2, Section 2.
29 On questions relating to Say's law see T. Sowell, *Say's Law*, Princeton UP, 1972.
30 *Capital*, vol. I, book I, quoted by J. P.Benassy (*Revue Economique*, 1976) in an article on modern disequilibrium theory, which like the Marxist theory of crises, refutes the notion that individual decisions are co-ordinated *a priori*.
31 'As the forces of production develop, they enter into sharper conflict with the narrow confines of commodity relations', *Capital*, vol. III, Book X.
32 In modern theory, this is described as the 'echo effect' and is especially prevalent in shipbuilding.
33 *Capital*, vol. III, Book X.
34 See Chapter 11.

CHAPTER 2 PRE-KEYNESIAN THEORIES OF GROWTH AND FLUCTUATIONS

1 In various publications between 1913 and 1923.
2 Keynes was to capture Foster and Catchings' idea in this way: 'if . . . marginal propensity to consume falls off steadily as we approach full

employment . . . it will become more and more troublesome to secure a
further given increase of employment by further increasing investment'
(*General Theory*, Macmillan, 1974, p. 127). I. Fisher, *The Purchasing Power
of Money*, Macmillan, 1911, p. 71.
3 According to T. S. Kuhn *The Structure of Scientific Revolutions*, Chicago
UP, 1st edition 1962, 2nd edition 1970 'normal science' is engaged in
extending the range of facts relating to a 'paradigm' accepted by a scientific
community. Extraordinary research seeks to discover new principles which if
adopted lead to a scientific revolution.
4 F. A. von Hayek, *Prices and Production*, RKP 1931, 2nd edition Kelley
1978.
5 Or of 'high-powered money'. Bank credit will be considered, following the
'Banking Principle', as a means of accelerating the circulation, rather than
increasing the stock, of money.

CHAPTER 3 THE KEYNESIAN REVOLUTION

1 Expected revenue net of user cost to be more precise: that is to say with due
deduction for purchases between entrepreneurs for replacement of
equipment and for intermediate consumption in the period.
2 As we noted above, the idea of equilibrium being determined exclusively by
producers was already present in Marshall. The notion is reinforced in
Keynes by the fact that the role of consumer demand is replaced as an active
component by the expectations formulated about it by entrepreneurs.
3 In 1937, for example, he wrote: 'the theory of effective demand is
substantially the same if we assume that short-period expectations are always
fulfilled' and also, 'if I were writing the book again, I should begin by setting
forth my theory on the assumption that short-period expectations were
always fulfilled', *The Collected Writings of J. M. Keynes*, vol. XIV, p. 181.
4 It would seem unnecessary to introduce a 'mark-up' component,
representing the margin required by firms in their price setting, as suggested
for example by M. K. Evans, *Macroeconomic Activity*, Harper & Row, 1969,
p. 361. Rather it would seem more appropriate to consider a firm's profits as
a quasi-rent, the average productivity of labour being higher than the
marginal productivity.
5 We here take the point of view of O. Lange and R. Kuenne, which would
seem the most logical in the context of neoclassical theory. For a more
extensive discussion, see M.Morishima, *Walras' Economics: a pure theory of
capital and money*, CUP, 1977.
6 The terms 'fall' and 'rise' are used for ease of expression. Strictly speaking,
in comparative statics one ought to say 'at a lower level' or 'at a higher level'
etc.
7 As we printed out above it is only in this hypothetical case that Keynesian
underemployment equilibrium can be reconciled with Walras' law.
8 The diagram becomes more meaningful if Allen's assumptions are reversed.
With N exogenously given, the point of intersection of the curves
determines the general level of prices. We may therefore deduce that only a
horizontal supply price curve will render this pseudo-equilibrium compatible
with involuntary unemployment.

9 This exposition derives from the work of Benjamin Friedman, who distinguishes 'transaction crowding out' from 'portfolio crowding out' in 'Crowding out or Crowding in? Economic consequences of financing Government Deficits', *Brookings Papers*, No. 3, 1978.

CHAPTER 4 THE CONSUMPTION FUNCTION

1 *General Theory*, pp. 90–91. Among the objective factors, it is important to note variations in wealth. A. Leijonhufvud, *On Keynesian Economics and the Economics of Keynes*, pp. 192–3, believes one must consider this wealth-consumption relationship as 'the second psychological law of consumption'.
2 Ibid., p. 96.
3 Ibid., p. 114
4 Formally: for all finite values of income.
5 In particular by S. Kuznets, *Uses of National Income in Peace and War*, NBER, 1942, and subsequently by R. Goldsmith, *A Study of Savings in the United States*, NBER, 1955.
6 'Forecasting Post-War Demand', *Econometrica*, January 1945.
7 The group to which the individual belongs, as distinct from the group from which he takes his reference. The latter influences the consumer through demonstration effects.
8 J. Duesenberry, 'Income Consumption Relations and their implications', first published 1948, reprinted in Lindauer, *Macro-economic Readings*, Free Press 1968, p. 10.
9 Duesenberry's formulation differs on two points: saving remains an endogenous variable in place of consumption and historical income is introduced in a factoral form. Ibid., p. 14.
10 T. M. Brown, 'Habit Persistence and Lags in Consumer Behaviour', *Econometrica*, July 1952.
11 For a comparison of individual effects, such as the relative income effect, and of temporal processes, such as partial adjustments, within a different context see P. Y. Hénin, 'Individual and Time Effects in the Dividend Behaviour of Firms', in *The Econometrics of Panel Data*, special issue, *Annales de l'INSEE*, September 1978, No. 30–31.
12 Determinate rather than stable, as the propensity to consume is a function in particular of the rate of interest, as shall later be seen.
13 dR_{t+1} measures the divergence from the initial value (in $t = 0$), not from that in the preceding period.
14 The same phrase also designates a different notion: the sequential play of the Keynesian multiplier. Clearly the two analyses do not coincide in any way.
15 On these conditions, see for example H. A. Green, *Consumer Theory*.
16 I. Fisher first expounded this theory in *The Theory of Interest*, first edition 1930. For a modern, yet simple exposition, see Friedman, *Price Theory*, or J. Hirschleifer, 'On the Theory of Optimal Investment Decision', *Journal of Political Economy*, August 1958.
17 More precisely:

$$\left(\frac{\partial U}{\partial C_0} \Big/ \frac{\partial U}{\partial C_1}\right) = 1 + i \quad \text{or equivalently} \quad \left(\frac{\partial U}{\partial C_0} - \frac{\partial U}{\partial C_1}\right) \Big/ \frac{\partial U}{\partial C_1} = i.$$

The market rate of interest is equal to the subjective discount rate, or the marginal rate of preference for the present.

18 Similarly for savings, if the relationship R_0/R_1 is not modified.

19 It is better not to confuse an income effect, which is positive in this sense (of widening the possible consumption range) with a growth of current wealth. The graphic illustration in this section illustrates a possible divergence between these two criteria.

20 We note the symmetry with the definition of the average duration θ of a flow of income in the Hicks-Macaulay sense:

$$\sum_{t=1}^{T} \frac{R_t}{(1+i)} = \sum_{t=1}^{T} \frac{R_t}{(1+i)}\theta = \frac{1}{(1+i)}\theta \sum_{t}^{T} R_t$$

21 The reader is invited to reflect on the fact that it is only in this case (an infinite time horizon) that permanent income corresponds to the Hicksian definition in *Value and Capital*, that part of one's inheritance one knows one may spend without growing poorer.

22 Formally, if U is homogeneous of degree k in C_0 and C_1, the marginal utilities are homogeneous of degree $k - 1$ and the marginal rate of substitution (MRS) is homogeneous of degree zero and, therefore, unchanged under any proportional growth of present and future consumption.

23 Derived from A. Ando and F. Modigliani, 'The Life Cycle Hypothesis of Saving', *American Economic Review*, March 1963, p. 58.

24 See J. Tobin, 'Life Cycle Saving and Balanced Growth', in Fellner, *Ten Economic Essays in the Tradition of I. Fisher*, J. Wiley, 1967.

25 See J. Tobin, 'Wealth, Liquidity, Propensity to Consume', in *Essays in Honour of G. Katona*.

26 In *Macro-economic Theory*, McGraw-Hill, 1975, p. 89.

27 More strictly, it has been shown that a process of revision of this kind is justified, if and only if either the permanent and transitory components are uncorrelated or if they are perfectly correlated. J. F. Muth, 'Optimal Properties of Exponentially Weighted Forecasts', *Journal of American Statistical Association*, 1960.

28 On the other hand, there is an essential difference in the econometric expression of the two theories. The Friedmanite derivation implies an auto-correlation of the residual of the function, unlike that of Brown.
  The more recent definition of permanent income in terms of rational expectations (studied in Ch. 11) leads, on the contrary, to some questioning of the formal similarity with adjustment models. With revisions of permanent income following a random walk, the variation in consumption itself follows a similarly hazardous path, without any auto-correlation over time and statistically independent of variations in current income; see R. Hall, 'Stochastic Implications of the Life Cycle-Permanent Income Hypothesis: Theory and Evidence', *Journal of Political Economy*, 1978, pp. 971–87.

29 Particularly the works of A. Zellner, 'The Short Run Consumption Function', *Econometrica*, October 1957.

30 D. Patinkin, *Money, Interest and Prices*.

31 *Ibid.*

32 *Ibid.*

33 *Ibid.*

34 For further econometric analysis of the effects of inflation, see D. Hendry

and T. von Ungern-Sternberg, 'Liquidity and inflation effects on consumers' expenditure', in *Essays in the Theory and Measurement of Consumers' Behaviour*, ed. by A. S. Deaton, Cambridge University Press.

35 For a more elaborate exposition, see J. Flemming, 'The Consumption Function When Capital Markets are Imperfect: The Permanent Income Hypothesis Reconsidered', *Oxford Economic Papers*, 1973, pp. 160–72, and C. Pissarides, 'Liquidity Considerations in the Theory of Consumption', *Quarterly Journal of Economics*, 1978, pp. 279–96.

36 Clower employs the expression 'expenditure constraint' in the same sense but in a slightly different context: 'A Reconsideration of the Micro Foundations of Monetary Theory', *Western Economic Journal*, December 1967, reprinted in *Monetary Theory*, Penguin Economic Readings collection.

37 J. Tobin, 'Wealth, Liquidity, Propensity to Consume', Extract from the volume of essays in honour of G. Katona, reprinted in *Essays in Economics*.

38 'In such a situation, his labour is an illiquid good, that is to say it cannot be converted into cash.' (A. Leijonhufvud, *Keynes and the Classics*, IEA, 1969)

39 'The Keynesian Counter Revolution: A Theoretical Appraisal', in *The Theory of Interest Rates*, F. Hahn and F. Brechling, Macmillan, 1965, p. 118.

40 A. Leijonhufvud, *op. cit.*

CHAPTER 5 INVESTMENT AND FACTOR DEMAND

1 Productive services in neoclassical terminology.
2 Or multi-dimensional surface, if there are more than two inputs.
3 $y = f(x_1 \dots x_n)$ is homogeneous of degree v, if $f(\lambda x_1 \dots \lambda x_n) = \lambda^v f(x_1 \dots x_n)$.
4 Constant Elasticity of Substitution. The properties of the CES function are studied in detail in the NBER volume, *The Theory and Empirical Analysis of Production*, (ed.) M. Brown, *Studies in Income and Wealth*, vol. 31, 1967.
5 The following isoquants correspond to the three cases considered:

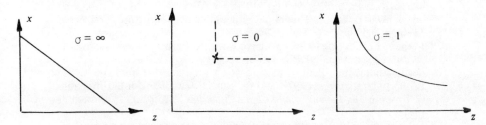

6 User cost u combines financial cost (interest at the rate i) and depreciation cost (at the rate δ), applied to the purchase price of capital goods p_k. Thus:

$$u = (i + \delta) p_k$$

7 Only in this case is marginal cost λ independent of output y.
8 'The Theory of Investment Behaviour' in R. Ferber, *The Determinants of Investment Behaviour*, NBER, 1967.
9 *A Study in the Theory of Investment*, Chicago, 1960.
10 See chapter 2, section 2.

11 For an analysis of this type, see Witte, 'The Microfoundations of Social Investment', *Journal of Political Economy*, Oct. 1963.
12 Remember that Marshall uses the term price for what we would call value, hence $P_K = p_K K$. See above, chapter 3.
13 The implications of this have been discussed in chapter 3.
14 *General Theory*, p. 135.
15 On the other hand, the rise in the supply price is not sufficient to compel abandonment of the marginal efficiency of capital concept in favour of that of the marginal efficiency of investment (which will be presented later), at least as long as the capital goods market remains competitive. On this point, we differ from several authors.
16 *Ibid.*, p. 141.
17 *Ibid.*, p. 148.
18 *Ibid.*, p. 315. Also: 'Being based on shifting and unreliable evidence, they (expectations) are subject to sudden and violent changes.'
19 See J. Hirschleifer, 'On the Theory of Optimal Investment Decisions', *Journal of Political Economy*, August 1958.
20 M. Kalecki, *Theory of Economic Dynamics*, Allen & Unwin, 1965.
21 'Le comportement d'autofinancement des entreprises', *Economie Appliquée*, December 1968.
22 However, studies undertaken for the 'D.M.S.' model show that the influence of profits would be clearest in services, that is to say a protected sector.
23 This hypothesis is presented and discussed in M. Evans, *Macro-economic Activity*, pp. 124–30.
24 In his thesis, *Croissance, profits et investissement: Une étude économétrique*, Paris, 1978, p. 294.
25 In his article, 'Investment Behaviour of French Industrial Firms: A Study on Longitudinal Data', in *The Econometrics of Panel Data*, *Annales de l'INSEE*, September 1978, p. 127.
26 As a sequel to the works undertaken for the STAR model, see J. Mazier, *La macroéconomie appliquée*, PUF, 1978, pp. 53–6.
27 See Schwartz, 'On the Theory of Optimal Financial Structure', *Journal of Finance*, 1959.
28 In their contribution to the collective work: R. Ferber, *Determinants of Business Investment*, NBER, 1967.
29 See E. Malinvaud, 'Peut-on mesurer le coût d'usage du capital productif?', *Economie et statistique*, 1970, and the collective work under the direction of G. Fromm, *Tax Incentives and Capital Spending*, Brookings Institution, 1971.
30 In his study on investment under disequilibrium in *Economie du déséquilibre*, Economica, 1977.
31 'The Non-Linear Accelerator and the Persistence of Business Cycles', *Econometrica*, January 1951. In the following year H. Chenery established an analogous formula entitled the capacity principle, 'Over-capacity and the Acceleration Principle', *Econometrica*, January 1952.
32 L. M. Koyck, *Distributed Lags and Investment Analysis*, North Holland, 1954.
33 At least, not enough information which can be utilised by the usual econometric methods.
34 Each coefficient $a(\theta)$ of the lag distribution is equal to the value of the polynomial $A(L)$ where $L = \theta$.

$$a(0) = \alpha_0$$
$$a(1) = \alpha_0 + \alpha_1 + \alpha_2 + \ldots + \alpha_r$$
$$a(2) = \alpha_0 + 2\alpha_1 + 4\alpha_2 + \ldots + 2^r \alpha_r$$
$$a(3) = \alpha_0 + 3\alpha_1 + 9\alpha_2 + \ldots + 3^r \alpha_r$$

35 For a clear presentation, which in particular explains the calculation of $a(\theta)$ from $b(\theta)$ and $c(\theta)$, see K. Wallis, *Topics in Applied Econometrics*, Gray-Mills, London, 1973, pp. 70–2.
36 'The Distributed Lags Between Capital Appropriation and Expenditures', *Econometrica*, January 1965.
37 In their study, 'Fonction d'investissement et retards échelonnés', *Annales de l'INSEE*, No. 21, 1976. They owe their method to Tinsley, 'An Application of Variable Weight Distributed Lags', *Journal of American Statistical Association*, December 1967.
38 The lag structures are estimated for the period 1954–1974, using the Almon method with a polynomial of degree 3.
39 P. A. Muet and P. Zagamé, *op. cit.*, pp. 128–9.
40 'Investment Behaviour and Neo-classical Theory', *Review of Economics and Statistics*, August 1968.
41 In particular by Ando, Modigliani, Rasche and Turnovsky, 'On the Role of Expectations of Prices and Technological Change in an Investment Function', *International Economic Review*, vol. 15, No. 2, June 1974.
42 See, for example, the study by de Menil and Yohn, 'La formation de capital fixe par des entreprises', *Annales de l'INSEE*, Nos 26–7, March 1977. The redefinition of user cost under the 'putty-clay' hypothesis is applied to the demand for labour in our study on 'L'offre d'emploi en longue période avec une technologie Putty-Clay', *Annales de l'INSEE*, Nos 38–9, April-September 1980.
43 On this point consult the work of M. Aitkinson and J. Mairesse, 'Length of Life of Equipment in French Manufacturing Industries', *Annales de l'INSEE*, Nos 30–31, April-September 1978.
44 See above, section 1 (D).
45 Causality in the sense of Granger. This technique will be later mentioned with regard to monetarist controversies (chapter 11).
46 'Are there Exogenous Variables in Short-Run Production Relations', *Annals of Economic and Social Measurement*, 1973.
47 'A Choice Theoretic Model of Income Investment Accelerator', *American Economic Review*, September 1972. Note that Grossman justifies the introduction of realised sales in the investment function according to the same principle which Clower applied to the consumption function.
48 Cf. H. Grossman, *op. cit.*
49 'L'investissement en déséquilibre', in *Economie du déséquilibre*, Economica, 1977.
50 See for example, 'Les modèles néo-classiques et l'impact du taux d'intérêt sur l'investissement', *Revue Economique*, No. 2, March 1979.
51 Introduced by Gould, 'Adjustment Costs in the Theory of Investment of the Firm', *Review of Economic Studies*, January 1968. See also P. Duharcourt, *op. cit.*, pp. 92–4.
52 See R. Craine, 'Optimal Distributed Lag Responses and Expectations' *American Economic Review*, 1971.

53 Especially the exposition in W. Brainard and J. Tobin, *Asset Markets and the Cost of Capital*, Cowles Foundation, 1976. See R. Hall, 'Investment, Interest Rates and the Effects of Stabilization Policies', *Brookings Papers on Economic Activity*, No. 1, 1977, pp. 85–90.
54 According to his study, which is confirmed by others, a realistic value of the elasticity of investment with respect to q is 0.7. On this point and for a discussion of the 'q theory' see G. von Furstenberg's article, 'Corporate Investment: Does Market Valuation Matter in the Aggregate' and the commentaries which follow it. (*Brookings Papers on Economic Activity*, No. 2, 1977.)
55 Cf. Oi, 'Labour as a Quasi-Fixed Factor', *Journal of Political Economy*, October 1962.
56 Such studies have been conducted by F. Brechling, 'Short Run Employment Functions in Manufacturing Industries: An International Comparison', *Review of Economics and Statistics*, August 1967 and in France by Limet and Salais, 'Essai de prévision à court terme dans le domaine de l'emploi et des salaires', *Economies et Sociétés*, 1971.
57 On this point see T. Boyer and P. Petit, 'L'estimation de fonctions d'emploi pour trois secteurs industriels dans six pays européens. Leur stabilité après 1973'. *Annales de l'INSEE*, Nos 38–9, April–September 1980.
58 See Schramm, 'The Influence of Relative Prices, Production Conditions and Adjustment Costs on Investment Behaviour', *Review of Economic Studies*, 1970. Also Nadiri and Rosen, *A Disequilibrium Model of Demand for Factors of Production*, NBER, 1973. We may deduce this formula from a generalised adjustment cost model, as does Schramm for example.
59 Which may be defined if the process is convergent or equivalently if the matrix (I-B) is non-singular.
60 In his study, 'Estimation de demande de facteurs en termes d'adjustements croisés', *Annales de l'INSEE*, Nos 38–9, April 1980.

CHAPTER 6 FINANCIAL BEHAVIOUR AND THE DEMAND FOR MONEY

1 The latter in his work of 1923, *A Tract on Monetary Reform*.
2 M. Friedman for example. We will return to this idea in the context of 'monetarised' growth models in chapter 8.
3 See B. J. Loasby, *Choice, Complexity and Ignorance*, Cambridge University Press, 1976.
4 In several applications, Government bonds are seen as preferable to money, being considered assets with a positive return and no risk. This is no longer true when the future rate of interest is risky, as bonds then bear a risk of capital loss or gain.
5 The reader will verify the similarity with the concept of efficiency in the theory of production, chapter 5, section 1.
6 One might refer to the work of C. de Boissieu, 'La Structure des taux d'intérêt', *Economica*, 1975.
7 See for example G. P. Dwyer, 'The Gibson Paradox: a Cross-Country Analysis', *Economica* 51, 1984.
8 Which we will call static, or long-term.

9 In their article, 'Pitfalls in Financial Model Building', *American Economic Review*, 1968.
10 Studied in chapter 5, section 3, part D.
11 Including savings deposits. See the first formula which appears in the *Treatise on Money*.
12 Tobin, *op. cit.*, pp. 157–8.
13 In his article, 'Liquidity Preference as a Behaviour Toward Risk', 1958, in Thorn, *Monetary Theory*.
14 M. Friedman, 'The Quantity Theory of Money: A Restatement', 1956, reprinted in R. Clower, *Monetary Theory*.
15 This ratio w should not be confused with the wage rate. It is, however, equal to the ratio of the permanent incomes from capital and property to permanent wage incomes.
16 The above function is not modified by the introduction of firms' demand for cash balances.
17 For money in the broad sense M_2, including bank savings deposits. On the other hand, it has not been proven that the permanent income-elasticity of demand for money in the narrow sense (M_1) significantly exceeds unity.
18 G. C. Chow, 'On the Long-Run and the Short-Run Demand for Money', *Journal of Political Economy*, April 1966.
19 E. L. Feige, 'Expectations and Adjustments in the Monetary Sector', *American Economic Review*, May 1967, pp. 462–73.
20 See, *The General Theory*, Chapter XV, p. 195.
21 Baumol, 'The Transaction Demand for Cash: An Inventory Theoretical Approach', 1952, in Thorn, *Monetary Theory*.
22 M. H. Miller and D. Orr, 'A Model of the Demand for Money by Firms', *Quarterly Journal of Economics*, August 1966.
23 The notion of a money record of past exchanges is one of the principal aspects of the informational concept of monetary exchange studied in Ostroy, 'The Informational Efficiency of Monetary Exchange', *American Economic Review*, September 1973.
24 A good appraisal of these is given in C. A. Goodhart, *Money, Information and Uncertainty*, Macmillan, 1975, Chapter I.
25 We employ the term 'means of settlement' as it is more precise in this context than the 'Means of payment', employed by Shackle for example. See Goodhart, *op. cit.*, p. 3.
26 As in the case of the 'Robertson lag' for example.
27 'Alternative Theories of the Rate of Interest', *Economic Journal*, June 1937, p. 247.
28 J. M. Keynes, 'The Ex-ante Theory of the Rate of Interest', *Economic Journal*, December 1937,pp. 667–8.
29 S. C. Tsiang, 'Walras' Law, Say's Law and Liquidity Preference in General Equilibrium Analysis', *International Economic Review*, September 1966, p. 332.
30 In his article, 'Foundations of Monetary Theory', 1967, reprinted in *Monetary Theory*, Penguin economic Readings Collection, 1969.
31 *Ibid.*, p. 206.
32 In periods of severe disequilibrium and strict rationing, such as in time of war, barter operations can actually become advantageous.
33 G. L. S. Shackle, *The Years of High Theory*, Cambridge University Press, 1967, p. 91.

34 For a discussion of the Clower-Shackle thesis, one is advised to consult Goodhart, 'Money and Disequilibrium', in Harcourt (ed.), *The Micro-foundations of Macroeconomics*, Macmillan, 1977, p. 222.

CHAPTER 7 THE REPRESENTATION OF GROWTH, AND ITS SOURCES

1 Total productivity formulae may be interpreted as implicit production functions.
2 The theory of aggregation was developed by H.Theil (1944–1954), W. Léontief (1947), Nataf (1953) and E. Malinvaud ('L'agrégation dans les modèles économiques', *Cahiers du séminaire d'économétrie*, No. 4, 1956). Green provides a good overview in *Aggregation in Economic Analysis*, 1964, Princeton University Press.
3 See the definition given in chapter 5, Section 1(A).
4 See, for example, the classical work of V. Smith, *Investment and Production, A Theory of Capital Using Enterprises*, Harvard, 1964. For an econometric example, see M. Kurtz and A. Manne, 'Engineering Estimates of Capital Labour Substitution in Metal Machining', *American Economic Review*, 1962, p. 662.
5 With the possible exception of the constant term a_{io}. Remember that one must distinguish between a linear function and a function which is homogeneous of degree one.
6 The classical reference on this theory is H. Theil, *Linear Aggregation of Economic Relations*, North-Holland, 1954.
7 See the capital vintage models further on, in part C (1).
8 See above, chapter 4.
9 Note the analogy with the definition of a cost function. In general, there is a range of possible costs at which a given quantity may be produced, each corresponding to a different technique. The cost function is the locus of minimum costs, corresponding to the best factor combinations.
10 As a way of testing out the scope of this criterion, M. Brown examined groups of producer goods, whose prices remained linked over a given economic period. *Cf.* M. Brown, 'Output and Capital Aggregation by Means of Composite Commodity Theory', in *Essays in Modern Capital Theory*, North-Holland, 1976.
11 K. Borch, 'Effects on Demand of Changes in Distribution of Income', *Econometrica*, 1953.
12 H. Houthakker, 'The Pareto Distribution and the Cobb-Douglas Production Function in Activity Analysis', *Review of Economic Studies*, 1955–56, pp. 27–31.
13 Houthakker's aggregation method differs from equilibrium aggregation in that he takes the distribution of capital as given rather than as optimal.
14 We will point out straight away a serious consequence of this finding: there is a high chance that the shape of production functions estimated from aggregate data will be quite random. In particular, it has been shown by a number of writers that the good performance of the Cobb-Douglas could be merely the result of fortuitous circumstances, such as the constancy of the wage share.

15 In Bliss's words, 'While our conclusions on general aggregation of capital are highly unfavourable to this notion, research has not however confirmed the idea that the aggregation of capital should be difficult, relatively speaking. The conditions for the general aggregation of capital are identical to those required for the aggregation of output or labour. We may thus conclude that the widespread belief that capital aggregation poses a particular problem of its own is at best a badly developed idea, and at worst based purely on ignorance.' *Capital Theory and the Distribution of Income*, North-Holland, 1975, p. 162.

16 And not on Y_t, nor directly on K_t, because of the production function's homogeneity of degree one.

17 One can, therefore, say that Hicks neutrality postulates distribution is invariant *ceteris paribus*, while neutrality in the sense of Harrod (or Solow, which is equivalent) makes the same postulation, *mutatis mutandis*.

18 J. Fei and G. Ranis, 'Innovational Intensity and Factor Bias in the Theory of Growth', *International Economic Review*, May 1965.

19 The notation A_0', A_1' is used to indicate that we are dealing with coefficients, which differ *a priori* from those used in the case of Hicksian neutrality.

20 Remember that factors are here measured in terms of efficiency units, which is why the unconventional terms 'labour-increasing' and 'capital-increasing' are employed in describing the direction of technical change. For a fixed volume of output, 'labour-increasing' technical progress reduces the number of man-hours required and so is equivalent to 'labour-saving' progress in standard terminology.

21 M. Beckman and R. Sato, 'Aggregate Production Functions and Types of Technical Progress: a Statistical Analysis', *American Economic Review*, 1969, p. 88.

22 On this notion, see chapter 5, Section 2.

23 The *ex ante–ex post* distinction often made is not very appropriate to the present argument.

24 In loose language, one might in this case speak of complementary factors. 'Restrictive factors' would be a more precise expression.

25 R. Solow, 'Investment and Technical Progress', in K. Arrow, *Mathematical Methods in Social Science*, Stanford, 1960, p. 89.

26 A constant ratio is maintained between the variables N_{tv} and K_{tv}. They are affected only by an exogenous process of physical deterioration of machinery, which in certain analyses can be ignored.

27 We owe the concept to Kennedy, 'Induced Bias in Innovation and the Theory of Distribution', *Economic Journal*, 1964, p. 541.

28 See W. Hirsh, 'Firm Progress Ratios', *Econometrica*, January 1956.

29 K. Arrow, 'The Economic Implications of Learning by Doing', *Review of Economic Studies*, 1962, pp. 159, 160.

30 There should in addition be some reference to the sociology of behaviour.

31 Nordhaus, 'An Economic Theory of Technical Change', *Cowles Foundation Discussion Paper*, February 1969, p. 265.

32 K. Wicksell, *Lectures on Political Economy*, vol. I.

33 Which explains her conclusion: 'This point of Wicksell's is the key to the whole theory of accumulation and the determination of wages and profits.' *The Accumulation of Capital*, p. 396.

34 P. Samuelson, 'Parable and Realism in Capital Theory: the Surrogate
     Production Function', *Review of Economics and Statistics*, 1962.
35 The presentation is inspired by G. Harcourt.
36 As $k_A > k_B$ at every point.
37 Otherwise, it would be superior to B, which would not be used at any rate of
     profit.
38 In his work, *Production of Commodities by Means of Commodities*,
     Cambridge University Press, 1960.
39 We will here present the model in terms of coefficients for input and price
     units, rather than for quantities of input and output.
40 A mathematical condition which is satisfied if one considers only basic
     goods, that is goods required directly or indirectly in the production of all
     others.
41 We thus obtain a system formally akin to the von Neumann model, which
     will be studied in chapter 9.
42 R. Solow, *The Theory of Capital and the Rate of Return*; L. Pasinetti,
     Technique changes and the 'Rate of Return' in the Theory of Capital.
43 *Cf.* G. C. Harcourt, *Some Cambridge Controversies in the Theory of Capital*,
     Cambridge University Press, 1972.
44 For example, if a technique A employs at least as much of each capital good
     as another technique B, then they may be unambiguously classified. *Cf.* B.
     Scarfe, *Cycles, Growth and Inflation*, McGraw-Hill, 1977, pp. 166–7.
45 Amidst an abundant literature, note in particular the controversy between
     J. Robinson and F. M. Fisher, 'The existence of Aggregate Production
     Functions', *Econometrica*, 1971, p. 405.
46 G. C. Harcourt, *op. cit.*, 1972.
47 *Ibid.*
48 *Ibid.*
49 In the collective work edited by Shell, *Essays on the Theory of Optimal
     Economic Growth*, MIT Press, 1967.
50 The implications for the debate on capital re-switching have been studied by
     Paul Zagamé, *op. cit.*
51 'In commerce bygones are forever bygones', said Jevons as long ago as 1871.
     Theory of Political Economy, Pelican Classics, 1970, p. 186.
52 R. Solow, 'Technical Change and the Aggregate Production Function',
     Review of Economics and Statistics, August 1957.
53 In addition, aggregation of factor quantities in terms of volume would in this
     case be possible – an incidental but by no means secondary consideration.
54 M. Abramovitz, 'Resources and Output Trend in U.S. since 1870', *American
     Economic Review*, May 1956, p. 11.
55 David and Van de Klundert, 'Non Neutral Efficiency Growth and
     Substitution Between Capital and Labour in the U.S. Economy', *American
     Economic Review*, June 1965.
56 See note 20.
57 Massel, 'A Disaggregated View of Technical Change', *Journal of Political
     Economy*, December 1961.
58 See section 1 (B), part 2 of this chapter.
59 Denison and Poullier, *Why Growth Rates Differ*, Brookings Institution,
     1967, chapter XVII.
60 Germany, France and Italy, *cf.* 'Le potentiel de croissance rapide et sa
     réalisation', *Communication au Congrès mondial de l'Association Inter-*

nationale de Science Economique, Tokyo, August 1977.

61 By convention, the American residual is interpreted as representing the 'development of knowledge', applicable to all countries. The excess of the French residual over the American is seen as the result of a closing of the 'technological gap'.

62 In their article, 'The Explanation of Productivity Changes', *Review of Economic Studies*, July 1967.

63 For their application in this context, see Jorgenson and Griliches, 'Divisia Index Numbers and the Productivity Measurement', *The Review of Income and Wealth*, June 1971.

64 On this notion, see chapter 5, section 1 (C).

65 'The Measurement of U.S. Real Capital Input 1929–1967', *Review of Income and Wealth*, December 1969.

66 Kendrick, *The Formation and Stock of Total Capital*, NBER, 1976.

67 Kaldor, 'A Model of Economic Growth', *Economic Journal*, 1957, pp. 591–624, and in the context of capital cycle models Kaldor and Mirrlees, 'A New Model of Economic Growth', *Review of Economic Studies*, 1962, pp. 174–92.

68 Appendix to his inaugural Cambridge lecture, 1966, published by Cambridge University Press, 1967.

69 These two concepts are not always kept sufficiently distinct in many studies. One of the merits of the work of Carré, Dubois and Malinvaud is that they make an unambiguous distinction between them.

CHAPTER 8 THE STABILITY AND REGULATION OF GROWTH

1 See the Introduction pp. 2–3. Also R. Harrod, 'An Essay in Dynamic Theory', *Economic Journal*, March 1939, p. 15.

2 See chapter 10 for complementary developments of stability.

3 Harrod's initial article refers to the ex ante/ex post distinction, although he was aware that his use of the term 'ex ante' was not exactly the same as that of the Swedes (*ibid.*, p. 21).

4 In his original article (Harrod, 1939, p. 22); see also his *Money*, Macmillan, 1969.

5 Hahn and Matthews, 1964, pp. 36–7. Their first model, presented in the original article, led – after correction of an error – to the conclusion of stability.

6 This term encompasses a set of properties needed for the determination of production equilibrium: continuity, differentiability, concavity and restrictions on the behaviour of marginal productivities.

7 Among the most important are Neville (1962) and, more subtle, Encarnacion (1965).

8 This idea was introduced by Baumol as early as 1949.

9 In the models examined above, which do not consider intermediate flows of consumption, the notions of investment and consumption goods coincide.

10 An Indian economist writing from an economic planner's point of view.

11 Total employment $N = N_c + N_m$ is exogenous and grows at the natural rate n.

12 This also ties in with the principle of causality in the sense used in physics,

applied to economics by Samuelson, *Foundations of Economic Analysis*, Harvard Press 1966.
13 For a rigorous exposition, see for example, Burmeister and Dobell, *Mathematical Theories of Economics Growth*, Macmillan,1970, pp. 112–13.
14 In the case of fixed coefficients, on the other hand, it has been shown that the condition on capital intensities is at once necessary and sufficient.
15 This specification, due to Svennilson, was developed by Bliss (1968).
16 This optimisation is not, however, possible if the elasticity of substitution is too great, the threshold being in general greater than 1.
17 See above, Chapters 2 and 3.
18 Concerning Kurz's similar demonstration see above, Section 1.

9 GROWTH: TRENDS AND LIMITS

1 The second order condition

$$\frac{d^2c}{ds^2} = \frac{dk^*}{ds}\ f''(k^*)\ +\ (f'_{k^*} - n)\ \frac{d^2k^*}{ds^2} < 0$$

is also verified.
2 Identical with those of Solow's model.
3 In his article 'The Golden Rule of Accumulation', *American Economic Review*, 1961.
4 Orally in 1932, then published in 1938 and translated into English under the title 'A Model of General Economic Equilibrium' in 1945 in the *Review of Economic Studies*, pp. 1–9, with an introduction by Champernowne.
5 The text follows the proof given by H. W. Kuhn in 'Lectures in Mathematical Economics', in Dantzig and Veinott (eds), *Mathematics of the Decision Science*, vol. 2, American Mathematical Society, 1968.
6 Historically the first exposition is due to Dorfman, Samuelson and Solow, *Linear Programming and Economic Analysis*, McGraw Hill, 1958.
7 This method has been mentioned with regard to Jorgenson's theoretical model (D. W. Jorgenson, *Optimal Replacement Policy*, North-Holland, 1967).
8 We exclude here technical progress, whose introduction in 'Harrod-neutral' form complicates the form of the model, though it can be incorporated if the utility function is homogeneous. See K. Arrow, 'Applications of Control Theory to Economic Growth' in Dantzig and Veinott (eds), *Mathematics of the Decision Science*, American Mathematical Society, 1968, pp. 97–115.
9 The exposition which follows is purely for reference.
10 The Hamiltonian is expressed here in current values, so that the discount factor, assumed to be constant, is omitted. We shall, however, need to reintroduce it later on.
11 Formally, the solution must be completed by 'resetting' the evolutions thus described to start from the initial conditions, and so-called 'transversality' conditions.
12 The relative price of capital, p_t is included in its shadow price q_t, so that $\dot{p}_t = \dot{q}_t$.
13 The stationary solution is then said to be a 'saddle point'.
14 For a more precise exposition, see Arrow, op. cit., p. 101.
15 For more precise presentation, see Samuelson (1965) or Cass (1966).

16 See above (p. 223).
17 This model is derived from that presented by Dixit (1976), pp. 163ff.
18 Under the simplified assumptions of the model, the user-cost reduces to the rate of interest, as the reader may verify for himself.
19 We saw earlier that indeed $\dot{p}/p_t = \alpha/v_t$.

CHAPTER 10 THE ANALYSIS OF FLUCTUATIONS

1 Studied in Chapter 2 of this book.
2 The standard derivation is to build the demand function conditionally to money market equilibrium and the supply function conditionally to labour market equilibrium. Thus, the aggregate supply and demand are reduced form equations rather than structural behavioural ones.
3 Chapter 8, Section 1, p. 212.
4 In the sense that there is no effect beyond that on prices called in the following period.
5 Depending on the size of this domain, we shall refer to local or global stability.
6 The model described here is adapted from Henderson and Quandt, *Microeconomic Theory*, 3rd edn, McGraw-Hill, 1980, p. 162ff.
7 The economic interpretation of this decomposition is easy to grasp: the homogeneous equation determines the path of the deviation from the equilibrium price $(P_t - P^*)$. The full solution must 'restrict' the solution of the homogeneous equation by adding in the equilibrium value.
8 The limiting case $R = 1$ leads to complete adjustment in a single period.
9 The term 'discrete' is used to distinguish an oscillation in discrete values, which may be represented by a cobweb diagram, from continuous oscillations corresponding to complex roots of the characteristic equation associated with second-order difference equations.
10 The limiting case $R = -1$ leads to oscillations of constant amplitude. Equilibrium is stable only in Samuelson's second sense.
11 An inappropriate name, since it is now clear that the cobweb diagram characterises a family of solutions rather than a particular model.
12 We have constant amplitude oscillation (Type II stability) if $c/a = 1$.
13 We know that the condition $b - s < 0$ is necessary for the convergence of the generalised multiplier $1/(1 - c + b)$.
14 This condition was proved by Samuelson in his *Foundations of Economic Analysis*, Harvard University Press, 1966. See also Gandolfo, *Economic Dynamics, Methods and Models*, North-Holland, 1980, pp. 258 and 216.
15 *A fortiori*, the condition $b = 0$ of the ordinary Keynesian model is itself sufficient.
16 For example, the solution of a first-order dynamic adjustment process, the continuous time equivalent of the tatonnement model of page 276 above, would be of the form $A \exp(k(a - c)t)$. Clearly, for $k > 0$ the absolute value of the coefficient does not affect stability, which depends only on the sign of $(a - c)$.
17 The main alternative assumptions needed to prove global stability in a tatonnement process are:
(a) that demand functions satisfy the weak axiom of revealed preference;
(b) that the matrix of derivatives $\dfrac{\delta E_j}{\delta p_j}$ is negative semi-definite; or

(c) that this matrix has a 'quasi-dominant' diagonal.

18 For a detailed study of this subject, see F. M. Fisher, 'The stability of general equilibrium results and problems' in Artis and Nobay, eds, *Essays in Economic Analysis*, Cambridge University Press, 1976, pp. 3ff.

19 See for example K. J. Arrow and F. H. Hahn, *General Competitive Analysis*, Holden Day, 1971.

20 Either $\alpha\beta$ or $\sqrt{\alpha\beta}$ may of course equivalently be compared to 1.

21 For a fuller treatment of this model see M. K. Evans, *Macroeconomic Activity*, Harper & Row, 1969, pp. 362ff. or R. G. D. Allen, *Macroeconomic Theory*, Macmillan, 1967, pp. 336ff., and for a discussion see R. C. D. Matthews *The Trade Cycle*, CUP, 1959.

22 The accelerator implies that a slowing down of expansion induces a fall in investment and, through the multiplier, a greater fall in income.

23 See above, Chapter 3.

24 This solution may be found in Evans, op. cit., p. 384 or, more fully, in Allen, op. cit., p. 417.

25 On this subject see also J. Mazier's, *La Macroéconomie appliquée*, Presses Universitaires de France, 1978, Chapter III.

26 In 'Economic fluctuations and growth', *Econometrica*, Jan. 1957. For an exposition see Evans, op. cit., pp. 407–9.

27 For an exposition with examples, see M. Guillaume, *Modèles économiques*, PUF, 1971, and Evans, op. cit., Chapters 15 and 18 to 21.

28 Boule, Boyer, Mazier and Olive, 'Le Modèle STAR', *Statistiques et Etudes Financières* 15, 1974.

29 From E. P. Howrey, 'Dynamic Properties of a Condensed Version of the Wharton Model' in B. Hickman ed., *Econometric Models of Cyclical Behavior*, NBER Studies in Income and Wealth, no. 36, 1978, vol. 2, p. 637.

30 A very simple introduction to this problem is given by van Doorn, *Disequilibrium Economics*, Macmillan, 1975.

31 Oudet, op. cit. pp. 1, 2 and 8, and Aoki, *Optimal Control and System Theory in Dynamic Analysis*, North-Holland, 1976, p. 8.

32 B. M. Friedman, *Economic Stabilization Policy: Methods in Optimization*, North-Holland, 1975.

33 M. Aoki, op. cit.

CHAPTER 11 INFLATION AND UNEMPLOYMENT

1 See above, Chapter 3, p. 50.

2 A formalisation of a similar process was proposed by J. A. Trevithick, 'Keynes, Inflation and Money Illusion', *Economic Journal*, March 1975.

3 This dealt with the deflation following the return to the gold standard in 1925.

4 From Nicolai's article under this title in the *Revue Economique*, 1962.

5 The demand curve $Y_o(P_t)$ remains invariant, as it is assumed that wages can only affect demand through P (i.e. there are no distributional effects.)

6 A very good survey of this literature is given by Silberston in 'Price Behaviour of Firms', *Economic Journal*, Sept. 1970, pp. 511ff.

7 Especially regarding British and American experiences, in W. D. Nordhaus and W. A. H. Godley, 'Pricing in the trade cycle', *Economic Journal*, Sept. 1972, pp. 853ff.

8 See Boyer and Mistral, 'Formation de capital, prix relatif et inflation', *Economie et Statistique*, April 1976, p. 35.
9 In an American study, L. Sahling found that the two components of the cost of capital, interest and depreciation contributed about equally to an explanation of industrial prices: 'Price behavior in U.S. manufacturing: an empirical analysis of the speed of adjustment', *American Economic Review*, Dec. 1977, pp. 911–25.
10 Defined above, p. 103.
11 Chapter 6, p. 154.
12 This derivation can be compared with that of the simple Keynesian multiplier as a reduced form equation $C = cY + C_0$; and $Y = C + A$.
13 See Chick, 1977, p. 34 and also Chapter 10, p. 284, of this book.
14 Andersen and Carlson, 1970 and Andersen and Jordan, 1968.
15 See, among many discussions of this subject, Goldfeld and Blinder's critique 'Some implications of endogenous stabilization policies', *Brookings Papers*, vol. 3, no. 3, 1972, p. 585.
16 See *A Theoretical Framework for Monetary Analysis*, NBER, 1971. A discussion of this model by Davidson, Patinkin and Tobin can be found in the *Journal of Political Economy*, Sept/Oct 1972, pp. 837–950 (sic). See also Hahn's critique, 'Professor Friedman's views on money' (sic), *Economica*, Feb. 1971, pp. 61–80.
17 See above, Chapter 3, Section 3.
18 This explanation is due in particular to L. Dicks-Mireaux (1961). See also Hines (1964), pp. 221–42 + appendix.
19 The second case has been more frequent in recent years, which could be explained by high growth rates relative to the level of unemployment. See Phan (1971).
20 It was noted above (Chapter 7 Section 1) that the properties of a global relationship may result from the process of aggregation as much as, and sometimes more than, from the microeconomic relationships.
21 In his book *Inflation, équilibre et chomage*, Editions Cujas. See also S. C. Kolm, 'La théorie de la courbe inflation-chômage', *Revue Economique*, March 1970.
22 The transition from a Phillips curve determining the growth of money wages to one giving directly the rate of inflation, by assuming the profit margin and rate of growth of productivity to be stable, goes back to Samuelson and Solow (1960).
23 Developed historically by Phelps (1968) and Friedman (1968), pp. 1–17.
24 Economic policy then operates by inducing systematic errors of foresight by agents.
25 See Chapter 4, p. 97, and Chapter 5.
26 This model is fully developed by Hénin (1980).
27 A systematic policy can however reduce the variance of y_t if the monetary authorities have an informational advantage over private agents. For a detailed study see Buiter (1980).
28 See Brunner, ed. (1976) and Sargent (1976) pp. 631–40.
29 It is this implicit assumption, even more than the idea of uncertainty, which marks a departure from the Walrasian framework as generalised by Arrow and Debreu.
30 It is in a situation of 'dynamic monopsony' as Phelps puts it in his article 'Money wage dynamics and labor market equilibrium' in Phelps et al.,

Microeconomic Foundations of Employment and Inflation Theory,
Macmillan 1971, p. 131.
31 This analysis is due to Holt. The exposition was suggested by Giran (1976).
32 In 'Le mirage du plein emploi', *Banque*, Oct. 1977, p. 1045. They took the
view that the deficiency of world demand in 1974/5 and 1975–77 'cannot
anyway explain more than a fairly small proportion of total unemployment'.
They take the duration of unemployment as an autonomous variable under
the control of the unemployed, an assumption not usually made even by 'job
search' theorists.
33 This idea seems to be due to Grossman; see also Alchian, Lucas and
Rapping (1973) p. 1365. 'In particular, Alchian argues that firms know from
experience that workers will not continue working at reduced wages, so they
simply effect lay-offs without bothering with wage negotiations'.
34 On Phelps's book and the theories of search unemployment, consult the
excellent critique by Hines 'The microeconomic foundations of employment
and inflation theory: bad old wine in elegant new bottles' in Worswick
(1976).
35 The principle behind this decomposition is due to Thirlwall (1969), pp. 31–4.
The interested reader can find a different line of argument in Poncet and
Portait (1980).

CHAPTER 12 DISEQUILIBRIA IN THE PRESENT DAY

1 In September 1984, unemployment levels remained as high as 12.9% in the
UK, 11.4% in France and 7.5% in the USA (*Employment Gazette*, HMSO,
Sept. 1984).
2 In contrast, one earlier approach takes a Marxist standpoint and lays stress
on the processes of accumulation and distribution. This also will be studied.
3 Kaldor starts from the following propositions:
(1) Combined growth in the aggregate volume of output and in labour
productivity.
(2) A sustained increase in capital per worker.
(3) A steady rate of profit.
(4) Steady long-term capital output ratios.
(5) A high correlation between the share of profits in income and the share of
investment in output and long-term stability of distribution of wages and
profits.
(6) Differences between countries in rates of growth and investment, though
these be stable.
In F. A. Lutz and D. C. Hague (eds), *The Theory of Capital*, Macmillan
1961, reprint 1968, pp. 178–9. Note Kaldor says: 'My purpose here is to
present a model of income distribution and capital accumulation which is
capable of explaining at least some of these "stylized facts"'.
4 The diagram is taken from CEP I. 'The world economy: increasing tensions',
Economica, 1983, p. 169.
5 J. Mazier, B. Loiseau and M. B. Winter, 'Rentabilité du capital dans les
économies dominantes', *Economie et Statistiques*, Feb. 1977.
6 'Rentabilité économique et comptable des sociétés en France de 1959 à
1975', *Annales de l'INSEE*, Nov. 1976.

7 'Is the Rate of Profit Falling?', *Brookings Papers on Economic Activity*, no. 1, 1977.
8 Ibid., p. 217.
9 Ibid., pp. 222–3. The Feldstein/Summers study was written in reply to an earlier and less rigorous study by Nordhaus (1974).
10 In Monti (1976), p. 207.
11 Monti (1976), p. 289.
12 On employment in the US during the 1975 crisis, see the article 'Recent Labour Market Developments', *FRB*, Jan. 1976 (vol. 62), pp. 1–10.
13 Quoted by Tatom (1979), pp. 3–16.
14 Among numerous references the following should be mentioned:
W. Nordhaus, 'The recent productivity slowdown', *Brookings Papers*, 1972, no. 3; E. Denison, 'Explanations of declining productivity growth', *Surveys of Current Business*, Aug. 1979, no. 8, pt II, pp. 1–24; J. R. Norsworthy, M. J. Harper and K. Kurtz, 'The slowdown in productivity growth: analysis of some contributing factors', *Brookings Papers*, 1979, no. 2, pp. 387–421; J. Kendrick, 'Productivity trends and the recent slowdowns, historical perspective, causal factors and policy options', *Contemporary Economic Problems*, 1979.
15 For example Tatom, op. cit., p. 7: 'To the extent that estimated series do not capture these losses in normal measures of "discords" and depreciation, the net capital stock measures tend to an overstatement of the growth of the net capital stock in the seventies.'
16 See above Chapter 5, Section 4, C3.
17 See above Chapter 7, Section 3, 3.
18 A similar line of enquiry will be pursued regarding the wage explosion of 1968–72, below, p. 406.
19 See Bardes (1978) and Rostow (1980).
20 K. Marx, *Capital*, vol. III, Part 3, Chapter 15, p. 360, Penguin, 1981, (with introduction by Mandel).
21 See above Chapter 1, Section 2 A.
22 A good summary of the theories arising from this perceived contradiction is M. Bleaney, *Underconsumption Theories*, Cambridge University Press, 1978.
23 The 'long wave' is advocated by E. Mandel (1975 and 1980).
24 P. Boccara (1976), p. 295.
25 Ibid., pp. 225–7.
26 From his Marxist perspective, J. Valier (1976) suggests that 'the notion of structural devalorization amounts to a confusion between devalorization and valorization at a reduced rate or in an alternative capital circuit. Valorization in an alternative capital circuit and, for certain types of capital, valorization at a reduced rate have nothing to do with the process of devalorization in the Marxian sense (in the sense of a reduction in the value of capital).' (Quoted in G. Abraham Frois et al., 1976, p. 222.)
27 See M. Bleaney, op. cit., 1978.
28 M. Aglietta (1976), p. 250.
29 Ibid., p. 251
30 By a reduction in the value of labour power, through technical progress and the intensification of work.
31 M. Aglietta, op. cit., p. 261.
32 In his article 'Money and inflation: some lessons from American experience',

Economie et statistiques, April 1976, p. 55. See also 'Capital devalorization: the links between accumulation and inflation', *Economie Appliquée*, 1980, no. 2, p. 387.

33 An increase which will only be temporary if the capital-output ratio remains constant. In effect, each generation of capital equipment is retired more quickly, but fewer generations are retired. The two effects cancel each other if the capital-output ratio is constant over all generations, old and new.

34 As does Aglietta, op. cit., p. 55.

35 See above, Chapter 1, Section 2 B.

36 See E. Mandel (1975 and 1980).

37 P. Boccara, op. cit., p. 136.

38 B. Billaudot, op. cit., p. 549.

39 In 'A Reconsideration of the microfoundations of monetary theory', *Western Economic Journal*, Dec. 1967.

40 In 'The Keynesian Counter-revolution: A Theoretical Approach', in F. H. Hahn and F. P. R. Brechling (eds), *The Theory of Interest Rates*, Macmillan, 1966, pp. 103–25.

41 Geary has shown that this type of utility function is associated with a linear expenditure function. On the problems of interpretation, see Hénin (1976).

42 Following a method of exposition first used by Barro and Grossman and developed by A. D'Antume.

43 This function was first investigated by D. Patinkin in Chapter XIII of *Money, Interest and Prices*, Harper & Row, 1965. If the possibility of holding stocks is introduced, firms will have two distinct reaction curves as have households. For the derivation of these curves, see J. Muelbauer and R. Portes, 'Macroeconomic Models with Quantity Rationing', *Economic Journal*, Dec. 1978, p. 803.

44 In the manner of J. Drèze, 'Existence of an Exchange Equilibrium under Price Rigidities', *International Economic Review*, June 1975 (vol. 16), pp. 301–20.

45 In Hénin (1972).

46 Bénassy (1974), pp. 81–113. Grandemont (1976), pp. 829–32 compares the Drèze and Bénassy models.

47 It has, however, been shown that the aggregation may depend crucially on the distribution of variables in the population under consideration. For example, the distribution of initial money endowments may affect the response of the unemployment rate to a variation in the wage rate in a Keynesian situation. See K. and W. Hildenbrand, 'On Keynesian Equilibria with Unemployment and Quantity Rationing', *Journal of Economic Theory*, no. 18, 1978.

48 In the context of this fixed-price model – or where in the short term at least prices are exogenously given – one should more strictly speak of repressed inflation.

49 In their article, 'Suppressed Inflation and the Supply Multiplier', *Review of Economic Studies*, January 1974, (vol. XLI), pp. 87–104.

50 If firms can keep stocks a complete symmetry with the classical case is obtained. See J. Muellbauer and R. Portes, op. cit., p. 807, who use the term 'under-consumption'. In a model with fixed capital, it seems justifiable to label this case 'over-capitalisation'. See P. Y. Hénin and P. Michel, 'Equilibrium with Rationing in a Two Sector Fix-Price Flex-Price Economy', presented to the 4th World Congress of the Econometric Society, Aix-en-

Provence, France, 1st September 1980 (under the heading 'Fixprice equilibria II').

51 Because $dw/dm = (-)/(-) = (+)$.

52 See for example his article in *Revue Economique*, Jan. 1978 (special issue on employment).

53 In his book, *Theory of Value*, John Wiley, New York/Chapman Hall, London, 1959. Uncertainty is introduced by the idea of markets contingent on a state of nature. Equilibrium is then defined over $N \times T \times S$, there being S states of nature.

54 See Grandmont (1976).

55 See above Chapter 10, Section 1 B.

56 See Section 3 of this chapter.

57 For example the article by V. Bohm, 'Disequilibrium dynamics in a simple macroeconomic model', *Journal of Economic Theory*, vol. 17, 1978, p. 179.

58 S. Honkapohja, 'On the Dynamics of Disequilibria in a Macro Model with Flexible Wages and Prices', in Aoki and Mazzolo (1979).

59 See above Chapter 11, Section 1 C.

60 See Chapter 3, Section 2.

61 An idea due to Simon (1957).

62 For this view see the theories of R. Cyert and J. March, *Behavioural Theory of the Firm*, Englewood Cliffs, 1963.

63 Developed systematically in Day and Groves, *Adaptive Economic Models*, New York, Academic Press, 1975.

64 Which depends on the degree of constraint imposed by the environment according to the state of the economy; cf. Echaud and Hénin (1970).

65 The substitutability between these measures can be appreciated by a detailed simulation; cf. Hénin and Prost (1977).

66 Alongside Perroux's 'theory of the subject', Lesourne's 'theory of the individual' suggests some relevant replies to the questions raised by the behaviour of agents in disequilibrium.

67 Op. cit., p. 829.

68 'The value of the ability to deal with disequilibria', *JEL*, September 1975, pp. 827–46, quote on p. 829.

69 Op. cit. (Frisch, 1933).

70 In his article cited above.

71 In his article, 'A new theoretical approach to the problems of economic growth', as cited.

72 A masterful tableau of the evolution of systems of production has been assembled by W. W. Rostow, op. cit.

73 This surplus may be linked with the technical progress term introduced into the production function. This surplus productivity is not to be confused with the global surplus of Ricardo or Baran nor with consumer surplus, nor yet with organisational surplus.

74 From the name of the Swedish economist David Davidson who thus explained the tendency for prices to fall between 1870 and 1896, at the same time as Wicksell sought a monetary explanation.

75 For an evaluation, see the writings of P. Temple, and *INSEE* (1974).

76 In his article (Kolm, 1966).

77 See Aglietta, op. cit.

78 For which C. Pallois uses the term neo-Fordism, quoted by Aglietta.

79 Op. cit., p. 326.

80 See above, Chapter 11.
81 In his article, 'Inflation and recession in the world economy', *Economic Journal*, Dec. 1976.
82 Ibid., p. 706.
83 See Lindbeck, 'Stabilization Policy in Open Economies with Endogenous Politicians', *American Economic Review*, May, 1976, pp. 1–19.
84 See W. Nordhaus, 'The worldwide wage explosion', *Brookings Papers*, no. 3, 1972.
85 Certain Marxists maintain that the present world crisis has its roots in a 'crisis of imperialism'. See S. Amin et al. (1975).
86 Blondel and Pauly, op. cit., p. 155.
87 The relationship between liquidity crises and financial spillover has been studied by J. P. Pollin (1973) and by Aglietta (op. cit. and 1975).
88 The first specific discussion of the financial spillover in disequilibria was Blondel and Pauly (1979).
89 This assertion should be considered both under fixed and flexible exchange rates. Monetarists had claimed that fixed rates were a factor preventing adjustment. Experience equally well shows the destabilising role of flexible rates.
90 Boyer and Mistral (1977), pp. 36–70.
91 CEPREMAP (1977), p. 555.
92 Op. cit., p. 559.
93 The concept of passing from competitive to monopolistic regulation was developed by Boyer and Mistral (1978). See also Aglietta et al. (1978).
94 'The great stagflation swamp', *Challenge*, December 1977, p. 8.
95 See above, Chapter 3, Section 3, and also Hénin (1979).
96 W. Rostow notes in his book (op. cit.) the failure of Keynesian macroeconomics to regulate this uneven development. Rejecting the liberal alternative, he advocates instead 'French-style' indicative planning.
97 As J. P. Pollin (1975), p. 47 ' as shown.
98 These ideas are developed in Hénin (1979).

Bibliography

CHAPTER 1 GREAT DYNAMIC THEORIES OF THE PAST

1 On the Ricardian dynamic system

(*a*) *Principal texts*
Blaug, M., *Economic Theory in Retrospect*, 3rd edition, CUP, 1978, Chapter IV.
Ricardo, D., *The Works and Correspondence*, ed. by P. Sraffa, CUP, 1955–62, vol. I.

(*b*) *Articles*
Kaldor, N., 'Alternative Theories of Distribution', *Review of Economic Studies*, March 1956.

2 On the Marxian dynamic system

(*a*) *Principal texts*
de Brunhoff, S., *La Monnaie chez Marx*, Editions sociales, 1967.
Desai, M., *Marxian Economics*, Basil Blackwell, 1979.
Gillman, J., *The Falling Rate of Profit: Marx's Law & its significance to twentieth century capitalism*, Dobson, 1957.
Maarek, G., *Introduction au Capital de K. Marx*, Calmann-Lévy, 1975.
Robinson, J., *An Essay on Marxian Economics*, Macmillan, 1966.
Sweezy, P. M., *The Theory of Capitalist Development*, Monthly Review Press, 1968.

(*b*) *Articles*
Abraham-Frois, G. (selected articles), 'Problématique de la croissance', *Economica*, 1974, Vol. II.
Bettelheim, C., 'Variations des taux de profit et accroissement de la productivité', *Economie Appliquée*, vol. 12, 1959.
Borkiewiez, L., 'Value and Prices in the Marxian system', in A. Peacock (ed.), *International Economic Papers*, No. 2.
Wright, E., 'Alternative Perspectives in Marxist Theory of Accumulation and Crises', reprinted in J. Schwartz, *The Subtle Anatomy of Capitalism*, Goodyear Publishing, 1977.

CHAPTER 2 PRE-KEYNESIAN THEORIES OF GROWTH AND FLUCTUATIONS

Principal texts on pre-Keynesian theory
American Economic Association, *Readings in Business Cycle Theory*, George Allen & Unwin, 1950.
Evans, M. K., *Macro-economic Activity*, Harper & Row, 1969.
Guitton, H., *Les Fluctuations économiques*, Sirey, 1951.
Haberler, G., *Prosperity and Depression*, Leagues of Nations, 1941 (3rd edition).
Hayek, F. A., *Prices and Production*, Routledge, 1931.
Schumpeter, J., *Business Cycles. A Theoretical, Historical and Statistical Analysis*, McGraw-Hill, 1939.

Principal texts on the development of Keynesian thought
Paquet, A., *Le Conflit historique entre la loi des débouchés et le principe de la demande effective*, Armand Colin, 1953.
Shackle, G. L. S., *The Years of High Theory*, CUP, 1967.

Principal texts on the history of crises
Flamant, M. and Singer-Kevel, J., *Crises et récessions économiques, Que sais-je?*, PUF.
Mandel, E., *Long waves of capitalist development: the Marxist interpretation*, CUP, 1980.
O'Connor, J., *The Fiscal Crisis of the State*, St Martin's Press, New York, 1973.

CHAPTER 3 THE KEYNESIAN REVOLUTION

I On the *General Theory* and its interpretation

Barrere, A. et al., *Controverses sur le système Keynésien*, Economica, 1975.
Davidson, P. and Smolensky, E., *Aggregate Supply and Demand Analysis*, Harper & Row, 1964.
Keynes, J. M., *The General Theory of Employment, Interest and Money*, Macmillan.
Kurihara, K., *Post-Keynesian Economics*, Allen & Unwin, 1955.
Millar, J., 'The Social Accounting Basis of Keynes' Aggregate Supply and Demand Functions', *Economic Journal*, June 1972.
Minsky, H., *John Maynard Keynes*, Columbia University Press, 1975.
Patinkin, D., *Keynes' Monetary Thought: A Study of its Development*, Duke University Press, 1966.

II On Anglo-Saxon Keynesianism and its critique

(a) Principal texts
Ackley, G., *Macroeconomic Theory*, Macmillan, 1961.
Denizet, J., *Monnaie et financement*, Dunod, 1967.
Hansen, A. H., *A guide to Keynes*, McGraw-Hill, 1953.
Harris, S., (ed.), *The New Economics*, New York, A. Knopf, 1948.
Klein, L., *The Keynesian Revolution*, Macmillan, 1961.

Leijonhufvud, A., *On Keynesian Economics and the Economics of Keynes*,
    Oxford University Press, 1968.
Mattick, P., *Marx et Keynes*, Gallimard, 1972.
Samuelson, P., *Economics*, McGraw-Hill, 1980 (11th edition).

(*b*) *Articles*
Hicks, J. R., 'Mr Keynes and the Classics: A suggested Interpretation',
    Econometrica, 1937, reprinted in M. Mueller, *Readings in Macroeconomics*,
    Rinehart, 1971 (2nd edition).
Hutson, J., 'The Fall of Bastard Keynesianism and the Rise of Legitimate
    Keynesianism' in J. Schwartz, *The Subtle Anatomy of Capitalism*, Goodyear
    Publishing, 1977.
Smith, W. L., 'A Graphical Exposition of the Complete Keynesian System',
    1956, reprinted in M. Mueller, *op. cit.*, 1971.

CHAPTER 4 THE CONSUMPTION FUNCTION

I General texts

Deaton, A., 'Involuntary saving through unanticipated inflation', *American
    Economic Review*, December 1977, pp. 899–910.
Evans, M. K., *Macroeconomic Activity*, Harper & Row, 1969, chapters II, III
    and VI.
Ferber, R., *The Theory of Consumption*, Economica, 1976.
Friend and Jones, *Consumption and Saving*, University of Pennsylvania Press,
    1960.
Henderson J. M. and Quandt, R.E., *Microeconomic Theory: A Mathematical
    Approach*, 2nd edn, McGraw-Hill, 1971.
Houthakker, H.and Taylor, L., *Consumer Demand in the United States:
    Analysis and Projectives*, Harvard University Press, 1970.

II Theoretical applications

Wallis, K., *Topics in Applied Econometrics*, Gray-Mills, 1973, chapter I.

CHAPTER 5 INVESTMENT AND FACTOR DEMAND

I General texts

Greenberg, E., 'Fixed Investment' in D. Heathfield, *Topics in Applied
    Macroeconomics*, Macmillan, 1976.
Jorgenson, D. and Siebert, C., 'A Comparison of Alternative Theories of
    Investment Behaviour', *American Economic Review*, September 1968.

II Advanced studies

Ando, A., Modigliani, F., Rasche, R. and Turnovsky, J., 'On the Role of

Expectations of Price and Technological Change in an Investment Function',
International Economic Review, June 1974.

Hénin, P. Y., 'Modèles de production sous contraintes financières', *Economies et Sociétés, ISEA*.

Zagamé, P., 'L'investissement en déséquilibre', in *Economie du déséquilibre*, Economica, 1977.

III Theoretical applications

Artus, P., Muet, P. A., Palinkas, P. and Pauly, P. 'Economic Policy and Private Investment since the oil crisis: A comparative study of France and Germany', *European Economic Review*, April 1981.

Clark, P., 'Investment in the 1970s: Theory, Performance and Prediction', *Brookings Papers on Economic Activity*, No. 1, 1979.

Hall, R. E., 'Investment, Interest Rates and the Effects of Stabilization Policies', *Brookings Papers on Economic Activity*, No. 1, 1977.

Malgrange, P. (ed.), 'Fonctions de production et demandes de facteurs', special issue of *Annales de l'INSEE*, Nos 38–9, April 1980.

de Menil, G. and Yohn, F., 'La formation de capital fixe par les entreprises', in *Metric, Annales de l'INSEE*, April 1977, Chap. VII.

Muet, P. A. and Zagamé, P., 'Fonctions d'investissement et retards échelonnés', *Annales de l'INSEE*, January–March 1976.

Schramm, R., 'Neoclassical Investment Models and French Private Manufacturing Investment', *American Economic Review*, 1972.

CHAPTER 6 FINANCIAL BEHAVIOUR AND THE DEMAND FOR MONEY

Akerlof, G. A. and Milbourne, R. D., 'The short run demand for money', *Economic Journal*, December 1980, pp. 885–900.

Clower, R,. *Monetary Theory*, Penguin Economic Readings, 1969.

Goodhart, C. A., *Money, Information and Uncertainty*, Macmillan, 1975.

Hendry, D. F., 'Predictive Failure and Econometric Modelling in Macroeconomics: the transactions demand for money', in *Economic Modelling*, ed. by Hendry and Ormerod, Heinemann, London, 1979.

Miller, M. H. and Orr, D., 'A Model of the Demand for Money by Firms', *Quarterly Journal of Economics*, August 1966, pp. 913–935.

Saunders, P. and Taylor, D., 'The Demand for Money', in D. Heathfield, *Topics in Applied Macroeconomics*, Macmillan, 1976.

Thorn, R., *Monetary Theory and Policy*, Praeger, 1976.

Tucker, 'Macroeconomic Models and the Demand for Money Under Market Disequilibrium', *Journal of Money, Credit and Banking*, February 1971.

CHAPTER 7 THE REPRESENTATION OF GROWTH AND ITS SOURCES

I The production function and technical progress

Brown, M., *The Theory and Empirical Analysis of Production*, NBER, 1967.

Hahn, F. and Matthews, R., 'The theory of economic growth: a survey', *Surveys of Economic Theory*, vol. 2, Macmillan, 1965.

Johansen, L., *Production Functions*, North-Holland, 1972.

II The controversy between the two Cambridges

Blaug, M., *The Cambridge Revolution, Success or Failure*, Institute of
    Economic Affairs, London, 1975.
Bliss, C., *Capital Theory and the Distribution of Income*, North-Holland, 1974.
Harcourt, G. and Laing, F. (eds), *Capital and Growth*, Penguin, 1973.
Zarembka, P., 'Real Capital and the Neo-classical Production Function', in F.
    Altman et al., *On the Measurement of Factor Productivities*, Vandenbroeck
    and Ruynecht, Göttingen, 1976.

III The sources of growth

Nadiri, I., 'Some Approaches to the Theory and Measurement of Total Factor
    Productivity: A Survey', *Journal of Economic Literature*, December 1970.
Sen, A. (ed.), *Growth Economics*, Penguin, 1970, Sections 9 and 10.

CHAPTER 8 THE STABILITY AND REGULATION OF GROWTH

General references on economic growth theory

Allen, R. G. D., *Macroeconomic theory*, Macmillan, 1967.
Dixit, A., *The Theory of Equilibrium Growth*, Oxford University Press, 1976.
Hahn, F. and Matthews, R., 'The theory of economic growth: a survey'.
    Economc Journal, 74, 1964.
Jones, H., *An Introduction to Modern Theories of Economic Growth*, Nelson,
    1975.
Mirrlees, J., Stern, H. H. et al., *Models of Economic Growth*, Macmillan, 1973.
Pasinetti, L., *Growth and Income Distribution – Essays in Economic Theory*,
    Cambridge University Press, 1974.
Sen, A. et al., *Growth Economics*, Penguin Economic Readings, 1970.
Solow, R., *Growth Theory*, Oxford University Press, 1970.
Stiglitz, J. and Uzawa, H., *Readings in the Modern Theory of Economic
    Growth*, The M.I.T. Press, 1969.
Wan, H., *Economic Growth*, Harcourt, Brace, Jovanovitch, 1971.

CHAPTER 9 GROWTH: TRENDS AND LIMITS

Arrow, K., 'Application of Control Theory to Economic Growth' in
    Mathematics of the Decision Science, edited by Dantzig and Veinott,
    American Mathematical Society, 1968.
Beckerman, W., *In Defense of Economic Growth*; Jonathan Cape, 1976.
Burmeister, E., and Dobell, R., *Mathematical Theories of Economic Growth*,
    Macmillan, 1970.
Cass, D., 'Optimum Growth in an Aggregative Model of Capital Accumulation:
    A Turnpike Theorem', *Econometrica*, October, 1966.
Dixit, A., *The Theory of Equilibrium Growth*, Oxford University Press, 1976.

Dorfman, Samuelson and Solow, *Linear Programming and Economic Analysis*, McGraw-Hill, 1958.
Hotelling, H., 'The Economics of Exhaustible Resources', *Journal of Political Economy*, vol. 39, pp. 137–75.
Kuhn, H. W., 'Lectures in Mathematical Economics' in Dantzig and Veinott, *Mathematics of the Decision Science*, vol. 2, American Mathematical Society, 1968.
Mishan, E., *The Cost of Economic Growth*, Stoyles Press, 1967.
Nordhaus, W. and Tobin, J., *Is Growth Obsolete?* Columbia University Press, 1972.
Phelps, E. S., 'The Golden Rule of Accumulation', *American Economic Review*, 1961.
Ramsey, 'A Mathematical Theory of Savings', *Economic Journal*, 1928.
Samuelson, P. A., 'A Catenary Turnpike Theorem Involving Consumption and the Golden Rule', *American Economic Review*, June 1965.
Stiglitz, J., 'Monopoly and the rule of Extraction of Exhaustible Resources', *American Economic Review*, October 1976, p. 657.

CHAPTER 10 THE ANALYSIS OF FLUCTUATIONS

I Problems of stability and cyclical models

Allen, R. G. D., *Macroeconomic Theory*, Macmillan, 1967.
Gordon, R. and Klein, L., *Readings in Business Cycles*, Irwin 1965.
Hansen, B., *A Survey of General Equilibrium Systems*, McGraw-Hill, 1970.
Kalecki, M., *Theory of Economic Dynamics*, Allen & Unwin, 1965.
Lucas, R. E., *Studies in Business Cycle Theory*, Basil Blackwell, 1981.
Warnowitz, R., *The Business Cycle Today*, NBER, 1972.
Readings in Business Cycles, American Economic Association, Allen & Unwin, 1966.

II Macroeconomic models

Hickman, B., *Econometric Models of Cyclical Behavior*, Columbia University Press, NBER, 1972.
Holden, K., Peel, D. A. and Thompson, J. L., *Modelling the UK Economy*, Martin Robertson, Oxford, 1982.
Ormerod, P. (ed.), *Economic Modelling*, Heinemann, 1979.
Turnovsky, S., *Macroeconomic Analysis and Stabilization Policy*, Cambridge University Press, 1977.
Wallis, K. (ed.), *Models of the UK Economy*, Oxford University Press, 1984.

CHAPTER 11 INFLATION AND UNEMPLOYMENT

I Books

Gordon, R. A. and Gordon, M. S., *Prosperity and Unemployment*, J. Wiley, 1966.

H M Treasury, *The Relationship of Employment and Wages*, 1985.

Lundberg, E. (ed.), *Inflation Theory and Anti-Inflation Policy*, Macmillan, 1977.

Parkin, M. and Sumner, M. T. (eds), *Inflation in the UK*, Manchester University Press, 1978.

Phelps, E. S., *Microeconomic Foundations of Employment and Inflation Theory*, Norton, 1970.

Pissarides, C. A., *Labour Market Adjustment*, Cambridge University Press, 1976.

Popkin, J. (ed.), *Analysis of Inflation: 1965–1974*, NBER, Ballinger, 1977.

II Articles

Akerlof, G. A., 'The Case Against Conservative Macroeconomics: An Inaugural Lecture', *Economica*, 1979.

Buiter, W., 'The Macroeconomics of Dr. Pangloss', *Economic Journal*, March 1980.

Cain, G. G., 'The Challenge of Segmented Labor Market Theories to Orthodox Theories', *Journal of Economic Literature*, Dec. 1976.

Desai, M., 'Wages, Prices and Unemployment a Quarter of a Century after the Phillips Curve', in D. F. Hendry and K. Wallis (eds), *Econometrics and Quantitative Economics*, Blackwell, 1984.

Laidler, D. and Parkin, M., 'Inflation. A Survey', *Economic Journal*, Dec. 1975.

Sachs, J., 'Real Wages and Unemployment in OECD Countries', *Brookings Papers*, 1983.

Santomero, A. and Seater, J., 'The Inflation–Unemployment Trade off: A Critique of the Literature', *Journal of Economic Literature*, June 1978.

Tobin, J., 'Inflation and Unemployment', *American Economic Review*, March 1972.

CHAPTER 12 DISEQUILIBRIA IN THE PRESENT DAY

I The rise of disequilibria

Caves, R. and Krause, L., *Britain's Economic Performance*, Brookings, 1980.

Muellbauer, J. and Mendis, L., 'British Manufacturing Productivity 1955–83: Measurement Errors, Oil Shocks and Thatcher Effects', *Centre for Economic Policy Research Discussion Paper* No. 32, Nov. 1984.

Buiter, W. and Miller, M., 'The Macroeconomic Consequences of a Change in Regime: The UK under Mrs Thatcher', *Brookings Papers*, 1983.

II The Marxist approach: overaccumulation and crisis

Aglietta, M., *A Theory of Capitalist Regulation: the US Experience*, NLB, 1979.

Cowling, K., *Monopoly Capitalism*, Harvester Press, 1982.

Desai, M., 'Growth Cycles and Inflation in a Model of the Class Struggle', *Journal of Economic Theory*, vol. 6, 1973.

Pasinetti, L. L., 'Rate of Profit and Income Distribution in Relation to the Role of Economic Growth', *Review of Economic Studies*, 1962.
Rowthorn, R., *Capitalism, Conflict and Inflation*, Lawrence & Wishart, 1980.
Steedman, T., *Marx After Sraffa*, New Left Books, 1977.

III The modern disequilibrium theory

Benassy, J. P., *The Economics of Market Disequilibrium*, Academic Press, 1982.
Fisher, F. M., *Disequilibrium Foundations of Equilibrium Economics*, Cambridge University Press, 1983.
Gale, D., *Money: In Equilibrium*, Nisbet, 1982, and *Money: In Disequilibrium*, Nisbet, 1984.
Hahn, F. H., *Money and Inflation*, Basil Blackwell, 1982.
Hahn, F. H., 'On Non-Walrasian Equilibria', *Review of Economic Studies*, 1978.
Harcourt, G. et al., *Microeconomic Foundations of Macroeconomics*, Macmillan, 1977.
Malinvaud, E., *The Theory of Unemployment Reconsidered*, Basil Blackwell, 1977.
Malinvaud, E., *Profitability and Unemployment*, Cambridge University Press, 1980.
Muellbauer, J. and Portes, R., 'Macroeconomic Models with Quantity Rationing', *Economic Journal*, Dec. 1978.

IV Disequilibria and macroeconomic regulation

Aoki, M., *Optimal Control and System Theory in Dynamic Economic Analysis*, North-Holland, 1976.
Kydland, F. and Prescott, E., 'Rules Rather than Discretion: The Inconsistency of Optimal Plans', *Journal of Political Economy*, June 1977.
Turnovsky, S., *Macroeconomic Analysis and Stabilization Policy*, Cambridge University Press, 1977.

Index

Abramovitz, M., 200, 205
accelerationist theory, 333–6
accelerator, flexible, 121–6
accelerator, the, 110–12
Ackley, G., 317
Adelman, I. and F., 299–301, 306
Adelsheim, P.D., 410
adjustment: costs, 131; income and interest, 282–5; ordered in real time, 280–2; process, 130–3
Aftalion, A., 34–5
Aglietta, M., 362, 366–8, 404
Alchian, A., 347–8
Algeria, 262
Allen, R.G.D., 70, 220, 291
Almon, Shirley, 124–5
America, 182, 310, *see also* USA
Ando, A., 96, 97, 128, 324
anticipation theory, 144
Aoki, M., 313
Archibald, G.C., 333
Arrow, K., 182, 183, 286, 320, 373
assets, return on, 143–6
Aujac, H., 317
Australia, 309
Austria, 31
Austrian School, 37

Baird, R., 73
Balance of trade, 17
Bank of England, 17
Baran, P., 365
Barro, R., 344, 381, 383
barter economy, 161
Baumol, W.J., 9, 13, 157
Beckman, M., 178
behaviourist school, 400–1
Benassy, J.P., 380–1, 384, 387
Bettelheim, C., 22

Beveridge curve, 345
Beveridge Plan, 72
Billaudot, B., 369
Black, 209
Blaug, Mark, 70
Blinder, A., 77, 291
Bliss, C., 235
Boccara, P., 363, 364–6
Bodin, Jean, 17, 314
Boisguilbert, 10, 137
boom/slump, 32, 353
Borch, K., 149, 171
Bowers, D., 73
Boyer, R., 410, 411
Brady, D., 86
Brainard, W., 146
Branson, W.H., 409
Britain: depressions, 31, 63; fall in profitability of capital, 354; Keynesian influence, 72; price-levels, 306; stop-go cycle, 413; 'Treasury View', 74; unemployment, 326; *see also* UK
Bronfenbrenner, M., 317
Brown, A.J., 345
Brown, M., 198
Brown, T.M., 87–8, 90,98
Brumberg, 96
Brunhof, S. de, 366
Bruno, M., 199, 322
Buiter, W., 341, 343
Burger, A., 356
Burmeister, E., 229, 257
Burrows, P., 76
Business cycle, 274, 287, 341

Cagan, P., 155, 156
Cambridge: critique, 189, 194, 197, 199; model, 235; school, 137, 165–7, 184, 197–9, 240, 317